LEEDS

An A to Z of
LOCAL HISTORY

by

JOHN GILLEGHAN
MBE

Kingsway Press

First published in Great Britain
by the Kingsway Press

British Library Cataloguing in Publication Data
A catalogue record for this book is available from the British
Library

Printed by BAF Printers Ltd Leeds LS6 2TG

ISBN 0 9519194 3 1

Cover photograph: John Gilleghan
Leeds Civic Hall 2001

John Gilleghan outside Buckingham Palace
the day he received the MBE from Prince Charles
in March 2000

INTRODUCTION

The idea for this book of Leeds local history emerged during a broadcast on BBC Radio Leeds with John Boyd's Sunday Brunch: "Who What Where?". The phone-in asks listeners for local history questions many relating to Leeds buildings and characters with consequent pauses while memory is recalled for the relevant information. The need for a ready reference book for instant answers seemed essential. This book mainly concerns the area around Leeds City Centre and there is inevitable cross referencing to obtain the maximum information.

JOHN GILLEGHAN

John was born in 1936 at The Halton Pharmacy in East Leeds and attended Leeds Grammar School from where he went to Bede College Durham University. He gained an Honours degree in Botany and Zoology together with an Education Diploma before starting his teaching career in 1960 as a Biology master at Temple Moor Grammar School Leeds.

John was involved in many school trips both at home and abroad and also was an ASM in the school scout troop. Many generations of boys were introduced to his beloved Yorkshire Dales on day and weekend outings and in 1970 John started an adult evening group in Halton Leeds featuring the Dales. This was followed by a complementary group at Roundhay in 1977 and today the two leisure groups have a membership of over 200 with outings, theatre visits and visiting speakers enhancing the attractive and popular programmes through the year.

In 1974 John was appointed head of sciences at the new Halton Middle School from where he took early retirement in July 1991. He then was able to develop his growing interest in local history: he had already started a weekly column in The Skyrack Express in June 1982 - this reached the 1000th edition in August 2001. The first book called "Scenes from East Leeds" was published in 1992 and this popular book was followed by "Highways and Byways from Leeds" (1994) and "Worship North and East of Leeds" (1998).

Local history involvement features regular contributions to

BBC Radio Leeds "Who What Where?" on a Sunday lunchtime, annual exhibitions in an East Leeds shopping centre and numerous illustrated lectures in local libraries and to groups throughout the county. John has written a regular column on Interesting Churches for the colour magazine Down Your Way from early 2000. He arranges regular lectures and walks at Temple Newsam Leeds and in Summer 2001 led his 15th series of local history evenings. John has written the guides for Aberford, Garforth and Saxton parish churches and contributed various articles to a number of magazines.

Travel has always been a major leisure interest and John has visited nearly 100 countries including flights on Concorde to the USA, cruising in the Caribbean, Baltic, Alaska's Inside Passage and the Mediterranean. John was invited to present his travel talks at numerous centres in the Swiss Bernese Oberland and on the new Silversea cruise ship "Silver Cloud" in 1999. He was on the maiden voyage of the luxury "Silver Shadow" named at Civitavecchia Italy in September 2000 and cruised the Mediterranean on "Silver Wind" in August 2001 where he again presented a slide show. The many experiences are presented to a variety of audiences throughout the year.

He recorded two programmes about his life for BBC Radio Leeds and was involved with the presentation of a programme on BBC Look North concerning the life of John Smeaton - he also advised for BBCTV's "Local Heroes" with Adam Hart Davis.

John Gilleghan was invited to a Buckingham Palace Garden Party in July 1998 and was awarded the MBE for services to local history, education and the community in the Millennium New Year Honours List 2000. He was presented with this prestigious award by HRH Prince Charles in March 2000 and remembers this occasion as the highlight of an active life.

John's grandfather was Walter Castelow who died aged 98 in 1974 - he ran a chemist's shop on Woodhouse Lane from 1907 and was still working at the age of 97. The shop was given to Hull Museums who exhibited it at their Wilberforce House Museum and it is now a feature of the newly restored Streetlife.

FOREWORD
by

JOHN BOYD
BBC RADIO LEEDS

It's always a pleasure to welcome a new guide to Leeds, which I unashamedly rate as my favourite place on earth. I note that others list locations that they have merely visited as tourists: to love the place where you live is I think far more important.

I'm a proud Loiner and delighted that this guide has come about as a result of the author's appearances on the Sunday Brunch on BBC Radio Leeds - it's nice to know that we did our bit!

I collect as much material as I can about the place and being of more mature years nowadays I love to recall buildings of a bygone era. Now I can also look at those which have survived and discover more about them.

Can there be a better way to spend a spring morning than just walking the city centre with this guide and as they say in the modern style "checking it out".

Read and enjoy as I will myself.

April 2001

LEEDS
A TO Z OF LOCAL HISTORY

AARON, ARTHUR LOUIS (1922-43) was born on March 5th 1922 in Gledhow and educated at Gledhow Primary and Roundhay Schools and in 1939 moved to the architectural section of the Leeds College of Art, where he stayed to the second year. He was a cadet with the Leeds University Air Squadron and joined the RAF Volunteer Reserve in 1941. He was awarded his pilot's wings in June 1942 and took part in many missions over Germany including attacks on Dortmund and Hamburg. He was posthumously awarded the Victoria Cross for bravery and the Distinguished Flying Medal - the five medals were given to Leeds in 1947 by his parents and are displayed in a case at Leeds Civic Hall. On the night of August 12th 1943 he was the captain and pilot of a Stirling aircraft attacking Turin, his aircraft was seriously damaged and he continued to fly the stricken plane to Bone in Algeria: he died from his injuries in the station hospital and was buried in the Commonwealth War Cemetery at Bone. A 5 metre high bronze statue of Flight Sergeant Aaron with children from the period of 1950 to 2000 climbing a tree was unveiled at the Eastgate Fountain on Saturday March 24th 2001 by Malcolm Mitchem from Andover Hampshire who is the last surviving member of Aaron's crew - the vote was taken by readers of the YEP, commissioned by Leeds Civic Trust and funded by the Scurrah Wainwright Trust. The sculptor was Barnsley born Graham Ibbeson who has depicted Flt Sgt Aaron in his flying jacket and pilot's helmet. The artist sculpted the figure of Eric Morecambe which was unveiled by The Queen in 1999 at Morecambe as well as statues of Thomas Chippendale in Otley and William Webb Ellis at Rugby - among more than 300 life size figures in his professional career.

ABATTOIRS in Leeds started with those located east of Briggate on the Shambles and Cheapside. The Leadenhall Wholesale Carcass Market off Vicar Lane close to the Shambles was opened pre 1831. These unhealthy places were swept away with redevelopment and in July 1899 a wholesale meat market opened on New York Street designed by Walter Hanstock & Son. The building featured a clock tower and was replaced with a new abattoir on Pontefract Lane: the foundation stone was laid in October 1964 and it opened on October 26th 1966. The New York Street site is Harper Street multistorey car park and the National Express coach station. The Pontefract Lane abattoir closed in April 1988 and was demolished in 1991.

ABBEY HOLFORD ROWE is an architect's practice on South Parade - they were originally Abbey Hanson Rowe of St Paul's Street. Among many projects are the design of No 1 City Square for the Norwich Union Investment Management and the restoration of Park Row House.

ADAMS, RICHARD (died 1883) was an architect in partnership with John Kelly on Park Row and was architect to the Leeds School Board in 1873; he later was in partnership with Edward Birchall. He was responsible for Church Institute Albion Place (1868), the old St Patrick's Church York Road (1891) with many Leeds Board Schools.

ADDLESHAW BOOTH & CO is a firm of solicitors based in Sovereign House on Sovereign Street, where they opened in June 1998. The business was started as Booth, Wade, Lomas-Walker & Co in 1775; they were in Central Bank Chambers Infirmary Street in the early 20th century as Booth Wade Farr & Lomas-Walker and in the 1930's became Booth Wade Lomas-Walker. Colbeck. Booth. Wade Lomas-Walker continued through to the 1970's at their Infirmary Street offices until transfer to Phoenix House on South Parade and a move in the 1980's to Sovereign House (Bank of England). A new office block was built at a cost of £1.5 million on David Street (Manor Road): officially opened in November 1993. The firm merged with Addleshaw & Sons in February 1997 - they started in Manchester as Addleshaw Sons & Latham in 1873.

AINSLEY'S BAKERS opened shops in the city following their foundation in 1938: the factory is at Victor House on Manor Road Sheepscar, which has 44,000 sq ft of floor space. Ainsley's have over 30 retail outlets with 12 within the city centre.

AIR RAIDS in Leeds included September 1st 1940: hit the Marsh Lane railway station and on March 14/15th 1941 incendiary bombs caused many buildings in the city centre to be severely affected by fire: Schofield's Arcade, Mill Hill Chapel, Kirkgate Market, Royal Exchange, Wellington Road Goods Yard, Infirmary, Town Hall and

Leeds City Museum on Park Row. August 31st 1941 with a bomb hitting near Quarry Hill destroying the Woodpecker Inn, damaging St Patrick's RC Church and shattering many windows in the Quarry Hill Flats. Kirkstall Forge was bombed on August 8th 1942 and there was damage or destruction of 130 houses in the Cardigan Road area of Headingley. There had been a total of nine bombing raids on Leeds with 87 alerts between August 25th 1940 and August 28th 1942: there were 77 fatalities.

AIRE is the river flowing through Leeds having its origin at Aire Head Springs near Malham. The water from the springs joins with streams from Malham Cove and Gordale Scar to begin the 72 mile course to the River Ouse at Airmyn. It has been associated with industry over many centuries and there has been much success to prevent further pollution. The Aire has a drainage area of 429 square miles. The longest Yorkshire river is the Swale (83 miles) and the shortest is the Bain (2.5 miles).

AIRE STREET links City Square with Whitehall Road and is the road to the restored car park and new west entry to Leeds railway station as well as Prince's Exchange and Whitehall. City Square House replaced a block of shops and offices including Barstow's newsagents on the corner. Businesses included S Grant paper merchant and Brown & Co woollen manufacturers.

AIREDALE, BARON The first Baron Airedale was James Kitson MP who was Mayor in 1896 and Lord Mayor in 1897, living at Gledhow Hall. He was made an Honorary Freeman of Leeds in 1906 and died in Paris in March 1911. The Airedale Foundry under James Kitson Snr built their first locomotive in 1838. The Monkbridge Iron & Steel Co was bought by James Kitson Snr in 1854. He laid the foundation stone for the first Leeds Infirmary in March 1864 - he died in 1885 and was buried at St John's Church near his home of Elmete Hall.

AIRESIDE RETAIL CENTRE was a £7.5 million development designed by DY Davies Associates for Countrycross Ltd and funded by the Post Office Staffs Superannuation Fund. A feature of this shopping centre is one of the three stone built waggon hoists dating from the 1850's - it is a protected listed building (Grade II). The goods yard around Central Station was on two levels: the low level North Eastern Railway/Great Northern Railway with the high level sidings and warehouse of the London & Yorkshire Railway.

Waggons were raised by hydraulic power and by the 1930's were electrically operated, from the low level to the viaduct on which the warehouse was sited - the line of the viaduct can still be seen. The third lifted waggons from the bonded warehouse on Whitehall Road to Central Station sidings. The plans for the Centre were unveiled in 1979 and the first occupant was in 1983.

ALBION is an old name for England meaning literally "white island". *Albion Street* was first laid out on vacant crofts in 1792 by Thomas Johnson and was extended to Woodhouse Lane in 1870. The Leeds Stock Exchange was on Albion Street (1847): later known as the Exchange Rooms (Denby & Co) - the building was demolished to make way for the new YMCA; Leeds & Holbeck Building Society had offices on Albion Street in 1886; the United Institute for the Blind, Deaf and Dumb was also initially based in Albion Street; Norton's Oyster Rooms were founded in Boar Lane in 1826 by John Norton and his nephew William Norton moved the shop to Albion Street in 1868 and there was a transfer to nearby premises in 1885. The Leeds Industrial Co-operative Society was based on Albion Street with the corner of Commercial Street occupied by a branch of Starbucks - built in 1852 for the Leeds & Yorkshire Assurance Company. *Albion Place* was the home of the Scala cinema and ballroom on Lands Lane, with the Church Institute, Leeds Club and William Hey's House: now the Leeds Law Society and Scarborough Building Society. The Church Institute was formed in 1857 and the foundation stone laid for the new Institute in 1866. Albion Place also had the County Court (now WH Smiths) and the YMCA (now partly Austin Reed). The section of Albion Place to Briggate was completed in 1904: the Briggate shops demolished in 1903 included Render's, William Elliott and the Hygienic Gas Stove Co together with the site of the Leopard Hotel in Wheat Sheaf Yard. *Albion Walk* was the site of the Albion Chapel which had the foundation stone laid in March 1793 and the "Zion" Chapel opened in May 1794. In 1796 it became an Anglican Chapel and on September 30th 1801 was consecrated as St James Chapel. It was reopened on January 2nd 1802 as a Scottish Presbyterian Chapel and in 1836 the Congregationalists moved to Belgrave Chapel. In February 1837 Albion opened as another Congregational Chapel and in July 1840 it became the New Connexion General Baptist Chapel - in 1842 Rev Jabez Tunnicliff became a new minister. On February 7th 1847 the Swedenborgians took over Albion Chapel until 1883 when they moved to Willow Terrace Road (New Jerusalem Church). The old chapel became a wool warehouse and later storage for the Leeds Mutual Supply Co - the chapel building was burnt down on July 12th 1889: parts of the graveyard were discovered in 1973.

ALBRECHT, MARTIN HENRY (1852-1909) of Lake Side Roundhay was a wholesale clothier. Albrecht & Albrecht opened on Park Place and moved to Oxford Row moving to Hudson Road in 1898. In 1920 the factory was sold to Burtons and Albrechts moved to the Friends Meeting House on Woodhouse Lane prior to the sale to the BBC. Walter Albrecht (1852-1923) was Martin's brother who was born in Manchester and came to Leeds in c1883. He formed a working partnership with his brother c1903 but then moved to his own business in Mabgate Mills manufacturing ladies skirts and blouses - he died in Harrogate.

ALDERMEN of Leeds were appointed with the first charter of 1626: the first one was Sir John Savile of Howley Hall. The first mayor of Leeds under the second charter of 1661 was Thomas Danby-remembered in Thomas Danby College.

ALEXANDRE LTD was founded in 1906 by Samuel Lyons on Skinner Lane and in 1910 opened Alexandre's tailors shop on County Arcade. In 1915 the firm moved to Templar Street and a factory was built in 1921 known initially as SH Lyons and in 1926 became Alexandre Ltd. By 1929 the firm ran 46 shops and 600 suits a week were being made at their factory: in 1937 there were 74 shops. The factory was extended to Lady Lane in 1938 and in the 1960's moved out to West Park Ring Road (WIRA) following a merger with UDS in 1954.

ALLBUTT, SIR CLIFFORD FRS (1836-1925) was born at Thornhill where his father was the Vicar and was educated at St Peter's School York and Cambridge University. He settled in Leeds and was appointed physician to the House of Recovery in 1861 and in 1863 joined the staff at the Infirmary and Dispensary. He introduced the ophthalmoscope into clinical medicine and was a respected physician and scholar. He built Carr Manor in 1881 - later the home of Lord Moynihan - and he retired in 1884 practicing in Leeds until 1889. He moved to Cambridge and became Regius Professor of Physic during which period he was knighted - he died at Cambridge in 1925.

ALLDER'S STORE on The Headrow was originally Lewis's department store: this was opened on 17th September 1932 at a cost of £1 million. The store became a member of the Owen & Owen Group after going into receivership in 1991 and was opened by Allders in September 1996. Allders was founded in 1862 by Joshua Allders in Croydon, where the present head office and main store is based. The company now have 36 stores throughout Britain with two in Leeds: The Headrow and Kirkstall. The Allders store at Kirkstall traded as Clover until October 1995: Clover was already a name within the Allders Group.

ALMSHOUSES in the city included *Harrison's Almshouses* built 1653 for 40 poor women being the gift of merchant John Harrison who left £1000 as an endowment. The Wade Lane almshouses were one site and there was another in Raglan Road Woodhouse Moor (Harrison Potter Almshouses). There were 12 houses added 1790-1817 being the gift of Arthur Ikin and eight more added on Harrison Street in 1826-45. The main block was rebuilt in 1849/50 to the designs of John Dobson who had a practice on Park Row: Dobson also was involved with St Matthew's Church Camp Road and St Stephen's Church Burmantofts. The Harrison Almshouses Wade Lane were demolished in 1960 for redevelopment. *Ibbetson's Almshouses* were opened in 1715 on Call Lane for poor men - the funding was by James Ibbetson. *Iveson's Almshouses* were founded near the workhouse c1695 as a gift of 3 houses by Lancelot Iveson. *Jenkinson's Almshouses* were founded by Josias Jenkinson at Quebec with eight cottages by his will of August 10th 1643: these were rebuilt on Mill Hill (Basinghall Street) in 1806-07 and removed to new buildings on St Mark's Road Woodhouse about 1838 providing nine dwellings. Jenkinson's will left a farm at Great Woodhouse in trust and the rents from the farm provided the money to build the Mill Hill almshouses. *Potter's Almshouses* on St Columba Street/Wade Lane (1736/1853) provided by Mary Potter widow of Thomas Potter merchant and Leeds alderman. Her will was dated 1st April 1728 and the almshouses were founded in 1736 and opened in 1738 for ten poor widows: Mary died on May 31st 1729 and left £2000 to found the almshouses which were rebuilt in 1853 and demolished for the development of the Merrion Centre. In 1765 Barbara Chantrell bequeathed the interest on £400 to the almshouses. The 40 Harrison & Potter's almshouses on Lovell Park Road (Camp Road) were opened in May 1967.

ALTMAN, MARK (1876-1951) came to Leeds and opened his ballroom on Great George Street in 1902: he also bought the old Vicar Lane Post Office and a house at Headingley for dancing. His son Dennis Altman took over and changed the name of the ballroom to the Dennis Altman School of Dancing. The school closed in 1990 and the building was demolished to be replaced with Crown House opened in 1996.

AMBLER, THOMAS (1838-1920) was the son of Leeds engineer Joseph Ambler; he was an architect who set up a practice on Park Row in 1860 and in the 1890's took George Bowman as a partner. Thomas Ambler designed the Trevelyan Temperance Hotel (1878) on Boar Lane for John Barran, along with other buildings on the street, St Paul's House as a factory and warehouse for Sir John Barran (1878) and Parcmont at Roundhay (1883) for the Barrans. Other Leeds buildings by Thomas Ambler included St James Hall York Street and Victoria Arcade (1898) - demolished 1959. He bought land in Far Headingley in 1874 and laid out Hollin Lane. Thomas Ambler lived at Broomhill on Harrogate Road, which was sold by the family in 1949 to the Diocese of Leeds. The house is the presbytery of the Immaculate Heart Church-the church opened in 1956 and was consecrated in 1959.

ANDREWS, SIR WILLIAM LINTON (1886-1972) was born and educated at Hull; he was the editor of the Leeds Mercury from 1923 until 1939 and editor of The Yorkshire Post from 1939 to 1960. He was knighted in 1954, chairman of the Press Council from 1955 to 1959 and Director of the Yorkshire Newspaper Group from 1956 until 1968.

APPLEYARD, JOHN ERNEST opened his first car showroom on Park Row in June 1919: this burnt down in 1921. A new depot opened in September 1921 on Albion Street and new showroom opened on St Anne's Street. The North Street showroom opened in October 1927 and Appleyard's rotunda petrol station at the bottom of Eastgate was restored and redeveloped as a fountain feature in 2000.

ARCADES *Burton's Arcade* was rebuilt in 1972 and refurbished at a cost of £1 million in 1996/97 by owners Gold Bay Developments Ltd - the arcade became part of the Trinity Quarter development;

County and Cross (after the nearby market cross) arcades were built on the site of Cheapside and the Shambles (1898-1903) designed by Frank Matcham who was responsible for the Empire Palace Theatre. County Arcade was the site of the Mecca Locarno Ballroom and this was converted into a café in 1994: the floor is mainly marble and mosaic-the County and Cross Arcades were sold to Prudential Assurance in July 1955; *Empire Arcade* developed following the demolition of the theatre in 1962: it opened in 1964 and has been redeveloped as Harvey Nichols; *Grand* (1897) was built by the New Briggate Arcade Company and there is a Potts clock inscribed "Time and Tide wait for no man": new glass doors and restored shops and floor were completed in 2001; *Market Street Arcade* was completed by 1930 with the covering of Market Street from Briggate to Central Road. Restoration followed purchase in 1959 by Metrovincial Properties, further restoration is planned; *Queen's* (1889) was built on the site of the Rose & Crown public house (Bink's Hotel) to designs by architect Edward Clark of London; it was sold on December 7th 1965 for £830,000 and restored in 1994; *Thornton's Arcade* opened on May 12th 1877 on the site of the Old Talbot Inn built by Charles Thornton to the design of George Smith of Leeds and restored in 1993 and 1997; the William Potts clock features characters from Ivanhoe and was installed in 1878. On the east end of the arcade is a representation of the Duchess of Devonshire: about the time that ths arcade was opened a Gainsborough portrait of the Duchess of Devonshire was stolen and Charles Thornton commissioned the head in the likeness of the Duchess for his arcade; *Trinity Street Arcade* was opened by Jimmy Savile on July 3rd 1973; *Victoria Arcade* on The Headrow was designed by Thomas Ambler in 1898 to mark the Queen's Jubilee and demolished in 1959 to be incorporated into Schofield's Store; *Victoria Quarter* (1990) is a glass covered arcade built on Queen Victoria Street with the County & Cross arcades at a cost of £6 million. Prudential sold the property in June 2001 to Paul Sykes (Highstone Estates of Harrogate) for £45 million. In recent years Paul Sykes has sold Meadowhall Centre (£1.2bn) and Planet Online (£46 million).

ARCADIA is Britain's second highest clothing retailer and owns Top Shop, Burtons and Dorothy Perkins - the 12 high street names once included Richards and Principles.

ARK ROYAL The first ship was named in 1587 when the Ark Raleigh received a name change as the Lord High Admiral's flagship (Lord Howard of Effingham) - the ship sank in the fight against the Spanish Armada in 1588. The second Ark Royal was that of a former merchant vessel launched in 1887 and received the new name to serve as a sea plane carrier in the First World War with action in the Dardanelles (1915): the name was changed to Pegasus in 1934. The third Ark Royal was launched on November 13th 1941 and commissioned in November 1938: the carrier saw action in Norway (1940), Spartivento (1940), Mediterranean (1940), in action against the Bismark (1941) and served on the Malta convoys (1941) - it was torpedoed off Gibraltar at 4.30am on Friday November 14th 1941 and sank at 6.30am after Captain Maund had ordered abandon ship - only one life was lost of the 1600 on board. The fourth aircraft carrier was adopted by the City of Leeds on February 7th 1942, which raised £9,301,297 for the Leeds National Savings Appeal during Leeds Warships Week from January 31st - February 6th 1942 meeting 40% of the construction costs. General de Gaulle took the salute at Leeds Town Hall for the march past of Allied troops during Ark Royal Week in May 1942. The new ship was launched by HM The Queen Mother on May 3rd 1950 and completed on February 25th 1955; the ship was decommissioned and was broken up in 1978/79 - a plate marking this event is displayed in the Civic Hall. The fifth Ark Royal (20,000 tons) was the ex-Indomitable (Invincible Class) launched on June 2nd 1981 and completed on November 11th 1985. On October 25th 1973 HM Queen Mother granted the Freedom of Leeds to the Ark Royal-it had been resolved in council on April 20th 1972. A ship's plaque is displayed in the Civic Hall which was presented to the City of Leeds by the Ark Royal in February 1955. A miniature silver ship's bell was presented to Leeds by the ship's company on October 25th 1973; a glass bowl which commemorates the 25th anniversary of granting the Freedom of Leeds to the Ark Royal is dated November 1997. A scale model of the ship by Julian Glossop is displayed in the Civic Hall.

ARMLEY MILLS. There was a fulling mill on the site in 1590 known as Casson's Mills: Peter Casson died in 1617 and the mills were run by his wife and sons before having new owners and tenants. One of the tenants was John Walker in 1782 who had a 20 year lease terminated in 1797. In 1788 the mills were bought by Col Thomas Lloyd for £5250 and the mills were reconstructed with a dam and watercourses to direct the river under his woollen mill. The Lloyd mill was burnt down in 1805 and it was bought for £23,790 by Benjamin Gott and rebuilt as a fire resistant construction. The main occupation at Armley Mills was fulling cloth but by the mid 19th century the mills saw a variety of use. Until 1969 Bentley & Tempest continued the production of woollen cloth at Armley Mills and in that year they were bought by Leeds City Council and opened as the Leeds Industrial Museum - an impressive museum complete with a 1930's cinema.

ART GALLERIES The ***Bruton Gallery*** is based in Trafalgar House Park Place and was opened as a commercial gallery by Helen Robinson in September 1998: it specialises in early 20th century French and European sculpture and contemporary paintings by established and emerging artists. The gallery was founded by Michael & Sandra Le Marchant in the village of Bruton Somerset between Frome and Castle Cary in 1968 and had a branch in Bath (closed 1998) and an affiliated gallery in New York. There are close links with the Henry Moore Sculpture Gallery and Yorkshire Sculpture Park at Bretton Hall. ***City Art Gallery*** was the inspiration of Col Walter Harding: he promoted the cause and bought and presented paintings to the new gallery as well as persuading friends such as Sir James Kitson, Alderman George and his father Thomas R Harding to donate paintings. The Art Gallery was opened as an £9000 addition to George Corson's Municipal Buildings (1884) on October 31st 1888 by Lord Mayor Archibald Scarr and the painter Sir Hubert Herkomer: the key for the art gallery was made by goldsmiths Pearce & Son and is on display in the Abbey House Museum. The gallery was opened with the transfer of the JG Umpleby bequest (1858) from the Town Hall. The money came from public subscription established to mark the golden jubilee of Queen Victoria: the art gallery was the former reading room of the Municipal Buildings and was converted to a sculpture gallery. Outside is the Garden of Remembrance opened in October 1937 with the War Memorial moved from City Square in the same year: the area was created by using a vacant site - the buildings having been demolished in 1929/33. Col Thomas Walter

Harding (Lord Mayor 1898/89) was also the prime motivator for City Square (1903). The foundation stone for the £1 million Henry Moore Gallery extension to the art gallery was laid on April 10th 1980: it was opened by HM The Queen on November 26th 1982. The Reclining Figure by Henry Moore 1980/82 was presented by the Henry Moore Foundation. On display in the art gallery is the Henry Moore Reclining Figure "Festival 1951" in bronze and loaned by the Moore Danowski Trust. *Craft Centre & Design Gallery* is on the lower level and is independently run with exhibitions: it was opened in 1982. *Henry Moore Institute* is east of the original art gallery and occupies three 19th century wool merchants office buildings. Designs were made for reconstruction in March 1992 and the £5 million Institute designed by Jeremy Dixon and Edward Jones was opened on April 22nd 1993. *Leeds Metropolitan University Art Gallery* is a part of the City Campus (Woodhouse Lane entrance). *The University Art Gallery* was opened in 1970 in the Parkinson Building and extended in 1974: improvements were financed by the Henry Moore Foundation and the Museums & Galleries Improvement Fund - the gallery reopened in November 1992. Temporary exhibitions were held in Parkinson Court prior to 1970 and there is a large collection mainly of European paintings, drawings and prints. The Vice Chancellor of Leeds University Sir Michael Sadler donated many pictures to the University Art Gallery when he left Leeds in 1923 as well as the City Art Gallery.

ASPDIN, JOSEPH (1778-1855) was a Leeds bricklayer who invented Portland cement: patented October 21st 1824. There is a plaque in the Town Hall unveiled on September 6th 1924: he died in Wakefield in March 1855 aged 76 and was buried at St Joseph's Church. Portland cement is made by burning a mixture of clay and chalk of the colour of Portland stone. Aspdin lived in Pack Horse Yard (Slip Yard) and sold his cement in the Angel Inn Yard off Briggate.

ASSEMBLY ROOMS were a part of the 3rd White Cloth Hall and were opened on June 9th 1777: they were built over the north wing at a cost of £2500 and became a centre of Leeds social life. The first White Cloth Hall was in Kirkgate (1711) with the second built south of the river in 1756. Only a part of the assembly rooms remain due to the construction of the rail link between Marsh Lane

(1834) and Leeds New Station (1869). A fourth White Cloth Hall was opened on King Street-the Metropole Hotel was built on this site in 1899 and included the cupola from the old Hall on the roof. The entrance to the 3rd Hall has been restored and the bell replaced. From the 1860's the Assembly Rooms became a Working Men's Institute, William Towler's Globe Foundry Warehouse, in 1923 Hirst's Tobacco occupied the building and named it Waterloo House. It became the Waterloo Antiques Centre in 1990 and is today Café Rouge (Whitbread) with the Pitcher & Piano bar.

ASSEMBLY STREET is a development of outdoor café/bars on two sides of the old Third Cloth Hall: the buildings include a restored Tower House as a café-bar concept The Townhouse (Chris Barton) in the former three storey warehouse of Regent Printers.

ASSOCIATED DAIRIES (ASDA) Headquarters Building south of the river was opened in 1988: designed by the John Bruton Partnership. The firm was founded in 1920 and became Associated Dairies & Farm Stores by 1949: in 1965 it became Asda Stores with headquarters on Kirkstall Road. The company merged with Wal-Mart (founded by Sam Walton - first store in 1945) which is the world's biggest retailer in August 1999: there are more than 240 stores throughout Britain. The company invested £450 million in new stores during 2001.

ATKINSON, JOHN FLS (1787-1828) was the son of Rev Miles Atkinson and was educated at Leeds Grammar School becoming a surgeon and amateur naturalist. He was the founder of the Museum at the Leeds Philosophical & Literary Society and became the first curator. He was the founder of the Yorkshire Agricultural Society in 1820 and a surgeon at the Leeds Lying-in Hospital of which he was the founder.

ATKINSON, REV MILES (1741-1811) was the son of the rector of Thorp Arch and born at Ledsham. In 1783 he was inducted as Vicar of Kippax and in September 1791 laid the foundation stone of St Paul's Church Park Square; he became the first minister of St Paul's Church Park Square, consecrated on September 10th 1793 by the Archbishop of York. The church was demolished in 1905 and a few memorials were transferred to Holy Trinity Church Boar Lane.

ATLAS CHAMBERS is an office block on the corner of King Street/ St Paul's Street built in 1910 (dated) and designed by architects

Henry Perkin and George Bertram Bulmer for the Atlas Insurance Company: the building is of Burmantofts Marmo Faience with a figure of Atlas over the entrance. The Atlas had been founded in London in 1808 and opened a branch in Leeds during 1885 - they acquired the Manchester Fire & Life Assurance. In 1959 The Atlas was taken over by the Royal Exchange Assurance and moved a few years later to Greek Street: Guardian Royal Exchange became part of AXA Insurance with Atlas House becoming the offices of the Royal Irish Bank.

AUSTICK'S BOOKSHOP was first opened in February 1928 by Bertie Lister Austick on Park Cross Street and on October 31st 1930 opened another shop on Cookridge Street: closed 1990. Bertie's sons David and Paul expanded the business in 1984: Barker's Headrow music shop closed in June 1984; in 1988 the map and travel bookshop opened on The Headrow. Austick's shops were sold to Blackwells in April 1998 who retained the shop on Blenheim Terrace as Blackwell's University Bookshop.

AWMACK'S was a china shop which opened first on Boar Lane in 1852 and transferred to New Briggate in 1880 and to The Headrow in 1931. They moved to Albion Street in 1957 but closed in December 1961. JH Awmack died aged 70 in September 1921.

BAINES, EDWARD (1774-1848) was the senior proprietor of the Leeds Mercury magistrate and MP for Leeds. He was educated at the Grammar School and in 1801 bought the paper on which he had worked: the first edition published by him appeared on March 7th 1801. In 1798 he married Charlotte Talbot and they had eleven children. The newspaper became the organ of the Whig and Dissenting interest in Leeds - it was the forerunner of the Yorkshire Post. Edward Baines was buried at Woodhouse Cemetery after a service at East Parade Chapel. His statue in the Town Hall is by William Behnes: at first it was placed in the Victoria Hall but in 1916 was removed to the rear vestibule along with the statue of Robert Hall.

BAINES, EDWARD JNR. (1800-90) was the Liberal MP for Leeds 1834-41 and again 1859-74. He became associated with his brother Frederick in the proprietorship of the newspaper and lived in Hanover Square.

BAIRD, WILLIAM The clothing supply group bought Centaur

Clothes Ltd in 1989 for £14 million: Centaur was created by John Jackson and based at Centaur House Grove House Lane. The business moved to Great George Street at Centaur House (Marlbeck House) in the late 1970's. William Baird sold its Leeds based Baird Menswear Brands for £19 million in 1998-now based at Quayside House on Canal Wharf; it is a development of an 18th century granary building by St James Securities & CTP Ltd. William Baird is to focus on the Winsmoor Group - women's retail clothes business.

BAKEWELL, WILLIAM (1839-1925) had an architect's practice on East Parade in 1892 and Park Square (1914-23). He became FRIBA in 1892 proposed by Edward Birchall and JW Connon. He was responsible for Carlton Hill Masonic Hall (1872), Queen Anne's Buildings New Briggate (1874), Coliseum (Gaumont) Cookridge Street (1885), Athenaeum Buildings Park Lane (1890), London & Midland Bank Kirkgate (1892), City Square layout (1903) and Pearl Buildings East Parade (1911).

BALMFORTH, LEONARD PERCY (1881-1936) was a violin maker trading in Cookridge Street c1906 moving to Park Lane and Merrion Street. His son Leonard Geoffrey Balmforth continued the business and was recognised as an expert in the county.

BAND OF HOPE was started in a house on the south side of Leeds Bridge in 1847 by Rev Jabez Tunnicliff (1809-65), who promoted the evils of drink to the youth of the town through this Temperance Movement.

BANKS *Abbey National* on Park Row was opened in December 1959: the Building Society became a bank in 1995. The Abbey National was established in 1849 as the National Building Society and in 1944 merged with the Abbey Road Building Society (1874). *Allied Irish Bank* building on Infirmary Street was opened in 1905 on part of the old infirmary site: the bank came to Goodbard House in December 1992 from previous premises on Albion Street. The Allied Irish Banks Ltd was formed in 1966 on the amalgamation of the Royal Bank of Ireland (1836), Provincial Bank of Ireland (1925) and the Munster & Leinster Bank (1885). *Bank of England* in Leeds established a branch on August 27th 1827 on Bank Street in the premises of failed bankers Fields & Greenwoods: it was opened by Thomas Bischoff on August 23rd 1827. They moved to Albion Street in 1835 and to new premises in 1864 on South Parade (architect Philip Hardwick). These were replaced by a new building on King Street (Bank House) opened in July 1971; the old building (Sovereign House) became offices with a bar in the old vaults. The Court of the Bank of England held its first meeting in Leeds in January 2001-the first meeting in Yorkshire since it was founded in 1694. ***Barclay's Bank*** on Albion Street opened in a new building in 1958 and on Park Row in 1967 (1922/23) - the branch closed on September 3rd 1999. Becketts Bank is a JD Wetherspoon Free House opened in the building on January 17th 2001. The branch on The Headrow/Vicar Lane corner was completed by Sir Reginald Blomfield in 1936-his only building on the south side. Barclay's Bank had its origins when John Freame and Thomas Gould opened their business on Lombard Street in 1690. In 1736 James Barclay became a partner: he had married Freame's daughter. In 1896 The Quaker Bank was a new joint stock bank with 182 branches and in 1918 Barclays Bank Ltd amalgamated with the London, Provincial and South Western Bank. By 1926 there were 1837 outlets and in 1986 Barclays acquired Martins Bank (an amalgamation of a London clearing house and the Bank of Liverpool in 1918). The Black Spread Eagle symbol was from the Quaker goldsmithing and banking firm of James Freame in 1728: the symbol was made official in 1937. ***HSBC (Hong Kong & Shanghai Banking Corporation)*** bought the Midland Bank in 1987 and changed the name to HSBC in 1998. HSBC was incorporated in Shanghai in 1866. The office (Midland Bank House) on Park Row/Bond Court was opened in June 1969 on the site of the Leeds Museum & Philosophical Hall. The Midland occupied the round building on the corner of Boar Lane/Bishopgate Street: opened in 1899 and designed by WW Gwyther for the Yorkshire District Banking Co which had been founded in 1834. The building became the Yorkshire Crown (1977) having been a temporary exhibition centre where in 1974 there was a special exhibition celebrating the discovery of Oxygen by Joseph Priestley in 1774; Bistro 5 in 1981, Huckleberrys (1986); it was converted to a restaurant: opened as The Observatory on March 31st 1989 and in 1992 went into receivership. ***Halifax*** took over the Leeds Permanent Building Society on May 1st 1997 and their offices on Lovell Park Road: the LPBS Corporate Centre was opened by the Duke of Edinburgh on June 6th 1993. The Leeds

Permanent was opened on November 8th 1848 as the Leeds Permanent Second Building & Investment Society on the site of WH Smith Lands Lane. They moved to Park Row in 1858 and to Park Lane/Calverley Street in 1878. Permanent House was opened on The Headrow on May 15th 1930, until the merger with Halifax. The Halifax became the bank Halifax Group plc on June 2nd 1997 and merged with the Royal Bank of Scotland in May 2001. *Leeds City Credit Union* was launched in 1987 serving employees of the City Council: based in Westminster Buildings. It is a co-operatively owned bank run by unpaid directors. *Lloyds/TSB* on Bond Street/Park Row was opened in August 1976 having taken three years to build and stands on the site of the Marshall & Snelgrove's department store. Lloyds Bank came to Leeds in 1900 on the amalgamation with William Williams Brown Bank: there is a Greek Street entrance of the old Lloyds Bank to the café bar All Bar One (Bass Leisure Retail). They first opened on the Headrow/ Vicar Lane corner and rebuilt the premises in 1930 set back further north allowing for a wider road: this was the second main block on The Headrow to be opened: designed by Kitson, Parish, Ledgard & Pyman to the original conception of Sir Reginald Blomfield. The bank in Kirkgate was originally the London and Midland by William Bakewell (1892) with carvings by JW Appleyard of Leeds who included the statue of Midas whose touch turned everything to gold. Lloyds Bank was founded in 1765 by Sampson Lloyd in Birmingham - Taylor & Lloyds Bank. In 1865 it became the Lloyds Banking Co Ltd - John Taylor had died in 1775. *Midland Bank* started in Birmingham in 1836 amalgamating with the Leeds & County Bank and Exchange & Discount Leeds in 1890; in 1891 it became the London & Midland and in 1923 The Midland Bank. The HSBC bought the Midland Bank in 1987 and changed the name in 1998. *National Westminster* on Park Row started as Beckett's Bank on the same site opening on June 3rd 1867 designed by George Gilbert Scott (foundation stone laid August 19th 1863): it had transferred from Beckett & Blayds Old Bank Briggate. The Park Row building was demolished and new premises opened in January 1967. John Beckett became a partner in Lodge & Arthington (1758) and in 1867 Cooke & Co amalgamated with Beckett's Bank. NatWest was created in 1968 following the merger of District Bank (1829), National Provincial (1834) and

Westminster (1834). *Royal Bank of Scotland* on Park Row occupies the Scottish Union & National Insurance Company Office of 1909 built in white Marmo blocks: the branch opened in 1983. The bank bought NatWest in 2000. *Woolwich* became part of the Barclays Group in November 2000 having become a bank in 1997: it was founded in 1847 as The Woolwich Equitable Benefit Building & Investment Association. The Park Row building the bank now occupies was built for the York City & County Bank in 1892: the branch transferred from Bond Street in 1988. *Yorkshire Bank* on Infirmary Street opened on the site of the first Infirmary in 1894 to the designs of George Bertram Bulmer, as the Yorkshire Penny Bank. The bank was opened by the Duke of Devonshire on August 17th 1894 using a golden key. The company changed from Yorkshire Penny Bank to Yorkshire Bank in May 1959. The head office on Merrion Way was opened by the Duchess of Kent on September 19th 1981; Brunswick Point was opened on Wade Lane as an office extension in 1991. The Market branch on New York Street was opened in 1900 and was closed in September 1999. Yorkshire Bank was acquired by the National Australia Bank in 1990 and it was announced in November 2000 that the Yorkshire was to be merged with the Clydesdale Bank of Scotland-acquired in 1987. The National Australian Bank Group is the largest Australian investor in the UK and Ireland with assets of more than £104 billion.

BANK MILLS are east of the city centre near Leeds Lock on East Street. They were built for Hives & Atkinson by John Clark in 1824, 1831-32 and the 1856 addition is by the outflow of Sheepscar Beck to the river. The site was originally a cotton spinning mill using a water wheel on Sheepscar Beck built in 1791 by John Sutcliffe (Armley Mills); in 1823 the mills were bought by Hives & Atkinson but a fire the following year necessitated complete rebuilding for their growing flax spinning industry. The mills were sold in 1882 to become a paper firm - producing packaging materials, carrier bags and general printing. Other parts of Bank Mills were at various times used by Marsh, Jones & Cribb, corn millers Letham & Sons, shirtmakers, fruit preservers, Dixon & Gaunt clothiers and waste paper merchants. The 1830's listed building has been converted into offices by Carey Jones (Rose Wharf).

BANK STREET (Boar Lane) was the first home of the Bank of England in 1827: the area has been redeveloped. In the mid 19th century Bank Street had the premises of printer DI Roebuck and the first location for William Williams Brown bank was on the corner of Bank Street and Commercial Street.

BARKER'S MUSIC SHOP The business was founded by Richard Barker in 1913 mainly selling pianos. It was sold to Horace Pickersgill in 1927 and created a limited company. In 1929 the premises were at Lands Lane/Albion Place corner and developed trading in sheet music and later records. In 1968 the shop moved to The Headrow and the shop closed in June 1984: the premises were taken by Austick's Bookshops.

BARRACKS *Carlton Militia Barracks* opened in 1865 for the 4th West Yorkshire Militia and had a new drill hall built in 1888 (dated): the headquarters of the 3rd battalion West Yorkshire (Leeds) Rifle Volunteers; the building became the Medical Training Centre for 212 Field Hospital RAMC Volunteers in October 1986. The Carlton Hill old entrance still bears the name "Carlton Barracks-Leeds Rifles" and the Old Carlton Barracks (Ministry of Defence) is the HQ of the 3rd VB Prince of Wales's Own WY Regiment and is the BHQ of WR Artillery 269 Observation Post Battery. The New Carlton Barracks is the HQ of the Leeds University OTC and 49 Signals Squadron. The site includes Carr Lodge which is now the Officer's Mess. Carlton Barracks featured a captured German field gun, which was once on a plinth outside Fenton Street Barracks from c1920 to 1962. Five years later it was moved to Collingham and stayed there until 1986 when the gun was taken to the Old Carlton Barracks; it was restored at York and displayed again at Carlton Barracks in 1989. The *Chapeltown Cavalry Barracks* were built on an 11 acre site in 1820 at a cost of £28,000 a mile from the town centre: the builders were Craven & Co. There were soldier's quarters, officer's accommodation, canteen, stables, hospital and infirmary with a riding school. At one time the barracks overlooked Rosebud Gardens to the south. The Leeds Rifles met at the old riding school and parade ground for 80 years prior to transfer to Harewood Barracks in 1967. The barracks were demolished in 1988 and a part of the site became the home to the Reg Vardy dealership opening in January 1995. *Fenton Street Barracks* dated from the 19th century being built of brick in a castellated style and were extended in 1903 and had a riding school added in 1911. They were the headquarters of the 1st WR York Artillery Volunteers formed in 1860 and later the 69th WR Field Brigade RA (TA). There was an extensive enclosed drill hall designed by Fox & Fraser and the area was demolished in 1962/64. *Gibraltar Barracks* were between Claypit Lane and Camp Road (north of Grove House Lane) and were opened in 1889: the headquarters of the Royal Engineers Northern Command Telegraph Companies (RE) which had been formed in 1908. The barracks were demolished by January 20th 1967. The *Harewood Barracks* on Woodhouse Lane were Artillery Barracks based at St James Lodge which was built for Richard Lee in c1860 and in 1877 the Lodge became the first home of Leeds Girls High School. When the school moved to Headingley St James Lodge became Harewood Barracks and the headquarters of the Army Service Corps (Territorials) and 1st West Riding (Leeds) Volunteers: TA from 1910. The barracks were also the meeting place of the Royal Army Medical Corps (TA) HQ 49th Division; 146th WR Field Ambulance; Yorkshire Hussars Yeomanry A Squad and 49th WR Division Training (TA). It was also the HQ of part of the 249 (West Riding Artillery) Regiment RA TA. The area was cleared in 1964 with the last block demolished by February 1967: the site became Leeds Polytechnic. The *Harewood Barracks* transferred to Skinner Lane/Regent Street which were opened on February 18th 1963: it is the HQ of the Harewood Cadet Detachment Yorkshire ACF, HQ of A Squadron 212 (Yorkshire) Field Hospital and the Leeds Detachment (Leeds Rifles) Imphal Company the East & West Riding Regiment from 1967. *The Churchill Barracks* on Whitelock Street are the HQ of 217 Transport Squadron. *Woodhouse Lane Barracks* were the temporary headquarters of the 70th Royal Sussex Regiment: the barracks were closed in July 1844 and were adapted for commercial use.

BARRACLOUGH, ZERUBBABEL & SONS were diamond merchants and jewellers having shops in Briggate and Commercial Street. The firm was established in 1805 and was advertised as being watchmakers to the Admiralty: the firm closed in December 1957.

BARRAN, SIR JOHN (1821-1905) was born in Surrey and married twice; he became MP for Leeds 1876-85 and was knighted in 1895.

He came to Leeds in the 1840's and opened a pawnbrokers shop at 30 Bridge End Street but soon started dealing in clothes. John Barran moved to No 1 Briggate (part of the site of the Golden Lion Hotel) and devoted his energy to the development of the ready made clothing trade and saw the advantage of the Singer Sewing Machine - invented in 1855. In 1858 he was inspired by Greenwood & Batley's band saw and started to use a band knife which allowed many thicknesses of cloth to be cut at one time. Barran then moved to larger premises at 1 Boar Lane and was to form a partnership with Nussey of Carlinghow Mills Batley and succeeded to this business. John Barran opened in Alfred Street Boar Lane and moved to the Commercial Buildings Park Row, where his son joined the firm. He had a new factory St Paul's House on St Paul's Street/Park Square designed by Thomas Ambler in 1878, which dealt in wholesale ready made clothing. In 1898 a new factory opened on Hanover Lane, now known as Joseph's Well. Sir John Barran bought Roundhay Park at an auction at the Great Northern Hotel in October 1871 for £139,000: the Council bought the property from Barran with interest and the park was opened to the public by HRH Prince Arthur on September 19th 1872. John Barran also paid for a fountain to be erected in the park at a cost c£2000. He was the Chairman of the YMCA and one of the founders of the Yorkshire College. He died a devout Baptist on May 3rd 1905 and was buried at Beckett Street Cemetery: he lived at Chapel Allerton Hall.

BARRASFORD, THOMAS (1860-1910) was born in Jarrow and came to Leeds to manage the Princess Palace - he changed the name to The Tivoli. He invented the Flickerless Barrascope which he used in Leeds to show short news films; he also designed and produced a new starting gate mechanism for use on race courses. Tom Barrasford died of Bright's disease at Brighton.

BARRY, DR ALFRED (1826-1910) was appointed headmaster of Leeds Grammar School in 1854 and two years later suggested that the school be transferred from the John Harrison building. The Woodhouse Moor site was chosen in 1857 and the architect appointed was Dr Barry's brother Edward Middleton Barry. The foundation stone of the new £9776 building was laid on April 6th 1858 by the Bishop of Ripon and the school opened on June 27th 1859. In May 1862 Barry decided to erect a chapel on the site again designed by Edward Barry: the chapel was opened in 1863 and consecrated on January 13th 1870 dedicated to St Wilfred. Dr Alfred Barry was appointed Principal of Cheltenham College in May 1862, later Principal of King's College London and later Bishop of Sydney and Primate of all Australia. He was followed as headmaster of Leeds Grammar School by Dr William Henderson who stayed at the school until 1884.

BARS There were six bar stones which were placed in 1725 marking the medieval boundaries of the town. *Burley Bar* was at Albion Street/Headrow junction and is preserved in a glass case in the Leeds & Holbeck Building Society. The *East or York bar* was by the parish church: it is in the exterior wall of the church; *North Bar* at the junction of Vicar Lane and Lady Lane on the site of the old workhouse and West Yorkshire Bus Station. The North Bar stone was originally on the old workhouse wall and was replaced in April 1937. *South Bar* was across Leeds Bridge. *West Bar* was at the end of Boar Lane - a blue plaque marks the site. *Woodhouse Bar* was at the south end of Woodhouse Lane (Dortmund Square).

BASINGHALL STREET links The Headrow with Boar Lane and was the site of the automatic telephone exchange, affected by an air raid during the last war. The site was cleared in October 1911 being once McCorquodale (printers) - the building is dated 1913 and bears the royal coat of arms; the exchange moved to Burley Street (1965) and Butts Court (1993). The street had the offices of film distributors Grand National Pictures as well as being the site of the Leeds Parish Church Middle Class School in 1870. The warehouse of Marsh, Jones & Cribb was in Basinghall Street as well as the office of the French Vice-Consul. It was on Basinghall Street that the Leeds & Bradford Relay Station was opened by Lord Mayor Sir Edwin Airey on July 8th 1924: this allowed radio links to London and the development of local broadcasting with the BBC- the site is now the Leeds Shopping Plaza.

BASS BREWERIES were founded in Burton on Trent in 1777 by William Bass: grandson Michael Bass (died 1884) was MP for Derby. In 1837 the business was Bass, Ratcliffe & Gretton and in 1926 Bass bought Worthington Breweries. In 1962 Charrington & Co (London 1766) merged with United Breweries (Carling & Jubilee) and in 1967 Bass Charrington was created: the group bought Holiday Inns in 1987. Bass run many hotel and bar operations in the city. Bass became Six Continents in 2001/2 after the sale of the brewery business in 2000.

BATEMAN, MARY (1768-1809) was born near Thirsk and came to Leeds in 1788; after 20 years of crime the so-called witch Mary Bateman was condemned to death for murder by poisoning. She was hanged at York Castle and her body was taken to Leeds General Infirmary where over £30 was raised for Infirmary funds following public viewing; her skeleton was retained and displayed at the Thackray Medical Museum in 2001.

BATHS *Holbeck Baths* were opened in 1898 and were closed in 1979. *Hunslet Baths* opened on December 17th 1898 and were closed on December 22nd 1979. *The International Pool* on Westgate designed by disgraced architect John Poulson was opened on September 23rd 1967: 220,000 swimmers enjoyed the facility in the first six months. *Kirkstall Baths* opened on June 8th 1895 and closed on March 15th 1977. *Meanwood Baths* were opened in March 1879 and closed in 1977. *Oriental Baths* on Cookridge Street were designed by Cuthbert Brodrick and opened on February 19th 1867 at a cost of £13,000 - with crowning domes and minarets: the building was resurfaced and altered in 1882 they were closed on February 4th 1965 and later demolished. The area became a car park and in 2000/01 became part of Millennium Square. *Union Street Baths* opened to the rear of Millgarth Police Station on August 24th 1895: designed by baths specialist Walter Hanstock (1842-1900) and closed on January 4th 1964. The baths and police station were built on land cleared of 222 houses. *Waterloo Swimming Pool* on the Leeds & Liverpool canal basin used river water and opened in 1833/34. *Wellington Baths* on Lisbon Street designed by Henry Walker were opened on May 1st 1869 at a cost of £6000. *Wellington Road Baths* opened on May 15th 1819 designed by Robert Chantrell opposite the pleasure grounds of the Infirmary: the cost was £7000. *York Road Baths* opened on April 4th 1905 and the Russian Baths were closed on January 4th 1964: the baths finally closed in the late 1970's.

BAY HORSE YARD is on the east side of Briggate near The Headrow: once the site of the Bay Horse Inn and now with few of the 19th century buildings. The original public house was run by a Mr Molineaux as a stone sign indicates - the yard retains reminders of the original gas lighting. The area south of this yard to Cheapside was demolished and redeveloped by The Leeds Estate Company 1898-1902, including the loss of the White Hart, Boy & Barrel and Boot & Shoe Inns.

BAYNES, ADAM (1621-1670) was the first Parliament man for Leeds during the Commonwealth: he was an officer in the Parliamentary army under General Lambert and was returned as MP for Leeds in 1644. He married Martha Dawson and lived at Knowsthorpe Hall.

BAZAAR was the market development on the east side of Briggate in 1826 following the demolition of the Moot Hall and Middle Row. One of the main occupiers was the carpet warehouse of W & T Kettlewell who also had a store at 100 Briggate.

BEAN, WILLIAM H was a Leeds bookseller established in 1795 and based on Lower Basinghall Street. The business moved in 1974 to premises on Dolly Lane due to the redevelopment of the Basinghall Street area. Dolly Lane is the continuation of Cherry Row in the Newtown area: the firm closed in 1983. In the mid-20th century the business was run by the brother of the Scholes/Crossgates GP Dr William Harold Bean.

BEAN ING MILL or Park Mills was built by Benjamin Gott in West Leeds in 1792 as the world's first woollen mill. He was soon also operating Armley Mills (rebuilt 1805) and Burley Mills - by 1813 Gott was running 133 looms. Bean Ing became the premises of other manufacturers including Joshua Wilson & Sons worsted spinners. The mills were demolished in the 1960's and the 16 acre site became the home of Yorkshire Post Newspapers. The new development was opened by the Prince of Wales in September 1970; the first premises were on Albion Street.

BECK & INCHBOLD were printers with premises on Bond Street who moved to new premises on Ring Road Seacroft in 1960. Thomas Inchbold (born 1786) was apprenticed in 1800 to Mr Fawdington a bookseller in Back of Shambles: in 1808 he joined as a partner. In 1819 Thomas became a partner with Thomas Kirkby and William Bawtress but a year later was bankrupt. In 1821 Thomas started again in Back of Shambles (Empire Theatre site) but in 1832 died in the great cholera epidemic. In 1860 William James Beck (died in Harrogate 1919) joined the business then based in Bond Street together with Henry Inchbold: the firm became Inchbold & Beck in 1865 and in 1890 was known as Beck &

Inchbold. The business was closed as Beck & Partridge in June 1979.

BECKETT, SIR EDMUND (1816-1905) was the first Baron Grimthorpe created in 1886: he was responsible for the restoration of St Alban's Cathedral and his interests included clocks, architecture and astronomy. Lord Grimthorpe was responsible for the design of Leeds Town Hall clock as well as the clocks of Leeds Parish Church, St Chad's Church Headingley and Big Ben at the Houses of Parliament. There are 320 steps to the clock tower at Leeds Town Hall and the clock has a diameter of over 11 feet with the minute hand measuring 5 feet 11 inches and the hour hand at 3 feet 10 inches.

BECKETT, SIR JOHN (1743-1826) was the grandson of Gervase Beckett of Barnsley and he married Mary Wilson: daughter of Rt Rev Christopher Wilson Bishop of Bristol & aunt to Richard Fountayne Wilson MP. They had eight sons and three daughters: William (born 1784) married Frances Adeline sister of Hugo Meynell Ingram of Temple Newsam. Sir John Beckett was created a baronet in 1813 and was twice mayor of Leeds (1775/1797). He was the principal partner of Beckett, Blayds Bank Co: he was succeeded by his eldest son Rt Hon Sir John Beckett MP FRS who in 1816 married Lady Anne Lowther daughter of the Earl of Lonsdale. On September 23rd 1826 he was interred at St John's Church Leeds in the family vault: mourners included John Blayds and Benjamin Gott.

BECKETT, RT HON SIR JOHN (1775-1847) was the eldest son of Sir John Beckett and educated at Leeds Grammar School continuing studies under Rev William Sheepshanks vicar of St John's Church. He gained distinction at Trinity College Cambridge and was called to the bar at the Inner Temple 1803. He held parliamentary posts and was returned as MP for Leeds in 1835: he was the head of Beckett & Co Bankers of Leeds and was a keen promoter of the railways. He died at the York Hotel Brighton intestate and the estates devolved to his brother banker Thomas Beckett. He was buried at Fulham where rested his maternal grandfather Christopher Wilson Lord Bishop of Bristol. His brother was Sir Thomas Beckett (1779-1872) who became the 3rd baronet and his other younger brother was Sir Edmund Beckett (1787-1874) who changed his name by royal licence to Sir Edmund

Beckett-Denison. It was his son Sir Edmund Beckett (1816-1905) who became the 5th baronet and was created the first Baron Grimthorpe in 1886. His sons were Christopher Beckett (1825-84) and William Beckett (1826-90) of Nun Appleton who married Helen Duncombe - daughter of the Earl of Feversham of Duncombe Park. William's son was Ernest William second Baron Grimthorpe (1856-1917) senior partner in Beckett's Bank and his son Ralph William Ernest Beckett (1891-1963) was the third Baron Grimthorpe of Westow Hall: his son Sir Christopher John Beckett became the fourth Baron Grimthorpe.

BECKETT, HON RUPERT EVELYN (1870-1955) was the chairman of the Yorkshire Conservative Newspaper Co from 1920 until 1950: the company was formed in 1866. His career started in the family banks - he steered the amalgamation with the Westminster Bank in 1921. Rupert Evelyn Beckett became an Honorary Freeman of Leeds in October 1930.

BECKETT, WILLIAM (1784-1863) was the principal partner of Beckett's Bank and MP for Leeds & Ripon (1841-57) and lived at Kirkstall Grange. He was a great benefactor for many charities as well as offering donations to the Philosophical Hall, Leeds Infirmary, Mechanic's Institute and St Chad's Church Headingley. He was the fifth son of Sir John Beckett and bought the New Grange estate in 1834 and it was renamed Kirkstall Grange. William Beckett was buried at Kelsall Green Cemetery London.

BECKETT PARK was opened as a teacher training college in 1913: in 1541 New Grange was leased to Robert Pakeman and was later in the hands of Thomas Cranmer, Isaac Foxcroft and in 1590 was bought by Anthony Wade. It was Benjamin Wade who built the New Grange in 1626 and it remained in the family until 1834 - the land once was part of Kirkstall Abbey property The Beckett family bought the estate in 1834 and renamed it Kirkstall Grange. In 1908 Lord Grimthorpe sold the estate to the City of Leeds who opened a college on the site. In the Great War it became Beckett's Park Hospital and by 1926 it resumed the teacher training facilities. In 1933 the Carnegie UK Trust set up a men's PE College (Carnegie College) which became part of the College of Education and is now part of the LMU. An archway was built in Beckett Park to mark the visit of Queen Victoria to Leeds when she opened the Town Hall in 1858.

BEDFORD STREET had the offices of Buckley wholesale clothiers-the building featured sheep's heads.

BEDFORD, FRANCIS WILLIAM (1867-1904) had an architect's practice in Leeds and was in partnership with Sydney Decimus Kitson (1871-1937). They were responsible for the School of Art (1903) and the Public Dispensary North Street (1904) - now Centenary House.

BEECH GROVE ESTATE is now an integral part of Leeds University situated on both sides of University Road (College Road). Beech Grove was built in 1796 for Benjamin Murgatroyd; Beech Grove House was built in 1799 for Abraham Rhodes and is now the Department of Education. In 1840 the house was sold to iron founder John March who became partner with Matthew Murray at the Union Factory Dewsbury Road-the last member of the family died there in 1925.

BEHNES, WILLIAM (1795-1864) was the son of a Hanover piano maker and came to London in 1802 and attended the RA schools: he was a RA Silver Medallist in 1816/17 and 1819. William Behnes became Sculptor-in-Ordinary to HM The Queen in 1837: he exhibited at the Royal Academy (1815-63) and at the Great Exhibition (1851/1862). He produced the statues of Henry Hall in the LGI (1852), Sir Robert Peel on Woodhouse Moor (1852) and Edward Baines (1858) in Leeds Town Hall. He died bankrupt and was buried at Kelsall Green Cemetery London.

BELGRAVE STREET was the site of the Great Synagogue opened for the United Hebrew Congregation in August 1861: architects were William Perkin and Elisha Backhouse. The first synagogue in Leeds was a converted house in Back Rockingham Street (Merrion Centre site) in 1846. The Belgrave Street synagogue was rebuilt in 1878 and the building closed in 1983: it was demolished and the site rebuilt as offices (Zicon House). Belgrave Hall is a period office building which was originally a warehouse built c1890. The building was refurbished in 1995 and is now office accommodation. Leeds Register Office was opened in 1979 (Belgrave House). Symons House was opened in 1989 by Elizabeth Symons in memory of her late father Ernest Vize Symons Chief Inspector of the Inland Revenue Department (1973-75).

BELLWIN, LORD (1923-2001) was born Irwin Norman Bellow and educated at Leeds Grammar School and Leeds University where he gained a degree in law. He worked in his father's textile firm Bellow Machines which had been founded in 1913, becoming chairman in the 1960's. The company was bought by Staflex in 1969 - Irwin Bellow served as its chairman from 1972 to 1978; it was sold again in 1982 to Willcox-Gibbs. He entered politics in 1965 winning Potternewton Ward for the Conservatives. He was later Shadow Housing Chairman and in 1968 became an Alderman. In 1973 he was elected Leader of the city's Tory Group and was Leader of the Council from 1975 until his creation as a Life Peer in 1979. He was appointed a junior minister for local government at the Department of the Environment and in 1983 was promoted to Minister of State. He was a magistrate in Leeds in 1969 and became Deputy Lieutenant for West Yorkshire in 1991. He was a governor of Leeds Grammar School and the Vice Chairman for 12 years; Lord Bellwin was married in 1948 to Doreen Saperia and has a son and two daughters.

BENNETT, ALAN was born in May 1934 and educated at Leeds Modern School (1946-52) and Exeter College Oxford (1954-57): he was a junior lecturer at Magdalene College 1960-62. His first play was "Forty Years On" in 1968 and wrote for Beyond the Fringe together with The Madness of George III, Talking Heads and A Private Function amongst many TV scripts. Alan Bennett has received the Tony Award (1963), Royal Television Society Award (1984 & 1986) and The Olivier Award (1990).

BERRY, HENRY & CO was established in 1883 on Balm Road manufacturing machine tools, hydraulic machinery and products for shipbuilding and railways.

BERWIN & BERWIN was founded by Barnett Berlyn who came to Leeds in 1900 from White Russia to work for John Barran and lived with his family in The Leylands. They moved to Coburg Street (Merrion Centre) and set up his own business in 1920. The expanding firm moved to Bridge Street and then acquired extra space by 1936 in St Peter's Building for the manufacture of Berbourne raincoats: by 1933 they had changed their name to Berwin. The Roseville Road factory (Heaton's old site) opened in 1935 and they moved to Westland Road (Dewsbury Road) after the last War. The 1960's further expansion saw the firm in three separate sites in Leeds including Harehills Lane (1962) but they moved to a single site in Roseville Road in 1971: producing clothing for Austin Reed, Harrods and Burberry. The firm closed in June 2000 with managing director Simon Berwin announcing the loss of 105 jobs. The business continues at South Kirby: in 2001 the firm bought the Hungarian clothing manufacturer Elit Group.

BINKS, MARTIN (born 1940) is the conductor of the Leeds Symphony Orchestra from 1970 and Artistic Director and Conductor of West Riding Opera from 1968. He was born at Knaresborough and educated at Newcastle, Southampton and the Universities of Birmingham and Cardiff; Martin was appointed Head of Music at Aireborough Grammar School. He is conductor of Knaresborough Choral Society, guest conductor of Oslo Conservatoire Orchestra and York Opera. The French Government appointed him Chevalier de l'Ordre des Arts et des Lettres in 1993 for his services to French music.

BIRCHALL, EDWARD (1838-1903) of Moorland Road came from a Leeds Quaker family and was the architect for the Friends Meeting House Woodhouse Lane (1868), Walter Stead's Wellington Street warehouse (1868), United Institution for the Blind, Deaf & Dumb Albion Street (1875), St Agnes Church Burmantofts (1889), Central High School Woodhouse Lane (1889) and Marsh Jones & Cribb Basinghall Street premises (later on York Road). Edward Birchall was in partnership with William Perkin and trained in the London office of Gilbert Scott; he was in partnership with John Kelly in 1883. He was the President of the Leeds & Yorkshire Architectural Society and in his will left £1000 to the Society of Friends.

BISCHOFF was one of the many families who were cloth merchants; the Blayds and Denisons were also family concerns. Sheepscar Hall (Bishoff House) on Hartley Hill was built by William Etty for Nathaniel Denison in 1692. It was later bought by Bernard Bischoff who came from Switzerland; his eldest son John James Bischoff (1775-1845) lived at the renamed Bischoff House - the façade was revealed in 1967 having been Arthur English's electrical showroom: it was demolished in 1968 - the site is the car park for Centenary House. James Bischoff married Miss M Stansfield and they had three sons and five daughters: the two elder sons lived in Hamburg and the youngest son was a partner with his father in London.

BISHOPGATE STREET by the station was once envisaged as

railway development; it includes the Scarbrough Hotel - named after Henry Scarbrough (landlord 1823-47) - the site of the Leeds Manor House and the Comfort Inn (2000). The street takes its name from the Rt Rev Christopher Wilson (1715-92) Bishop of Bristol; he was the son of Richard Wilson (1678-1761) who was the Leeds Recorder and he was the grandfather of Richard Fountayne Wilson MP. Christopher was educated at Leeds Grammar School and Cambridge; he married Anne Gibson daughter of the Bishop of London and became Bishop of Bristol in 1783. He gave the ground on which was built St Paul's Church Park Square. His eldest son Richard married Elisabeth Fountayne Dean of York and their son was Richard Fountayne Wilson - he became a Yorkshire MP and gave to Leeds a piece of land in front of the LGI. Bishopgate Street once featured Beecroft's Hotel - demolished in 1874 for road improvements.

BISHOPS The Catholic Bishops of Leeds were first appointed in 1878 when the first was Robert Cornthwaite. It was in October 1862 that the Bishop of Beverley Robert Cornthwaite came to live in Hanover Square and he made Leeds the centre of the Diocese of Beverley prior to the creation of the Diocese of Leeds. The Bishops of Leeds: Robert Cornthwaite (1878-1890), William Gordon (1890-1911), Joseph Robert Cowgill (1911-1936), Henry John Poskitt (1936-1950), John Carmel Heenan (1950-1957), George Patrick Dwyer (1957-1965), William Gordon Wheeler (1966-1985) and David Konstant.

BLACK PRINCE (1330-1376) is the centrepiece of City Square: Edward the Black Prince was sculpted by Thomas Brock - it was unveiled on September 16th 1903. The Black Prince was the eldest son of Edward III and was said to have stood for good government, democracy, chivalry, patronage of arts and encouragement of industry. Edward was born in 1330 and wore black armour at the battle of Crecy in 1346. He captured the French king at Poitiers (1356) and ruled Aquitaine (1360-71); in 1367 he invaded Castille and restored Pedro the Cruel to the throne. The Black Prince died in 1376. Col Harding was a keen medieval historian and the inscription reads: *"Hero of Crecy and Poitiers. The flower of England chivalry. The upholder of the rights of the people in the Good Parliament"*.

BLACKBURN, ROBERT OBE (1885-1955) was educated at Leeds

Modern School and Leeds University and started work at Thomas Green, where his father George was works manager. In 1910 he formed Blackburn Aeroplanes of Spencer Place - the business became the Blackburn Aeroplane Co and Robert bought the old Olympia roller skating rink on Roundhay Road in 1914. Plane manufacture moved to Brough in 1929 although 1936 saw the Roundhay factory reopened prior to closure in 1946. The site is now a supermarket and related car parks.

BLACKMAN LANE leads from Woodhouse Lane to Leicester Place: the Blenheim Baptist Chapel and Sunday School is on the corner and on the east side was Carlton Lodge - home of Sir Edwin Gaunt and the Houchin family of dentists: the house was demolished and replaced with a road system connected to the Inner Ring Road. Blenheim Place and Ella Street were also demolished with Lofthouse Place being the site for the Blenheim Primary School and Nursery. Blenheim Lodge faces along Blackman Lane it was once the home of Ada Bulmer and soon became a Nursery - it is still an Early Years Learning Centre. All Soul's Church and Blenheim Square are 19th century features of Blackman Lane.

BLAYDS was one of the merchant woollen families of Leeds. Blayds Yard in Lower Briggate were the workshops and the house faced the main road - seen today with the central section protruding slightly; the house became Owen & Robinson jewellers, later Bass and Bligh. John Blayds became a partner in Beckett's Bank in 1777 and invested heavily in land, building up estates at Oulton and Rothwell. He died childless in 1804 and left his property to a banking partner John Calverley as long as he changed his name to Blayds. In 1850 Oulton House burnt down and the present Oulton Hall was built in 1851-54 by John Blayds - he changed his name back to Calverley in 1852. Oulton Hall is a five star luxury hotel which opened in June 1993.

BLAYDS MEWS & YARD connects Swinegate with Lower Briggate: the narrow street features Blayds House, the restored entrance to the old stable yard to the rear of the Golden Lion Hotel and the Travelodge (Forte). In 1870 George Corson designed shops and offices in Blayds Yard for JD Heaton. Blayds Bar includes a restored plaster ceiling.

BLENHEIM is the area on Woodhouse Lane with All Soul's Church Blackman Lane and the Blenheim Baptist Church. The Baptist

Church was formed in 1848 on Park Lane and a chapel built on Great George Street in 1851. In 1864 the chapel was demolished to make way for the new Infirmary and land was bought on Woodhouse Lane/Blackman Lane with the new chapel opening in 1864. The Woodhouse Lane frontage was added in 1892 - the main church was sold in 1980 for office development. The row of houses called Blenheim Terrace was started in 1824 - it had been suggested for demolition in 1951. An area adjacent to Blenheim Square was once the ground where the Leeds Archery Club (1848) held their meetings. Blenheim School on Blenheim Walk opened on August 11th 1879: after closure and demolition the site was developed as the Student Medical Centre. Blenheim Walk was once the site for the Home & School for Blind and Deaf Children, which was opened on July 5th 1899.

BLENKINSOP, JOHN (1783-1831) was the manager of the Middleton Collieries and in 1811 took out a patent for a locomotive steam engine manufactured by Fenton, Murray & Wood: this was the first engine to use two cylinders and improved on Trevithick's design. The engine started running 3.5 miles from Middleton Collieries to Leeds on August 12th 1812. He died on January 22nd 1831 and was buried at Rothwell Church.

BLIND, DEAF AND DUMB INSTITUTE was in Upper Albion Street with the new building opening on October 22nd 1877 designed by Edward Birchall: demolished to become the site of Dudley House. The United Institution was formed with the amalgamation of the Deaf and Dumb Association and the Blind Institution established in 1866. The Leeds Society for Deaf and Blind People is based in the old Dispensary on North Street/ Hartley Hill.

BLOMFIELD, SIR REGINALD THEODORE (1856-1943). He was the son of Rev GJ Blomfield and was articled to his uncle Sir Arthur Blomfield: he designed Lambeth Bridge and Barker's of Kensington together with the RAF memorial on The Embankment and a few country mansions - his other claim to fame was the design of the electricity pylon. The London architect was engaged to design the new avenue for the city of Leeds - Eastgate and The Headrow in 1925 with the project commencing in 1927. The original narrow Upperhead and Lowerhead Rows were widened to 80 feet by the demolition of the north side. He was keen on cricket and was buried in Golders Green Cemetery on December 31st 1943.

BLUE COAT SCHOOL opened as a charity school on Lady Lane in the converted workhouse in 1705: this was intended for the education of 40 poor children. The workhouse opened again in 1726 and the Blue Coat School re-opened in the Harrison's Almshouses Chapel - there were 120 children in 1806. This was rebuilt in 1815 and there was a change of use to the education of 80 girls for domestic purposes.

BLUE PLAQUES have been placed on many important buildings of Leeds by the Leeds Civic Trust founded in 1975: the first blue plaque was for the Burley Bar stone in 1977. The Civic Trust have placed 67 blue plaques on important sites in Leeds (July 2001) including the site of the Leeds Philosophical Hall Park Row placed in June 2001.

BOAR LANE or Bar (Borough) Lane is one of the original streets of old Leeds leading from Briggate to City Square (West Bar): Bore Lane in 1572. The narrow street was widened 1867-69 to 66 feet by the demolition of the south side: the improvement scheme was completed at a cost of £60,590. Thomas Ambler was engaged to design the new buildings which included Barran's Temperance Hotel - now the Leeds Marriott. On the north side stands Holy

Boar Lane c1905 *(Dorothy Burrows Collection)*

Trinity Church (1726) and adjacent on the site of the C&A store was Alexander Monteith's Grand Pygmalion (1880's) department store. The north side was once the site of attractive gentlemen's residences including that of Sir William Lowther.

BODINGTON, SIR NATHAN JP (1848-1911) was the first Vice Chancellor of Leeds University from 1904 to 1911. He was born at Aston Birmingham and educated at Birmingham GS and Wadham College Oxford. He married Eliza Barran - daughter of Sir John Barran; taught at Manchester GS and Westminster School before appointment as Professor of Classics at Mason College Birmingham. He was the Vice-Chancellor of Victoria University (1896-1904) and Professor of Greek at the Yorkshire College (Leeds) from 1882 to 1904. Bodington Hall was opened at Lawnswood in November 1961.

BOGG, EDMUND (1850-1931) was a picture framer of 3 Wade Street who was the founder and head of the Leeds Savage Club. During the 1880's he lived at Yarm Cottage Holywell Lane Shadwell. Edmund Bogg started this Club in 1891 from artists, musicians, journalists and other friends: he was usually dressed in war paint, feathered head dress and Indian robe being known as T'owd Chief. The meetings were held at Whitelock's public house in Turk's Head Yard. He was born in the East Riding and was a great lover of Yorkshire, coming to Leeds in c1869. He wrote six Yorkshire books including The Old Kingdom of Elmet in 1902 reprinted as Round about Leeds and the Old Villages of Elmete in 1904. The books are still much sought after and were originally sold by James Miles of Upperhead Row. Edmund Bogg's wife Fanny died on February 3rd 1931 and they had two children - one of whom lived in Australia. Edmund Bogg died at his home at Caledonian Road (demolished) on November 24th 1931 and was buried at Lawnswood three days later - there were many members of the Leeds Savage Club including artist Owen Bowen of East Keswick at the service.

BOND COURT was developed as part of the Comprehensive Development Scheme in the mid 1960's and further restored in the 1990's complete with square and chess tables. No 9 Bond Court is the main offices of the Royal & Sun Alliance Insurance Group: opened in 1978 - the building includes the offices of Price Waterhouse Coopers and is managed by Jones Lang La Salle of

Leeds. A bronze sculpture by Roger Burnett showing boules players was unveiled by the Deputy Mayor of Lille Raymond Vaillant on Friday November 9th 2000 - it was a gift of the Scurrah Wainwright Trust.

BOND STREET is the extension of Commercial Street: the intention was to create a east/west route through Leeds from Kirkgate and included the demolition of the prison at the Briggate end. The whole line was initially called Bond Street: features included Marshall & Snelgrove department store. The Leeds Savings Bank (1818) built their headquarters on Bond Street (1835). The first traffic lights were placed at the junction of Bond Street and Park Row in 1928.

BOND STREET CENTRE was started on September 16th 1974 on a three acre site: the foundation stone was laid by Chancellor of the Exchequer Rt Hon Denis Healey on February 8th 1975: it was completed in September 1976 and opened in September 1977. The scheme was by John Brunton & Partners which replaced many 19th century buildings. It became the Leeds Shopping Plaza in March 1996 under new owners Tops Estates (Yorkshire) following a complete restoration and rebuilding. City Square Mall was opened as a main shopping precinct and the Grosvenor Shopping Mall was opened by Mina Goodman on October 22nd 1997. Albion Tower is a 7 storey office block completed in 1975 and occupied by 1977: the original owners were the Guardian Royal Insurance.

BOOT, JESSE (1850-1931) was the son of John Boot (1815-60) of Radcliffe on Trent: in 1849 John opened his British & American Botanical Establishment at Goose Gate Nottingham. His wife Mary took over on his death helped by his young son Jesse - in 1871 he became a partner in the herbalist business and traded as M & J Boot Herbalists. In 1877 he controlled the shop and became the largest dealer in patent medicines in Nottingham. The shop expanded to additional premises in 1881 and two years later became Boot & Co Ltd; he opened other shops throughout the city and in 1884 opened in Sheffield appointing his first dispensing chemist. In 1888 the company became Boots Pure Drug Co Ltd and following his marriage to Florence Rowe of Jersey in 1886 his son John was born in 1889. In 1891 the first Nottingham Department Store opened and a year later the Island Street Works were completed. In 1893 there were 33 stores and in 1900 there were 250 shops with Florence founding a series of subscription libraries and cafes in their shops. In 1920 the United Drug Co of America bought Boots and in 1933 with 1000 stores and John Boot as Chairman: Boots was sold to a group of British financiers. The Beeston Works were built in 1929-33 and by 1935 there were 450 libraries: they all closed in 1965/66. Jesse Boot was knighted in 1909 becoming a baronet in 1917 and the First Baron Trent in 1929.

Halfords was bought by Boots from Ward White Group in 1989- they had bought Halfords from Burmah Oil in 1984. The firm of Halfords was founded in 1907 by hardware merchant FW Rushbrooke (died 1953) in Birmingham and now have 410 stores and 9000 staff.

Boots opened their first Leeds shop in 1902 on the corner of Briggate and King Edward Street and at 7/9 Bond Street in 1905 which featured the subscriber's library. In 1915 Boots third Leeds shop opened on Boar Lane, replacing the Saracen's Head. The all night Boots service ended in 1964 and on July 7th 1977 Boots new store opened in the Bond Street Centre - now Leeds Shopping Plaza.

BORDERS BOOKSHOP on Briggate was opened in May 1999: it is the second largest UK bookstore. The company was founded in 1971 by Louis and Tom Borders in Ann Arbor Michigan USA and sold to Kmart in 1992. The present chain of stores employs 10.000 and there are nearly 6,000 book stores which were spun off from Kmart in May 1995 as Borders Group Inc.

BOSTON, RICHARD (1843-1908) of Croft House Burley was born at Kirkby Wiske; he was a member of the Leeds Council for 12 years: elected for Headingley Ward (1891). Boston paid for the statue of John Harrison in City Square: he was Chairman of the Planning Committee.

BOTTOMLEY, ALFRED (died 1909) of Ingledew Crescent Roundhay was born at Whitby and a prominent member of the Leeds Savage Club.

BOTTOMLEY, JOHN MITCHELL (died on the Isle of Man 1935) was an architect with offices in Albion Street prior to moving to Harrogate. He was responsible for the Masonic Hall Great George Street (1900).

BOURSE is an office development off Boar Lane from 1993 by the

Sir Basil Spence Partnership.

BOWER, JOHN RICHARD (1845-1928) was Mayor of Leeds in 1884 and lived at Newton Hill Chapeltown Road. He was a member of the firm Joshua Bower & Sons who once owned Allerton Main Collieries: they were sold to Bowers Allerton Main Collieries Co and bought back by his brothers T & RW Bower.

BREWERIES In 1900 there were 16 common brewers and more than 50 home brew houses in Leeds. *Albion Brewery (Youngs)* was on the corner of Woodhouse Lane and Kelsall Street (50 Woodhouse Lane) opened in 1897 with its familiar lion symbol and was closed in 1933: the buildings were demolished in 1939 and the site is now part of the Merrion Centre, opposite the old Central High School. *Brunswick Brewery* was started in 1830 on St Thomas's Square in The Leylands area by William Singleton & Co manufacturing black beer. *Hemingway's Brewery* on York Road was founded on Regent Street by John W Hemingway in 1866 and under Albert Hemingway moved to Beckett Street: the York Road brewery opened in 1923 with William Hemingway. In August 1967 the brewery with its five public houses was taken over by Tetley's Brewery and closed. The site became a car showroom and a Co-op supermarket and in February 1987 it was rebuilt and opened as Great Clothes. *Kirkstall Brewery* was opened in 1833 by Thomas Walker and was bought by Whitbread's Brewery in 1982 and the brewing of Mackeson Stout ceased. The brewery closed in January 1983: acquired for £235,000 by Leeds City Council for a £17 million redevelopment as student flats for the LMU: the Earl of Harewood officially opened the complex on October 8th 1996. *Melbourne Brewery* was started by Dickenson & Co in 1846 at the brewery on Plum Street off Regent Street and in 1875 Kirk, Matthews & Co of Leeds took control, merging with Carter & Co (Leeds & Wakefield Breweries) in 1889. The Wakefield brewery ceased trading in 1915 and in 1935 Leeds & Wakefield Breweries bought Waller's Bradford Brewery Ltd and in 1958 took over Russells & Wrangham Ltd of Malton. Leeds & Wakefield Breweries changed their name to Melbourne Brewery (Leeds) Ltd in 1958 using the Courtier trademark - introduced in 1926. It was taken over by Tetley's on April 1st 1960 which included the Regent Street Brewery and 245 public houses. The brewing of Melbourne beers ceased in 1960 - Tetley Mild was brewed there until 1962

Regent Street – Melbourne Brewery on right

when the brewery was used by Minster Minerals - the soft drinks firm controlled by Tetleys until closure in 1964. The buildings were demolished in 1973 for redevelopment. *Musgrave & Sagar* were founded in 1793 in Kirkstall being maltsters and brewers: in 1858 they moved to the Rutland Brewery on Marlborough Street but brewing ceased in 1948 and they continued bottling Guinness until 1992 and in 1993 moved to new premises at Carr Crofts at Armley. In 1802 Margaret Musgrave married Richard Hartley Sagar of Bramley at Leeds Parish Church and their son was John Musgrave Sagar-Musgrave JP (1835-1906) who lived at Red Hall Shadwell. They had their offices on Cavendish Street. *Tetley's Brewery* had its origins with maltsters William and John Tetley of Armley in the 18th century. William Tetley married Mary Vevers whose father was Joshua Vevers after whom they named their youngest son, who was born in June 1752. The eldest son was William Tetley born in September 1749 and in 1771 married Elizabeth Rimington of North Hall off Burley Road. They had eight children including Joshua Tetley who was born on July 20th 1778 - his mother Elizabeth died aged 36 on Christmas Eve 1788 at Armley Lodge. Following many financial difficulties William Tetley & Sons were trading well in malt, spirit and wines in 1801; Joshua Tetley married Hannah Carbutt in 1808 and lived in Albion

Street and they had five children. They moved to Park Square and had two more children including the only boy Francis William; their last child was born at their Brewery House in Salem Place in 1824. In October 1822 Joshua Tetley bought William Sykes Brewery of Salem Place founded in 1792 and also carried on with their maltings at Armley. Joshua Tetley & Son was created in October 1839 with son Francis William as partner and in 1862 Francis has Foxhill Weetwood built for his family (now Moorlands School). Land was bought from the Blayds-Calverley family of Oulton Hall adjacent to the Sykes Brewery and the building of the New Brewery started in 1852. Joshua and Hannah Tetley are buried at Hampsthwaite Harrogate: Joshua died aged 81 in August 1859 - the brewery was run by partners Charles Ryder and Francis William Tetley from 1858. The acquisition of the Old Sykes Brewery site was achieved in 1864 and architect George Corson and builder William Nicholson became involved in the building of new premises: Crown Point Maltings. Francis's eldest son Charles Francis joined the Leeds Brewery in 1873: Francis died in 1883 leaving partners Charles Ryder (died 1902) and Charles Francis Tetley (died 1911) to continue the business. The first two pubs purchased were the Duke William in the brewery yard in July 1890 (closed 1953) and The Fleece Farsley in November 1890. Tetley's went public in 1897: in the 1950's there were mergers with Duncan Gilmour (Sheffield), William Whittaker (Bradford), Melbourne (Leeds), Thomas Ramsden (Halifax) and Charles Rose (Malton). The parent company became Tetley-Walker in 1960 (after the merger with Walker Cain of Liverpool & Warrington). In May 1961 Tetley Walker, Ind Coope (Burton) and Ansells (Birmingham) merged to become Allied Breweries which became Allied Lyons in 1981, following the acquisition of J Lyons in 1978. Improvements were made to the Hunslet site including the opening of Huntsman House in 1968, new brewhouses in 1967 and 1989. In 1978 Tetley Heritage Inns were being designated and in August 1985 about £10 million was spent on a redevelopment of the Leeds site. In January 1993 Carlsberg Tetley Brewing Ltd was formed from a merger between Allied Lyons and Carlsberg A/S and in 1997 Carlsberg A/S in Denmark became the majority shareholder in Carlsberg Tetley Brewing Ltd. *Willow Brewery* was founded in 1863 on Willow Place Kirkstall Road.

BREWERY WHARF was a museum of brewing opened on the Tetley's brewery site by the river on March 19th 1994: the attraction was closed on April 7th 2000. The museum building is to become a restaurant and bar in a £100 million development scheme by Brewery Wharf Ltd (Allied Domecq) - a joint venture between Rushbond and Swanhill of London. Work on the five acre site started in 2001 and completion is expected to be in 2004. The scheme includes over 300 flats, a hotel with over 100 bedrooms, health club, leisure units and office space.

BRIDEWELL was the prison accommodation in the Town Hall opened in 1858; until 1847 convicted prisoners were taken to Wakefield Gaol. In July 1847 Armley Borough Gaol was opened; the Town Hall had 13 cells and 3 police offices with living quarters for a civilian gaoler and his wife. The name comes from St Brides Well in London - a prison for petty offenders; the official name was the Central Charge Office. In 1864 Leeds became an assize town with courts in the Town Hall: more cell accommodation was completed beneath the front steps, which were reshaped. The cell block was on the west side of the building with access from Oxford Place and from the front west entrance. The cells were improved in 1937-41 with 11 new cells added and the Bridewell remained the same until closure and transfer to the new building on Park Street.

BRIDGES *Centenary Bridge* designed by Ove Arup was opened on December 20th 1993 by Lord Mayor Keith Loudon, marking the centenary of the city of Leeds; *Crown Point Bridge* was built in 1840 and designed by George Leather: tolls were ended in February 1868. The bridge was reconstructed and widened by Birse of Doncaster: reopened on December 19th 1995. *Leeds Bridge* was designed in wrought and cast iron by Thomas Dyne Steele of Newport and built by John Butler Iron Works Stanningley. It was opened on July 9th 1873; the foundation stone was laid by John Barran on September 20th 1871, there had been a stone bridge from about 1376 and had the chapel of St Mary and later used as a school to 1728 - the chapel was demolished in 1760; the bridge was widened in 1730, 1760 and 1796 with removal in 1869. *Monk Bridge* was designed by George Leather in 1827 for Whitehall Road - a new bridge was built by Thomas Hewson and opened by Ald Gaunt on June 1st 1886. *Victoria Bridge* was designed by George Leather Jnr who was engineer to the Aire & Calder Navigation and built in 1837-39 at a cost of £8000 on the former School Close; an earlier footbridge opened September 18th 1829 was washed away in 1837. **Wellington Bridge** was originally designed by John Rennie and had the foundation stone laid by Benjamin Gott on March 12th 1818. The bridge opened in 1819 to improve connections with Gott's Bean Ing Mill - widened in 1873 under the direction of AW Morant - it is hidden by a modern concrete bridge; the tolls were ended on March 1st 1867. The small Timble and Lady Bridges once crossed Sheepscar Beck and have both been demolished: Timble Bridge was probably named after John Tymble who was buried at Leeds in 1400.

BRIDGE END The area south of Leeds Bridge and the junction of Dock Street, Hunslet Road and Meadow Lane. The triangular building is Leeds Bridge House built at the end of the 19th century: Hunslet Road dates from the 1870's. The site became the property of banker John James Cousins of Allerton Park and he built a Temperance Hotel (Cobden's Temperance Hotel) in 1879 but by c.1899 the hotel closed. In 1910 it was taken by Tunstall & Co (manufacturing chemists) and in 1960 the building was bought by the Council and it was refurbished and reopened in 1981 as offices. The Adelphi public house was first opened in the early 19th century and The Old Red Lion dates from the 18th century. It was in the Georgian house at Bridge End that Jabez Tunnicliffe founded the Band of Hope in 1847 and from a window in the same house Louis Le Prince made the first moving pictures of traffic crossing the bridge in October 1888 using his single lens camera.

BRIDGE STREET (Lady Bridge) is the home of the Pentecostal Church which was opened in May 1931: the adjacent building was a bullion store and bought by the church as an activity centre and offices - opened in 1989. The Centrica Call Centre and offices were formerly the headquarters of British Gas North Eastern. Some of the buildings date from the mid 1930's for the Leeds Gas Company as a meter and cooker repair shop. The Leeds Gas Company became part of the North Eastern Gas Board in 1947/48. In 1962 the main office tower block was completed and the "Sugar Cube" was built in 1969: in 1979/80 the computer block was added and in the mid-1970's the cooker and meter repair shops were demolished for the construction of the car park. In the 1970's a building for Grid Control was completed but in 1996 this was demolished to create the BGT Leeds Area Office.

BRIGG SHOTT was the food and ale provided at local inns for the weavers coming to trade at the Leeds cloth markets. The meal consisted of a pint of ale, trencher of beef and bowl of porridge.

BRIGGATE means the road to the bridge: the name first appearing in the early 16th century. There was a ford across the river in the early days with a bridge first mentioned in the early 14th century. In 1207 Maurice Paynel Lord of the Manor of Leeds granted the first borough charter. There was a market held on Briggate with 30 burgage plots on either side - many retained today with houses and inns. The cloth market was held on the bridge with the lower part of Briggate known as the Clothmarket (Cossin's map of 1740). On Briggate were the market cross (1619) with the corn market, moot hall (1618-1825) - part of Middle Row outside the present Debenhams store: Middle Row was demolished by May 30th 1825. In the 1820's a corn market was built above The Headrow (outside the Odeon) and when this was demolished in 1868 New Briggate was constructed. The first arcade was built by Charles Thornton in 1877 and the Leeds Estates Company redeveloped much of the east side of Briggate 1989-1903. The last bow windowed shop was

Briggate

Buck & Jackson adjacent to Turk's Head Yard and demolished in 1922 - replaced by Thornton's shop. There is a large oil painting of Briggate at night by Wilfred Jenkins dating from 1884 in the Abbey House Museum. A one way traffic flow (upwards) was introduced on January 4th 1965 and on Lower Briggate in January 1980. Cars were banned from Briggate in January 1993 when there was a £0.75 million facelift completed in 1995; all traffic was banned on August 3rd 1997.

BRIGGS, ARTHUR CURRER JP (1855-1906) of Gledhow Grange was the Chairman of H Briggs of Whitwood Collieries - founded by his grandfather Henry. He was Lord Mayor of Leeds in 1903-04 and established the Mining Department at Leeds University. A portrait in the Civic Hall was painted by Ernest Briggs (1866-1913).

BHS (BRITISH HOME STORES) opened in the Bond Street Centre (Leeds Shopping Plaza) on Albion Arcade in August 1977 by the site of West Bar - the Civic Trust plaque is on the outside of the arcade. This was their first store in Leeds and opened in the White Rose Shopping Centre in 1997. Bhs was founded in 1928 in the USA and incorporated in 1933 - in 1969 there were 94 stores. Bhs was sold by Storehouse in 2000 to Philip Green. Storehouse was created in 1986 on the merger of Habitat (1964), Mothercare (1960's) and Bhs by Sir Terence Conran - Mothercare (incorporated 1972) was sold in 1991.

BROCK, SIR THOMAS (1847-1922) The sculptor of the Black Prince in City Square: born in Worcester he was an RA in 1891 and knighted in 1911. He sculpted the large statue of Queen Victoria outside Buckingham Palace and The Moment of Peril exhibited in the Tate Gallery London.

BRODETSKY, SELIG (1888-1954) was born in Moldavia Ukraine and in 1893 the family travelled to England, where the boy attended Hanbury Board School and the Jewish free School and gained a place at Cambridge University. He was a lecturer in Applied Maths at Bristol University and he married Manya Barenbaum in 1919. He was appointed a lecturer at Leeds University in 1920 with Sir Michael Sadler obtaining his membership of Leeds Luncheon Club. He joined the Zionist synagogue in Brunswick Street and was very active in the Jewish community. He was appointed to the chair of Applied Mathematics at Leeds University which he held until 1948.

BRODRICK, CUTHBERT (1822-1905) The Hull born architect who had offices at 30 Park Row: his works included Leeds Town Hall (1858), Corn Exchange (1860/63), Leeds Mechanic's Institute (Leeds Civic Theatre) from 1860-65, Brodrick's Buildings on Cookridge Street: built in 1864 and restored 1988, King Street Warehouse (1862) now the Bank of England site and Oriental Baths Cookridge Street (1867). Brodrick settled in France in 1876 and died in Jersey. *Brodrick Court* was developed in Millennium Square/Cookridge Street in 2001 as 19 luxury apartments with The Qube Bar Café terrace, overlooking the new square (Trinity Agencies & Services Ltd).

BROTHERTON, LORD EDWARD ALLEN (1856-1930) was born at Ardwick Green Manchester; in 1878 he opened a chemical works in Wakefield and afterwards acquired more factory space for his works - a rose bowl is on display in Leeds Civic Hall which marked his 25 years of business on August 31st 1903. He became Lord Mayor of Leeds in 1913-14 with his niece Dorothy Una Ratcliffe as his Lady Mayoress. He was knighted in June 1918 having bought Roundhay Hall in 1916. In June 1929 he was created Baron Brotherton of Wakefield and died at his Kirkham Abbey home on October 21st 1930 - buried at Lawnswood Cemetery after a service at Leeds Parish Church. Lord Brotherton's wife died in childbirth and there were no direct male heirs. Sir Edward was a benefactor to Leeds University to whom he donated £200,000 between 1927 and his death. He laid the foundation stone for the Brotherton Library in June 1930 - it was his last public ceremony: it officially opened in October 1936. The Brotherton Collection of books was presented to the University in 1935. His sister Florence married Frederick Edwin Ratcliffe and there were six children. One of their sons was Charles Frederick Ratcliffe Brotherton (1882-1949) who was the benefactor for the Brotherton Wing extension for Leeds General Infirmary - built in Portland stone and opened on November 14th 1940 at a cost of £50,000.

BROWN, WILLIAM WILLIAMS (1788-1856) was a banker and alderman of Leeds: head of the Union Bank in Commercial Street (corner of Bank Street). He lived at Allerton Hall and founded the Leeds Union Bank in March 1813 with partners Thomas and Stephen Nicholson of Roundhay and Timothy Rhodes: following Stephen Nicholson's death in 1858 William became the senior partner of the bank which bore his name. The bank was designed by Thomas Taylor and transferred to Park Row in 1898 (architect-Alfred Waterhouse): it was taken over by Lloyds Bank in 1900.

BRUDENELL, JAMES THOMAS (1797-1868) was the 7th Earl of Cardigan being remembered for leading the Charge of the Light Brigade at Balaclava on October 25th 1854 during the Crimean War. He was an MP from 1818-1829 and was appointed a Lt-General in 1861. GEORGE THOMAS BRUDENELL (1880-1963) inherited the Cardigan estates which included holdings in Leeds; he lived at the family home Deene Park Corby. The Brudenell and Cardigan names are remembered in some streets of Leeds.

BRUNSWICK STREET The site of the Brunswick Chapel opened in 1825 and closed in 1972: demolished and developed as offices for Yorkshire Bank. The chapel war memorial is retained at the front of this building on Wade Lane. The Beth Hamedrash Hagadol Synagogue was moved from Hope Street and was consecrated in March 1908: this closed and the foundation stone for a new synagogue was laid in June 1936 in Chapeltown; the Brunswick Street building was sold to the Salvation Army.

BUCK, SAMUEL (1696-1779) came to Leeds to visit Ralph Thoresby in October 1719 and in 1745 published his Prospect of Leeds with his brother Nathaniel.

BUCK & JACKSON in Briggate was the last bow fronted shop on Briggate demolished in 1922 for Thornton's shop: prior to the last business it was William Green & Sons.

BUILDING SOCIETIES *Bradford & Bingley* in Albion Street opened their new premises in early 1993: planning approval was granted in March 1992 to demolish the turn of the century building on the site. The Bradford & Bingley opened their Leeds branch in 1963 on the site of the demolished King Charles public house in Lands Lane. *Britannia* was based on Albion Street/ Commercial Street which had been built for the Leeds & Yorkshire Assurance Co by William Bruce Gingell of Bristol in 1852/55 - it became the Leek & Westbourne for a few years. The Britannia closed in 2000 and moved to Commercial Street premises: the site opened as a Starbucks Coffee Bar with exterior restoration. A plaque inside states that the building was a branch of the Leeds & Yorkshire Assurance Company (Liverpool & London & Globe Insurance) established in 1824. *Leeds & Holbeck*: the Leeds

Union Operative Building Society opened in the old schoolroom Marshall Street Holbeck in 1845 followed by four other terminating societies; the sixth society was founded in 1875 on a permanent basis in Holbeck Mechanics Institute with bankers William Williams Brown of Park Row. The Albion Street premises were bought in 1886 and the head office of the Leeds & Holbeck Building Society was formed. New premises were opened on Albion Street/Headrow in 1930 which were extended in 1970; the Burley Bar Stone is displayed inside the offices. *Norwich & Peterborough* in Albion Street transferred from Albion Place in 1995.

BULMER, GEORGE BERTRAM (died 1916) was an architect in partnership with Henry Perkin (1847-1925). His works include Atlas Chambers on King Street/St Paul's Street and the Yorkshire Bank Infirmary Street.

BURGAGE PLOTS were plots of land held by the burgesses or free men of the borough - Briggate had 30 on each side of the street. They were essentially building plots with gardens and in Leeds the burgesses were granted tofts (Burmantofts).

BURMANTOFTS POTTERY started in 1842 when land was acquired by William Wilcock and John Lassey who sank a pit for coal and clay: in 1845 the firm was known as Lassey & Wilcock Rock Colliery. In 1858 Lassey died and in 1863 John Holroyd came into the business: a cloth finisher and dresser from Carlton Mills Woodhouse. The name changed to Wilcock & Co with a store and office on Infirmary Street - the property of Holroyd's textile business. In 1875 new offices on Quebec Street were acquired and the company became an important contributor to brick manufacture. In 1878 Wilcock died and Holroyd's brother James came to Burmantofts as manager in 1879. He designed and built new works for the production of glazed bricks and terra-cotta. The glazed clay was known as Burmantofts Faience and sold both at home and abroad. An association developed with architect Alfred Waterhouse who came to Leeds in 1883 to design the Yorkshire College - faience and tiles were used in the entrance and staircase at the Great Hall. In 1888 the company was renamed The Burmantofts Company Ltd and a year later became The Leeds Fireclay Co Ltd. Production of art pottery ended in 1904 with the eventual closure in 1957 - the buildings were demolished and the site redeveloped as a housing estate.

BURTON, SIR MONTAGUE MAURICE (1885-1952) was the son of Charles and Rachel Burton who came to England in 1900 from Lithuania: he set up a men's outfitters shop in both Chesterfield (1908) and Sheffield (1913) prior to coming to Leeds, from where he bought his clothes wholesale. In 1909 Montague Burton started manufacturing in Sheffield and acquiring Progress Mill and Elmwood Mill in Leeds where he settled in 1915: he became a limited company in 1929. By 1919 he had 40 shops and enlarged his Leeds factory and in 1920 he bought the Hudson Road factory from Albrecht & Albrecht. The factory was the largest clothing factory in the world by 1925 and by the 1930's 10,500 were employed in the factory. A Leeds Civic Trust blue plaque was unveiled on the Hudson Road buildings on March 30th 2001 by his twin sons Arnold and Raymond Burton. In 1939 there were 20,000 employees with a further 4000 in retail: in 1952 there were more than 600 shops. The Burton Group acquired Peter Robinson (1946), Dorothy Perkins (1979), Collier Group (1985) and Debenhams (1985-86); many shops were closed in 1977 with the Hudson Road factory reduced to a cloth cutting and warehousing centre. Clothing production ceased in 1981 and by 1994 Burton suits were made by Centaur. The Burton Group is part of Arcadia who also have Dorothy Perkins, Evans and Topshop. Montague Burton was a Leeds JP from 1924, received a knighthood in 1931 and an Hon LlD from Leeds University in 1944. He was married to Sophia Marks, daughter of a Worksop antiques dealer in 1909 and they had four children; after his death the firm was continued by Stanley Burton until his retirement in 1985. There were a few shops in the city centre including the Briggate superstore which was opened on February 4th 1972.

BUS COMPANIES *Arriva* was formed by Tom Cowie's Sunderland Group who bought British Bus - the holding company was the Yorkshire Bus Group. On privatisation Caldaire Holdings included West Riding Automobile Company, Yorkshire Woollen and Selby & District who held their own operators licences. Arriva took the West Riding Automobile Co to become Arriva Yorkshire with the Yorkshire Woollen as Arriva Yorkshire West. Arriva Yorkshire is based at Belle Isle Wakefield (West Riding HQ). *Black Prince* is based in Fountain Street Morley with several bus routes operating.

In 1968 Brian Crowther started his commercial services with one coach: in 1969 he formed a partnership with Bert Colley and a new name for their firm came from the Black Prince statue in City Square. There was an increase in private hire, school journeys and contracts; Brian became the sole proprietor when Bert Colley died in 1976. In 1975 the firm operated the Blackpool Express under contract to National and after partial regulation in 1981 Black Prince operated this as a commercial enterprise. *First Leeds* is a subsidiary of First Group plc which in 1996 took over Yorkshire Rider. First Group was based at Bristol and was Trevor Smallwood's Badgerline. Leeds City Transport was taken over by a worker's cooperative in 1986 who were taken by Yorkshire Rider. *Quickstep Travel Ltd* was formed in 1990 and is based at Kirkstall Road. *Wallace Arnold* brought together Wallace Cunningham and Arnold Crowe who were running a coaching business by 1922: they sold their business in 1926 to Robert Barr. The haulage section was R Barr (Leeds) Ltd and the coaching was Wallace Arnold Tours Ltd: by 1955 the firm had 200 vehicles. In the 1950's Robert Barr developed a chain of car dealerships with a car showroom on Hunslet Road and bought the Kippax & District bus company in June 1958. Wallace Arnold continued the service until March 1968 when the route was sold to Leeds City Transport together with seven double decker buses. In 1957 the new coach station on The Calls was opened and there was a booking office in the Corn Exchange. The Calls site was developed as Chancellor Court from 1989 with Wallace Arnold selling the area in July 1994. In 1997 the parent company sold Wallace Arnold Tours to the management. In 2001 Wallace Arnold bought National Holidays from retiring owner Godfrey Burley: National Holidays was formed in 1997 following a demerger from the East Yorkshire Motor Group. *West Yorkshire Roadcar* was taken by Blazefield Holdings of Keighley who operate Keighley & District, Harrogate & District and Yorkshire Coastliner. The WY Roadcar operations at Bradford, Leeds and York were taken by Yorkshire Rider.

BUS STATIONS. *City Bus Station* (Central) was opened on August 31st 1938. The bus station was rebuilt at a cost of £6,000 and was reopened by the Lord Mayor Ald EJ Wooler on September 30th 1963. The newly rebuilt £2 million bus station opened on March 25th 1996 by Coun Brian Walker and Coun Michael Lyons of the WYPTA. *Vicar Lane Bus Station* (West Yorkshire) closed on March 31st 1990: built on the site of the workhouse and north bar in 1936/37. *Wellington Street Bus Station* opened in 1929 on the site of a former timber yard and was closed in 1996 with the opening of the £1.8 million *National Express Coach Station* in July 1996. The site was developed as Springfield House. *West Riding Bus Station* on Cross York Street was on the site of the demolished St James Church (erected 1794 and consecrated 1801) in 1954, from where buses departed for Wakefield and Rothwell: the red WRA buses operated on the old tram routes. The Express service from Leeds to Wakefield originally used Cross York Street as a departure point. The small bus station closed in 1972 and services transferred to the main bus station. The site became Pilkington's Glass and now Autoglass. *Rockingham Street Bus Station* was on the site of the Merrion Centre and opened in 1954: closed c1961. On-street bus stations were completed in 1997 on Infirmary Street and Corn Exchange.

BUSK, HANS (1717-92) was a prominent Leeds merchant with a large house on South Parade: when he died he left a small fortune of £15,000 to his widow Martha (1798-1802). They were buried at St John's Church and there is a memorial plaque in this church.

BUSINESS SCHOOL, LEEDS UNIVERSITY was officially opened on March 23rd 2001: the school moved into the former Leeds Grammar School buildings which had undergone a £10 million transformation: the site includes the Maurice Keyworth Building (former chapel). There is an academic staff of 80 including 18 professors and 1200 undergraduates.

BUTLER, ALD AMBROSE EDMUND JP (1849-1923) was the fourth generation of the family who ran Kirkstall Forge from 1779. He married the sister of Col Thomas Harding and was a director of the Yorkshire Penny Bank and Lord Mayor (1901); he died at Kirkstall Abbey House (Abbey House Museum) - his father JO Butler (1812-83) had also lived at the House.

BUTT'S COURT The street to the west of Albion Street leading to the Headrow and now part of the one way traffic system: it was first known as Turner Street. This was the area where archers practised and was built in c1778: it was on Merryboys Hill (Albion Street-Park Row).

C & A STORE on Boar Lane was built to the west of Holy Trinity Church and replaced Monteith & Hamilton's Grand Pygmalion department store (1888) in the 1930's: the store was completely rebuilt and reopened on November 16th 1970. The first British store was opened in London in 1922 and grew to 108 branches. The Leeds store closed on January 27th 2001 and the stores in Britain closed on May 31st 2001. C & A takes the initials of the Dutch founders Clemens and August Brenninkmeyer who opened their first store in Holland in 1841. The C & A store in the White Rose Centre was taken by Littlewood's in January 2001 as one of their 112 stores. The Trinity Centre is to be rebuilt which includes the demolition of the C & A store.

CAFES IN LEEDS There were many hundreds of cafes and restaurants in the city open and closed during the 20th century and the following are a few of the most memorable. *Betty's* in Lands Lane: shops founded by Frederick Belmont about 1900. Betty's opened in Leeds on November 10th 1930 and closed March 30th 1974. *Collinson's Café* opened c1900 and closed on Wellington Street 1958. *Fuller's* of Bond Street opened c1911 and closed as a Forte property in June 1964. *Gambit* opened c1905 on Park Row as the Mecca and had the name change after becoming headquarters of Leeds Chess Club - closed August 1961. *Jacomelli's* of Boar Lane opened 1906 by Anthony & Francis Jacomelli and sold to Hagenbachs 1949: closed September 29th 1967 and to the Berni Inn chain who opened in December 1968 (demolished November 1973). *Kardomah* opened on Briggate 1908 (closed August 14th 1965) and bought Collinson's Café in Albion Street 1962 (closed c1972). *King Edward Restaurant* was opened in 1903, designed by Frank Matcham. *Lyon's Café* opened in County Arcade 1903 - closed 1938; Lyon's Café Bond Street opened c1915 - closed 1966; Lyon's Café Briggate closed 1957. *Nash's Tudor Fish Restaurant* opened in December 1963 in the old building once occupied by Kemplay's Academy: the first location for Nash's Restaurant was on Park Lane - closed November 1963. *Perry's Café* was on Commercial Street 1933-1963. *Powolny's Café* Bond Street opened c1858 and closed 1960-reopened as Yates Wine Lodge 1961. *Victoria Tea Rooms* were opened in Leeds Town Hall by Leader of the City Council Jon Trickett on December 20th 1995. *Wray's* of Duncan Street & Vicar

Lane (closed 1947). Other popular cafes included *Civic Restaurant* in the Town Hall (1942-66), *Fields* Commercial Street opened c1908 and closed on March 15th 1958 with development as a Hepworth's store, *Ceylon Tea Centre* The Headrow was opened on December 21st 1964 and closed in November 1981, *Lyon's Cafes* were in Leeds from 1903 (County Arcade) to 1966 (Bond Street), *Milkmaid Milk Bar* on Albion Street opened in 1962 and closed in 1975, *White Horse Restaurant* Boar Lane (c1900-1970) was owned by Fairburns and developed from the Leeds Public Cocoa House Company's café/Golden Fleece. There were store café-restaurants at Marshall & Snelgroves of Bond Street/Park Row (closed 1971), MC Hitchens of Briggate and Kirkgate (closed 1952), Matthias Robinson's restaurant, Marks & Spencers restaurant (1951-61), Schofields Old English Café in the King's Chamber of Red Hall opened in 1912 and Woolworths self service restaurant on Briggate opening in 1928.

CALLS was one of the original medieval streets of Leeds together with Briggate and Kirkgate. The origins of the name (caul) are obscure but it could mean either "weir on a river to divert water to a mill stream" or from the Latin "callis" meaning a track. The area has been substantially upgraded in the 1980's/1990's with at the west end the warehouses of William Turton Crown Point Provender Mills (corn merchants & supplied food for horses running the Leeds horse trams); dated 1876 - converted into The Chandlers 120 apartments opened in October 1987 - opposite was the Church Army Labour Home. Chantrell Court and House (Yorkshire Metropolitan Housing Association; Fletland Mills were operated in 1887 by the Wright Brothers corn millers who acquired the late 18th/19th century mills providing flour and horse corn for the Leeds district: in 1991 the mills were converted into a hotel (42 The Calls); Calls Landing warehouse was converted to a restaurant opened in 1994 as the Hereford Beefstouw - the franchise ended in 1997 and was renamed The Calls Grill by Stewart Graham; Old Brewery (High Court) was converted into offices in 1989; Langton's Wharf (Langtons were builders merchants) was restored as 67 flats in 1992 and the Design & Innovation Centre was converted from Simpson's Fold - a 1930's warehouse; Chancellor Court/Harcourt House was built as offices in 1990 for £2.5 million. Thistle Hotel Group (Mount Charlotte) occupied No 2 The Calls prior to their relocation and The New Penny public house was once known as the Hope & Anchor. The large metal globe on a plinth was placed by the Leeds Development Corporation who attracted £70 million of private sector investment into the Riverside at a cost to the taxpayer of £6 million from 1988 to 1995.

CALL LANE The road connects Swinegate/Lower Briggate with Kirkgate. Pitfall Street is a reminder of George Sorocold's pumping system for the transfer of water to a reservoir near St John's Church and thence to local housing: it used a water powered pump supplied from a goit of the Bondman's Dam. The system was abandoned with the opening of Eccup Reservoir in 1842. Tay House was a new building dating from 1990 with apartments on Riverside Court.

CALVERLEY STREET The street dividing the Town Hall from the Municipal Buildings named in the years prior to the building of the Town Hall and continued to divide the Civic Hall from the LGI. It is a reference to the Calverley family of land owners in the city: they owned Park House on which site was built the Town Hall. Park House was the family residence for many years and was sold in 1851 to the Corporation for £9500; at the time of sale Park House was the home of Dr Richard Hobson. John Calverley (1718-83) was Mayor of Leeds (1772) and his son John Calverley of Oulton Hall (1753-1804) was also Mayor in 1785 and 1798. The street was extended northwards with the demolition of property that included a sign works, Sunny Bank Street and The Queen's Arms public house.

CAMP ROAD The original name was Long Balk Lane/Wade Lane and was the home of farmer-clothiers. In 1588 a field was known as Townes Cliff which by 1677 was the site of Wade Hall: home of the benefactor Thomas Wade. St Matthew's Church was consecrated on August 13th 1851 and the architect was Charles Walklett Burleigh of Albion Street: a vicarage and church schools were part of the complex demolished in June 1967.

CAMBODUNUM A Roman site possibly on Quarry Hill but not confirmed archaeologically. The traces of a Roman ford, road and several artefacts provide evidence of Roman occupation in Leeds. It is likely that the Quarry Hill site was used by the Saxon settlers.

CANALS *Aire and Calder Navigation Canal* was passed by Act of Parliament in 1699 with Leeds at the western end: the canal opened to Leeds Bridge in 1700. The first boats to use the Leeds canal basin entered on Friday November 17th 1700. The five mile stretch of canal from Haddlesey to Selby was opened in 1778: the canal from Leeds joined the Ouse at Goole. A warehouse on Call Lane was built by William Hurst for the company in 1828 (demolished). In 1906 the new office building between Leeds Bridge and Dock Street was opened for the company: this was once the site of William Milner's gardens and summer house in c1720. The terminus of the canal was at first on the north bank but later transferred to the opposite side where a basin was opened in 1821. *Leeds and Liverpool Canal* is the longest in Britain with a total length of 127 miles linking Liverpool with the Aire & Calder Navigation Canal at Leeds. It was in Yorkshire that a canal was proposed in 1766 and the merchants were keen to improve the supply of lime and limestone from the Dales and to expand the cloth market via Liverpool to the developing colonies. In 1773 the canal opened from Bingley to Skipton and the next year from Skipton to Gargrave. By 1777 the canal opened from Liverpool to Wigan (for coal transport) and from Leeds to Gargrave; construction stopped due to a lack of available cash and it was started up again in 1791 from Gargrave westwards. The proposed route was altered and it was fully opened in 1816: every year there was over a million tons of coal carried with 50,000 tons of limestone although more economic were the carriage of other merchandise - grain, machinery, cotton, wool and cement. Trade declined after the Great War as road transport improved: in 1953 British Transport Waterways was set up and took over the running of the canal. In 1960 regular traffic ceased across the summit and the canal had no regular traffic from 1964. One of the most impressive features of the canal east of the Pennines is the Bingley five-rise locks, lowering the canal by 60 feet.

CANAL BASIN was the terminus of the Leeds & Liverpool Canal: the basin dates from c1820 and in 1845 reached the river with access to Bean Ing Mill. The Dry Docks date from c1790 and c1819 and the canal warehouse was built in 1777. The old coal depot (Coop) site became Victoria Gate (Privilege Insurance/Green Flag) in 1998.

CANAL WHARF has been redeveloped with new offices including those of The Pensions Trust at Verity House-the foundation stone was laid by Lord Mayor Keith Parker on May 17th 2000. The other businesses located at Canal Wharf include The Leeds Hospital Fund and Allied Dunbar.

CANKERWELL was one of 28 Leeds wells and spas on Cankerwell Street. Cankerwell was an iron rich chalybeate spring: two other town wells provided popular cures - St Peter's (rheumatism) and Eyebright wells. Cankerwell Lane led to the Sunny Bank district: the site is now part of the Leeds Metropolitan University.

CARBUTT, SIR EDWARD HAMER (1838-1910) of Chapel Allerton was a member of the Council in 1876 and Mayor of Leeds (1877-78). He was the President of the Institute of Mechanical Engineers (1886/87), retired to live in Surrey and was buried at Woodhouse Cemetery.

CAR PARKS Two of the many car parking areas in the city are Albion Street opened on February 7th 1974 and the secured Woodhouse Lane multi-storey with 1100 spaces opened on August 6th 1970. Criterion Place multi-storey car park on Swinegate was opened in 1999 (LCDC and British Land).

CAREY JONES (Gordon Carey & Chris Jones) is an architects practice with the head office at Rose Wharf - the firm designed the refurbishment of the large, listed old flax mill. The business was started in 1989 and by 2001 had been responsible for £250 million worth of redevelopment in Leeds; including the refurbishment of Debenham's on Briggate, City Station Concourse (1999), No16 Park Row with the wall of plate glass (1997) and the Princes Exchange in Aire Street. Royal Mail House on Wellington Street and the Clarence Dock development are Carey Jones projects.

CARLING & WRIGHT was formed as a TV and radio retailer when Christopher Carling and John William Wright opened their shop on Park Lane in 1949. Increased business saw a move to The Headrow with gradual expansion into adjacent shops and the use of an old clothing factory to the rear as a service department. In January 1957 a fire badly damaged the premises but on rebuilding there was further expansion and the opening of shops in Harrogate (old Fullers café), Ripon, Kirkstall Road and Bramley. The shops were all closed by 1972.

CARLTON HILL Carlton Hill was opposite the first Leeds Girls High School in St James Lodge (1876): there is a small garden where the street once started (a few yards from the Dry Dock). The streets were demolished for the inner ring road/multistorey car park with the completion of a housing estate: Carlton Towers were built in 1957-59 being the first tower blocks in the City. The ZamBuk Company was part of patent medicine firm CE Fulford with their manufacturing base and offices at 23/25 Carlton Hill on the corner of Jowitt Lane. Fulford's business also included Bile Beans, Vitapoint hair conditioner and Peps Pastilles. Zam Buk was made from 1914 until the firm closed - sold in small tins at 1/3d it was a green ointment put on with lint and rubbed into the affected place: used for skin ailments, sores, arthritis and lumbago. The Fulford garage, warehousing and packaging departments were on the corner of Dorington Road on the east side of Carlton Hill. Carlton Hill also had a masonic hall, Particular Baptist Meeting Room as well as the extensive Carlton Mills and Carlton Cross Mills (Brigg & Sons woollen and cloth manufacturers) with their mill ponds, Magee's Coach Works and a lamp works on the south corner of Jowitt Lane. The continuation north-eastwards was Carlton Street with the Carlton public house, Carlton Barracks, Windsor Castle public house and Carlton Cinema which was opened in March 1920 and closed in April 1965 - premises demolished for redevelopment as a housing estate. The Somnus bedding factory and showroom (William Rhodes Ltd) was based in Carlton Cross Mills (Exeter Place) prior to transfer to the Ring Road Leeds 16.

Carlton Hill today leads from the Inner Ring Road with the new development of LMU student's flats by Holmes Building plc and the old entrance to Carlton Barracks - the new entry is from Carlton Gate. Dorrington Road Mills were the home of Camrass & Sons clothing manufacturers: Solomon Camrass was one of the first Jewish immigrants to Leeds in the 1860's later producing coats in his Lower Headrow shop for John Barran. Fire destroyed part of the building in 1915 and the firm closed in c1982 being then known as Cap-Art House. The clothing manufacturer Morris & Co was on Jowitt Lane until c1935 when it moved to Sydmor Works on Crimbles Street.

CARPENTER, ANDREW The sculptor of the statue of Queen Anne in the Art Gallery. It was originally placed on the Moot Hall (1710) at a special unveiling with procession and festival on May 12th 1713 in the centre of Briggate. It was paid for by merchant

William Milner JP (1662-1740) at a cost of £200. The statue was placed on the first corn exchange in 1828 and when this was demolished in 1868 moved to the Town Hall and was put into the art gallery in 1887. A reproduction of the front of the Moot Hall was made for the City Tercentenary in 1926 at Wellington Station which included a copy of the Queen Anne statue.

CARR, JOHN (1723-1807) was born at Horbury and lived at Askham Richard Hall. He was responsible for Jeremiah Dixon's house Boar Lane (1753), Leeds Infirmary (1771) as well as many mansions including Harewood House (1771).

CASHDISIA was opened in 1912 as a one unit overall shop by Wilkinson and Keighley. In 1922 the business was sold to Frederick Taylor and John Ackroyd and in 1956 to Harry Sternberg. In 1934 the various departments were brought under one roof - the junction of Vicar Lane/Queen Victoria Street. The firm closed on October 30th 1982.

CASTELOW, WALTER THOMAS (1876-1974) was one of the oldest working pharmacists in Leeds. Walter Thomas was born at the Palace Inn near the Parish Church (his father Benjamin William was the landlord and lived at Beulah House Cross Gates).

He was educated at the Church Middle Class School on Vernon Road and then at The Yorkshire College (University) prior to qualifying as a dispensing chemist at Edinburgh University and in 1894 was apprenticed to Abbott & Anning of 145 Woodhouse Lane (corner of Fenton Street). He joined Johann Reinhardt's business on Queen Victoria Street in 1897 and married Elizabeth Wilton of Birmingham in 1901. In 1907 he took over Brown's Pharmacy at 159 Woodhouse Lane (opposite the Friends Meeting House and Louis Le Prince's workshop). Edward Brown had

Walter Thomas Castelow
outside his Pharmacy Woodhouse Lane

Interior WT Castelow's Pharmacy 1956 – *JE Castelow*

a well established pharmacy on Woodhouse Lane. There were four children: Violet (born 1904), Constance (1908-75), Walter (1909-77) and John (1910-79). At the age of 97 Walter Thomas Castelow was working a full day in the shop and was known as the oldest practising chemist in England. The shop contents and fittings were donated in 1979 to Hull Museums and were on show initially at the Wilberforce House Museum, prior to recent transfer to Streetlife.

CASTLE The Normans built a moated fortification on Mill Hill as a local base on "castelhyll" serving as a manor house. There was later another manor house near the Parish Church and in late Norman times the North Hall manor was created with the hall on the junction of Vicar Lane/Lady Lane. The original manor house had been swept away by the 14th century and the Wilson family altered the 16th century house and rebuilt it in 1765. In 1815 a wing became the King's Arms on the site of the Scarbrough public house on Bishopgate Street.

CASTLETON MILLS to the west of the city centre were opened in 1836 for Hargrave's flax spinners - they ceased trading in 1853. Until 1935 linen was made at the Mills and BY Clothes restored the building in 1986.

CATHEDRAL OF LEEDS St Anne's Church became a Cathedral in

1878: the new diocese was formed from the Diocese of Middlesborough on December 20th 1878. The church had been dedicated on October 24th 1838 and was sited at the top of Park Row/Guildford Street.

CATHOLICS IN LEEDS The celebration of Catholic Mass in Leeds started with the Killingbeck family at Allerton Grange and in 1712 the Leigh family established a Catholic Chapel at Middleton Hall: this moved to Ebor House Belle Isle and Stourton Lodge at Thwaite Gate. The Savile family and the Duke of Norfolk had a Catholic Chapel at their home of Red Hall Shadwell. In the 1780's Father Underhill established a mission and helped by Joseph Holdforth started a small chapel adjacent to the Pack Horse Inn Briggate over a blacksmith's shop in 1786. A new chapel was built at the junction of Lady Lane and Templar Lane with the foundation stone laid in April 1793 and it opened the following year. In July 1831 St Patrick's Chapel was opened on York Road to the designs of John Child: he was also appointed to design a new St Anne's Church in the centre of the town for which the foundation stone was laid on August 12th 1837.

CAVENDISH ROAD by Leeds University leads from Woodhouse Lane: the Presbyterian Church was designed by James Barlow Fraser, opened in 1879 and converted in the 1960's into the Clothworker's Centenary Concert Hall with the original entrance intact: entry to the concert hall is by new additions to the rear. The inaugural concert was held on May 5th 1976: the development had been made possible with £60,000 from the Clothworkers Company of the City of London. The housing was completed between 1859 and 1892

CEMETERIES *Armley Cemetery* was opened in 1892, *Beeston* in 1859 and *Cottingley Hall* in 1938. *Farnley Cemetery* on Tong Road was consecrated on March 16th 1860 with *Gildersome* in 1865 and *Guiseley* in 1922. *Harehills* was opened on November 8th 1908: extensions in 1916 and 1956. *Holbeck* was opened on July 1st 1857, *Horsforth* in 1881 and *Hunslet* in 1845. *Jewish Cemetery* is on Whitehall Road New Farnley opened in 1840 on land given by the Earl of Cardigan. *Killingbeck RC Cemetery* was opened on July 14th 1895. *Lawnswood* was consecrated as Headingley Cemetery on December 20th 1875. The chapels were designed by George Corson and the first burial was registered was on January 23rd 1876; the first cremation was on January 4th 1905. **Leeds Burmantofts** opened on August 14th 1845 on 16 acres of land bought from William Beckett MP with two chapels for Anglicans and Dissenters. Over 150 years there have been c180,000 burials in 28,000 graves. The war memorial was designed by Sir Reginald Blomfield. The cemetery has the graves of Sir John Barran, Jabez Tunnicliff, George Leather and a model chimney memorial to Sarah and Thomas Kidney. **Morley Cemetery** was opened in 1884, **New Wortley** in 1863, **Pudsey** in 1875, **Upper & Lower Wortley** in 1865 and **Whitkirk** opened in 1874. **Woodhouse** was opened on July 23rd 1835 by the Leeds General Cemetery Company. The perimeter wall, lodge and chapel were designed by John Clark. The 10 acre site was formed as St George's Fields by Leeds University in 1969: among the many graves is Edward Baines Senior, editor of the Leeds Mercury (Yorkshire Post). The last coffin burial was in 1978.

CENTAUR Marlbeck House was built by Thomas Marshall & Co (Marlbeck) Ltd c1922 on the site of wholesale clothiers J & N Campbell (1889) and later Gaunt & Hudson's hat and cap and wholesale clothiers (1903) which had moved to Elland Road. Marlbeck Fashions remained at Great George Street until closure. Centaur Clothes was started in the 1950's by John Jackson in Grove House Lane and moved in the 1960's to Great George Street Marlbeck House: renamed Centaur House when the factory closed in 1991. The building was converted to 41 apartments and a leisure centre in 1997-98. Centaur Clothes was bought in 1989 by the William Baird Group; Baird Menswear Brands (Baird's men's suits business) was bought by Harold Tillman and Peter Lucas for £19 million in December 2000. The business is based in Granary Buildings on Canal Wharf and owns the Alexandre Savile Row tailoring business and manufactures men's suits under brands such as Jasper Conran, Centaur, Pierre Cardin, Jeff Banks and British Tailor. BMB makes 700,000 suits a year and with the bespoke suits for Austin Reed made in Goole - the suit number reaches a million. Harold Tillman (born 1945) founded the men's clothing companies Honorbilt and Lincroft Kilgour; his first job was a trainee merchandiser with Lincroft Clothing who used to manufacture suits for the Co-op.

CENTENARY HOUSE is the old Leeds Dispensary opened in 1904:

it closed on November 27th 1971. The building was sold in 1972 for £71,000 and in 1975 was bought by the Centre for Deaf and Blind People: opened by the Duke of Edinburgh on February 13th 1976. There were two chapels in the building and the combined Chapel of the Holy Spirit was dedicated on March 3rd 1991.

CENTRAL GARAGE occupied the corner site of the south end of Woodhouse Lane - now St John's Centre. Looker's of Leeds closed their premises on February 11th 1983 at Central Buildings. Looker's of Leeds also closed Cox & Co of Regent Street in January 1985.

CENTRAL ROAD links Kirkgate with Duncan Street, Market Street Arcade and New Market Street. There is a development of 24 loft apartments by Town Centre Securities (Vassalli House) and House of Fraser.

CENTRAL STREET features Central House (1988) built by Jack Lunn and Eyton House whose foundation stone was laid on January 1st 1931 by Albert Jones.

CHAMBER OF COMMERCE, INCORPORATED LEEDS The first Chamber started in 1785 and continued until 1793 meeting at the Rotation Office Kirkgate: the first president was George Goodman and one of the founding firms was Booth, Wade, Lomas-Walker & Co. (now Addleshaw Booth). They moved to offices in the Commercial Buildings on Boar Lane in 1826 (demolished 1872) and in 1851 the Chamber met at the Court House Park Row. The Chamber was in Benson's Buildings on Park Row and on the completion of the Royal Exchange Building on Boar Lane (City Square) the Council Room was in this building from 1884 until 1914; this was followed by the Chamber meeting in the Scottish Union Building on the corner of Park Row and South Parade. The Chamber then met at Quebec House before opening their new £750,000 headquarters at Commerce House Wade Lane on September 14th 1978. In 1993 the Leeds Chamber merged with Bradford to form Leeds & Bradford Chamber Services and on merging with York in 1995 Chamber Management Services were created serving North Yorkshire. The Chamber moved to Phoenix House (Green Flag) near Owlcotes in December 1997 and then moved to the present offices at Thornbury in 1998. In April 2001 the three Chambers of Leeds, Bradford and York separated again with the Thornbury site becoming Bradford Chamber and Leeds

Chamber opened on Wellington Street. The **Junior Chamber of Commerce** was started in 1956 by a group of young businessmen: it was not an offshoot of the Leeds Chamber of Commerce & Industry but a collection of individuals who gave voluntary service. Their headquarters on Mill Hill were opened in 1977 and the Junior Chamber is now based in Albion Place.

CHANGE ALLEY links Albion Street with Lands Lane parallel to Albion Place precinct: it features two old gas lamps inscribed Stock Exchange.

CHANTRELL, ROBERT DENNIS (1793-1872). He was an architect who set up a practice on Park Row in 1819. He was responsible for the Philosophical Hall Park Row (1820), Wellington Road Baths (1819-20), William Hey's shops Bond Street (1820), South Market (1824), Leeds Library alteration (1835), Court House additions (1835), Leeds Parish Church (1841), Holy Trinity Church new steeple (1839) and St Philip's Church Wellington Street (1847).

CHANTRY CHAPELS The Chantry Chapel of St Mary the Virgin was opened on the north east end of Leeds Bridge c1327: from the Dissolution it was a school until 1728 maintained by charities. The building became a warehouse and was demolished in 1760. There was a chantry chapel to St Mary Magdalene founded in 1470, a medieval chantry in Lady Lane on the site which was to become the workhouse and a chantry chapel near to the Vicarage in Kirkgate founded in 1430 by Thomas Clarell.

CHARITIES include **Baynes Charity**: founded in 1807 by the will of Ann Baynes. It was distributed by the minister of St Paul's Church Park Square. **Dixon's Charity**: founded 1742 through the will of Rachel Dixon (1719) for the benefit of the widows of clergymen - the money came from the house rents of properties in the Lower Head Row. **Leighton's Charity** was founded in 1653 by the will of Isabella Leighton: the rents from land at Greater Woodhouse were distributed to the poor. **Milner's Charity** was founded by William Milner in 1739 to support poor widows. The **Pious Uses Charities** were sums of money from land, rents donated to charities in the Parish of Leeds. **Wade's Charity** was founded in 1530 by the will of Thomas Wade initially for the repair of local roads: from 1890 the funds were used for the creation of public open spaces of which the Merrion Street Garden of Rest is an example opened in 1933.

CHARLES, JOHN (born 1932) made his first team debut for Leeds United in 1949 and scored 153 goals in 308 appearances prior to playing for Juventus. He returned to England in 1962 for playing and management before leaving football for the licensed trade and involvement with charities. He was awarded the CBE in June 2001.

CHARTERS OF LEEDS The first Charter of Incorporation was granted to the burgesses by King Charles I on July 13th 1626. The corporate body was called *"The Alderman and Burgesses of the Borough of Leedes in the County of York"*. The council had one alderman (Sir John Savile), nine burgesses and 20 assistants. There were 35 aldermen who succeeded Sir John Savile. A plaque marking the 350th anniversary of the incorporation was unveiled at Leeds Civic Hall on July 13th 1976. The second charter was granted by King Charles II in 1661 thus providing for the appointment of Mayors - the first was Thomas Danby and the third charter was granted by King Charles II in 1684. The second charter was restored in 1689 by William and Mary. The title of City of Leeds had been conferred upon the Borough by Royal Charter on February 13th 1893; in her Jubilee Year Queen Victoria declared and ordained by Letters Patent that the First Citizen should be "styled, entitled and called Lord Mayor of Leeds". The Leeds Corporation Act of 1899 declared that the corporate body should be styled "The Lord Mayor, Aldermen and Citizens of the City of Leeds". On April 1st 1974 the former County Borough of Leeds, Boroughs of Morley & Pudsey, Urban Districts of Aireborough, Garforth, Horsforth, Otley & Rothwell and parts of the Rural Districts of Tadcaster, Wetherby and Wharfedale were all amalgamated to form the new Metropolitan District: the MDC decided that the area be known as Leeds.

CHILD, JOHN (1790-1868) was the Leeds architect responsible for St Patrick's RC Church York Road (1831), St Anne's Cathedral (1838) and St Joseph's Church (1860).

CHILDREN'S DAY The first event was held in 1920 and led to the formation of the Leeds Elementary Schools Sports Association and the camp at Ben Rhydding. The 1921 event was abandoned due to stormy conditions and the following year there was a week's delay due to rain before the first Queen Elsie Oldfield was crowned on July 15th - the crown is on display in the Civic Hall. The Children's

Day at Roundhay Park in 1923 raised £2000 for the camp but by 1962 interest was dwindling - the last Queen was crowned by Ronnie Hilton in 1963. The events in 1964 were combined with Leeds Printer's Gala and briefly revived again in 1968.

CHORLEY, CHARLES ROBERTS (1829-1914) commenced his Leeds architectural practice in 1854 and was in partnership with John Dobson (1856-70) and with John Connon (1885-97). He was responsible for Yorkshire Post offices Albion Street (1887), Liberal Club Quebec Street (1890) and the Metropole Hotel (1899). Charles Chorley was the Honorary Architect to Leeds Parish Church and for 30 years was a churchwarden.

CHORLEY, ROBERT (1842-1904) started work at Messrs. McCorquodale Newton-le-Willows and then transferred to Leeds as manager. He started in Cookridge Street with Joseph Pickersgill establishing a letterpress, printing and lithographic firm. Robert Chorley died as a result of an accident in the Cookridge Street works in September 1904.

CHORLEY LANE leads from Little Woodhouse Street to Clarendon Road and was named after Francis Chorley - in 1818 he developed the area on which Joseph's Well now stands. Belmont House was built in 1786 by the Oates family and it was the home of Joshua Tetley from 1839 to 1856 - it was demolished in 1978 for the building of the Clarendon Wing of the LGI.

CHURCHES AND CHAPELS *All Souls Blackman Lane* was built as a memorial to Dr Walter Hook Vicar of Leeds (1837-59) and designed by Sir George Gilbert Scott and completed by his son John Olrid Scott. The church had the foundation stone laid by William Page Baron Hatherley Lord Chancellor of Britain on September 2nd 1876 and was consecrated on January 29th 1880 with the church tower designed by John Olrid Scott and dedicated in November 1907. The chancel's stained glass is by Charles Eamer Kempe and there is a memorial window to architect Elisha Backhouse who lived in Hillary Place. *Emmanuel Church* is the University Chaplaincy for Anglican, Baptist, Catholic, Lutheran, Methodist, Quakers, Salvation Army and United Reformed Church members. The foundation stone was laid on October 28th 1876 and consecration followed on September 15th 1880 by Bishop of Ripon Robert Bickersteth; architects Richard Adams and John Kelly. Emmanuel Church was built in memory of Leeds surgeon William

Hey and solicitor Thomas Dibb. The spire was designed by Harry Chorley and was dedicated in November 1906; there was restoration after a fire in 1968. *Friend's Meeting House* of the Carlton Hill Religious Society of Friends (Quakers) opened their new meeting house on Woodhouse Lane in 1987 having transferred from a room in the Soroptimist's building at Hyde Park. The Quakers first met in Leeds on Water Lane with a meeting house in which their first meeting was held on September 24th 1699. The meeting house was rebuilt in 1672: this was sold in 1946 and the site was cleared in 1967. In 1864 the Carlton House estate was sold by John Jowitt (1811-98): the new meeting house had the foundation stone laid by Ald George Tatham (later Mayor of Leeds) on June 6th 1866 and it was opened on Woodhouse Lane on February 23rd 1868; the building was designed by Edward Birchall. In 1921 two of the rooms were sold to wholesale clothiers Albrechts Ltd with the Meeting using the schoolroom and rear library area. The last meeting for worship was held on April 22nd 1979. The BBC obtained use of part of the building in 1938 and BBC Radio Leeds moved from the Merrion Centre to their new studios in 1980. *Holy Trinity Church* or the Chapel of the Holy and Undivided Trinity was consecrated by the Archbishop of York Lancelot Blackburne on August 10th 1727: the procession was led into the church by Lady Betty Hastings. The foundation stone was laid by Rev Henry Robinson on August 23rd 1721 and the cost of £4563 was offset by Lady Betty Hastings of Ledston Hall who contributed £1000 with help from many leading Leeds merchants and Ralph Thoresby: the site of Kid Stack Garth was bought for £175. The church was designed by William Etty who added a wooden spire to the original design. The church has a high nave with Doric columns and chancel with an oak pelican and young above the altar. Galleries were inserted in 1752 and the present pews installed in 1887. A hurricane on Monday January 7th 1839 seriously damaged the spire, although the vane and Cross remained in place. The spire was later demolished and a new 186' structure was designed by Robert Chantrell, who rebuilt the three upper stages. *Leeds Parish Church* There seems little doubt of a Saxon church existing in the 8th/9th century: this would have been replaced by the Normans - in 1812 Norman stones were found during repairs. In the mid-14th century the church was rebuilt or enlarged but a fire about 1500 necessitated rebuilding. On April 15th 1837 Dr Walter Hook was inducted Vicar of Leeds: he was unhappy with the arrangement of the church for worship and a restoration was planned by Robert Chantrell - except for the south wall which had been rebuilt in 1809/12 by Thomas Taylor. A report in 1810 by Charles Watson of York found a cracked tower but it was in 1837 that a report envisaged a cost of £4500 which within months rose to £6000. In March 1838 the monuments were removed and major problems were discovered: tenders were invited to rebuild the whole church except for the south wall-the final cost was £30,000. The new church was consecrated on September 2nd 1841: in 1868-69 a railway viaduct separated the church from Leeds using the old north graveyard. South of the Leeds Cross which was restored in 1986 is the effigy of a 14th century knight who was a member of the Manston family. The Hardwick memorial remembers Thomas Hardwick of Potternewton who died in February 1577: it is a rare Elizabethan table tomb which was behind the altar in the old church - the tomb has frescoes and also remembers his wife Anne and seven children. A tablet on the south wall is to the Leeds historian Ralph Thoresby (1658-1725) - the canopy once was a feature of the piscina from the 14th century church. His father John Thoresby (died September 20th 1661) is remembered in a plaque/bust on the west wall of the Lady Chapel by Andrew Carpenter. The memorial in the north chancel chapel to Dr Hook was designed by Sir George Gilbert Scott and made by William Day Keyworth Jnr of Hull: Dr Hook is buried at Chichester Cathedral where he became Dean in 1859. The Chapel of the Holy Spirit and St Katherine was furnished in memory of Rev Geoffrey Studdert Kennedy "Woodbine Willie" and opened on May 11th 1986. It is near the site of a chantry chapel founded by Thomas Clarell who appointed William Sheafield as the chantry priest. The £1 million restoration of the Parish Church was completed in 2000: stained glass windows, rebuilding north entrance, restoring the organ and the historic monuments. The Good Shepherd Mission was in St Peter's Square opened in 1882 on a slum site which included the Falstaff Inn and the Parish Church Sunday School. The Mission was demolished for the building of the Quarry Hill Flats: the last service was in 1936. The Railway Arch Mission was in the Lloyd's Arms Yard (Marsh Lane):

opened in 1895 with the communion cup on display in the Civic Hall. *Mill Hill Unitarian Chapel* was first built near Alms House Garth and was opened on March 25th 1674. The church was founded by a group of non-conformist English Presbyterians and attended by Ralph Thoresby's father. Richard Stretton was the first minister and together with John Thoresby became early trustees of The Presbyterian Fund. Richard Stretton who left for London in 1678 and died in 1712 is the first name on a brass plate listing the ministers - it was erected in 1897. One of the most eminent of the ministers was Rev Joseph Priestley who was born at Birstall in March 1733 into a weaving family. He moved to Mill Hill Chapel from Warrington in September 1767 and lived in the minister's house north of the chapel. He preached his last sermon on May 16th 1773 and took up the offer of a position with the Home Secretary Lord Shelburne William Petty Fitzmaurice (1737-1805) - he was prime minister in 1783. During his time in Leeds foundations were laid for his discovery of Oxygen in 1774 and he worked with Thoresby to found the Leeds Library and Infirmary. His statue is in City Square and there is a chair in the chapel today, restored by Mrs Currer-Briggs and said to have belonged to Joseph Priestley. The foundation stone for the new Mill Hill Chapel was laid by Ald Hamer Stansfield (died at Ilkley 1865) on April 26th 1847 and the chapel was designed in Potternewton and Meanwood stone by Henry Bowman and Joseph Stretch Crowther. The opening of the £7300 chapel was on December 27th 1848 with minister Rev C Wicksteed: during the period of building services were held at Call Lane Chapel. Priestley Hall was built in 1858/59 by George Corson as the chapel school; it was adapted for wartime use in 1915-19. In 1924 the chapel chancel floor was laid in marble to mark the chapel's 250th anniversary. In 1956 Priestley Hall was sold to Ocean Accident Assurance with the top floor leased for chapel use, resold and demolished in 1968 by new owners National Provincial Bank. The hall is now included at the south end of the chapel and is in constant use today by many groups. The building of the nearby shopping centre caused the removal of many graves with re-interment elsewhere. Chapel Yard was re-laid in 1978 using some old gravestones and in 1970 Mill Hill Chapel became a listed building. The organ was built by Norman & Beard in 1910 enhanced and enlarged by JM Spink under the supervision of Mill Hill Chapel organist Anthony Norcliffe. The site for the **Oxford Place Methodist Chapel** was bought on December 2nd 1834 and James Simpson was asked to prepare plans. The foundation stone was laid on February 4th 1835 by Rev Robert Wood. The opening service in the new £10,000 chapel was on October 9th 1835, having been built by Boothman and Woolley. The preachers at the opening services were Rev Robert Newton, Rev James Dixon and Rev Theophilus Lessey with the use of a temporary organ. The Sunday School moved from their basement room to the new Oxford Row buildings in September 1841. In 1889 the rooms were used by Leeds Board School as the precursor of the City of Leeds School. In 1894 Oxford Place was made into a Methodist Mission: in 1896 plans by George Danby and William Thorp were being put into effect with the completion of a new Baroque-style building. New schools were opened in June 1897 and the new chapel was opened on September 22nd 1898: the whole scheme completed in 1902 at a cost of £30,000. Oxford Place benefited from a rapidly increasing congregation but tragedy struck in the morning of September 4th 1911, when fire severely affected the Chapel. Rostrum, organ and seating were destroyed and the Coliseum on Cookridge Street was used temporarily for services for six months as restoration work proceeded. The present premises were reconstructed to designs by Trevor Wilkinson Associates of York-the old Sunday School building was sold and money also came from Brunswick closed in 1972; the new sanctuary and ground floor rooms were opened on May 12th. 1979. The basement rooms were refurbished and completed by May 1982 and the adjacent Oxford Place Chambers were also refurbished at a cost of £250,000. **St Anne's Cathedral** The Catholic church in Leeds was first established at the junction of Lady Lane and Templar Lane with the foundation stone laid in April 1793, opening the following year. In July 1831 St Patrick' s Chapel opened on York Road. John Child was appointed to build a new Catholic Church for the city centre: the foundation stone was laid on August 12th 1837. St Anne's Church cost £10,000 and was dedicated by Bishop John Briggs on October 24th 1838. A new altar and reredos by A W Pugin were installed during a two month closure of the church, when there was painting and decorating carried out: the reopening was held on June 22nd. In 1875-76 the church was restored for £4000 with a new organ chamber by Richard Adams and John Kelly. St Anne's Church became a Cathedral in 1878 - the new diocese was formed from the Diocese of Middlesborough on December 20th 1878. Dr Robert Cornthwaite was installed in the Cathedral as Bishop of the new diocese in October 1879. On December 1st 1899 the Council announced the compulsory purchase of the Cathedral for road widening: the church stood at the head of Park Row and was demolished during November 1904. The Council offered land at the junction of Great George Street and Cookridge Street and in 1900 John Henry Eastwood (1842-1913) was appointed to design a new Cathedral Church in collaboration with Sydney Kyffin Greenslade (1866-1955). The foundation stone for St Anne's Cathedral was laid on July 26th 1902 by Bishop Robert Brindle of Nottingham. The last Mass was held at the old church on April 24th 1904 and the first service held in the new building on May 1st being celebrated by William Gordon. The formal dedication was held on June 16th 1904: the whole project including presbytery and schools cost £52,000. The consecration was held on July 18th 1924 and in 1963 the sanctuary was re-ordered by Weightman & Bullen of Liverpool for Bishop Dwyer: this followed a previous re-ordering in the 1950's. *St Augustine's Church Wrangthorn* was consecrated on November 8th 1871 to designs by James Barlow Fraser; the spire was built in 1878. *St George's Church* was designed by John Clark in 1836-38: the foundation stone was laid by Bishop of Ripon Charles Longley on December 16th 1836. The church had two main features: a 160' spire and extensive vaults originally intended for burials which ceased in 1855. The church cost about £11,000 and was consecrated on Wednesday November 7th 1838 by the Bishop of Ripon. The builders were Atack & Baxter and there had been a delay in completion with the construction of the vaults. The church was restored in 1874, 1886 and again in 1900 when the eastern apse was added and a chancel arch and vestry erected. The Long Room extension to the north was opened in 1974 and an interior restoration by James Thorp costing £400,000 was dedicated on September 9th 1990. This included the removal of the galleries and insertion of a central section of the south stained glass window, which remembers Christopher Beckett who was one of the original founders. The city was hit by high winds on

Sunday February 11th 1962 and some of the church tower pinnacles were blown down causing considerable damage: the north staircase and part of the balcony were brought down leaving a large hole in the roof. The church had to find £20,000 for repairs and the removal of 60 tons of stone enabled the church to be reopened the following Sunday. The vaults found another use when Rev Don Robins founded St George's Crypt as a hostel for homeless men with accommodation and food: it opened on October 14th 1930 by Sir Benjamin Turner. The Crypt Chapel was dedicated to St Francis of Assisi by Bishop Burroughs in July 1932. Rev Percy Donald Robins became the Vicar in 1931: prior to this he had been the curate of St John the Baptist Church Croydon. He was at St George's Church until 1948; the Don Robins memorial window shows St Francis offering food and shelter. The Crypt launched a £1 million appeal and in December 1997 succeeded in raising £120,000 in two weeks: funds were used for a £1.5 million restoration scheme to meet health and safety requirements which opened in 1999 and for the setting up of a community church. *St John the Evangelist Church* The consecration of John Harrison's church took place on September 21st 1634. The Harrison memorial window inserted in 1885 shows scenes from his life including the building of the church, the market cross, almshouses and the apocryphal scene at Red Hall in 1647 when King Charles passed through Leeds a prisoner of the Scots: John Harrison brought him a tankard of ale which the King found to be full of gold coins. Harrison was tried at York in 1649 for supporting the Royalist cause where he was fined: he died on October 29th 1656 aged 77. His tomb in the chancel was restored in 1884 and has an inscription by Dr John Lake Vicar of Leeds (1660-1663). The portrait of the founder hangs at the west end and was possibly donated to the church by John Harrison's great-nephew Rev Henry Robinson: the painting was displayed in the Town Hall until c1920. On the north wall is a memorial to Godfrey Lawson (1629-1709) who provided the first public library at Leeds Grammar School and was Mayor of Leeds in 1669. In 1765 the west and south galleries was built by John Blayds (1730-1807) who was three times Mayor of Leeds. A main feature of the church are the black Jacobean wooden screens with their coats of arms together with the ornate ceilings. The strap cresting was removed in the

1860's and was replaced in 1890/91 by Temple Moore and new sections inserted - his panels are now on the west wall. The pew ends and brasses all relate to the prosperity brought to Leeds by the weaving and fabric trades: one pew has the iron holder for the alderman's mace used by John Harrison. In 1802 Thomas Johnson who designed the Leeds Library in Commercial Street worked on the church; in 1816 Thomas Taylor was at St John's Church as was John Clark in 1838 when he rebuilt the church tower. Richard Norman Shaw suggested an extensive restoration scheme and with the support of Sir George Gilbert Scott prevented demolition. A scheme was prepared which included the removal of the galleries and building a new south porch with stone sundial and vestry: the church reopened in 1868. During the time of Rev John Scott (1836-1906) - cousin of Gilbert Scott - new choir desks were installed and Harrison's tomb was given a new setting in 1884. Temple Moore worked at the church from 1890 adapting the Harrison Chapel for weekday services; he restored the screens but did not replace the removed coats of arms which were later placed on the west wall - they were reinstated to their original positions and display the arms of Charles I as Prince of Wales and those of James I. Closed in October 1974: maintained by the Churches Conservation Trust from 1977. The St John's Vicarage was once on Albion Street near the junction with Woodhouse Lane. *St Patrick's Roman Catholic Church* was opened on April 30th 1891 to designs by John Kelly and Edward Birchall: the church was consecrated on April 22nd 1926. The last service was held on Saturday April 28th 2001 and a new church designed by Michael Bateson Associates was opened on Torre Road adjacent to St Patrick's RC Primary School on Sunday April 29th. The old social club became the new home of East Street Arts and the church was renovated as rehearsal space for the West Yorkshire Playhouse. *St Mark's Church Woodhouse* was consecrated on January 13th 1826 to designs by Peter Atkinson Jnr and RH Sharp: it was a Waterloo or Million Church. The church was restored by Adams & Kelly in the 1870's; the St Stephen's Window is the memorial to Jane Hopkinson (1810-42). The graveyard was opened in 1831 and closed for burials in 1958: it is an area of special scientific interest. The final service was held on 15th July 2001. *Salem Chapel* on Hunslet Lane was built in 1791 for the Congregationalists with a Sunday School added in the 1860's. The curved front of the chapel is part of the 1907 rebuilding and the chapel is now the United Reformed Church. This was one of several Congregational Chapels which included Belgrave (1836), East Parade (1841), Headingley Hill (1866) by Cuthbert Brodrick, Kirkstall (1878) and Queen Street (1825).

CHURCHES CONSERVATION TRUST has maintained St John's Church from 1977. The Historic Churches Conservation Trust (Redundant Churches Fund) was established by Parliament in 1969 - a partnership between State and the Church of England. From 1970 to 2000 there have been 1566 parish churches declared redundant and 320 churches have been vested with the Trust. The Trust has adopted William Morris (1834-96) as its guiding light: in 1877 he helped to found the Society for the Protection of Ancient Buildings.

CHURCH INSTITUTE was formed in January 1857 and the foundation stone for their building on Albion Place was laid on October 29th 1866 by the Archbishop of Canterbury. It opened on May 16th 1868 to designs by Adams & Kelly at a cost of £7300. The British Deaf Association was founded in the Church Institute on July 24th 1890. The building is now Albion Court and La Senza. In early 1981 the Church Institute moved to Basinghall Street and then to Leeming House in 1994 where two suites were leased. The Institute moved again to premises on the corner of New Market Street/Central Road in August 1999.

CHURCHILL, SIR WINSTON LEONARD SPENCER (1874-1965) was the Prime Minister of an all-party administration from May 1940 until May 23rd 1945 leading Britain through the Second World War. Churchill visited Leeds on May 18th 1942 and on June 6th 1945: he was granted the Freedom of the City of Leeds on October 28th 1953.

CINEMAS *ABC Cinema* was opened on the site of Sheepshanks House as The Ritz on Vicar Lane on November 19th 1934 featuring a British Crompton organ: the cinema was designed by WR Glen. The name changed in May 1959 to the ABC (Associated British Cinemas) and was converted to a twin cinema in April 1970 (opened by Beryl Reid) and a triple screen cinema in March 1974. There was another name change to Cannon in March 1987 and to MGM (Metro Goldwyn Mayer) on May 23rd 1993 with a reversal to ABC in 1996: the cinema was closed by owners Cinven on

ABC Cinema Vicar Lane and Hope Inn *(demolished for Inner Ring Road)*

Thursday February 17th 2000. It is proposed that the cinema be demolished and replaced with a 15 storey tower block containing 123 apartments. *Assembly Rooms* on New Briggate was built in 1898 as a concert hall in the Grand Theatre complex by George Corson and James Watson with 1100 seats. The Assembly Rooms became a cinema in April 1907: in August 1958 it became The Plaza (Star Cinemas) and the cinema closed on February 14th 1985. The Assembly Rooms showed the first colour film in Leeds on January 8th 1912. The building became a rehearsal room for Opera North from August 1986. *Gaumont* on Cookridge Street opened as the first full time cinema in Leeds The Coliseum in April 1905, having been a concert hall and theatre designed by William Bakewell which had opened on July 15th 1885 by the Prince of Wales (future King Edward VII). In 1906 it was bought by Sydney Carter at auction who presented his New Century Films until 1907 when he moved to the Assembly Rooms. The name changed to the Gaumont in 1938 and it closed in December 1969. The premises were used for bingo; it became a TV centre from October 1981 to March 1991; the Town & Country Club opened in 1992 (Ollie Smith & Mick Whelan) and closed in 2000; it was bought by night club chain First Leisure who restored and altered the listed building at a cost of £7 million and opened the new club on May 18th 2001 as The Creation designed by Blueprint. *Majestic* on City Square was designed by Pascal Stienlet and opened in June 1922 on the site of Eye Bright Place and later the Recruiting Office demolished 1918: it was closed as a cinema on July 10th 1969. The old cinema was known for its dances and it became a bingo hall (Top Rank) until April 1996 and the Majestyk nightclub from November 1996. *New Gallery* on South Parade opened in 1920 in the old Baptist Chapel: it closed in June 1922. *News Theatre* in the Queen's Hotel Building City Square was opened in August 1938 becoming the Classic (1966), Tatler Film Club (1969) and Classic (1979). The cinema closed in 1981 and became a night club (Bondi Beach Bar). *Odeon* on The Headrow was opened by Lord Mayor Fred Brown Simpson as The Paramount on February 22nd 1932 being built on a site which was occupied by small shops and ale houses and bought for £110,000. The building cost £230,000 and the auditorium had a seating capacity of 2590; there were 1, 235, 674 patrons in the first year. The first film was *"The Smiling Lieutenant"* with Maurice Chevalier and Rex O' Grady playing the organ to 1500 paying patrons and VIP's as well as the Paramount Symphony Orchestra. The name changed to the Odeon in April 1940. Conversion to twin cinemas followed in May 1969; a third screen opened in July 1978 in the old restaurant and it became a five screen cinema from March 1988. The 17 ton Wurlitzer organ had 2000 pipes and 160 stops being worth £10,000: it was sold on July 9th 1968; the 3 manual 19 rank organ was played for the last time by Arnold Loxam and broadcast on BBC Radio Leeds on July 27th 1968. It was moved to the High Wycombe Organ Centre in Buckinghamshire and is now preserved at the Thursford Steam Museum Norfolk. There were many stage appearances at The Odeon including The Beatles (November 1963), Gracie Fields, Gene Autry, Tom Mix, Paul Robeson, pianist Myra Hess and Laurel & Hardy. The Odeon Cinema closed in October 2001 - the Odeon Group opened a 13 screen new cinema at Thornbury Bradford in July 2000 as part of the Gallagher Leisure Park. Plans were made by architects Broadway Malyan to create 52 apartments on five floors above ground level leisure units retaining the listed façade. The plans were submitted by the Headrow Development Company (Craiglair Property Co). *Odeon Merrion Centre* opened in August 1964 and closed on October 30th 1977. The Odeon Cinemas were founded by Oscar Deutsch in Birmingham (1930): the name stands for Oscar Deutsch Entertains Our Nation: JA Rank bought the cinemas on Oscar Deutsch's death in 1941 and the Odeon chain was bought by London based Cinven from Rank in February 2000. *Playhouse Film Theatre* opened on Calverley Street in the University Sports Hall in September 1970. Films were last shown in the year that the Playhouse transferred to their new theatre on Quarry Hill. *Rialto* on Briggate opened in April 1911 as the Briggate Picture House and became the Rialto in March 1927: the cinema closed in March 1939 and became the site for the Marks & Spencer department store. *Savoy* was in Queen's Arcade (Boots) and closed in 1918. *Scala* in Albion Place opened in June 1922 and closed on August 31st 1957, becoming a furniture showroom. The organs of the Scala and Majestic were sold for scrap on July 15th 1954. *Tatler* opened as the City Cinema on Boar Lane in October 1915 and changed to the Savoy in 1925, Academy (1931) and Tatler News Theatre (1936). The cinema was in the Royal Exchange Building and closed in January 1964. *Theatre de Luxe* opened on Kirkgate in 1910 and closed 1934. *Tower* on New Briggate opened in the converted Grand Arcade in April 1920: the cinema closed on March 7th 1985 and became a night club from October 1986.

CITY CENTRAL is a development on Wellington Street in the old Great Northern (Wellesley) Hotel. Taywood Homes completed a £4.8 million restoration programme to create 65 apartments retaining original features including marble fireplaces, mouldings and cornices especially in communal areas.

CITY CENTRE LOOP ROAD was built at a cost of £15 million between 1993 and 1998: complete with 18 junctions from City Square (1) to Bishopgate Street (18).

CITY HOUSE dominates the railway station: opened in 1962 and designed by John Poulson (1911-1993) - built by Taylow Woodrow. The office block is 248' high and has 13 floors. It is owned by Roy Star Ltd with agent Weatherall Green & Smith.

CITY OF LEEDS was created in 1893: the charter was sealed by Queen Victoria on February 13th.

CITY OF LEEDS AWARD FOR ARCHITECTURE is sponsored by the Halifax and promoted by the City Council, Leeds Society of

Architects, Landscape Institute, Leeds Civic Trust and Institute of Historic Building Conservation. The 14th annual awards were announced in January 2001.

CITY SQUARE The plans for a City Square were announced by the Mayor of Leeds John Ward the day after the charter was signed by Queen Victoria which raised Leeds to city status. The first step was to demolish the already deserted Coloured Cloth Hall, which the town had bought for £66,000 in 1889 together with the large Quebec House, for which negotiations were protracted. The council derived some financial input from the sale of land for the new post office opened in 1896 and offices to the north. The plans for the new square were drawn up at Col Harding's request by architect William Bakewell and work taking two years was started in 1897. Demolition of the old hall was complete by 1890 and in 1886 Col Thomas Walter Harding of the Tower Works commissioned Thomas Brock RA to design and cast an equestrian statue of the Black Prince for the new square. It was in 1898 that the city elected Col Harding as Lord Mayor; he later commissioned other statues for the square. Due to the lack of large casting facilities in England Brock had the statue cast in bronze in Belgium taking seven years to complete the commission for Leeds. The

City Square – Norwich Union Building and Post Office

Black Prince travelled from Antwerp to Hull by ship and then by the Aire & Calder canal to New Dock (Clarence Dock) over two days in August 1903. The Black Prince was sited in the square on August 31st 1903 and City Square was officially opened on September 16th 1903. Col Harding covered the cost of the Black Prince, lamp statues of Morn and Even by Alfred Drury and the statues of Rev Walter Hook (Vicar of Leeds 1837-59) and Joseph Priestley (1733-1804). The statues of John Harrison (1576-1656) and James Watt (1736-1819) were paid for by Coun Richard Boston (1903) and Richard Wainwright (1898). The War years saw City Square with air raid shelters surrounding the Black Prince. The layout of City Square was changed in 1966 with the closure of the road in front of the post office and in the new millennium when a £1.6 million restoration project was completed. The square was remodelled by city architect John Thorp and includes new seating, planting and re-siting of the statues to echo the original layout. The original granite balusters were replaced after rediscovery and a fountain feature was introduced at a cost of £186,000. There are six red K6 telephone kiosks outside the Post Office - designed by

City Square/Boar Lane – *from Queen's Hotel*

Sir Giles Gilbert Scott in 1935 - the boxes are protected and listed.
The Standard Life Assurance building north of the square was built in 1901 on the site of the old courthouse - there were 50 suites of offices: the Norwich Union demolished and rebuilt this in 1969. The second building was demolished in 1995 to be replaced by No 1 City Square: this opened in 1996 for Norwich Union and was designed by Abbey Hanson Rowe. On the east side is the other tall office block of No 1 Park Row which was built in 1996 designed by Fletcher Joseph. This had replaced the NatWest building of Priestley House - on the site of the original Priestley Hall demolished in 1968.

CIVIC HALL was opened on Wednesday August 23rd 1933 by King George V and Queen Mary; designed by E Vincent Harris with 90% of the workers being taken off the unemployment register during the construction period (The Unemployed Grants Committee). The cost of the building was £360,000 (c£40 million today). The towers are 170 feet high and topped by gilt bronze owls by John Hodge: they weigh half a ton each and are seven feet six inches high. The key used to open the Civic Hall was returned from New Zealand on June 7th 1993 after having been missing since 1933. The gardens created in front of the Civic Hall once included the £3000 Coronation Fountain erected in 1953 and demolished a year later. The old St George's Works, St James Square and Back Portland Crescent were demolished to prepare the site for the Civic Hall area. A plaque marking the Golden Jubilee of the Civic Hall was unveiled by Lord Mayor Martin Dodgson on August 23rd 1983 when the Council Leader was George Mudie. The dates described on the façade are 1626 and 1933.

CIVIC THEATRE was designed by Cuthbert Brodrick based on the style of the Bibliotheque St Genevieve Paris and opened as the Leeds Mechanics Institute on June 1st 1868 costing £60,000; used for lectures (seating for 1500), concerts and having a library, reading room and art gallery. The building was also partly used as the forerunner of Leeds Modern School. The main lecture hall for the Leeds Institute was known as the Albert Hall and was converted to a theatre and opened on October 7th 1949. The theatre was refurbished in 1983 by Clare Ferraby: the theatre has 523 seats. There was a proposal in 2001 that the building be converted in a £20 million project as the new City Museum, complemented with a new building at Clarence Dock.

CIVIC TRUST was founded in 1965 as an independent voluntary organisation to encourage high standards of architecture and planning; conservation and enhancement of the city heritage; improvement of public amenities and quality of life. The Trust has a Heritage and Design Centre in a pair of renovated Victorian cottages in Wharf Street near the Parish Church and The Calls: it opened in 1993. The houses were once the home of the Rayton family who lived there until 1938: the present shop was once a storeroom for lamps and electrical goods. The Heritage Open Days featured 43 buildings of historic interest opened in 2000.

CIVIL WAR was the struggle between King Charles I with the Royalists or Cavaliers and the Parliamentarians or Roundheads under Oliver Cromwell. On August 22nd 1642 the King raised his standard at Nottingham and this was followed by the Battle of Edgehill (October 1642) and Marston Moor on July 2nd 1644 with a Parliamentarian victory. In June 1645 Cromwell defeated the King at Naseby and on January 30th 1649 the King was beheaded: the last major battle of the Civil War was the Battle of Worcester in 1651. Leeds was held for the King by Sir William Savile until January 23rd 1643 when the town was taken by Sir Thomas Fairfax. The Royalist victory at Adwalton Moor in June 1643 brought the town into the hands of the King again until the aftermath of Marston Moor in July 1644. The King eventually surrendered to the Scots and taken to Newcastle-on-Tyne: he came to Leeds on February 9th 1647 as a prisoner and passed the night at Red Hall. There is a story that the King was supplied with gold coins by John Harrison in an ale tankard - the event is pictured in stained glass in St John's Church.

CLAPHAM, JOHN WILLIAM was a botanical chemist and licensed herb distiller who started his herbalist shop at Clapham's Buildings on Wade Lane in 1859: the laboratory, herbal distillery, grinding mills and store rooms were on Meanwood Road. Clapham's botanic gardens on Meanwood Road were "open on Wednesday afternoons in the summer months". His residence was on Woodhouse Ridge and then Oakdale House Meanwood Road; by 1902 Sarah Clapham was in Kelsall Street; by 1917 the shop was in New Market Buildings on Vicar Lane and later in County Arcade (1947). The present shop is on Ludgate Hill in the market buildings: owned by Buckles it was sold to the Birmingham firm Rippleglen Ltd in 1995. The shop sells over 200 different varieties of herbal remedies, health foods, vitamins, herbal teas, oils and aromatherapy products.

CLARELL, THOMAS (died 1469) belonged to the family who lived at Clarell Hall near Tickhill. He became Vicar of Leeds on November 8th 1430 and remained in that post until his death. It was his will dated 1469 which provided the money to found the Chantry of St Katherine at the Parish Church. The origins of Leeds Grammar School are thought to be associated with this chantry.

CLARENCE DOCK or New Dock was the terminus for the Aire & Calder Navigation Canal (1700) and is the site of the Royal Armouries opened in 1996. The Leeds Development Corporation contributed £11.8 million between 1990 and 1995 to restore Clarence Dock and the Armouries site. The Crosby Group whose parent company is the Berkeley Group, is building the biggest single mixed use scheme in Leeds: combining 450 luxury apartments with a 250 bed hotel, office, cinema and a health and fitness centre. The £100 million development on 15 acres will have bars, restaurants, club and casino and is due to open in late 2003. The Crosby Group's other Leeds projects include Portland Place, Whitehall 2 (149 one and two bedroom apartments) and Merchant's Key (apartments and penthouses) overlooking the river.

CLARENDON ROAD was created c1838 through the inspiration of John & John William Atkinson of Little Woodhouse Hall - once called the Judges Lodging (1864-1913). The Hall was converted into flats in 1973 and is the property of the Bradford and Northern Housing Association. John William married Marian Heaton in 1851 and moved to Woodhouse Square (Waverley House). Dr John Deakin Heaton (born 1817) and his wife Fanny (Heaton) bought Claremont on Clarendon Road in 1856, while his sister Ellen lived at Woodhouse Square (Swarthmore Centre). Fanny's father was John Heaton (unrelated) and lived at St John's Cottage which was demolished for the site of St Michael's College. Clarendon Road had many other large houses including Woodsley House (Fairbairn House) where Queen Victoria stayed on her visit to Leeds in 1858 to open the Town Hall: Mayor of Leeds Peter Fairbairn was knighted in the Town Hall on that occasion. Dr Heaton died in 1880 (buried at St George's Church) and Fanny continued to live at

Claremont until she died in September 1893 aged 65. It was bought by the Charles family and became a nursing home: it was bought in 1968 by the Yorkshire Archaeological Society. The large house at 67 Clarendon Road was bought for c£3000 by the Governors of Leeds Grammar School as the headmaster's residence in 1904: the first headmaster living at Sheafield was the Rev Canon Wynne Edwards (headmaster 1902-22). Sheafield was reconstructed and converted into the Junior School in 1937 and the boys moved in under headmaster SR Ince. The headmaster moved into a newly built house at Lawnswood. Sheafield continued as the Junior School until July 1997, when the whole school relocated to Alwoodley Gates. Sheafield has been converted into luxury en suite apartments and opened in September 2000. The Greater World Sanctuary of the Greater World Christian Spiritualist Association opened in a Clarendon Road house in 1935: it was the home of Dr Edwin Roberts and in the 1920's became the Clarendon Nursing Home. Springfield House was built on Well Close in 1792 for clothdresser Thomas Livesey and in 1836 was the home of the Quaker woolstapler Samuel Birchall (his son was architect Edward Birchall) until 1854. In 1865 the House was sold to the Roman Catholic Diocese (Leeds Clergy School 1876) who built the St Joseph's Diocesan Seminary (between Hyde Terrace and Seminary Street) opened in September 1876, held the property until 1969 when it was sold to the University and in 1981/83 became the Technology Department. Springfield House is now the headquarters of Covance (Development Services Company) involved in testing medications. (ref: Little Woodhouse)

Edward Hyde was the 1st Earl of Clarendon (1609-74): the Clarendon Code (1661-65) was a series of acts passed by the government directed at Nonconformists and designed to secure the supremacy of the Church of England.

CLARK, JOHN (died 1857) was born in Edinburgh and settled in Leeds following his success in the competition to design Leeds Commercial Buildings in 1829. His other work in Leeds included Bank Mills for Hives & Atkinson (1833), Bond Street Trustee Savings Bank (1834), Woodhouse Cemetery (1835), District Bank Boar Lane (1836), St George's Church (1838), Roundhay Hall (1840), Waverley House Woodhouse Square (1840), Woodhouse

Moor Almshouses (1840), Gledhow Grove (1840), Peter Fairbairn's Woodsley House Clarendon Road (1841) and Wilkinson's Mills (1842).

CLAYPIT LANE was mainly tenter fields in the 18th century and in 1791 the windmill caught fire. Queen Square was created in 1806: nearby is The Cobourg public house - a reminder of Cobourg Street. Cobourg was Prince Albert's home in Franconia Northern Bavaria. Claypit Lane is now the extension of the A58 Wetherby Road with a flyover across the Inner Ring Road.

CLOCKS *Dyson's* shop clock was installed in 1865 in their shop on Lower Briggate: the clock over the pavement in Lower Briggate was set in motion in 1910 to celebrate the birthday of John Dyson's wife. The clock has been restored and is now a feature of the Marriott Hotel. *Grand Arcade* clock was installed in 1898 at the Briggate end of the arcade designed by Smith & Tweedale and transferred to the Vicar Lane end in November 1939 after the arcade was sold - the parallel arcade was partly taken by the Tower Cinema in 1920 - the clock is by Robert James & Joseph Potts who depicted Windsor Castle with two knights striking the hours with their battleaxes. The original quotation from Macbeth was substituted with *"Time and Tide wait for no man"* in 1967. The original *Market Clock* (1904) by Leeming & Leeming was taken to Oakwood in July 1912 following agreement in Council in November 1911. *Thornton's Arcade* clock was made by William Potts in 1877 depicting characters from Ivanhoe: Robin Hood, Friar Tuck, Richard Couer de Lion and Gurth the Swineherd. The sculptor was John W Appleyard of Cookridge Street Leeds:the clock is 5'6" high and two feet wide. The *Town Hall* clock was designed by Lord Grimthorpe and other city public clocks include the *Post Office* City Square (1896), *Leeds Parish Church* (1841) by Potts of Leeds designed by Lord Grimthorpe and the *Markets Clock* presented by Marks & Spencers in 1984.

CLOTH HALLS The *First White Cloth Hall* for the sale of unfinished or "white" cloth was in Kirkgate in 1711 and the *Second White Cloth Hall* opened south of the river in Meadow Lane in 1755. The *Third White Cloth Hall* and Assembly Rooms over the north wing between The Calls and Kirkgate opened in 1776 to the designs of William Johnson at a cost of £4000 with 1210 stalls for the West Riding clothiers meeting every Tuesday and Saturday. The cupola was taken down from the second hall by William Johnson in 1786 and re-erected at the 3rd Cloth Hall. Due to the railway extension from Marsh Lane to New Station in 1869 the building was abandoned in favour of a **Fourth White Cloth Hall** built in King Street and opened on July 18th 1868 at a cost of £20,000 by the North Eastern Railway Co: markets were held on Tuesdays and Saturdays. This lasted until the building of the Metropole Hotel in 1899 - the last cloth hall's cupola is preserved on the roof. The First Hall is to be restored as Crown Court (Corn Exchange Walks) by Speciality Shops while all that remains of the Third Hall is a section of west façade with the old entrance (behind the Corn Exchange) and part of the Assembly Rooms. The restored entrance to the Third Hall was awarded the Ironbridge Award in 1992; architect John Lyall: restaurant and shops. Speciality Shops restored the old building at a cost of £720,000. **The Mixed or Coloured Cloth Hall** designed by John Moxon at a cost of £5300 opened in 1758 near the south end of Park Row (City Square): the building had 1770 stalls and the inner courtyard could hold 20,000 people. The octagon rotunda was a

Coloured Cloth Hall (centre) c1888

prominent feature and had the offices and the Council Chamber of the Trustees. The extensive building closed in 1889 and was demolished in 1890 and the first building on a part of the site was the new main Post Office in 1896. The 1758 brass bell is now on display at Armley Mills Industrial Museum. Cloth Hall Court was built on part of the Coloured Cloth Hall site and designed by TP Bennett & Son with builders Higgs & Hill: it was opened by Lord Mayor Eric Atkinson on September 25th 1980.

CLOTH HALL STREET links Crown Street and Call Lane/Duncan Street by the Corn Exchange. The large car park was opened on the site of demolished buildings which included the former premises of WH Smith (wholesale) and CH Johnson (manufacturing stationers). A £16 million scheme will have basement shops and 55 flats: the developers are Welfield Ltd and architects are Allford Hall Monaghan Morris with probable completion by October 2002.

CLOTH MARKET was first on Leeds Bridge and extended to Lower Briggate: this market continued in specially built cloth halls in the 18th century.

COAT OF ARMS of Leeds includes the three owls (coat of arms of Sir John Savile), three stars (coat of arms of Thomas Danby) and fleece (sign of a wool stapler). Sir John Savile of Howley Hall (1556-1630) was the first Alderman of Leeds and King Charles II granted a new charter in 1661 appointing Thomas Danby as the first mayor. In 1836 the motto Pro Rege et Lege (For King and Law) was added following the Municipal Corporations Act of 1835; the completion of the armorial bearings were in 1921 with the addition of a golden helmet and the original silver owls changed to brown.

COCKBURN, SIR GEORGE (1849-1927) was the chairman of the Education and Management Committee of the Leeds School Board from 1880: born in Glasgow he traded as an East India Merchant prior to his retirement from business and embarked upon his career as educational administrator. Cockburn High School was named after hin in 1904: he died on January 27th 1927.

COHEN, LEONORA (1873-1978) was a prominent suffragette: before the Great War she campaigned for enfranchisement and in 1912 was well known for throwing an iron bar through the jewel case in the Tower of London - a crime for which she was discharged. She became active in trade union work and was appointed a Leeds magistrate in 1922 and was awarded the OBE in 1928.

COLLEGES *College of Art and Design* The college started as the Leeds Government School of Design in 1846 (Leeds Mechanics & Literary Institution) and in 1851 was established the Department of Science & Art. In 1852 this became Leeds School of Art and in 1903 their new building designed by Bedford & Kitson was erected behind the Institute. The Jacob Kramer building on Blenheim Walk was opened by Rt Hon Denis Healey on March 1st 1985. The artist Jacob Kramer (1892-1962) trained at the school: the college was called Jacob Kramer College prior to 1993. *College of Building* on North Street originated as the Leeds Mechanics Institute from 1824. The Leeds School of Science was formed and in 1868 moved to the Leeds Institute on Cookridge Street. In 1908 Leeds College of Technology was formed and in 1931 the Department of Building was in Cross Stamford Street School - in 1946 it moved to Darley Street School. In May 1967 building started on the new North Street College, completed in November 1972. *College of Music* The Leeds College of Music moved into their premises on Quarry Hill in September 1997; the ground breaking ceremony was held in May 1996 with the foundation stone laid on February 19th 1997 by Chairman of the Governors Robert Tebb - the official opening was held on October 4th 1998. The college started as the Music Centre in the Leeds Institute on Cookridge Street and changed to become the Leeds City College of Music. *Joseph Priestley College* was formed in 1955 when the West Riding established Area Institutes with the amalgamation of Evening Institutes. The Joseph Priestley Institute of Further Education used part time teachers and in 1988 was one of nine further education colleges in Leeds: changing its name from Institute to College. The College is centred on Burton Avenue (Alec Beevers Centre) and has centres on Peel Street Morley and Marsh Street Rothwell. *Leeds College of Technology* originated in 1908 and the first stage of their new building on Cookridge Street was opened by Clement Attlee in January 1956 with the second stage in March 1959 and final stage in 1960: it was known as Kitson College in 1961 and became a regional college in 1962, providing further education for 16 to 18 year old students. This was the £750,000 Branch College of Engineering & Science with a

13 storey block catering for 1000 students: the completion of the complex was in September 1963 the site was once Rowland Winn's motor business. The Leeds College of Technology was opened as an incorporated institution on September 6th 1993. *Leeds Polytechnic* was formed in January 1970 when the Central Colleges of Art, Commerce, Education, Technology and Home Economics were combined into one college: this was granted University status in 1992 becoming the Leeds Metropolitan University. *North of England (Secretarial) College* based at Cavendish House Albion Street originated in 1913 by Sir Isaac Pitman & Sons with the present college founded in 1938 as the North of England Higher Secretarial College at Lands Lane/Albion Place corner. A branch of Pitman's College opened in Leeds in September 1958 and closed in July 1967; the Yorkshire Ladies Secretarial College was on Blenheim Terrace. *Park Lane College* had the foundation stone laid by Margaret Thatcher on November 3rd 1971: designed by JC Riddell and in August 1997 merged with the Airedale & Wharfedale College. It is one of the largest in the country with 30,000 students and 800 staff at 50 locations across Leeds. The Leeds Business School (Park Lane College) on Bridge Street was opened by Sir Leon Brittan on February 23rd 1990: the premises were originally opened on October 11th 1965 by Sir William Carron for the Amalgamated Engineering Union. *Thomas Danby College* transferred from Sweet Street (Marshall Mills School building) on the opening of the new building at Sheepscar on September 19th 1977 - it had taken 4 years to complete.

COLLIER, JOHN was a chain of clothing shops with a Boar Lane branch (closed 1955) and on Vicar Lane (United Drapery). In 1954 John Collier acquired Fifty Shilling Tailors and their factory on Burton Road closed in 1974; in 1980 the firm merged with Alexandres of Lady Lane and there was a management buy out in 1983 prior to eventual closure. Fifty Shilling Tailors was created by Sir Henry Price in 1928 (he retired in 1954) and was succeeded as chairman by John Collier in 1954.

COMMERCIAL BUILDINGS was a Georgian building on the corner of Boar Lane and Park Row (Quebec): designed by John Clark and opened on October 12th 1829 at a cost of £28,000. The foundation stone had been laid by Lepton Dobson on May 18th 1826. The exterior featured a series of 40' high columns and the interior had a staircase hall, ornamental dome and a reading room in which members could read the daily papers for an annual subscription - there was also a dining room, concert room and hotel. This impressive building of Leeds was demolished by June 27th 1872 for the Royal Exchange Building designed by Thomas Healey - opened 1875. There was also a Commercial News Room and Coffee Rooms on Briggate.

COMMERCIAL COURT is in Lower Briggate by the viaduct: it was once a tailor's shop and house in which took place the first Jewish wedding in Leeds. It was at 21 Commercial Court that Abigail Davis and James Pirani were married in June 1842: James Pirani was a manager at the shop (viaduct site) which was part of a chain of tailor's shops run by Hyam & Co - the Leeds branch opened in 1841 and moved to another shop in Briggate when the railway was built from Marsh Lane to New Station. The bride was the daughter of Gabriel Davis who became an optician on Boar Lane: he was the main inspiration behind the purchase of a plot of land on Gelderd Road from the Earl of Cardigan for Jewish burials. The Commercial Inn changed to The Viaduct in the mid-19th century.

COMMERCIAL STREET The street was cut in 1802 to Lands Lane and in 1807 was cut through to Briggate with the demolition of several old properties. The first wooden pavement was laid down in Commercial Street in 1872. The first buildings included the Leeds Library (north) and Nicholson & Brown's Bank (south).

COMMUNITY ENTERPRISE CONSORTIUM, LEEDS is a voluntary organisation created in 1998 with headquarters on Woodhouse Street from 1999. The Consortium is funded with lottery cash and lends a hand to groups keen to make Leeds a better place.

CONCORDIA STREET has the entrance to the 1915 City Transport building - now the Malmaison Hotel; Prospect House on the corner of Sovereign Street is the new offices of Regus who offer serviced offices to many clients; the building was the Concordia Works of Charles Walker & Co Ltd in 1887: manufacturers of belting and mill leather requisites. The Quays is a luxury apartment/ penthouse suite on the riverside, launched in November 2000. The development was by KW Linfoot: most of the 83 properties were pre-sold prior to the official launch.

CONNON, JOHN WREGHITT (1849-1921) was a partner with

Charles Chorley from 1885 to 1897; their projects included work of the Philosophical Hall Park Row (1862), LICS Stores Albion Street (individual project 1884), Yorkshire Post Offices Albion Street (1887), Liberal Club Quebec Street (1890), Metropole Hotel King Street (1899). John W Connon was a director of the Metropole Hotel and a chapel warden at Mill Hill Unitarian Chapel in City Square where there is a memorial plaque, placed by his wife Rhoda Anne.

CONSTANTINE & CO were cabinet makers of South Parade in the 19th century: a dressing stool made by the firm is on display in the Abbey House Museum.

COOKE, ALFRED (1842-1902) was born in Leeds and in 1866 married Annie Nickson - they raised ten children. He bought a lithographic press for his shop and in the early 1870's bought premises near Crown Point Bridge: destroyed by fire in 1880. He bought a new site on Hunslet Road with the help of a loan from William Beckett and in 1883 was appointed Chromo-lithographer to HM The Queen. The factory was destroyed by fire in 1894 and the factory was rebuilt to the designs of Thomas Ambler including a turret clock copying that of Leeds Town Hall: in 1895 it was the largest printing works in the world. The factory was extended in 1962 on the site of St Jude's Church - built in 1853 and demolished in 1954. Alf Cooke was Mayor of Leeds in 1890 and lived at Weetwood Hall, which in 1913 became the property of Leeds University.

COOKRIDGE STREET The street links The Headrow with Woodhouse Lane and includes the Civic Theatre (Leeds Institute), St Anne's Cathedral, Gaumont (Coliseum) Cinema, Brodrick's Buildings and Leonardo House - once the site of a timber yard and smithy. The street was blocked in 2000 in order to construct Millennium Square, which was opened officially by Nelson Mandela in April 2001. Other buildings once included the Oriental Baths - the site became a car park and during the construction of Millennium Square a few white tiles were revealed from the old baths. The Headrow end features the new complex of The Light constructed in the old Leeds Permanent Building of 1930 by Blomfield and Atkinson and c1955 - both from Portland stone. The LPBS was built on the site, which was once occupied by the Bishop's House and the Roman Catholic School.

CO-OPERATIVE SOCIETY The Leeds headquarters on Albion Street opened on November 8th 1873: a foundation stone was laid for a LICS Stores and People's Hall on October 6th 1883 with opening on July 19th 1884; designed by John Wreghitt Connon. The store on Albion Street (west) had the foundation stone laid on May 6th 1893 with opening on September 1st 1894. The LICS started as the Leeds Flour Society at Benyon's Mill Holbeck in 1847: in 1853 this became the Leeds Co-operative Flour and Provision Society. The Albion Street store was sold to CRS (merged with CWS in April 2000) in 1993 and the LICS rented space for a pharmacy/optician until 1996 when the departments transferred to Boar Lane (closed 1999). The Albion Street store was sold in January 1999 to Tops Estates who commenced a restoration and development scheme - they own the Leeds Shopping Plaza. Wilkinsons Discount Store is one of the businesses with a lease. The LICS runs two travel agencies in the Leeds city centre: Merrion Centre and Kirkgate.

CORN EXCHANGE was designed by Cuthbert Brodrick with the foundation stone laid in May 1861 and opening on July 28th 1863. The first Corn Exchange was held at the market cross and in 1826-28 a new Corn Exchange was built by Samuel Chapman north of Headrow junction with Briggate at a cost of £12,500. The foundation stone was laid by John Cawood on May 31st 1826 with work on the west and main wing starting by August 1827. The building had facilities for the sale of corn and there were offices and warehouses for corn merchants as well as a small hotel, inn and four shops. The building was demolished 1869. Brodrick's Corn Exchange was refurbished in 1990 by Laings, Addy of Leeds and Butler & Co - the architects were William Alsop and John A Lyall (Shoreditch London) with the John Bruton Partnership. The redevelopment was by Speciality Shops: there are 48 shops - the Corn Exchange was sold to Arcadia.

CORSON, GEORGE (1829-1910) was born in Dumfries and brother of William Reid Corson. George came to Leeds in 1854 having an architect's practice on South Parade (1860) and Cookridge Street from 1871 to 1901 when he retired. His extensive work in Leeds included Auction House East Parade (1863), Tetley's Brewery (1872), School of Medicine (1865), Shop Commercial Street 1868), Life Assurance Building Park Row (1869), Heaton's shops/offices

Swinegate/Blayds Yard (1870), Ramsden's Music Rooms (1871), layout of Roundhay Park (1873), Lawnswood Cemetery (1875), Grand Theatre (1876), Municipal Buildings (1876), School Board Building (1881) and Infirmary extensions (1892).

COURT BARON was a manorial court and the property of the Lord of the Manor: the court dealt with escheated estates, land transfers, manorial custom enforcements and the management of the commons and wastes. The court appointed the Reeve who collected manorial dues.

COURT LEET was a manor court in the public domain which dealt with minor offences presided over by the Lord of the Manor and meeting about twice a year. The court appointed the constable and pinder who looked after stray animals in the pinfold.

COURTS The *County Court* in Albion Place was opened in 1869 to the designs of Thomas Charles Sorby (1836-1924): the building is now a part of WH Smiths. The *Court House* had the foundation stone laid on Park Row on September 2nd 1811 by Mayor Charles Brown; it was opened two years later to the designs by Thomas Taylor. It was enlarged with another floor in 1834/35 by Robert Chantrell; when the *Town Hall* opened in 1858 the courts were moved and the old building became the main post office. In 1864 the Privy Council decided that the West Riding Assizes were to be based in Leeds and on August 6th 1864 the Commission Criminal List was opened. In 1872 another floor was added to the court house but when the new post office was opened in 1896 in City Square, the building was abandoned: it was demolished in 1901. The *Leeds Combined Court Centre* had the foundation stone laid on July 6th 1979 and the £9.5 million complex was opened in September 1982; the official opening was by the Duchess of Kent on February 4th 1983: the builder was Higgs & Hill. *The Leeds Magistrates Court* was opened by Lord Chancellor Rt Hon Lord Mackay of Clashfern on September 30th 1994: architects Leeds Design Consultancy/R Cornfield.

COX & CO was a motor dealing business created by Russell Rose in 1933 who bought a showroom in Albion Street - originally opened by Francis Cox. In 1935 Cox & Co moved to newly built showrooms on Regent Street at a cost of £50,000. During the last War the premises were used as an ambulance depot until 1945 and in 1945 the Rose family continued trading. The business closed in

January 1985.

CRABTREE, CHARLES HENRY was the chairman and managing director of Crabtree & Sons engineers and printing press manufacturers. The business was founded on May 6th 1895: the company was honoured with a visit by HM The Queen in October 1958.

CRICKET The Headingley ground opened on May 27th 1890 for the Leeds Cricket, Football and Athletic Company and the Yorkshire County Cricket Club played their first match in June 1891. The first County Championship match was played at Headingley in August 1891 and the first Test Match (Australia) was played in 1899.

CRISPIN HOUSE was built in 1911 for Heaton's factory - ladies costume and raincoat manufacturer. They had started in 1899 in York Street and moved in 1909 to King Street and Cookridge Street. In 1926 an extension on New York Road opened: the premises were sold to shoe makers HW Poole in 1979 and became known as Crispin House. In 1999/2001 plans were being carried out by Leeds based Cityfusion to construct 77 luxury apartments (Crispin Lofts) with 11 penthouses designed by London based Buschow Henley within the shell of the original building at a cost of £11.5 million (Urban Loft Co). St Crispin is the patron saint of shoemakers.

CROCKATT, JOHN (died 1854) was a shipmaster of Tayport who married Anne Campbell in 1847: Peter Campbell set up as a dyer in Perth in 1814 and married the widow of William Pullar whose relation John Pullar was taken by Peter as an apprentice. John founded Pullars of Perth. John & Anne Crockatt's son John (1852-1927) joined Leeds based William Watson in 1873 and moved to Bradford and was in London a year later. In 1875 he started his dyer and cleaners shop in Carlton Hill Leeds-his mother lived on Blenheim Mount. He expanded the business to Harrogate and Wakefield and opened his shop on Commercial Street Leeds: in 1903 he had eight Leeds shops. In 1910 Crockatt's works were on Stoney Rock Lane and in 1935 the firm merged with the Johnson Group of Dyers and Cleaners (Liverpool). Their Leeds premises are on Stoney Rock Lane, Albion Street and in the White Rose Shopping Centre.

CROSS PARISH was the old name for the top section of Briggate where the market cross was positioned: it was also the site of the old Borough Prison transferred to Kirkgate in 1655. Cross Arcade (County Arcade) is also a reminder of the market cross.

CROSS YORK STREET links New York Street with Kirkgate: the large building on the east side was opened in 1909 as the Canon Jackson Memorial Sunday School for St James Church. There is a plaque inscribed *"To the Glory of God. This stone was laid by Mrs Sydney Rumboll November 14 1908"*. The building became a carpet warehouse and was converted into The Northern Light bar in 2001. *Back York Street* was once the site of St Vincent's Roman Catholic Chapel.

CROWN POINT RETAIL PARK was opened for business on August 28th 1989: officially on September 25th 1989 - the project costing £10 million. The site was the former Hunslet Lane railway yard.

CROWN STREET links The Calls with the rear of the Corn Exchange and Call Lane. The Assembly Rooms were a part of the 3rd White Cloth Hall and were opened on June 9th 1777: they were built over the north wing at a cost of £2500 and became a centre of Leeds social life. Only a part of the Assembly Rooms remain due to the construction of the rail link between Marsh Lane and Leeds New Station (1869). The entrance to the 3rd Hall has been restored and the bell replaced: Orford's Garage and Raine Bros plumbers merchants once occupied the building. From the 1860's the Assembly Rooms became a Working Men's Institute, William Towler & Co Globe Foundry (iron and steel) Warehouse; in 1923 Hirst's Tobacco occupied the building and named it Waterloo House. It became the Waterloo Antiques Centre and is now a Café Rouge. Crown Street also featured the premises of United Photographers, Boocock & Wood wholesale clothiers and the Fox & Grapes Yard together with the Crown & Fleece Hotel.

DANBY, THOMAS became the first Mayor of Leeds in November 1661 under the second charter (Charles II). Three silver stars were a part of Danby's coat of arms which form part of the City of Leeds coat of arms.

DARK ARCHES were created when the railway was extended from Marsh Lane station to Leeds New Station in 1869. The railway was brought to the city centre from 1866 on a long viaduct through the cemetery of the Parish Church (on an embankment), across the site of the 3rd White Cloth Hall and over the river. The Dark Arches were formed as a result of the new through station slightly above the original Wellington station. In January 1892 there was a severe fire in the Dark Arches which resulted in partial rebuilding of the line and station. Granary Wharf was created in December 1988 in the Dark Arches: a popular craft market in a regenerated part of the city.

DEBENHAM'S STORE Briggate was once Matthias Robinson's Department Store. The building was erected by 1904 by the Leeds Estates Company with the first occupant being piano dealer Charles Fox. It became outfitters G Cooke & Son and Donald Hart: Hart's shop had moved from New Briggate and was bought by Matthias Robinson in 1936, who substantially altered the building. In 1962 Debenham's bought Matthias Robinson: the name changed on December 8th 1972. There was a £20 million conversion by Carey Jones which was started in March 1997 and completed in Autumn 1998.

DE LACY was the Norman family who held the Leeds area after the Conquest: they were centred at Pontefract Castle. Ilbert de Lacy was the first holder of this part of the Honour of Pontefract. It was Ilbert de Lacy who granted lands in Leeds to the Norman Ralph Paynel who then gifted the Parish Church to Holy Trinity Priory York. Thus was formed the rectory - manor of Leeds Kirkgate cum Holbeck: administered by a separate court (High Court Lane off The Calls). In 1152 Henry de Lacy gave the lands for the Cistercian Kirkstall Abbey: the monks had moved from Barnoldswick.

DENBY & SPINKS The firm was founded in 1849 by Alfred Denby in partnership with his two nephews; they were joined in the 1860's by Albert Ingham Spink. The shop first opened in Albion Place for a mainly wholesale business and in 1876 they acquired the old Music Hall (closed 1870) premises on Albion Street at the corner of Albion Walk: used from 1850 as the Albion Carpet Warehouse. In the same year the store was called Denby & Spinks: Alfred Denby died in 1891 and Albert Spink died in 1929 after buying the partnership. Albert's son Ingham Spinks was made a partner in 1901 and it became a private limited company in 1916: the Harrogate branch was opened in 1947. The store was sold in 1958 to Harrison Gibson of Essex.

DENISON, EDMUND BECKETT, 1ST LORD GRIMTHORPE (1816-1905) was the designer of the clock for Leeds Town Hall as well as Big Ben at the Palace of Westminster and St Chad's Church Headingley. He was created Baron Grimthorpe in 1886.

DENISON, JOHN (1758-1820) was formerly John Wilkinson who inherited Potterton Hall and Ossington Hall (Nottinghamshire) on the death of his maternal uncle in 1785. A year later he built Denison Hall (Hanover Square) living there until his first marriage in 1787 to the daugther of J Horlock when they moved down to Ossington Hall. His wife died in 1794 and he married Charlotte Eastwick by whom he had 12 children: the eldest being John Evelyn Denison (1800-73) who was the Speaker of the House of Commons and on his retirement was created Viscount Ossington. He died at his London home in Portman Square and was buried at Ossington Church.

DENISON, ROBERT (1720-1785) William's younger brother and Mayor of Leeds in 1755. He lived at Denison House (later Sheepshanks House) until 1737: the house was probably designed by William Thornton (John Bourchier's Beningborough Hall) at the north end of North Street (Vicar Lane) on the eventual site of The Ritz Cinema. The house at 10 North End was restored with a new frontage and became the power base of the brother's merchant business - it also featured a large garden. Robert Denison inherited Ossington Hall Nottinghamshire in 1782 having bought Potterton in 1771 from the Fretwell family and built a house which is now the west wing of Potterton Hall. Robert changed his will six times and in 1783 he made his housekeeper Mrs Dunn the main beneficiary although on his death the estates were inherited by John Wilkinson (1758-1820) who changed his name to John Denison and in 1786 built Denison Hall in Hanover Square. There are fine memorials to the two brothers at the west end of Ossington Church by Joseph Nollekens.

DENISON, WILLIAM (1714-1782). He lived in Kirkgate and bought the manor of Ossington in 1753 and was Leeds Mayor in 1758. He died unmarried and was succeeded by his brother Robert; William and Robert Denison were buried in the family vault at Holy Rood Church Ossington. The church was built in 1783 by John Carr with the eastern mausoleum demolished in 1838. Ossington Hall was demolished in 1963 and all that remains are the entrance gates in the village, a ha-ha and man made lake together with part of the old garden which became an extension to the church graveyard where Maxwell Denison was buried in 1972. **DENISON HALL** was built in 1786 by John (Wilkinson) Denison to designs by William Lindley. John Wilkinson had inherited the fortune of his uncle Robert Denison in 1785 while living at Potterton Hall (Lodge). He acquired land in Woodhouse for £8500 and had built his mansion of Woodhouse House in 101 days, living at the new hall for a short time before his marriage in 1787 moving to live at Ossington Hall. In 1796 a lease was taken on Denison Hall by Sir Richard van Bempe Johnstone who divided the mansion into two houses; Harry Wormald bought the property in 1806. In 1824 the estate was developed by George Rawson. In 1917 the Hall became a private nursing home and in 1962 it was an old people's home. The last residents left in 1989; in April 2000 it was announced that the Hall would be converted into apartments. The conversion by Columbia Design & Build London includes 13 apartments in the old Hall with new building to the rear providing additional apartment accommodation. Many interior features have been retained and restored including the staircase and vaulted cellars; completion was in November 2001.

DENTAL HOSPITAL An honorary dental surgeon was appointed to the Infirmary and Dispensary in 1881; in 1905 the Dental Department was established with honorary dental surgeons. The official opening of the Dental Department was on July 27th 1905 by the Lord Mayor of Leeds and a year later the department was recognized by the University. In 1914 the University Dental School was opened - in March 1928 a new Dental Hospital was opened built on Infirmary land: this was to be demolished. In 1979 the Duke of Kent opened the Worsley Medical and Dental Building.

DESIGN INNOVATION CENTRE on The Calls occupies a converted 1930's grain and flour warehouse and opened in 1988 - architect Allen Tod.

DEWHIRST, ISAAC JOWITT (1863-1937) was born in Huddersfield and came to Leeds in 1885 establishing his tailoring business in Kirkgate. He was a Leeds alderman in 1923 and lived at Whinmoor Lodge (demolished).

DICK, SIR WILLIAM REID (1879-1961) was the Administrator of the Tate Gallery London 1934-41: he sculpted the statue of Lord Moynihan in the LGI (1939).

DIOCESE OF LEEDS was created in 1878 with Robert Cornthwaite being the first Roman Catholic Bishop of Leeds. In October 1862 the new Bishop of Beverley Robert Cornthwaite came to live in Hanover Square from York.

DIOCESE OF RIPON was formed in 1836 with the first Bishop of Ripon Charles Thomas Longley: Leeds is in this Diocese. The Diocese of Ripon and Leeds was formed in 2000: the first Bishop being John Packer who was welcomed at Ripon Cathedral on July 16th 2000.

DISPENSARY was first opened on October 1st 1824 in the House of Recovery (1802/04) on Vicar Lane. In November 1828 a house was purchased at North Street/Templar Street and the institution bought a site in Belgrave Square from Francis Lupton for £1000. The foundation stone for a new Dispensary on the corner of Vicar Lane and New Briggate was laid by Mayor John Darnton Luccock on October 19th 1865 and it was opened by (Sir) Andrew Fairbairn on June 6th 1867 designed by Leeds architect William Hill (1828-89), who also designed the offices for the Poor Law Guardians in East Parade (1859). In 1900 the site was needed for street improvements and the new Dispensary built in Portland stone was opened on Hartley Hill on May 12th 1904 by Dr T Clifford Allbutt, physician to the Dispensary (1864-79): designed by Francis Bedford & Sydney Kitson. The Dispensary was extended in 1921-22 and again in 1931 when a children's ward was opened on October 15th by Lord Mayor Arthur Hawkyard - he presented a silver salver to Leeds which is displayed in the Civic Hall. The work of the Dispensary was transferred to St James Hospital in 1971: the old Dispensary remains a listed building being used as the Chest Clinic. The old Dispensary on Hartley Hill is now the headquarters for the Leeds Society for Deaf and Blind People and is called Centenary House: it was restored and externally illuminated in 2000.

DIXON, JEREMIAH (1726-82) was a cloth merchant of Leeds and asked John Carr to build him a large house on Boar Lane in 1750 - he sold this in 1763. Dixon then bought Gledhow Hall in 1764 from William Wilson. He remodelled the Hall and made many additions to the house and grounds, including the road bridge seen today with his initials and date 1768. The Hall was the home for the Beckett family and later other families took the estate: the estate was bought by Sir James Kitson Baron Airedale of the Monkbridge Iron & Steel Co who was Lord Mayor in 1896.

DOCK STREET is south of the river and once was the main site of the warehouses and offices of the Aire & Calder Navigation Canal. Their main office was on the corner of Dock Street by Leeds Bridge built in 1906: it became the British Waterways Offices prior to closure. The warehouses of the Aire & Calder Navigation on the south bank were built in the 1770's on the gardens of William Milner. The Victoria Quays is a housing development on the site of the old warehouses built in 1815-21; Barratts completed 120 units (1985-88) with Navigation Walk having Flax House, Chippindale House and Calder House. A foundation stone was laid at the east end of Dock Street for the new development on November 20th 1986. The dock area has a wooden footbridge (private) using roof beams from the flax warehouse - the new basin was made in 1821. The Bridge End/Dock Street area is to be developed with a 6 storey block including 97 flats with restaurant/ bars.

DODGSHUN, EDWARD JOHN (1854-1927) was an architect who commenced in Leeds in 1875: he was articled to Thomas Ambler in 1870 and worked with George Street for a year and afterwards with William Burges. He was elected an FRIBA in 1891 and had offices on East Parade moving to Basinghall Street (1914-23). Edward Dodgshun was in partnership with William Frederick Unsworth (1851-1912) and with George Dale Oliver from 1898; he was the President of the YAS 1894-96. His Leeds work included houses in Hyde Terrace, Peacock's Store (St Andrew's House) Park Row and the West Riding Union Bank Park Row.

DOMESDAY BOOK was a record of the survey of England carried out in 1086 by officials of William the Conqueror. This was completed in order to assess land tax and other dues, to ascertain the value of crown lands and to enable the king to estimate the power of his barons. One of the two entries for Leeds reads: *"In Leeds 10 carucates of land and 6 bovates top be taxed and land for 6 ploughs. Seven thanes held it in the time of King Edward as 7 manors. Now there 27 villeins, 4 sokemen and 4 bordars who have 14 ploughs. There a priest and church and a mill of 4s and 10 acres* *of meadow. The value was £6 now £7."* The Domesday book also mentions that the land of Leeds was given to the Norman baron Ilbert de Lacy.

DORTMUND SQUARE was named in 1980 and there were celebrations held between September 11th and September 13th. The bronze statue of the Dortmund Drayman is by Arthur Schultz-Engels, who also unveiled the work. The statue was placed in the new square in 1980 celebrating the 10th year of civic twinning.

DOYLES was a high class china shop established in 1842 by JA Doyle - father of SB Doyle (1882-1922): the Boar Lane shop was opened in 1872; the Albion Street shop was opened by Sir John Wedgwood in 1964. In 1979 Doyle's with the Junior Chamber of Commerce commissioned a limited edition of Leeds Civic Plate, produced by Caverswall of Stoke on Trent and artist John Ball. A set of this plate is displayed at Leeds Civic Hall. There were fears that the shops would close in 1990 until they were saved by the owner's son.

DRONY LAITH was an area in west Leeds on which there was a farm on the Wilson estate (sold to the family by Jeremiah Dixon in 1777): it had been converted in 1767 by John Close into a dyehouse and finishing shops, adjacent to Bean Ing mill. Coal came to the expanding dyeworks from the Middleton Colliery coal staith. In 1814 the Drony Laith dyeworks were bought by Wormald & Gott of Bean Ing from the Wilson estate - the partnership ceased in 1816. The new turnpike road across Wellington Bridge in 1819 caused the demolition of the buildings. It was after 1820 when the north part of Drony Laith was with Henry Wormald that the buildings were demolished. The area of Drony Laith became new housing and the extension of Wellington Street.

DRURY, EDWARD ALFRED (1856-1944) was the sculptor of Morn & Even statues and Rev Joseph Priestley in City Square as well as Circe in the centre of Park Square. He was born in London on November 11th 1856 and trained in Paris coming back to England in 1885: he was appointed an RA in 1913.

DUDLEY HOUSE was opened in 1969 on the former site of the Caxton Works (manufacturers of printer's furniture) being one time premises of the Leeds Education Department prior to transfer to the Merrion Centre. The building is owned by Norwich Union

Insurance and after a period of remaining empty, approval was given in late 2000 for conversion into a £20 million restaurant/bar on the first three floors with a 20 storey residential tower above: Persimmon Homes are converting it into 90 flats and penthouses.

DUKE STREET links St Peter's Street with East Street with an altered route as part of the Loop Road. The large block on Duke Street, St Peter's Square and York Street is St Peter's Buildings: the corner site was restored in 1983 as Munro House and on St Peter's Street are the Yorkshire Dance Centre and The Wardrobe. The building was used by a variety of woollen manufacturers and the United Yeast Co Ltd from 1930 at Unecol House - they took over from the Airedale Bottling Co and brush maker Thomas Cox. The United Yeast Company was created in 1874 with the amalgamation of Harvey Risk & Co, Blackmore, Leconte & Co and Brocklehurst & Co and had premises on Wellington Street: it was incorporated in 1899. In 1959 the business moved to Clarence Road.

DUKES OF LEEDS (1631-1712) The first Duke of Leeds was Sir Thomas Osborne, son of Sir Edward Osborne of Kiveton and elected high sheriff of Yorkshire in 1662; he was Lord President of the Council in 1689. He was elevated to the peerage as Viscount Osborne of Dunblane on February 2nd 1673 and became Baron Osborne of Kiveton & Viscount Latimer of Danby (Yorkshire) on August 15th 1673; Marquis of Carmarthen (1689) and the First Duke of Leeds in May 1694. He was succeeded by his son Peregrine (died 1729) and by Peregrine's son Peregrine Hyde (died 1731); the 4th Duke of Leeds was Thomas (1713-1789) and his son Francis Godolphin became the 5th Duke of Leeds. The successors included George William 6th Duke (1775-1838), Francis Godolphin D'Arcy 7th Duke (1798-1859) and George 8th Duke (1802-72). The more recent members are George Godolphin Osborne 9th Duke (1828-95), George 10th Duke of Leeds (1862-1927), John Francis 11th Duke (1901-63) and the last Duke of Leeds Sir Francis D'Arcy Godolphin Osborne (1884-1964). On the death of the last Duke on March 20th 1964 the title became extinct. The later members of the family lived at Melbourne House Jersey Channel Islands; the family country seat was at Hornby Castle, where some members of the family are buried at St Mary's Church including the 9th and 10th Dukes of Leeds.

DUNCAN, VISCOUNT ADMIRAL ADAM (1731-1804) entered the

Royal Navy in 1746 becoming a commander in 1759: he became an admiral in 1795 and received a peerage in 1797 - he has a statue in St Paul's Cathedral London. Admiral Duncan was involved with the relief of Gibraltar in 1779/80 and 1782 and he was involved in the victory over 30,000 Dutch at Camperdown who were intent on sailing to invade Ireland: he became Commander of the North Sea Fleet. He died on August 4th 1804.

DUNCAN STREET runs between Boar Lane and the Corn Exchange: opened through Willow Tree Yard in 1787/88, opened out to Kirkgate/Vicar Lane in 1868 and doubled in width in 1882, with many new buildings by Thomas Ambler. The first name of Duncan Street was Fleet Street but Admiral Viscount Duncan's victory at Camperdown in October 1797 caused the change in name. The Central Market was built on Duncan Street in 1824-27 to the designs of Francis Goodwin of London at a cost of £24,800 and in 1868 the Corporation bought the estate for £25,000. The market contained 67 shops, 56 stalls, offices and a hotel but was affected by fire in 1893: a new covered market hall was agreed in 1898. The north side of Duncan Street was demolished in February 1904 and was redeveloped: this work entailed the demolition of the Old King's Arms, which closed in 1813 and was used as shops and offices. The present Rawcliffe's Store was opened in 1914 transferring from Woodhouse Lane; the Duncan Street building was designed by Percy Robinson: the company was founded in 1897; the building was restored in 1992. The Admiral Duncan public house is on the south side (now The Duncan) originally the Willow Tree and rebuilt c1904: it changed the name in 1797. On the south side is the house with the Leeds coat of arms built by Thomas Ambler in 1882 for William Tunstall: an archway gains access to Hirst's Yard. The corner

Briggate/Duncan Street Corner c1890

98

shop on north Duncan Street/Briggate was Reid Brothers (1950's) and Paragon Jewellers (1960's).

DUNKIRK VETERANS ASSOCIATION was founded in Leeds in 1953 by members of the British Expeditionary Force who were rescued from the beaches of northern France in the summer of 1940. Between May 26th and June 4th 1940 Operation Dynamo evacuated about 338,000 Allied troops from a 10 mile radius stretching from the entrance to Dunkirk harbour. The veterans disbanded in summer 2000 placing their international standard in the Royal Armouries at a ceremony in November 2000.

DUNN'S MENS HATTERS GA Dunn opened at York House Boar Lane c1892 - they closed the Boar Lane shop in September 1981 and the Briggate shop closed in 1991.

DUTSON'S had their petrol station and showrooms on the central site between Woodhouse Lane and Wade Lane; this became Central Garage prior to demolition and the building of the St John's Centre.

DYSON'S CLOCKMAKERS John Dyson founded the firm of clockmakers and jewellers in 1865. He converted two cottages (26/27 Briggate) which dated from 1650 and placed a façade on the front of them: he used his name and house numbers for the clock hours. The shop was rebuilt and refurbished at a cost of £250,000-reopening on May 19th 1980. The shop was closed on February 10th 1990 and the sale of the stock was held at Sotherbys in May 1990. John Dyson Jewellers in Commercial Street opened in 1996 and has no connection with the family: it opened in the Watches of Switzerland premises. Dyson's shop became a restaurant in the Marriott Hotel (Whitbread) in the Time Ball Buildings. The clock bears the date 1865 being set in motion in 1910 and inscribed Tempus Fugit: it was restored in 2000; the ball used to descend exactly at 1pm.

EAGLE STAR INSURANCE opened on The Headrow in 1965. In 1994 they transferred to East Parade, on the site of Devereux House: demolished in 1993. In 1999 Eagle Star was bought by Zurich Insurance who now occupy the East Parade offices. The Headrow offices were bought by the Burford Group and re-named Gallery House in 1995: offices and café-bar.

EASTGATE is a 1930's creation linking Vicar Lane/The Headrow with the Bus Station, Quarry Hill and the old Regent Street/

Mabgate roundabout: it was built on Nelson Street and Pollards Yard which were demolished in 1928. The road was constructed as a continuation of Sir Reginald Blomfield's scheme of widening and improvement: opened in February 1932. In c1935 the council bought land in Eastgate to extend the markets but this never matured and c1960 the first large block (Yorkshire Hussar) was completed. The remainder of the land south of Eastgate was sold to a developer to build shops and offices. The 1930's roundabout (Appleyard's Ltd) was a petrol station and re-opened with the Millennium Fountain in January 2000. The Yorkshire Hussar public house occupied the lower building on the south side while the buildings between Lady Lane and the Inner Ring Road flyover included The Marquis of Granby public house, George Nelson's Billiard Hall and the Ministry of Labour Employment Exchange.

EAST PARADE had a Congregational Chapel opened in 1841 designed by William Hurst (1787-1844) and partner WL Moffatt and could hold 1600: Edward Baines laid the foundation stone in September 1939. It was demolished in 1899 and replaced with the offices of the North British & Mercantile Insurance Co. East Parade was developed initially as a part of the Park estates: Park Row (1767-76), South Parade (1776-78), East Parade (1779-89), Park Place (1778-1800) and the beauty of Park Square (1788-1810). There was more land sold on The Park Estate by absentee landlord Christopher Wilson Bishop of Bristol in 1805. East Parade Chambers were built in 1899 using Burmantofts Faience; Hepper House (Phillips) was designed by George Corson in 1863; on the east side of East Parade is Minerva House opened in 1966 and refurbished in the 1990's (owned by Roando Holdings Ltd) - the offices of the Royal Bank of Scotland. It was on East Parade that the Leeds School of Medicine transferred in 1834 from their rooms in the Dispensary: they moved in 1894 to Thoresby Place and a purpose built School of Medicine designed by WH Thorp. No 1 East Parade is the headquarters for Zurich Insurance Co and was built in 1992-94 for the Eagle Star Insurance Co - architect William Glover & Partners; the new building replaced Devereux House. Adjacent to East Parade Chambers was the headquarters of the Provident Life (1840) featuring a figure of Britannia on the roof: from 1872 it was the offices of the County Fire & Provident Life Association (County Fire Office & Alliance Assurance) - now The

Firehouse. East Parade was the site for the first Hospital for Women and Children which opened in 1853: in 1860 the Springfield estate was bought and the private house converted and opened by the Earl of Carlisle in October 1861.

EAST STREET has a development by Crosby Homes of 127 apartments on 8 storeys-completed in June 2000. The street once had the Steander Foundry (Frederick Dyson) the firm was established in 1840: the foundry was originally on Swinegate and transferred to East Street in 1887. Rose Wharf is a £3.5 million development by Caddick of the first flax mill (1820): the architects are Carey Jones.

e-HQ LEEDS Leeds has the largest internet server farm in Europe managed by Energis Squared handling 33,000 commercial web sites; more than 35% of internet traffic passes through Leeds; Freeserve was created and is based in Leeds with over 2 million users; Leeds has over 1000 companies in the computer software and IT sector and has one of the largest IT workforces in Britain outside London.

ELAM, SAMUEL (1773-1811) was a Leeds born Quaker who purchased Roundhay Park with Thomas Nicholson (1764-1821) from Baron Stourton in 1803 for £58,000. He became a partner in Thompson, Elam and Holtby's Leeds bank; he was to be declared a bankrupt and died at an early age: his portion of the estate to the south was developed with exclusive housing.

ELECTRIC PRESS BUILDING on Cookridge Street/Great George Street dates from the 1860's when it was the premises of Charles Roodhouse & Sons cabinet makers; when they moved to Albion Street c1897 the building was taken by Chorley & Pickersgill - printers and bookbinders. The building was restored in 2000/2001 as part of the Millennium project.

ELECTRICITY The first public display of electric light in Leeds was probably in August 1880 and in October 1881 a generator provided electric street lighting at the west end of Boar Lane. The Electric Lighting Company was appointed in 1882 and in October 1883 electric lighting was installed in the Town Hall. In June 1884 electric lights were installed in the new Municipal Buildings and the Coliseum had electric light installed for the visit of the Prince & Princess of Wales in July 1885 when they opened new buildings for the Yorkshire College. A new system was introduced for the

Municipal Buildings in December 1885 and in 1888 the new Art Gallery opened with electric lighting. Electric lighting was installed for the Yorkshire Post in July 1890 and Yorkshire House-to-House installed a new generator on December 12th 1892. A permanent electric supply was started from Whitehall Road in May 1893 when there was the official opening of the new station. The Town Hall was connected to the system in 1895; electric trams appeared in Leeds on October 29th 1891 - powered by a gas driven dynamo. The Crown Point Power Station between The Calls and Crown Point Bridge was opened in 1897 and in late 1897 the electric tramway was working. The Whitehall Road Generating Station was built in 1902 and the building was eventually demolished in 1994/95. Electric street lighting was further installed on Briggate, Boar Lane and Wellington Street in December 1897. The electricity supply business was bought by Leeds City Council on December 15th 1898. Kirkstall Power Station started operating in October 1930 and Crown Point was closed on March 31st 1932.

ELLAND ROAD was a turnpike road opened in 1785 and was later to feature The Leeds Greyhound Stadium opened on July 16th 1927, closed on April 3rd 1982 and demolished in October 1982. The Leeds United Football Ground (Leeds Sporting) is a major development on Elland Road, which is the A643 to Elland north west of Huddersfield. The road starts at Cemetery Road (Holbeck Cemetery) and continues to join the Ring Road at Cottingley Hall Cemetery and ascends Churwell Hill to Morley Bruntcliffe thence to Birstall, Cleckheaton and Brighouse.

ELMET, KINGDOM OF was created following the departure of the Romans c410 and this extensive kingdom was administered from Barwick in Elmet. It stretched from the Peak District to the headwaters of Wharfe and Nidd and from the western edge of the Plain of York to the Pennines: the old West Riding. The Anglo-Saxon invaders conquered Holderness, Wolds and Plain of York in the 6th century but westward invasion was prevented by the Kingdom of Elmet. The Saxon kingdoms of Deira and Bernicia united as Northumbria in 593AD but in 615AD the Saxon Hereric was poisoned in Elmet. Hereric was the nephew of Edwin who invaded Elmet in 617AD in retaliation for his murder: the kingdom was thus at an end. King Edwin was converted and baptised at

York in 627AD: the date of the commencement of the first Minster. Edwin was the King of Northumbria until 632AD and by that time all of "Yorkshire" was under Saxon rule.

EPIDEMICS in Leeds included plague in 1645, typhus in 1847, cholera in 1832 (first victim was on May 28th): there is a cholera graveyard on Mabgate west of the site of St Mary's Church Quarry Hill - the year recorded 700 killed. In 1849 there were occasional outbreaks of smallpox, scarlet fever and typhoid fever.

ERMYSTED, SIR WILLIAM He was appointed the Rector of Adel in 1536 and later was Vicar of Birstall, Master of the Temple, Canon of St Paul's and Chaplain to Queen Mary I. On August 20th 1555 he gave the income from his lands at Wike to Leeds Grammar School thus becoming one of the many important benefactors. In 1552 the will of Rev William Sheafield on July 6th gave the school the principal benefaction: the foundation of the school is officially in this year, although the origins were in the mid-14th century.

EXCELLENCE YORKSHIRE was set up in 2001 to promote business excellence and quality of management in the Yorkshire and Humber region. It is based at Bradford University School of Management and the awards scheme was established in association with the Yorkshire Post.

FACILITIES in Leeds include 16 main hotels with 1500 beds, 100 public houses and café-bars, c100 restaurants and cafes and c40 nightclubs. The city has 945 shop units, 15 department stores and including 392 multiples. There are four main shopping malls: Merrion Centre refurbished 1985, Leeds Shopping Plaza (1977) refurbished 1988 & 1997, St John's Centre was refurbished 1985 and Headrow Centre (1989) refurbished 1996. There are 110,000 working in the city centre (2000) and 425,000 in the Leeds District: the service sector employs 277,000 with 5300 in the legal services and 17,000 working at call centres. Since 1990 over £4 billion has been invested or is in the pipeline for major property schemes and £1 billion has been invested in the city centre.

FAIRBAIRN, SIR ANDREW (1828-1901) was the son of Sir Peter Fairbairn born in Glasgow and married Clara daughter of Sir J Lambton-Loraine in 1862. He became Chairman of Fairbairn-Lawson-Combe-Barbour and was Mayor of Leeds in 1866/67. He was the first chairman of the Leeds School Board, a Director of the

Great Northern Railway Co, High Sheriff of Yorkshire, West Riding JP and MP for the East Division (West Riding) and a Captain in the Yorkshire Hussar Yeomanry. He was knighted in 1868 following the opening of the Leeds Exhibition by the Prince of Wales. He bought Askham Old Hall in Askham Richard near York in 1879 but this was demolished and a larger house built in 1886: Askham Grange became an open prison in 1947. On Sir Andrew Fairbairn's death in May 1901 the property was inherited by his uncle William Wailes (1862-1933) who added the Fairbairn name to his own.

FAIRBAIRN, SIR PETER (1799-1861) was the son of Andrew Fairbairn of Kelso and became an apprentice millwright in 1800. He married in 1827 and the year after came to Leeds from Glasgow: he improved the construction of woollen machinery and for flax spinning. He ran the Wellington Foundry and became a councillor in 1836 and alderman in 1854. Peter Fairbairn was elected Mayor of Leeds in 1858 - the year of the meeting of the British Association for the Advancement of Science and when Queen Victoria opened the Town Hall. During her visit the Queen stayed at Peter Fairbairn's house on Clarendon Road (Woodsley House); he was knighted by The Queen in the Town Hall at the opening ceremony. Sir Peter Fairbairn died on January 4th 1861 and was buried at Adel Church. The statue of Sir Peter Fairbairn was erected through public subscription and placed at Woodhouse Square: it was made in bronze by Matthew Noble on a plinth of Peterhead granite costing £1000 and unveiled on May 14th 1868.

FAIRBAIRN HOUSE on Clarendon Road was formerly Woodsley House and was built in 1840 for Sir Peter Fairbairn: Queen Victoria stayed here in September 1858 prior to the opening of Leeds Town Hall. The Queen journeyed by train from London and lunched at Peterborough arriving in Leeds at 6.15pm. Queen Victoria, Prince Albert with Princesses Alice and Helena journeyed with the Lord Mayor and Lady Mayoress to Woodsley House for the night; Fairbairn House is now The Nuffield Institute.

FAIRBAIRN LAWSON COMBE BARBOUR was the company created in 1900 with the amalgamation of Peter Fairbairn's Wellington Foundry (founded 1828 by William Fairbairn) together with James Combe's Belfast company (founded 1845) and partner James Barbour (1851). Keighley born Samuel Lawson (1782-1866) opened the Hope Foundry in 1812 on Mabgate and this was to be merged with Fairbairn's enterprise. The company made machine tools, wood and flax machinery; during the Great War they made shell fuse caps and machine tools for boring tank guns. Upto the year 1900 the business was Fairbairn Greenwood & Batley, Fairbairn Kennedy & Naylor and Fairbairn Naylor & McPherson; in 1921 the firm amalgamated with Urquart Lindsay and Robertson Orchard of Dundee (the Dundee factory closed in 1958). The business made munitions in the last War and then again produced textile machinery for export. In April 1980 Fairbairn Lawson went into receivership and closure followed in 1985: the Wellington Street factory was demolished in 1990 and redeveloped as Citygate with TGI Friday's, Westgate Casino, Travelodge Hotel and offices.

FAIRFAX, SIR THOMAS (1612-71) was born at Denton Hall and knighted in 1641: during the Civil War Leeds was held by Sir William Savile until January 23rd 1643, when the town was taken by Sir Thomas Fairfax. He lived at Nun Appleton Hall and died in November 1671 - buried at Bilbrough Church, where there is restored marble tomb in the south chapel.

FAIRFAX HOUSE was in an area known as Lydgate on the corner of Wormald Row. The three storey house dated 1727 and was the home of Nathaniel & Katherine Fairfax prior to demolition.

FEHR, HENRY CHARLES (1867-1940) studied in the studio of Sir Thomas Brock: he sculpted the statues of James Watt (1903) and John Harrison (1903) in City Square and the War Memorial (1922) which was moved from City Square to the Garden of Rest. HC Fehr studied at the Royal Academy Schools and exhibited at the RA from 1887: his bronze Perseus rescuing Andromeda was bought in 1894 by the Tate Art Gallery London. He was a founder member of the Royal Society of British Sculptors in 1904.

FENTON STREET was started in 1842 with the Fenton public house on Woodhouse Lane built in 1853. Isabella Fenton lived at 112 Fenton Street and her friend was Henrietta Strickland who bought some fields in 1840 and was to live in a house which became the Fenton Hotel. Fenton Street once known for the extensive barracks was cut off in July 1964 for the completion of the Inner Ring Road and Leeds Polytechnic.

FIENNES, CELIA (1662-1741) visited Leeds on horseback in 1698 and wrote an account in her diary, which became one of the earliest descriptions of the city.

FIRE SERVICE had their first station on Fenton Street with their later headquarters on Park Street from 1883 as the Central Fire Station: used by Leeds Police/Fire Service until 1941. The stables were used by the Police mounted section until the building was demolished in 1972. The building was opened in 1883 at a cost of £5000 and included fire engine house, guard room, stables, offices, blacksmith's shop, joiner's shop and a water tank holding 6000 gallons; it was mostly demolished in the 1960's to allow redevelopment. The West Yorkshire Fire Service headquarters are now at Oakroyd Hall together with fire stations around the city.

FISH STREET was a narrow alley connecting Kirkgate with King Edward Street: this was the site of the fish market and the alleys were also known for their butchers businesses many years ago prior to upgrading in recent years. It was butchers Joseph and Frederick Rinder who developed the area between 1814 and 1823: Fish Street had covered stalls and an open octagon for the sale of vegetables and fish. The area now has banks: the Halifax is based in King Edward House.

FOLEY, PATRICK JAMES (1836-1914) was born in Ireland and worked as an engineer in Armley, became a clerk and in 1863 moved to London. He started a business association, which was to develop into Pearl Assurance. He was MP for West Galway and laid the foundation stone for the Pearl Building on The Headrow on July 14th 1910; his full size statue is featured on the building overlooking the Municipal Buildings and Art Gallery.

FORESTALLING was the act of selling cloth before the 8am bell and after the 9pm bell at the cloth court stalls: the act was a punishable offence.

FOUNTAINS IN LEEDS The £3000 *Coronation Fountain* in front of the Civic Hall was opened in 1953 and removed in 1954. The fountain in *Lands Lane* precinct as a part of Landmark Leeds was opened on April 12th 1972 by Peter Walker; it was to be scrapped in September 1978 but was renovated in 1979 and 1983 - removed in November 1989. The *Millennium Fountain* on the Eastgate roundabout was opened in 2000 and included the Graham Ibbeson statue of Arthur Aaron VC from March 2001. *Millennium Square Fountain* was opened on April 30th 2001 in a new garden which features two interlocking pools, jets and a mini-canal. *The Victoria Quarter* fountain was redesigned in 1991. A fountain which started life in the Fish Market was taken to **Victoria Square** (Town Hall) but was removed in June 1902 and replaced by the statue of Queen Victoria unveiled on November 27th 1905: it now stands on Woodhouse Moor.

FOUNTAINE STREET and **WORMALD ROW** are streets near The Headrow and remember two leading Leeds cloth merchants in the 18th century. In Wormald & Fountaine's counting house once worked a young apprentice called Benjamin Gott, who was to become a junior partner; his father was a consulting engineer to the Aire & Calder Navigation and lived in Butts Court - he founded the firm in 1758. Wormald, Fountaine & Gott had a rotative steam engine in their works built by Bolton & Watt of Birmingham in 1792; later Benjamin Gott ran this cloth merchants business prior to the building of Bean Ing.

FOWLER, JOHN (1826-64) ran his Hunslet factory (Fowler & Hewitson) from 1860 manufacturing his invention of the steam plough and later produced concrete mixers and equipment for the construction industry. On December 16th 1881 a third of the factory was destroyed by fire but a month later the machine shop was operating again: producing electric generating equipment from 1887. In the last War John Fowler's works were producing armoured fighting vehicles, tanks, generating sets, diesel locomotives and petrol engines. In 1950 the diesel manufacturing business was sold followed by the locomotive side in 1968. Fowler's were merged with Marshall & Sons in 1968: the factory was closed in 1974 and demolished in 1975

FOX, SAMSON (1838-1903) was apprenticed to Smith, Beacock & Tannett at The Round Factory. He opened a factory making specialised tools at the Silver Cross Works on Dewsbury Road and in 1874 formed the Leeds Forge Company on Armley Road.

FRAMPTON, SIR GEORGE JAMES (1860-1928) made the large statue of Queen Victoria which was transferred to Woodhouse Moor from outside Leeds Town Hall in 1937. This was taken to the Moor at the same time as the statues of Sir Robert Peel and the Duke of Wellington from outside the Town Hall.

FRASER, HUGH 1st BARON FRASER OF ALLANDER (1903-66) was born in Glasgow and educated at Glasgow Academy and Warriston School Moffat: he left school at 17 years old and joined his father's wholesale drapery business. He was made Managing

Director in 1924 and Chairman in 1927 buying his first Edinburgh store in 1940. In 1948 the House of Fraser was floated and in 1957 they acquired John Barker Group (London) and in 1959 bought Harrod's Store on Knightsbridge (Mohamed al Fayed bought Harrods in 1985). Hugh Fraser became a Baronet in 1961 and a Baron in 1964. In 1931 he had married Kate Hutcheon - son Hugh was born in 1936 who became Chairman in 1966: he succeeded to the baronetcy but disclaimed a peerage.

FRASER, JAMES BARLOW (1835-1922) was an architect who lived on Vernon Road: he designed Wrangthorne Church and the Festival Gallery at the Town Hall - he retired in 1914.

FREEDOM OF THE CITY was granted to the West Riding Regiment Prince of Wales Own on July 1st 1945; King's Own Yorkshire Light Infantry on June 7th 1945 and in 1979 this transferred to the Light Infantry; 49th (Yorkshire) Signals Regiment Royal Signals (TA) who were formed in 1861 as 2nd West Riding Royal Engineers Volunteers on April 1st 1967; RAF Church Fenton was granted the Freedom of Leeds on April 29th 1971.

FREEMEN OF LEEDS The Honorary Freemen of the City of Leeds are Col John Thomas North (1889), Lt Gen Sir John Denton Pinkstone French (1902), Col Thomas Walter Harding (1903), Sir James Kitson (1906), Lord Allerton (1908), Field Marshall Earl Haig (1920), Field Marshall Foch (1922), Admiral Lord Beatty (1922), Rt Hon David Lloyd George (1922), Major Rt Hon Edward FL Wood (1923), Ald Charles Henry Wilson (1923), Stanley Baldwin (1925), Earl of Oxford & Asquith (1925), Sir Berkeley Moynihan (1926), Col Sir Edward Brotherton (1929), Sir William Middlebrook (1926), Ald Charles Francis Tetley (1926), Ald Charles Lupton (1926), John Rawlinson Ford JP (1926), Henry Cawood Embleton (1926), Rt Hon Philip Snowden Chancellor of the Exchequer (1930), Rt Hon Arthur Greenwood MP Minister for Health (1930), Ald George Ratcliffe JP (1930), Hon Rupert Evelyn Beckett JP (1930), HRH The Princess Royal (1932), Thomas Thornton Town Clerk (1937), Rt Hon HV Evatt (1943), Rt Hon Clement Attlee (1951), Rt Hon Winston S Churchill (1953), Rowland Winn JP (1956), Ald William Hemingway JP (1956), Sir George William Martin JP (1966), Rt Hon Lord Milner (1966), Sir Albert King (1976), Sir Frank Shaw Marshall (1976), Henry Moore (1981), Lord Healey (1991), Lord Merlyn Rees (1993). The latest Honorary Freeman is Nelson

Mandela who visited Leeds on April 30th 2001 to officially open the Millennium Square and the new Mandela Gardens - as part of Celebrate South Africa Week.

FRIEND, HERMAN arrived in Leeds from Lotz Poland in 1847 and became a tailor in Templar Street. He worked with cloth supplied from John Barran's works and was responsible for the breakdown of the numerous tailoring tasks into minor operations; he ran the Ashton Road Mills in Harehills.

FULFORD CE were manufacturers of patent medicines on Carlton Hill: the business started at 15/16 Greek Street at the turn of the century and c1911 moved to the former premises of John Chaplin Warriner (coach builder) on the corner of Carlton Hill/Jowitt Lane. The first product was Pep Pastilles - they were produced throughout the war years with special supplies of sugar. The later products were ZamBuk ointment, Vitapoint hair conditioner (still manufactured by another company) and Bile Beans. Fulford's had an extensive warehouse and packaging department on the corner of Dorrington Road. The managing director was Frank Harris Fulford who lived at Headingley Castle. In c1958 Fulford's moved to Blythe in Northumberland and the former premises were demolished prior to redevelopment.

GARDEN OF REMEMBRANCE (VICTORIA GARDENS) was created in 1936-37 with the demolition of a block of shops and offices together with Pitman's School, Victoria Buildings and Wharton's Hotel (c1838) - on the site of the war memorial area. The Garden of Remembrance designed by JE Procter was officially opened on October 28th 1937 (the coronation of King George VI was on May 12th 1937): the area was paved and provided with floral displays. The War Memorial was moved from City Square (front of the Majestic) in January 1937: it had been unveiled in October 1922. The street in front of the Garden of Rest was Park Lane with Guildford Street to the east and Vicar Lane. The offices of the Leeds Permanent Building Society were at the west end of the Garden of Rest from 1876 (Victoria Chambers) and the offices were transferred to their new headquarters on The Headrow/Cookridge Street in 1930. Another block of offices adjacent to the old LPBS offices was Calverley Chambers - demolished c1930.

GASCOIGNE STREET was off Boar Lane: the location of Gascoigne

Chambers and the paperhanging manufacturer Lightbown, Aspinall & Co who opened their Leeds branch in 1891.

GAS LIGHTING was first introduced to Leeds streets on May 19th 1819: there are listed lamps and posts in Ship Yard, Bay Horse Yard, Change Alley, Minor & Scurr's Yard Albion Place and Queen Square. The Leeds Gas Light Co was incorporated in 1819 with works in York Street and a gasholder at Sheepscar.

GATEWAY YORKSHIRE is the tourist office in the railway station: opened in May 1995. The tourist office opened first in the City Library in 1982 and transferred to a Wellington Street basement in July 1987.

GAUNT, ALD SIR EDWIN (1818-1908) of Carlton Lodge Blackman Lane (later home of the Houchin family) was the Mayor of Leeds in 1885 and was knighted in 1886 - Queen Victoria's Jubilee year. He was born in Wortley and worked for 11 years at Eyres Mill (site of Central Railway Station); in 1843 he married Caroline Jowett - they had 4 daughters and worshipped at Mill Hill Chapel. He formed Gaunt & Hudson (hats & caps) in Hogg's Mill (later Lockwood's Mill) Hunslet, Grace Street and on Great George Street (later Centaur House). The firm ceased hat and cap production in 1930 and concentrated on clothing manufacture as Dixon & Gaunt (formed c1916) at Moorland Works Elland Road - the business was moved to Bank Mills in the 1950's. Sir Edwin Gaunt was a councillor for Holbeck and his portrait by Marmaduke Flower (1892) is in Leeds Civic Hall.

GELDERD ROAD is the main route from Leeds to Huddersfield and turnpiked in 1825 to Birstall. It was probably named after Billy Gelderd who was born at Armley in 1736 and moved to Gildersome where he died in 1819.

GEORGE STREET is north of Kirkgate Market and links with Vicar Lane by Ludgate Hill and St Peter's Street by Dyer Street. The car park bounded by George Street, Harewood Street, Union Street and Millgarth Street is to be developed by Town Centre Securities as a 98 bedroom hotel, 70 apartments, 15 large shops and parking spaces for 437 cars.

GILL, ERIC ARTHUR ROWTON PETER JOSEPH (1882-1940) was the artist who designed the University War Memorial, the oak font canopy at St John the Baptist's Church Adel (1921) and the statue of St Wilfrid in St Wilfrid's Church Halton.

GILLINSON, BASIL (1926-2001) was born in Leeds and educated at Leeds Grammar School before attending the School of Architecture at Leeds College of Art in 1940. He served with the RAF from 1943 to 1947 and returned to pass the RIBA examinations and set up in practice in Leeds in 1951. A first client was Arnold Ziff of Stylo Shoes and as the business expanded he took Clifford Barnett into partnership in 1956. The Gillinson Partnership designed the Merrion Centre and St John's Centre in Leeds as well as the CEGB building in Harrogate and Leeds United's north stand. Basil Gillinson became a Fellow of the RIBA in 1966 and retired in 1985 to become a senior teaching fellow in the Department of Civil Engineering at Leeds University. In 1990 he became a research fellow at the Institute of Advanced Architectural Studies at York University.

GILPIN, CRAVEN (1875-1951) was a well known Leeds caterer who took over in 1894 at The Mansion Roundhay from his father William who had taken the licence in 1884.

GLOBE FOUNDRY was south of the river and formed a part of Green & Jackson's woodworking machinery factory. The firm started in 1846 and William Jackson continued the business to the 1860's and the firm moved to Crown Point Road c1880. The Globe works was taken by William Towler producing castings, girders, bridges and steam driers. After 1900 parts of the old foundry were used for various light industries including Symington's printing & cabinets and Turner's tobacco factory where cigars were made until the late 1960's. The mill complex was demolished in 1996.

GOLF COURSES *Alwoodley Club* was founded in 1907. *Cookridge Hall* opened in 1993. *Gott's Park* was opened on April 8th 1933. *Leeds Club* was created on North Hill Fields Estate and was formed in 1896 with their clubhouse at Cobble Hall. *Middleton Club* was opened on April 8th 1933. *Moor Allerton Club* was founded in 1923 with the new clubhouse (Allerton Hotel) opened in April 1958 and moved to the Coal Road in 1970. *Moortown Club* was founded in 1909. *Oulton* was opened in 1991 on a former farmer's field and the grounds of Oulton Hall. *Sandmoor Club* was founded in 1926. *Temple Newsam Club* was opened in 1923/24. *Wike Ridge (Leeds) Golf Centre* was opened in 1994.

GOODALL & BACKHOUSE had an extensive riverside factory (now offices) east of Victoria Bridge and covered an 8 acre site having a five storey factory manufacturing Yorkshire Relish. They were manufacturing grocers: egg powder, baking powder, custard powder and blancmange powder. The factory north of the river was

Goodall, Backhouse & Co *Advertisement*
(Dorothy Burrows collection)

established in 1853 by Robert Goodall who was joined by Backhouse in 1858; the factory was demolished c1990 for office development. In the early 1880's Mrs Robert Goodall of Park Place married Henry Backhouse - he had a chemist's shop adjacent to Holy Trinity Church: it was her home made sauce that was the inspiration for Yorkshire Relish. The sauce sold 6 million bottles a year in the 1880's and the Abbey House Museum has an example of the bottle from c1885. The business was also a wholesale chemists and druggists (later Goodalls Leeds Ltd) in White Horse Street Boar Lane. In 1959 the business was bought by Hammonds Sauce Ltd. Goodall's moved to Phoenix Works Sheepscar Street and ceased trading in the late 1960's.

GOODMAN, SIR GEORGE (1792-1859) was the son of Benjamin Goodman (1763-1848) and was appointed the first Mayor of Leeds under the Corporation Reform Act in 1836 and again in 1850-52: he was knighted in 1852. He was the MP for Leeds from 1852 to 1857 and carried on his trade as a wool stapler in Leeds and Bradford. Sir George Goodman lived at Goodmans House Roundhay - later Beechwood and home of the Lupton family: he was buried in the south west corner of St Mary's churchyard Whitkirk. Portraits of Benjamin Goodman by CH Schwanfelder (1773-1837) and Sir George Goodman by J Simpson are in Leeds Civic Hall.

GORDON, JOHN (1854-1925) was born in Forfarshire and educated at Leeds Grammar School. The accountant and stockbroker was a partner in his uncle's business and represented Mill Hill Ward (1886-95) and was a Leeds Magistrate (1892): he was a member of the Leeds Rifles retiring in 1887 with a rank of Captain. He lived at Church Lane House Adel and died at his later home of Potternewton Hall. His wife Mary died in 1914 and her memory was perpetuated in the steam boat Mary Gordon which sailed on Waterloo Lake Roundhay Park. Potternewton Hall became the site of Riviera Gardens following purchase by the Council in 1966 and demolition of the old hall. John Gordon's portrait by George Fiddes Watt (1873-1960) was donated in 1921 and is displayed in the Town Hall Albert Room. George Watt was born in Aberdeen and studied at the RSA with residences in Edinburgh and London.

GOTT, BENJAMIN (1762-1840) came to Leeds and served an apprenticeship with Wormald & Fountaine and in 1790 controlled the firm of woollen cloth merchants. Gott established the Park Mills at Bean Ing (Yorkshire Post Newspapers) in 1792, which was the first woollen mill in the world. In 1797 there were 1200 folk working with both Armley Mills and Burley Mills in the Gott enterprise - Benjamin Gott died a millionaire.

GOTT, JOSEPH (1786-1860) was born at Calverley and was no relation to Benjamin Gott who became Joseph Gott's patron. Benjamin sent him to Rome where he worked until his death: he sculpted many works for Gott's mansion together with Sir John Barran and Miss Beckett in Leeds Art Gallery.

GOTT'S PARK was built in 1781 as Armley House for local merchant Thomas Woolrick. Benjamin Gott bought the estate in 1804 which was redesigned by Humphrey Repton and Sir Robert Smirke (1829) converted the house into a mansion. The end of the 19th century saw all the treasures dispersed-some went to the city council and are now in the library, art gallery and reference library. In 1928 Armley House and park were presented to the city by the Trustees of Wade's Charity: the hall is now Gott's Park Mansion and the Club House for the golf course.

GRACE STREET has Brotherton House which is the centre for Leeds Police CID, Immigration and Traffic Warden Departments. Brotherton House was built as the head office of the chemical manufacturers Brotherton & Co, opened in January 1957 and built at a cost of £350,000. The building became the headquarters of the Leeds Police in April 1965 prior to transfer to the new Millgarth Street headquarters. Netel House is the British Telecom Centre -

the foundation stone was laid by Director GG Brooks on April 23rd 1982 and the building was opened by the Duchess of Kent on May 10th 1984. The stone panel in the entrance foyer was a feature of Nelson Street Telephone Exchange in Bradford built by the National Telephone Company in 1898. The building was demolished and the plaque preserved and transferred to Netel House. Grace Street Mill was once the premises for hat and cap maker Gaunt & Hudson who built a factory in 1903 on Leighton Lane which was later to be Centaur House; Gaunt & Hudson ceased trading in c1930. Hipsley Works were once run by Hipps clothing manufacturers who by 1914 ran a chain of 70 shops and went to Grace Street in 1931. The factory caught fire in 1940 and the business re-located to Balm Road Mills.

GRAHAM, JAMES (1869-1931) was the Leeds Director of Education for 25 years from 1906 and one of the sponsors of Beckett Park Training College.

GRAHAME STOWE BATESON is a firm of solicitors based in Portland Street and was founded in 1981 by Grahame Stowe and Arthur Bateson.

GRANARY WHARF is a popular riverside craft market underneath the railway station and viaduct. In the 1970's Leda Securities acquired the dark arches for development: they had been used as storage facilities with Joseph Watson soap works occupying some of the western arches. In 1987 Leda and British Waterways extended this initial development for the council with craft shops and small businesses. In 1987 the Festival Market Place was planned used as a weekend craft market and there are programmes of entertainment: the craft arcade opened in December 1988. Granary Wharf has been developed by Leeds Development Corporation and Leeds City Council at a cost of £6 million. The Granary Wharf Festival Market Place was opened in 1998.

GREAT GEORGE STREET was created following the building of St George's Church in 1838: it connects Clarendon Road (Inner Ring Road pedestrian bridge) with Woodhouse Lane. The street features Centaur House converted to 41 luxury apartments and a leisure centre in 1998, Crown House was opened as a new office block in 1996 replacing Mark Altman's School of Dancing opened in 1902 and closed in December 1990: it was later run by Dennis Altman. The original ballroom was known as The Empress and was first opened on January 6th 1892; St George's Church; Leeds General Infirmary (1868 George Gilbert Scott); the Great George Street Post Office was on the south side opposite the LGI; St George House was opened on April 6th 1984 by Lord Mayor Martin Dodgson: the architects were Abbey Hanson Rowe - the development was by Bass Pensions and Leeds City Council. The Victoria Hotel opened in 1865 with 28 bedrooms serving the assizes held at the Town Hall; photographers Edmund & Joseph Wormald's house and studio designed by George Corson (1865); Masonic Hall built in 1865 and later used as the Juvenile Courts - opened as The Felon & Firkin in December 1995, Millennium Square (2000-01), Civic Hall (1933), School Board Building (Carpe Diem ale & wine bar and offices) built by George Corson in 1878-81 and now Civic Court, JW Clark's West Riding Carriage Manufactory: redeveloped as Portland Court; Alexander Court opened in 1997 as 60 flats for students at Leeds Metropolitan University; Chorley & Pickersgill premises (refurbished) and the Leonardo Building (Development Agency & Highways) built 1892 and rebuilt/restored in 1998, Cathedral House (residence of St Anne's Cathedral clergy), Thoresby School and Central High School (council offices) and the second Masonic Hall with the Shap granite foundation stone laid by the Rt Hon Earl of Warwick on July 18th 1900: designed by JM Bottomley this is now Cathedral Chambers which includes the office of City Centre Management.

GREAT WOODHOUSE HALL was built by 1720 by Thomas Pease and inherited by his grand-daughter who married Col St George Dalley in 1771 and looked over fields which became Leeds General Cemetery. It was later extended and converted to flats but the hall was demolished in 1958 to build the University Civil Engineering Department.

GREEK STREET features Greek Street Chambers built by Alfred Waterhouse (1898) as the William Williams Brown Bank: partly converted into The Old Monk. TH Sagar's City Ironmongery Warehouse at 6 Greek Street was a wholesale and retail ironmonger whose business features at Abbey House Museum. Bibi's Restaurant was opened on Mill Hill by Oliver & Dino in April 1975; a restaurant was opened in Greek Street as Gardiner's Terrazza and on the closure of the Mill Hill premises became Bibi's restaurant.

GREEN FLAG is an insurance company based on Neville Street opened in Victoria Gate in July 1998. The business was started in the 1960's by Dennis Thrustle in Hull offering cheap holiday insurance, including transport home in the event of a car breakdown. Gordon Sheard and Colin Wilkinson created The National Breakdown Recovery Club in 1971 based in Bradford.

GREEN, THOMAS (1811-1892) established his business in 1835 on North Street making a variety of products including wheelbarrows, pub tables and mowing machines. They made steam rollers, steam trams and vehicles for road sweeping and locomotives. The Smithfield Works, which expanded to include the Smithfield Hotel and St Thomas Church School were closed down after being sold to Atkinson's of Clitheroe in 1975. The façade of the old hotel (1850) was restored and is the only reminder of the Smithfield Works, which covered many acres across Bridge Street.

GREENWOOD, HON ARTHUR MP JP was the managing director of Greenwood & Batley: he was made an Honorary Freeman of the City of Leeds on September 11th 1930; the inscribed Freedom roll casket is on display in Leeds Civic Hall alongside those awarded to Charles Lupton and Charles Tetley. He was born in Leeds and was elected MP for Nelson and Colne in 1922; he was a lecturer in economics at Leeds University and a lecturer with the WEA. Greenwood & Batley was founded in 1856 by his father Thomas Greenwood - he worked at the Wellington Foundry as a draughtsman. The business was based on East Street in the Albion Works and manufactured hydraulic textile machinery, engines, generators, steam turbines, shell making machinery, cartridges and torpedoes; the business was closed in 1988.

GREENWOODS JEWELLERS was founded by William Greenwood in 1894 in Briggate, where he lived over the shop. The shop was rebuilt in 1924 and in 1959 William moved out of the shop in order to enlarge the premises. The business moved from Briggate to the Schofield's Centre in 1989 and closed in 1998.

GREENWOODS MEN'S WEAR had their shop on the corner of Briggate and Queen Victoria Street: now part of the Victoria Quarter. It was James Greenwood who opened a hatter's shop in Bradford in 1860 when he was 37 years old: the shop was demolished in 1865 and his son Moses carried on in other premises on Westgate. Moses made hats for the wool barons and in 1889 was making straw hats from another shop: son Willie decided that the business should become outfitters. The Greenwood family lived over the shop and Walter joined the family business in 1919 at the age of 18. In later years the business spread and in 1934 there were 36 shops for Greenwood's (Hosiers & Outfitters). In 1956 the head office building at White Cross Guiseley was opened and there are over 100 branches throughout Yorkshire, Midlands, East Anglia and the North of England.

GREYHOUND STADIUM (Leeds Stadium) on Elland Road was opened on July 16th 1927 at a cost of £67,000. It was closed on April 3rd 1982 and was demolished in October 1982. The Parkside Greyhound Stadium was opened on December 12th 1932 and was closed on October 15th 1963.

GRIMSHAW, ARTHUR EDMUND (1865-1913) was the son of Atkinson and Frances Grimshaw and was organist at St Anne's Cathedral for 30 years: he was buried at Woodhouse Cemetery.

GRIMSHAW, JOHN ATKINSON (1836-93) was railway clerk and a self taught local painter who completed views of Roundhay Park and Leeds City Centre - including Park Row. He lived at Knostrop Hall from 1870 after spending four years in a house on Cliff Road Hyde Park. His views of Park Row with the first St Anne's Cathedral and Boar Lane (1881) are on show in Leeds City Art Gallery - the Boar Lane picture was bequeathed to the Art Gallery in June 2000. Grimshaw's painting of Allerton Lodge Moortown was sold in April 2001 at Phillips Auctioneers.

GRIMTHORPE, BARON was the title conferred on Sir Edmund Beckett-Denison (1816-1905) in 1886. He was interested in the design of clocks and was involved with those at Big Ben, Leeds Parish Church and St Chad's Church Headingley: he designed and endowed this church with his father Edmund Denison - consecrated on January 11th 1868. The title passed down the family and the second Baron Grimthorpe was Ernest William Beckett-Denison who was born at Roundhay and educated at Eton and Trinity College Cambridge: he was MP for Whitby. In 1883 he married Lucy Tracey Lee (died 1891) of New York and lived at Kirkstall Grange. He was a partner in Beckett's Bank of Park Row until 1905, when he inherited the peerage on the death of his father. He died in a sanatorium in Scotland having lived at Ravello (Italy) until 1916.

GUILDFORD STREET was the continuation of Park Lane and was once Upper Head Row. The name was changed c1820 - it had been known as Butt's Hill and was popularly called Merryboys Hill. Guildford Street changed into a section of The Headrow in the widening and rebuilding scheme of the 1930's.

HALL, ROBERT (1801-57) was born in Kirkgate and educated at Heath Grammar School, Leeds Grammar School and Christ Church Oxford. In 1829 he married Maria daughter of Mayor of Leeds Thomas Tennant. He was deputy recorder for Leeds and Recorder for Doncaster (1845) and was elected Conservative MP for Leeds in 1857 a few months prior to his death: he was succeeded by George Beecroft. He campaigned for the reduction of working hours of children in factories and helped to bring Rev Walter Hook to be Vicar of Leeds. Robert Hall's statue is at the rear of the Town Hall and was carved in 1857 by Dennis Lee - unveiled on July 12th 1861 by George Skirrow Beecroft MP: it stands facing the statue of Edward Baines by William Behnes.

HALL, HENRY (1773-1859) of Bank Lodge was born in Kirkgate and his son was Robert Hall. He was made an Alderman in 1811 and was Mayor of Leeds in 1812 and 1825. He was a patron of Leeds vicarage - his coat of arms is included in the west window; he was a trustee of the Grammar School, treasurer of Leeds Library for 40 years and treasurer of the LGI for 39 years. He and son Robert campaigned for the election of Dr Walter Hook as Vicar of Leeds: Henry and Robert Hall were buried at St Mary's Church Whitkirk.

HAMMOND SUDDARDS EDGE The firm of solicitors was started in 1870 by Thomas Last of Suffolk in Bradford and his partners included Peter Harris, Arthur Betts and Cyril Reddihough. The other founding firm was JR Phillips of Bradford - Roger W Suddards was taken into partnership in 1952; in 1961 the two firms were merged as Last Suddards & Co. The firm opened in Leeds in 1984 in Britannia Chambers and Joseph's Well. In 1988 AV Hammond & Co and Last Suddards were merged and Hammond Suddards started trading on May 1st 1988. The new premises on Hanover Walk/Park Lane had the foundation stone laid by Sir Gordon Linacre on September 11th 1990 and the firm moved in during April 1991. Hammond Suddards merged with the Birmingham firm Edge Ellison in August 2000.

HANOVER SQUARE was laid out in 1827 in the grounds of Denison

Hall by James Pritchett (1789-1868) following purchase by stuff merchant George Rawson in 1824, although he never lived there (Benjamin Gott's son was a tenant). The square was completed in 1900 with houses on the site of the iron church for the Presbyterian and later Primitive Methodist Mission to 1882. The houses on the square included that of Edward Baines Jnr MP: the house (1840) was restored by the City Council and Unipol Student Homes for student accommodation; James Kitson later Lord Airedale lived at Hanover House between 1861 and 1870. The old Day Centre - now 8 flats - occupied the premises of the Methodist Chapel Sunday School (c1902): the chapel was built in 1888. The name refers to the family of George IV who was the great grandson of George 1st - son of the elector of Hanover. Hanover Place Wesleyan Methodist (St Peter's Hill) Chapel was built in 1847 designed by James Simpson and was renovated and enlarged in 1906; it was used as a storeroom from the 1960's and is now offices.

HARDING, COL THOMAS WALTER JP (1843-1927) was the head of the Tower Works - named after the two impressive chimneys, which had been founded by his father Thomas R Harding in 1829. The firm made steel pins for combs and cards needed for the textile industry. By the 1860's the firm occupied a five acre site and in 1892 was incorporated as TR Harding & Son Ltd. It amalgamated with two other firms in 1895 to become Harding, Rhodes & Co and the Tower works closed in 1981. Col Harding was the main inspiration for the Leeds Art Gallery and paid for the City Square scheme including Brock's Black Prince and Drury's lamp statues as well as those of Dean Walter Hook Vicar of Leeds and minister of Mill Hill Chapel Rev Dr Joseph Priestley. He also provided the money to improve Abbey House-the original gatehouse to Kirkstall Abbey. Thomas W Harding married Annie Heycock Butler (died 1923); he was the President of the Leeds Chamber of Commerce for two years and the first Chairman of the Art Gallery Committee (1888), Lord Mayor of Leeds 1898-99, elected an Hon Freeman of Leeds in 1903 and Chairman of Harding, Rhodes & Co Ltd. He lived for a few years from 1870 at the corner house on Cavendish Road/Hillary Place and died at his Cambridgeshire home of Madingley Hall on March 26th 1927. His portrait by Hubert von Herkomer is on display in the Town Hall's Albert Room.

HARDWICK, ROBERT GEORGE (1834-1864) was a physician

living in Park Square: he studied at Leeds Medical School and was house surgeon at the LGI. He became physician to the Leeds Dispensary and House of Recovery.

HARE, JAMES started work in the mid 19th century as an apprentice in a woollen mill: his own business in a cottage during the 1860's led to his establishment as a woollen and worsted merchant on Clare Street. He took a warehouse on Wellington Street and was joined by brother Samuel Hare and cousin Robert Sykes. In 1913 the firm started the manufacture of cloth and Arlington Mills soon spread over several acres. In 1922 a warehouse on Queen Street was bought and soon Coronet House was erected: in 1933 the firm bought Dixon & Gaunt Ltd and in 1952 there was a Hare company founded in Canada. James Hare of Fieldhead Thorner died in October 1965. In 1973 Hares of England was sold to Illingworth Morris of Bradford.

HARPER STREET crosses New York Street by the market and was once the site for the Leeds Wholesale meat market - now Harper Street 600+ space multi-storey car park. It was also the site of IJ Dewhirst Ltd., whose sign still remains opposite to the old Brougham Arms (Duck & Drake) public house and the premises of Smith Dixon & Lodge who were wholesale druggists, drysalters and oil manufacturers founded c1873.

HARRISON, JOHN (1579-1656) was a wealthy merchant and Alderman of Leeds in 1626. He was a trustee of the Grammar School which he had removed in 1624 to a field between the present Grand Theatre and North Street. In 1631 John Harrison founded St John's Church which was eventually to be his burial place. In 1653 he financed Harrison's Hospital (almshouses) built west of his church - they were rebuilt in 1850 and provided a new market cross (1619). In 1603 John Harrison bought property from the Falkingham family: the New Hall estate (Vicar Lane/Lady Lane) and Rockley Hall (Lower Head Row) - the Rockley family had their own chantry in the Parish Church. He married Elizabeth Foxcroft in 1603 and moved to a house on the east end of Boar Lane.

HARRISON STREET links New Briggate and Vicar Lane with the site of the Assembly Rooms, Grand Theatre stage door. The area was originally John Harrison's tenement with two acres known as the Nether Tenters.

HARRIS, EMMANUEL VINCENT (1876-1971) was born in

Devonport and articled to James Harvey and later was assistant to Leonard Stokes and Sir William Emerson. Vincent Harris worked for the London Council for 7 years and won a competition for designing Glamorgan City Hall (1908-11). His work included Sheffield's War Memorial Halls (1920-32), Leeds Civic Hall (1933), County Hall at Trent Bridge (1935), Council House Bristol (1937) and St Mary's College Durham University (1947-53). Later work included Whitehall Government Offices London (1951-59) and Central Library Kensington London (1958).

HART'S was a milliners and furriers shop on New Market Street which opened in 1893 (Martin Hart lived at Allerton Park) and moved in 1897 to New Briggate prior to re-locating to the corner of King Edward Street and Briggate in 1926: the New Briggate shop was demolished for the Paramount (Odeon) Cinema. The business trading as H & D Hart was acquired by Matthias Robinson in 1938. Donald Hart bought Hazlewood Castle near Tadcaster in 1960 from the Fawcett family and he started a programme of restoration and alteration including the Flemish Hall and demolishing the north east section leaving the chapel separated from the main castle. The Carmelite Friars bought Hazlewood Castle and grounds from Donald Hart in 1967 and he retained a flat at the castle until his death in 1972. The Carmelite Community established a retreat at Hazlewood until they sold it to be developed as a luxury hotel: the Community left in December 1995.

HARTLEY HILL is the truncated street that now only has the old dispensary and car park-now the Leeds Society for Deaf and Blind People at Centenary House. The street once featured Bischoff House (Sheepscar Hall) demolished c1969 for the route of the Inner Ring Road. Jonas Batley was a wholesale draper: the firm transferred from North Street c1880. The street was cut during the building of the Inner Ring Road in the 1960's. North of Hartley Hill overlooking the slip road to the Inner Ring Road is a five storey apartment block of 45 flats funded by the Joseph Rowntree Foundation at a cost of £3 million: the development is known as CASPAR (City Centre Apartments for Single People at Affordable Rents). The design was by Levitt Bernstein and built by Kajima: the flats were awarded a top prize in the 14th City of Leeds Awards for Architecture announced in January 2001. The first tenants moved in during June 2000 and the official opening was by Arts

Minister Alan Howarth in September 2000.

HARVEY NICHOLS glass fronted £15 million store was opened on Briggate on October 23rd 1996 built in the shell of the Leeds Empire/Empire Arcade. The project received an award in the Leeds Awards for Architecture 1997 - architects were Brooker Flynn with Hosker, Moore and Kent. The store opened every day of the week from September 2000. The store has its beginnings in 1813 when Benjamin Harvey opened a linen shop in Knightsbridge (London): in 1820 his daughter joined with Col Nichols in the business of selling linen with Oriental carpets, silks and luxury goods. In the 1880's the present Knightsbridge store was completed with a rear extension opened in 1932. In 1919 Harvey Nichols was bought by Debenhams and in 1985 it became part of the Burton Group. In 1991 Harvey Nichols was acquired by Dickson Concepts (International) Ltd and in April 1996 was listed on the Stock Exchange. In May 2000 the first store abroad was opened in Riyadh (Saudi Arabia) designed by Sir Norman Foster. A Birmingham store was opened in 2001 with branches in Edinburgh (2002) and Manchester (2003) to follow.

HEADROW is one of the original streets of the city known as Lower Head Row and Upper Head Row: the northern limit of the town. In later years the names were changed to Park Lane and Guildford Street and in the 1930's became The Headrow following widening and rebuilding; the latest scheme was designed by Sir Reginald Blomfield. The Headrow was developed into a precinct in February 1975 and there was a landscaping costing £9000 in the same year. Headrow House was opened in 1955 with an underground car park: the shops included Ceylon Tea Centre sponsored by tea planters: opening in 1964 and closed in 1981 - now Halifax, Vallance' s electrical goods, Dean & Dawson travel agents with the BEA and BOAC offices. Headrow House is the offices of Direct Line Insurance; it stands on the site of Guildford House demolished for Sir Reginald Blomfield's Headrow improvements of the 1930's. Direct Line was created by the Royal Bank of Scotland in 1985: the Leeds branch was opened by founder Peter Wood on March 1st 1994.

HEADROW SHOPPING CENTRE The £16 million Headrow Centre was built on The Headrow/Lands Lane Schofields site and was opened on September 6th 1990 by the Lord Mayor Bill Kilgallon.

The Centre is owned by Postel and was designed by Crampin & Pring.

HEATON, DR JOHN DEAKIN (1817-80) was an eminent Leeds surgeon: physician to the LGI, House of Recovery and the Public Dispensary. He was a lecturer at the Medical School and from 1856 lived at Claremont on Clarendon Road. John Deakin was born at his father John's book shop in Briggate and in 1850 he married Fanny Heaton (unrelated) at St George's Church; one of the groomsmen was Andrew Fairbairn (son of Sir Peter Fairbairn). John and Fanny frequently travelled abroad, often with Thomas Cook himself. Fanny died in 1893 and Claremont was sold in 1894. The tomb on the south side of St George's Church is that of the Heaton family: John Heaton (1769-1852), wife Ann and John Deakin Heaton.

HEATONS were a clothing firm based in New York Road/North Street: Crispin House. The firm was started by William Heaton in 1899 as a ladies costume and raincoat manufacturer in King Street. In 1914 they moved to North Street and in 1916 a new building was opened as Heaton House and in 1924 an extension on New York Road (Heatona House) was opened with the factory having an output of 3000 garments weekly. In 1970 the premises were sold to HW Poole shoe manufacturers and the property became known as Crispin House - now being developed as luxury apartments. St Crispin of Soissons is the patron saint of shoemakers - his date of martyrdom was October 25th 287.

HEMINGWAY, SIR WILLIAM was a member of Leeds City Council from 1915 and elected Lord Mayor in 1934: he became an Honorary Freeman of Leeds in 1956. He started work as a trapboy at Waterloo Main Colliery and from 1922 to 1946 was a check weighman at Water Haigh Colliery. William Hemingway was the Chairman of Leeds Corporation Waterworks Committee and knighted in 1965.

HEPPER, JOHN (1835-1915) was the son of John Hepper (died 1851) who had opened an auction house on Trinity Street. The business was established in 1820 when linen merchant Gilbert McIntyre started auctions and in 1825 John Hepper snr joined the business and McIntyre retired. He was joined by his brother Joseph Henry and in 1862 moved from the George & Dragon Yard Briggate to East Parade where they built a saleroom. John Hepper jnr lived in Clareville on Spring Road designed by George Corson in the 1870's and died at Ilkley. The business was merged with JW Watson of New Station Street in 1974 and in 1976 the auction business were bought by Phillips of London (founded 1796) with Hepper Watson continuing to trade as estate agents and property valuers. John Wainwright Watson founded his business in 1883 in his home and moved to Albion Street and then to New Station Street. There was a depository for Hepper Watson on Park Place.

HEPPER, JOHN (1925-1991) was the sixth generation of the family to join Hepper & Sons: he was educated at Leeds Grammar School and was a business partner from 1947 to 1961. John Hepper was a governor of the Grammar School, founder chairman of Leeds Civic Trust and the President of Leeds Junior Chamber of Commerce.

HEPTON BROS were tailors established by 1900 on Oxford Row and by the 1930's were on Sovereign Street. The factory on York Road opened in 1948 and was designed by Charlie Castelow: closed by the late 1970's with demolition - small firms now occupy the site (Hepton House).

HEPWORTHS was started on Bishopgate Street by Joseph Hepworth in 1865 and by 1881 were on Wellington Street and later occupied Marshall Mills. The factory on Claypit Lane was extended in 1896 in Queen's Square and in 1907 another block was completed. The premises are now Ventura - formerly Club 24. One of their retail shops was on the corner of Duncan Street and Briggate - premises which also included Walker & Hall (silversmiths and cutlers) of Sheffield.

HEPWORTH HOUSE was the home of the clothing firm on Claypit Lane - now the headquarters of Ventura. Contractors started work on the 10 storey building in August 1971 at a cost of £2 million.

HERKOMER, SIR HUBERT (1849-1914) was a portrait, historical, landscape and figure painter who was born in Bavaria. He came to England in 1857 and founded the Bushey School of Art and was the Slade Professor of Fine Arts at Oxford from 1895. He was knighted in 1907 and painted the portrait of Col Thomas Walter Harding in 1888 which is displayed in the Albert Room Town Hall.

HEY, RICHARD (1745-1835) was the brother of William Hey born at Pudsey and educated at Magdalene College and Sydney Sussex College Cambridge. He was called to the bar at the Middle Temple although devoted much of his life to writing social dissertations.

HEY, DR WILLIAM FRS (1736-1819) was a founder of the first Infirmary in 1767 in his Kirkgate house and was mainly responsible for the building of the new Infirmary in 1771. He worked as a surgeon at the LGI: his house was Albion Place dated from 1794/95 to designs by Thomas Johnson - the street was named from the house. He was Leeds mayor in 1786/87 and 1801/02: he married Alice Banks in 1761 by whom he had 14 children. The statue of William Hey in the LGI was sculpted by Sir Francis Legatt Chantrey (1781-1841) and was erected in 1819. Sir Francis Chantrey was born in Derbyshire and operated a bronze foundry in Eccleston Place London: he exhibited at the RA from 1804 to his death and was knighted in 1835.

HIGH AND MIGHTY is an independent men's outfitting retailer who opened their Merrion Centre shop in 1972 and moved to King Edward Street shop in 1986. The business was started by Bernard Levy in 1956 as a mail order concern based in Hull: his daughter Judith currently runs the business which has 23 branches throughout the UK and 8 in Europe.

HILLARY PLACE on Woodhouse Lane was developed by John Hillary Hebblethwaite following the death of his great uncle in 1840. He lived at Hope Villa which was sold in 1900 for the building of Trinity Church. Hopewell House (Leeds Innovation) was the home of Henry Littlewood of Briggate and later flax merchant Henry Pritchard. On the north side is the caretaker's house for Trinity Church built in 1901 and on the south side is the University Physics department replacing 19th century housing. The remaining houses are occupied by the Department of Education with the corner house being the home of Col Thomas W Harding in 1870.

HILTON, RONNIE (1926-2001) was born Adrian Hill in Hull but moved to Leeds in 1940: his break into show business was at a talent night at The Shaftesbury public house. He released many hit songs in a long career and moved from Shadwell to Eastbourne in 1991.

HILTON & HILTON were piano manufacturers of Saville Street (Wellington Street) who opened their premises in 1890 when they were awarded a Gold Medal at the Leeds International Exhibition: their business started at Mirfield c1870.

HIGH COURT LANE is by the Parish Church and is a reminder of the manor house near the church, where the courts were once held. It was Ralph Paynel who in 1089 gave the parish church and land in Holbeck to Holy Trinity Priory at York: they were mainly within the Manor of Leeds and known as the Rectory-Manor of Leeds Kirkgate-cum-Holbeck.

HIRST, JOHN was the first printer in Leeds: in 1718 he printed The Leeds Mercury newspaper and in 1726 printed his first book.

HIRST'S YARD links Call Lane with Duncan Street and is the site of the Whip public house: this was extended in Victorian times and was the last of the men only public houses - it is reputed to have sold more pints of beer weekly than any other inn in the city. The yard is named after William Hirst (1777-1858) a cloth manufacturer who had premises there. William Hirst was born near Huddersfield and came to Leeds in 1795 starting his own business in 1810 as a cloth dresser and manufacturer. In 1813 his cloth was made by machinery and he made many improvements to cloth manufacturing in Leeds from 1813 to 1825. He retired a wealthy man in 1825 but became a bankrupt in 1830 - he spent some time in Rothwell Gaol for debt.

HITCHENS was a draper's store on Briggate which was founded in 1879 on Lower Head Row; in 1886 the shop was sold to buy a hatter's business on Kirkgate. The founder was MC Hitchen and son Clarence Hitchen joined the expanding firm in 1906: he died in 1946. The shop was extended and remodelled during the 1930's but was closed on January 21st 1952. Littlewood's Store moved into the Hitchen's building in 1952 and expanded to the corner of Briggate in 1971 - the store was re-modelled and re-opened in 1984.

HOGSHEAD is a pub chain owned by Whitbread's Brewery. They opened on Albion Street in 1977 and in Watson Cairn's premises on Lower Briggate in 1997. Hogshead on Great George Street opened in March 1998.

HOL BECK is a tributary of the River Aire which originates as Low Beck and has its confluence with the river by canal basin at Victoria Bridge: Water Lane follows the last section of this beck.

HOLLIS, WALTER DAWSON (died 1914) founded the firm of Hollis & Webb (estate agents) with JS Webb: he was a director of the Leeds Permanent Building Society.

HOLMES, REV DR JOSEPH (1790-1854) was headmaster of Leeds Grammar School from 1830 to 1854. He was educated at Queen's

College Cambridge and was a minister at Trinity Church until the death of the Vicar. He was succeeded at the school by Dr Alfred Barry, son of Sir Charles Barry architect of the Houses of Parliament.

HOLROYD, JAMES (1839-1890) was the manager of Wilcock & Co (Burmantofts Pottery) from 1879: in 1861 he had founded James Holroyd woollen manufacturers and moved to Leeds from Barnard Castle. He lived at College Road which became part of the University site and was a Liberal and member of the Leeds Literary & Philosophical Society. He died at his later home Holly Bank Headingley - the week after his brother Thomas was buried at Lawnswood; James left his wife Margaret and seven children - the eldest James succeeded him as manager at Burmantofts. There is a memorial to James Holroyd in St Agnes Church Burmantofts.

HOMBURG, KARL ALBERT (1847-1922) was born in Berlin and came to England in 1868. He started his wig making business in Briggate and in 1916 his son William Albert Homburg took over the business. The firm moved to Lower Briggate and then moved to Call Lane for 40 years and then to Sovereign Street. WA Homburg are now based at King House Regent Street.

HOOK, WALTER FARQUHAR (1798-1875) was the Vicar of Leeds from 1837 to 1859, when he became Dean of Chichester. Hook was instrumental in rebuilding the Parish Church: architect Robert Dennis Chantrell was appointed. The medieval church was closed in March 1838 and the new church was consecrated on September 2nd 1841. During his vicariate the Church Institute was formed in 1857 and he was instrumental in raising the money to build 21 churches, 27 schools and 23 vicarages in addition to Leeds Parish Church. Walter Hook's grandfather was James Hook who was a Norwich organist and composer of light opera; his maternal grandfather was Sir Walter Farquhar - naval doctor and physician and adviser to the Prince Regent George IV. Walter's father was another James-novelist and clergyman: chaplain to George IV.

HOPE FOUNDRY was founded in 1812 on Mabgate by Samuel Lawson: it amalgamated with Fairbairn's Wellington Foundry (founded 1828). The firm closed in 1930: the grand stone entrance remains on Mabgate with the site taken by other businesses.

HOPKINSON'S MUSIC The shop was in Commercial Street selling pianos and sheet music: it was started by Jonathan Hopkinson c1845 and his son who were army bandmasters. The son married Miss Barker from Harewood and opened a shop on Wade Lane and his son founded the piano firm. Hopkinson's also had premises at East Street Mills: the business closed in 1967.

HORNE BROTHERS were men's outfitters on the corner of Briggate and Albion Place: in 1986 the shop transferred to the Austin Reed site in Bond Street which closed in 1991. Horne Brothers opened their Commercial Street shop in June 1992 - they closed a year later: the premises became Oasis.

HOSPITALS *Chapel Allerton Hospital* was built in 1926 in the grounds of Gledhow Grove and became a hospital for war pensioners. In 1960 administration was taken over by Leeds Group A and the main wards were moved to Newton Green Hospital by 1994: Gledhow Grove was sold in 1994 for redevelopment. The Duchess of Kent opened the new Chapel Allerton Hospital on July 22nd 1994. *Cookridge Hospital* The main wing was built in 1869 as a Hospital for the Convalescent Poor of Leeds and this remained until 1939. It was re-opened as Cookridge Hospital in 1943 and became part of the NHS in 1948. In 1952 beds were available for patients requiring radiotherapy. *Hospital for Women & Children* was first opened in 1853 on East Parade and in 1855 transferred to the Springfield Lodge estate: it was opened by the Earl of Carlisle in October 1861. After some rebuilding the hospital changed the name to Hospital for Women at Leeds and in 1974 it was transferred to Roundhay Hall with demolition of the old buildings. *Ida & Robert Arthington Hospital* at Cookridge started in 1886 with John North's gift of £6000 to open a convalescent home in memory of daughter Ida. Chorley & Connon were the architects and opening was on May 10th 1888; Robert Arthington financed the building of a new hospital on an adjacent site which opened in May 1905 - the two became known as the Ida & Robert Arthington Hospital: a nurses home was opened by The Princess Royal in 1954 and the hospital closed in 1997. *The Jewish Herzl Moser Hospital* at Hope Villa, Leopold Street was opened on November 15th 1905. The hospital enlarged with the purchase of more property and in 1936 the Newton Green Hall estate was purchased for a new hospital: this was to be used for allotments and in 1948 was transferred to the National Health Service who built a new hospital on the site in 1974. The Jewish Hospital was closed on January 31st

1970 with facilities transferred to St James Hospital. It was named after philanthropist Ald J Moser and Theodor Herzl a leading member of the Zionist movement. **Killingbeck Hospital** was developed from the Killingbeck Hall estate which was bought from Mrs Meynell Ingram in December 1898. The smallpox hospital was opened in September 1904 and from 1913 the Killingbeck Municipal Sanatorium specialised in TB cases. The extension to the Killingbeck Sanatorium was opened on July 9th 1936. Killingbeck Hall was demolished in 1978 and the hospital closed in 1997. The first **Leeds General Infirmary** was designed by John Carr and built 1768-1771 for £4599 on a site west of the Coloured Cloth Hall - this replaced temporary premises in William Hey's house on Kirkgate which had been acquired in 1767. The Infirmary was extended in 1782 with a new wing for £500 increasing the accommodation to 68 beds and a third floor added in 1786 with 20 beds and a top storey came in 1792 adding another 20 beds. The grounds of the Infirmary were extended in 1818 on 4000 square yards of land bought by Richard Fountayne Wilson for £1500 - he gave the land to the Infirmary. This first Infirmary was demolished in 1893: the only reminder is a single stone pillar to the rear of the Metropole Hotel. The site of the first Infirmary was taken by the Yorkshire Penny Bank. It was Sir George Gilbert Scott who designed the new Infirmary on Great George Street following visits with the chief physician Dr Charles Chadwick to French hospitals: the foundation stone was laid by James Kitson on March 29th 1864. The Prince of Wales opened the National Exhibition of Works of Art on May 19th 1868 and the building was ready for opening on May 22nd 1869. The Exhibition Committee built a glass and iron roof over the Central Hall and it was used also for concerts, tennis and an art gallery - the roof was demolished in 1911. The chapel is on the first floor with memorials to the Heaton family and George Corson added the east wing in 1891-92 following Scott's style and the nurses home was opened in 1897 - this had an extension opened on October 2nd 1937 by HRH The Princess Royal; the Weatherill Ward was opened by Lord Mayor Sir Wilfred Hepton on October 8th 1908. There was another extension in 1917 - inspected by HRH The Prince of Wales (the future King Edward VIII) commemorating his grandfather's reign. Charles Frederick Ratcliffe Brotherton (1882-1949) was the benefactor for the Brotherton Wing extension for Leeds General Infirmary and new outpatients department - built in Portland stone and opened on November 14th 1940 at a cost of £50,000. There is a proposal to demolish the Brotherton Wing and replace it with a new building which will include a hotel, offices, leisure and shops as part of the £200 million programme by the Leeds Teaching Hospitals Trust; the proposed completion date is 2006. The Martin Wing (Sir George Martin) was opened by the Duke of Edinburgh in 1961 and the Wellcome Wing followed in the same year. New buildings followed in 1974 - the foundation stone was laid by Prime Minister Edward Heath in 1972. The Clarendon Wing was officially opened in 1984 by the Duchess of Kent and the Jubilee Building was opened on March 25th 1998 by the then Secretary of State for Health Frank Dobson MP. Projects include Trauma Unit, £19 million children's hospital at the LGI, a £58 million cancer centre at St James Hospital and restoration of the Chancellor and Gledhow Wings at St James. *Malham House Day Hospital* is on Hyde Terrace and was opened in April 1996. *Nuffield Hospital (Leeds):* plans were announced on January 20th 2000 to build a new Nuffield hospital on the site of the former Centaur clothing factory on Leighton Street - it is to be a £30 million, 70 bed hospital due to open in Autumn 2002. *St James Hospital* was developed on land bought from the Beckett family by the Poor Law Guardians in 1846: the Leeds Moral & Industrial Training School was opened in October 1848 (Lincoln Wing). The Leeds Union Workhouse was opened in 1861 (Ashley Wing) with a workhouse chapel in between the two buildings, designed by Perkin & Backhouse. In 1874 the Leeds Union Infirmary was built on the site of the present Gledhow Wing. There was further building in 1904-06. In 1915 the Workhouse and Infirmary were taken over as the East Leeds War Hospital - visited by King George V in September 1915. The Poor Law Infirmary was renamed St James Hospital in 1925, honouring Dr James Allen and Sir James Ford. In October 1970 the hospital became St James University Hospital: the Chancellor's Wing was opened by the Duchess of Kent on February 23rd 1972 (the Duchess of Kent was Chancellor of Leeds University) with the Beckett Wing opening in the same year; the Gledhow Wing was opened in 1977 with the Clinical Sciences Building opening in 1979. *Roundhay Hall BUPA Hospital* was opened in 1989 having been bought in 1986. The hall was built for John Goodman in the 1820s and from 1916 was the property of Edward Brotherton. In the last war in was an LGI annexe and became a nurses training school and in 1974 was the Hospital for Women. *Seacroft Hospital* was opened on Edward Waud's New Manston Hall estate which was bought in June 1892: the Manston Infectious Diseases Hospital was opened in October 1898. A new complex was opened in September 1904 with ET Hall's famous clock tower (1903) built to hold the hospital water supply. The Leeds Teaching Hospitals NHS Trust was created in April 1998 and employs 15,000 staff.

HOSPITAL FUND, LEEDS. Frederick R Spark JP (1831-1919) founded the Leeds & District Workpeople's Hospital Fund in 1887. The Fund was to finance local hospitals and by 1939 £2 million had been handed over to the LGI and other local hospitals. The Fund opened a convalescent home at Horsforth in 1896 and a men's Bridlington home in 1949: a female home designed by William Backhouse opened in Bridlington in 1953. The Fund office in Park Square became too small and it moved to St Paul's Street - opened in November 1955. In 1981 the name changed to the Leeds Hospital Fund Ltd. The Leeds Hospital Fund moved their offices from St Paul's Street to Canal Wharf in August 2000.

HOTELS *Crowne Plaza* on Wellington Street was opened on May 31st 1990 by the Earl of Harewood as The Crest and when Bass bought the chain in 1997, the hotel became a Holiday Inn. The name changed to Holiday Inn-Crowne Plaza and then dropped the Holiday Inn name: architects were DJ Curtis & Associates. *42 The Calls* was opened in the old Fletland Mills which were operated in 1887 by the Wright Brothers corn millers who acquired the late 18th/19th century mills providing flour and horse corn for the Leeds district: in 1991 the mills were converted into the hotel by architect Allen Tod. *Golden Lion* Lower Briggate was designed by Thomas Ambler in 1879 and built on part of the site of The Commercial Hotel coaching inn, which was complete with stables. The hotel also stands on the site of No 1 Briggate which was bought in 1873 by John Barran and demolished for the hotel. The hotel once part of the Thistle Group became a member of Peel Hotels in October 1998: there has been much investment in refurbishing. *Griffin Hotel* on Boar Lane stands on an ancient site once used for travelling circuses. It was a private house for a wool merchant in the 18th century set in fields and was sold to a Sheffield cutler. In 1780 it became a coaching inn with the services to Bradford, Scarborough, York and London and was also used as a stage for transfer from Marsh Lane to Wellington Station prior to the link being built across the city. The hotel was rebuilt in c1880 (probably a short lived Temperance Hotel) and in 1919 was bought by the Griffin Hotel Syndicate from a Sunderland company. In 1923 the hotel was restored by Percy Robinson and refurbished in 1937. In 1976 Tetleys ceased their function room hirings and it was taken over by Jinnah who closed the hotel in July 1999. The Griffin re-opened after conversion of a derelict building on Bishopgate Street as the *Comfort Hotel* (Choice Hotels) in November 1999 and offers 80 en suite rooms. The lower floor of the old Griffin which retains the clock and name over the door is leased to the Bar Censsa (Scottish & Newcastle). *Guildford* on The Headrow was first built c1778 and was known as The Duncan, changing to the Green Dragon prior to 1820: it was rebuilt c1900. In 1921 the name changed with new ownership to Hotel Guildford and it was restored in 1986-88, after the threat of demolition. *Hilton* opened as the Dragonara on April 1st 1973 becoming the Ramada Dragonara in 1975 and the Leeds Hilton in 1988: the site was Whitley's School Close woollen mills. There was a £1.5 million refurbishment in 2000 and plans for a further £6 million restoration in 2001. Hilton Hotels were founded by Conrad Hilton (1888-1979) in 1919. *Holiday Inn Express* (Bass Hotels franchised to Premier Hotels) on Kirkstall Road was opened on October 25th 1999 with 112 en suite rooms. *Malmaison Hotel* on Swinegate opened in the old offices of the Leeds City Transport Department after conversion in June 1999 - there are 100 en suite rooms. The £11 million conversion was by the Ferrier Crawford Partnership. *Marriott* Trevelyan Square Boar Lane (Whitbread) incorporated the Trevelyan Temperance Hotel (Thomas Ambler 1878) and was opened by Rt Hon Betty Boothroyd Speaker of the House of Commons (retired 2000) on June 6th 1994: architects were Cobban & Lironi. The hotel was partly opened for business in October 1993. *Merrion Hotel* on Wade Lane was opened by the Duke of Devonshire on January 12th 1966 by Rank Hotels. It became part of the Kingsmead Hotel Group in 1977 and was taken over in 1987 by Mount Charlotte Thistle Hotels of Leeds; in 1998 Merrion Hotel became one of the Peel Hotels of London. *Metropole* on King Street was opened on the site of the Fourth White Cloth Hall on June 28th 1899: designed by Chorley & Connon in brick and terracotta, it incorporates the stone cupola from the old cloth hall on the roof. The Metropole became a Forte Hotel and sold to Crown Hotels in 1988 who sold in 1991 to Principal Hotels. *Le Meridien Queens* (Nomura Securities) in City Square had the foundation stone laid on October 7th 1936 by Sir Josiah Stamp (Chairman LMS): it was opened by the Earl of Harewood (Henry Lascelles 6th Earl of Harewood 1882-1947) on November 12th 1937 designed by W Curtis Green and LMS architect William H Hamlyn in Portland Stone; it was built on the same site of the original Queen's Hotel. This was first agreed by the Midland Railway on August 16th 1859: it opened in 1863 to the designs of William Belton Perkin with new wings added in 1867 and 1898. *Park Plaza* with 192 bedrooms was opened in Royal Exchange House in Winter 2002. *Radisson SAS International* is a 150 bedroom hotel opened in November 2001 as a part of The Light development. *Travel Inn Metro* (Whitbread) on Wellington Street opened in 1996 and was extended in 1998: there are 139 en suite rooms. *Travelodge* (Granada) on Swinegate was opened on August 8th 1999 with 100 en suite rooms.

Leeds hotels which have closed or have been demolished include the *Albion Hotel* on Briggate, demolished for the FW Woolworth store - the hotel had stables and coach houses - an archway led to Albion Yard. *Commercial Hotel* on the corner of The Headrow/ Albion Street (previously the AA shop). *Greyhound Hotel* was on Vicar Lane and was converted from the original House of Recovery. *King Edward Hotel* was closed on April 4th 1961 with the site becoming the office for Leeds Permanent Building Society in 1973. *Imperial Hotel* was a palatial building on the west side of Briggate opposite The Victory. The hotel closed on March 8th 1961 and it was demolished and rebuilt as a Burton's store, who already had traded in the old building. *Jubilee Hotel* (1904) on The Headrow opposite the Town Hall used Burmantofts terra-cotta in its construction: it is now Jubilee House and a café - the interior was modernised in 1973 and 1987. *Royal Hotel* on Lower Briggate was built originally in 1692 and known as The New King's Arms: coaches ran from the hotel in 1765. It was the New Inn from 1773 and became The Royal Hotel in 1834 following the departures of the Royal Mail coaches-the service stopped in 1840. The hotel closed and in 1979-83 the hotel was replaced with the Yorkshire Metropolitan Housing Association's development of single person's flats - Regent Court (architects: Booth Shaw & Partners). The flats were opened on February 25th 1983 with the reconstructed façade made of fibre glass. *Trevelyan Temperance Hotel* (1866-70) by Thomas Ambler for John Barran: now the Marriott Hotel. *Victory* on Briggate was an early coaching inn with the Loyal Duncan starting services in 1800: it was built as a private house c1810 and became the Bull and Mouth Hotel. The name changed to Grand Central Hotel in 1903 which displayed a William Potts clock designed by Lord Grimthorpe from 1903; it was bought in 1919 by the proprietors of the City Cinema Boar Lane with the intention to develop into a cinema and restaurant but became the Victory Hotel in 1921: it had a very large banqueting hall. The hotel closed on May 10th 1939 and the site became the extension to Woolworth's Store. *Wellesley* on Wellington Street was built as the Great Northern Hotel designed by Matthew Ellison Hadfield (1812-85) serving the Central railway station in 1858 but suffered a disastrous fire in July 1906: afterwards five floors were rebuilt. It became the Wellesley in 1973 and was converted to City Central by Taywood Homes at a cost of £4.8 million: there are 65 apartments including studios and penthouses. Taywood added two additional floors replacing those destroyed in the 1906 fire: City Central opened in December 2001.

HOUSE OF FRASER department store on Briggate opened as Rackhams in the original Woolworths building in 1986 into which Schofields had moved from The Headrow/Lands Lane prior to sale. Rackhams changed their store name to House of Fraser in October 1996.

HOUSE OF RECOVERY was housed on Ebenezer Street in temporary premises. A permanent building on Vicar Lane was completed in 1802. The House opened on November 2nd 1804 with the Dispensary opening in the building during 1824. The House of Recovery was moved to a new building on Beckett Street in 1846. The old House on Vicar Lane became The Greyhound Inn and was demolished in 1938.

HUDSON, ROBERT opened the engineering works in 1865; the

Gildersome works were sold in 1982 and the business closed in 1985.

HUDSWELL CLARK was established on the old Railway Foundry in 1860 and manufactured steam locomotives until the 1960's; the business closed in 1972.

HUNSLET ENGINEERING WORKS were established in 1864 on the old Railway Foundry workshops site - developing into a 7 acre site by the 1930's. The firm manufactured steam locomotives until the 1960's and was closed in 1996.

HUNTSMAN TRADEMARK for Tetley's brewery was produced in the 1920's by Causton & Sons who were commissioned by the Dorchester brewery of Eldridge Pope for their Huntsman ales as well as for Tetleys Brewery and Raymants of Hertfordshire. Eldridge Pope used the logo until 1935 and Raymants until 1951: the symbol was removed from the Leeds brewery premises and from cans of Tetley Bitter in 2000.

IBBESON, GRAHAM (born 1951) is the sculptor of the bronze statue of Arthur Aaron VC which was unveiled at the Millenniun Fountain Eastgate on March 24th 2001. He trained at the Royal

Infirmary Street c1935 *(Photo: Leeds Express)*

School of Art and made the first figures for the Jorvik Viking Centre York as well as the statues of Thomas Chippendale in Otley and Eric Morecambe (Bartholomew) in his home town. There are many works by Graham Ibbeson through Britain and in October 2001 a work commemorating the Jarrow March was unveiled.

INFIRMARY STREET remembers the first Leeds General Infirmary founded in 1771 - a stone pillar on Little King Street remains from this building. The Yorkshire Penny Bank was built on the site and Goodbard House was opened in 1905: this is owned by CIS of Manchester and now includes the offices of the Allied Irish Bank.

INITIATIVE, LEEDS The Leeds Initiative was founded as a partnership in July 1990 and is led by the City Council. By the end of the 1990's the Leeds Initiative had published The Vision for Leeds which identified aims for the city in key strategic agendas. There were eight founder partners and the Board now represents 20 large organisations in the city. Leeds Arts is part of the Leeds Initiative which is developing a co-ordinated approach to all forms of art in Leeds.

INSTITUTO CERVANTES is based at 169 Woodhouse Lane: it is a world wide organisation created by the Spanish government in 1991. There are more than 30 Institutes around the world and Leeds is one of three UK cities to have one.

ISLE OF CINDER is a few hundred metres west of Leeds Bridge: an island created by the waterways once serving the King's Mills. In 1836 Victoria Flour Mills were established by Roger Shackleton & Sons: there were four mills with wharfage on the river. The brass founding business of John Ogden was also on the Isle of Cinder.

IVESON, HENRY was the Mayor in 1695 and 1709 as well as a JP and High Sheriff: he lived at Black Bank and ran the Black Bank Colliery.

JACKSON, REV EDWARD (1812-92) was educated at Fulneck School and in 1845 was ordained to a curacy at Leeds Parish Church under Rev Walter Hook. He stayed at the church for 11 years until becoming the priest in charge of St James Church on York Street: in 1875 he was made an Honorary Canon of Ripon. Rev Jackson is remembered in the Memorial Sunday School built on Cross York Street opened in 1909.

JACKSON, RT HON WILLIAM LAWRIES JP (1840-1917) was born

in Otley and was a tanner and leather merchant in Buslingthorpe. He married Grace Tempest (1837-1901) in 1860 and became the first Baron Allerton in 1902. He was the Mayor of Leeds in 1895-96, MP for Leeds (1876-80), MP for North Leeds (1885-1906) and a Privy Councillor (1890) and was made an Honorary Freeman of Leeds in October 1908. He was the Financial Secretary to the Treasury, cabinet minister in Lord Salisbury's government and Chairman of the Great Northern Railway.

JENKINSON, REV CHARLES (1887-1949) was the Vicar of Holbeck in 1927 and became leader of the Leeds Labour Party. He was chairman of the Housing Committee and supplied the initiative to demolish many slum areas and build estates of council flats. The best known scheme inspired by Charles Jenkinson was Quarry Hill Flats - the largest scheme in Europe, based on the Karl-Marx-Hof in Vienna. Jenkinson was City Council Leader from 1947 and died with overwork two years later.

JESSOP'S PHOTOCENTRES The origins of the business can be traced back to a chemist's shop in Leicester in 1875; Frank Jessop founded the firm in 1935 in Leicester mainly dealing with the hiring and selling of 16mm film. In 1960 his son Alan took over the company and in 1978 opened premises on Hinckley Road Leicester making it the world's largest photographic store. In 1979 computerisation was introduced and in 1981 Jessop's opened their first store in London and three years later opened on Oxford Street. In 1985/87 they moved to new warehouses on Scudamore Road making it their Leicester headquarters. In 1988 there were 52 shops and in 2001 there are 192 photo stores around the country. In 1989 the firm was sold to the management and in 1996 the firm left the control of the Jessop family. In 2000 Jessop's bought the shops of Tecno from the Car Phone Warehouse making it a £127 million chain of stores. The Leeds branch on Wade Lane opened in part of the first site of Radio Leeds - the branch in Headrow House was the Tecno outlet.

JOHNSON, THOMAS (died 1814) planned the development of Albion Street, Blenheim Terrace Woodhouse Lane and was the architect for the Leeds Library (1808) on Commercial Street.

JOSEPH'S WELL was the clothing manufactury opened by John Barran in 1888 which after closure became derelict. The building was restored in 1980 as quality offices and a public house: it is owned by J Pullan & Sons Ltd Building Contractors, who also have Apsley House Wellington Street; their main office is at Manor Works Beeston.

KPMG is an accountancy business incorporated in 1897 as Marwick Mitchell & Co in New York with James Marwick and Roger Mitchell. In 1911 the business merged with Sir William Peat's UK firm and in 1999 KPMG was formed after the 1987 merger of Peat Marwick and KMG. The KPMG offices on Neville Street were opened by The Princess Royal on January 28th 1990 at No 1 Embankment for Peat Marwick McLintock (from 1999 KPMG).

KELLY, JUDE was born in Liverpool in 1954 - in 1976 she was artistic director with the Solent People's Theatre and in the 1980's launched the Battersea Arts Centre and was the Director of the National Theatre of Brent. In 1988 Jude Kelly was the Director of the York Mystery Plays and a Director at the Royal Shakespeare Theatre at Stratford on Avon. She was appointed the Chief Executive of the West Yorkshire Playhouse in January 1989 and is now Artistic Director: she was awarded the OBE in 1997 for services to the theatre. Jude Kelly has received honorary doctorates from the Universities of Bradford, Leeds and York, Dartington College of Arts and in April 2001 a doctorate from the Open University at a ceremony at Harrogate International Centre.

KELSALL STREET was created in 1863 from Woodhouse Lane to Wade Lane.

KEMPLAY, RICHARD (1770-1830) opened an Academy for Young Gentlemen in 1817, where they were taught copperplate handwriting using steel nibs. Richard Kemplay was a churchwarden at Leeds Parish Church and a commissioner of the Leeds Waterworks. He was buried in St Matthew's churchyard Chapel Allerton where his wife Elizabeth - daughter of Rev William Fryer of Spurriergate York and William (1809-12), Caroline (1803-30) and Annabella (died 1886) are also buried. The house off New Briggate was built for Matthew Wilson in 1720 and is now Nash's Fish Restaurant.

KENDAL LANE runs to Clarendon Road and was probably a medieval track to Woodhouse Moor. It was named after John Kendal the owner in Elizabethan times of the Little Woodhouse estate.

KENNEDY, REV GEOFFREY STUDDERT (1883-1929) was an army

chaplain in the Great War and awarded the Military Cross: taking part in the Battle of the Somme. He was affectionately known as Woodbine Willie: the Chapel of the Holy Spirit and St Katherine in the Parish Church was furnished in his memory and opened in May 1986.

KERSHAW, ABRAHAM (1861-1929) started work for Sir John Crossley of Halifax and set up his own shop in Park Place, moving to Dorrington Place in 1898. He founded his business in the 1880's producing cameras: he made a single lens reflex camera which went on sale in 1905. During the Boer War Kershaw's factory manufactured and repaired telegraphic and signalling army equipment. A factory was opened on Woodhouse Lane in 1910 producing the Kalee projector (derived from AK Leeds) and Harehills Lane from 1916/17. Kershaw manufactured the Electrocardiograph for the LGI (invented 1903 by Willem Einthoven). In the last War Kershaw's made gun sights, bomb sights, tank periscopes and over 250,000 pairs of prism binoculars. Kershaw's made Gaumont-Kalee film projectors from 1948 until 1958: the business was bought by Rank in 1947 and the firm closed in 1980.

KEYWORTH, WILLIAM DAY Jnr (1843-1902) was the son of monumental mason William Day Keyworth (1817-97) of Hull. In 1867 he sculpted the four lions outside Leeds Town Hall: the cost was £550. The lions were based on those guarding Nelson's column in Trafalgar Square London; the Leeds lions were carved in Portland stone and are made in two sections, he had many commissions including Andrew Marvell (Hull market place), William Wilberforce (Wilberforce House) and Rowland Hill for Westminster Abbey. He shot himself in his Hull studio on August 9th 1902 following a visit to London - there were business problems. The body was found by his daughter Martha and he was buried in Springbank General Cemetery

KING'S ARMS INN This one time coaching inn was first used as the home of John Harrison and became the earliest coaching inn in Briggate (the site subsequently became Woolworths). It was used in the 18th century by magistrates and meetings of the turnpike trusts: regular coaches left from here to London. The building was sold in 1802 and closed in 1813.

KING CHARLES CROFT featured Red Hall, Hippodrome and the

King Charles public house on the corner of Lands Lane: demolished November 1974. A temporary wooden circus was held here in 1848 run by W Danby.

KING EDWARD STREET is a street built by the Leeds Estates Company replacing Fleet Street and Leadenhall Street between 1898 and 1902: the King Edward Restaurant was a popular meeting place. The street is now a pedestrian precinct.

KING STREET features the Metropole Hotel (Chorley & Connon 1899) and the Bank of England: transferred from South Parade. The street was first mentioned in 1817 (as was Queen Street) and named after King George III & Queen Charlotte. CMA House was designed by John Poulson in 1964.

KING'S MILLS were on Swinegate and in 1839 the obligation to the Leeds people to grind their corn at the mills was relieved: a compensation was paid to proprietor Edward Hudson of Roundhay. There is a carved stone set into the riverbank inscribed "King's Mills" marking the site of the oldest industrial site on the riverside: recorded in 1086 when Leeds was an agricultural village of 1000 acres worked by 35 farmers. The water turning the mill wheels was supplied from the Leeds Dam: it was repaired with wood from Roundhay Park in the late 14th century after flood damage.

KIRKGATE is one of the original Leeds streets from the Parish Church to Briggate. The view was changed with the building of the railway bridge in 1869: the street was the site of the First White Cloth Hall and north-west of Vicar Lane was the house and museum of Ralph Thoresby (1658-1725). This was timber built by his grandfather in the early 17th century and it later had a turret and below this was Ralph's study - later a pigeon cote. The interest in collecting had been started by his grandfather with coins and Ralph developed the idea with books, manuscripts, rocks and minerals together with many unusual curiosities. The house was demolished in 1878 - the Thoresby collection had been dispersed in the late 18th century. The vicarage stood on the corner of Kirkgate and Vicar Lane - the site of the market. Kirkgate was the site of Barstow Mansion - named after Jeremiah Barstow (died 1679) - which was demolished in 1908. In 1883 the Central Cocoa House was opened: designed by William Perkin. The Theatre de Luxe opened on Kirkgate in December 1910 and was closed in May

1934; George Proctor ran a bakery at Constitutional House with another branch at 31 Lady Lane. Kirkgate and Central Road were remodelled in 1996.

KIRKSTALL ABBEY was first settled by Cistercian monks from Fountains Abbey in 1147 on the lands of Henry de Lacy at Barnoldswick. Abbot Alexander found a new site near Leeds belonging to William of Poitou-a vassal of Henry de Lacy. On May 19th 1152 the monks transferred from Barnoldswick to Kirkstall with the first abbey built from local wood. The abbey was later rebuilt using Bramley Fall gritstone and by 1182 most of the abbey was completed. The abbey had vast estates with granges or farms managed by the lay brothers: trade in wool developed and export orders sought and obtained. On November 22nd 1539 Abbot John Ripley surrendered the abbey to the king's commissioners. The abbey was bought by Sir Robert Savile in 1584 and it remained with this family until 1671 when it passed through marriage to the Brudenells - Earls of Cardigan. Stone was taken to build roads and local Kirkstall houses and from 1799 the Butler family of Kirkstall Forge (leaseholders) carried out a conservation programme. In 1889 the Trustees of the Earl of Cardigan sold the abbey to Colonel John North for £10,000, who presented it to the City of Leeds. Conservation works were planned by architect John T Micklethwaite and the abbey was formally opened to the public on September 14th 1895 by the Bishop of Ripon and Lord Mayor of Leeds. Two oil paintings of the Abbey by John Bouttas (1735) are in the Abbey House Museum and show the tower complete.

KIRKSTALL ABBEY HOUSE was the abbey gatehouse, which became separated in 1827 by the new turnpike road. It was built in 1152-82; the last abbot John Ripley altered the gatehouse as a home where he lived until 1568 and was later buried under the floor. The Savile family owned the property from 1584 and it served as a farmhouse for 300 years to 1899 the Butler family leased it from the Earls of Cardigan and converted it to a gentleman's residence. In 1841 Abbey House was altered with a west wing and restored gatehouse as a home for George Skirrow Beecroft MP (1809-69) of Kirkstall Forge. In 1869/70 more extensions were added by John Octavius Butler (1812-83) of Kirkstall Forge and in 1889 it was bought by Col Thomas Walter Harding of the Tower Works Holbeck who owned the property until 1912 - he completed a restoration which included stained glass and carved oak. The buildings were sold to the City Council in 1925 and it was opened as Abbey House Folk Museum on July 11th 1927. The Victorian streets were opened with Abbey Fold in 1954, Harewood Square in 1955 and Stephen Harding Gate in 1958. A bid was lodged with the Heritage Lottery in November 1996 - approval of £1.65 million was given a year later with the remainder from the City Council and the Friends of Leeds City Museums. In Spring 1998 the museum was closed for a £2.3 million restoration and alteration: it re-opened on Saturday 20th January 2001. The restored museum includes the history of Kirkstall Abbey, Victorian Leeds and a Childhood Gallery. There is an undertaker's workshop, Sunday School, Taylor's chemist's shop, pub and pawnbroker's shop on re-constructed streets.

KITCHINGMAN, ROBERT (1616-1716) was a merchant in Leeds who lived at Allerton Hall: the hall was sold in 1755 by James Kitchingman to Josiah Oates-another Leeds merchant. He married Mary Robinson, daughter of Alexander & Grace - she was the sister of John Harrison. Mary's brother was Rev Henry Robinson Vicar of Leeds from 1632 to 1646. Members of the family are buried in the old churchyard of St Matthew's Church Chapel Allerton: John Kitchingman (died 1818) with the Wibsey branch of the family represented by blacksmith John Charles Kitchingman. The family were concerned with civic life: Thomas was Mayor of Leeds (1688) with son James being Mayor in 1702 - they were both interred in Leeds Parish Church and the grave slabs are in the chancel floor. Allerton Hall became the home of banker William Williams Brown and afterwards Rt Hon William Lawies Jackson MP, 1st Lord Allerton (1840-1917). Allerton Hall was demolished and the site became Wensleydale Court.

KITSON FAMILY in Leeds trace their ancestors over four centuries: James Kitson died in 1551. James Kitson Snr (1807-1885) was the son of licensee Thomas Kitson of the Brunswick public house on Camp Road. He married Ann Newton (1806-65) and moved to Hunslet in 1835 to found his engineering business. This Airedale Foundry under James Kitson built the first locomotive in 1837 with Charles Todd. The Monksbridge Iron & Steel Co was started in 1851 and it was bought by James Kitson in 1854 for his sons James and Frederick. James Kitson of Elmete Hall was Mayor of Leeds in 1860-61 and he laid the foundation stone for Leeds General Infirmary on March 29th 1864. Sir James Kitson (1835-1911) of Gledhow Hall was a senior partner at the Monkbridge works: he was the last Mayor of Leeds in 1896 and the first Lord Mayor in 1897. He was created an Honorary Freeman of Leeds on May 23rd 1906 and was raised to the peerage as Lord Airedale in 1907. A silver punch bowl dated 1889 marking his election as Lord Mayor is on display at the Civic Hall. Lord Airedale died on March 22nd 1911 aged 75 and was buried at St John's Church Roundhay - a memorial service was held at St Margaret's Church London. The Hon Albert Ernest Kitson became Lord Airedale on the death of his father and with his wife Florence (Schunck) lived at Cober Hall Cloughton near Scarborough - the baronetcy has been dissolved with the last Lord Airedale having lived in Stamford. Frederick James Kitson became Lord Mayor in 1908 - he was the son of Frederick William Kitson (Lord Airedale's brother 1829-77). FJ Kitson's niece was Jessie Beatrice Kitson who was elected the first woman Lord Mayor following the death of Arthur Clark in November 1942. Col Geoffrey Kitson (died 1974) was Lord Airedale's grandson who was Pro-Vice Chancellor of Leeds University and a President of Leeds Chamber of Commerce: his wife Kathleen died aged 89 in 1992.

KNIGHTS TEMPLARS (The Poor Knights of Christ and of the Temple of Solomon) received the gift of the Manor of Whitkirk which included land within Leeds: in later times landholders of previous Templar property marked their property with a Templar Cross to signify their exemption from grinding their corn at the manorial corn mill in Swinegate. The Knights Templars had their origin in the Crusades, being the wars undertaken between 1096 and 1291 to recover the Holy Land from the Moslems. The pilgrims on the road to Palestine were protected by the Templars which was an order instituted in 1118/19. The Templars had their home in Jerusalem on the east side of the Temple given by King Baldwin II of Jerusalem: members of the order were divided into Knights, Squires and Servitors and all the classes had their characters of piety and courage. In 1146 the Pope allowed the Knights Templars to wear a red cross on their white cloaks, as a symbol of martyrdom to which they were being constantly exposed. The first Templar house was founded in 1128 and to raise money for their work they established preceptories. In England their centre was at The Temple London, where their round church survives. A preceptory was established at Neuhusum in 1155 by William de Villiers, who gave the Manor together with Whitkirk Church to the Templars; the order had about 50 preceptories in Britain. Their preceptory near the river was archaeologically investigated in 1989 but was destroyed by opencasting at the Skelton site in 1991-92. In 1308 King Philip IV of France with papal authority suppressed the order: the Templars were abolished in England by 1312 although their estates had been confiscated in 1308; their lands were bestowed on the Knights Hospitallers (Order of St John of Jerusalem).

KONSTANT, RT REV DAVID MA was born in London in June 1930 and ordained priest in June 1954 by Cardinal Bernard Griffin, Auxiliary Bishop of Westminster in 1977 and was appointed the Bishop of Leeds on July 23rd 1985: he was installed as the eighth Bishop on September 25th 1985.

KRAMER, JACOB (1893-1962) was born in the Ukraine and attended Darley Street School, trained at Leeds College of Art from 1905 and then The Slade London; he founded the Yorkshire Luncheon Club. He painted the portraits of many including Frederick Delius (1862-1934), JB (John Boynton) Priestley (1894-1984), Dame Sybil Thorndike (1882-1976), Gracie Fields (1898-1979) and Mahatma Gandhi (1869-1948). A bust of Jacob Kramer by Jacob Epstein (1880-1959) is displayed in Leeds Art Gallery.

LACY This was the family who were given the Manor of Leeds by William the Conqueror: they held Pontefract Castle. It was Ilbert de Lacy who also held estates in France, Midlands and in Lincolnshire as well his Honour of Pontefract. Ilbert granted the Manor of Leeds to the Norman baron Ralph Paynel who gave it to the Holy Trinity Priory York in 1089. In 1152 Henry de Lacy gave the site by the river to the Cistercian monks for the foundation of Kirkstall Abbey - this followed the initial foundation in 1147 at Barnoldswick.

LADY LANE links Vicar Lane with St Peter's Street: it was the site of the Lady Lane Chapel and the Leeds Workhouse on the corner of Vicar Lane - also the site of the North Bar. The name derives from the presence of a chantry chapel in medieval times. Henry Thorn

& Co was founded in 1832 and their cocoa works on Lady Lane was a familiar sight and smell. The company was concerned with chicory, cocoa, chocolate, toffee, and ginger grinding. The Catholic church in Leeds was first established at the junction of Lady Lane and Templar Lane - the foundation stone was laid in April 1793 and the chapel opened in 1794. There was a priest's house and stables in which opened a girls school with help from Joseph Holdforth. By 1810 a boy's school was opened: in July 1831 St Patrick's Church was opened on York Road to replace the Lady Lane Chapel. The chapel became the United Methodist Chapel of the Lady Lane Central Mission and after use as offices, the building known as Templar House became derelict. Lady Lane/Templar Lane is the site of Alexandre's Tailors founded by Samuel Henry Lyons in 1906: the buildings date from 1921 and 1925 (Saxon Hawke House) with the extension opened in 1938 (foundation stones were laid by Samuel and Sophia Lyons). Circle House on the corner of Bridge Street dates from the early 1940's being built on the site of the offices for Lockhart's Restaurants and was the headquarters of the National Union of Tailors & Garment Workers-the initials are over the door. Lady Bridge spanned Sheepscar Beck, which flowed under Timble Bridge east of the Parish Church prior to the confluence with the River Aire.

LAIDLER, FRANCIS (1867-1955) was born at Thornaby on Tees, the son of Dr Joseph Laidler and was educated at Wharfedale College Boston Spa and Darlington Grammar School. He worked in a Stokesley bank and in 1888 moved to Bradford as secretary of the Hammonds Brewery. In 1902 he became a partner with Walter J Piper of The Prince's Theatre (demolished 1961) and built The Alhambra Theatre in 1914. In 1909 he presented his first pantomime at the Theatre Royal (Babes in the Wood); in 1911 he acquired the lease of the Theatre Royal Lands Lane Leeds and assumed control of the Keighley Hippodrome Theatre. In 1944 the Theatre Royal was sold to the Yorkshire Theatres Ltd of which Francis Laidler was governing director. He became the King of Pantomime at his theatres and in 1945 his pantomime at the Theatre Royal ran over 22 weeks for 239 performances. In 1926 Francis Laidler married his second wife Gwladys Stanley who had been one of his principal boys; he was responsible for the success of Norman Evans and Albert Modley and featured The Sunbeams children's dance troupe from 1917. Francis Laidler's funeral service was held at Bradford Cathedral: buried at Nab Wood Cemetery.

LAMBERT'S YARD is named after Lambert's tea merchants and grocers: William Lambert died in 1919 aged 92. The Yard is the location of the oldest house in Leeds: a three decker half timbered house dating from about 1600. The site is one of the original 60 burgage plots and is earmarked for restoration: there are plans to develop 11 flats with three bars in the Yard.

LANDMARK LEEDS is represented by the Lands Lane pedestrianisation together with Albion Place, Commercial Street, Albion Street and Bond Street in 1991-92. The terracotta signs were made by Shaws of Darwen and the area featured a fountain opened in April 1972 and removed in November 1989. The pedestrian precinct on Commercial Street and Bond Street was opened in November 1970 - officially on March 17th 1971. This was also the year in which the shops on Albion Street/Bond Street corner and Upper Basinghall Street were demolished for redevelopment.

LANDS LANE The Lands were the fields of the Lords of the Manor. The Trinity shopping centre was opened in December 1970; Lands Lane precinct and fountain were opened on April 12th 1972 by the Environment Secretary Peter Walker MP. The street was known for the Schofield's Store, Theatre Royal, Scala Cinema of which the façade is intact together with the original ballroom floor and the Church Institute with Mowbray's Bookshop on the corner of Albion Place. Shops that have closed include John Peters furniture store which was opened by the Lord Mayor on October 1st 1958 and Fosters (closed October 1974). King Charles Croft with the King Charles public house led to Red Hall - taken over by Schofields expansion and later demolished.

LAWSON, GODFREY (died 1709) was an alderman and Mayor of Leeds in 1669: he gave to the school a library building as an extension of the school, built by John Harrison in 1624. This public library was the first in Leeds and opened in 1691/92: mainly for the use of adults including the schoolmasters and trustees. The private Leeds Library in Commercial Street was opened in July 1808 having been in the Rotation Office in Kirkgate from 1768.

LAWSON HARDY'S was a boys and mens outfitters who opened a shop in Otley and came to Leeds c1936. The firm bought two shops in New Briggate - corner of Merrion Street - and were known for their displays of school ties and blazers. The firm became a subsidiary of Tritire Ltd and went into liquidation in June 1983: caused by the rent being increased by the owners London Guardian Royal Exchange Co.

LE PRINCE, LOUIS AIME AUGUSTIN (1842-1890) Born in Metz as the son of a French army officer he came to Leeds in 1866 after meeting engineer Joseph Whitley: he married his sister Elizabeth in 1869. He ran a School of Art in Park Square with his wife and went to the USA in 1881. He was again in Leeds in 1886 at Whitley's workshop on Woodhouse Lane where he built a single lens 16 frames a second film camera taking out a patent in 1888. He used this to make the world's first moving pictures from Hick's Ironmongers in October 1888 - the warehouse south of Leeds Bridge. Initially the photographs were printed onto glass but flexible celluloid was invented in November 1888: the 200' film shows the traffic passing across Leeds Bridge. He sailed for New York where his wife and family had been living for three years and where she had prepared a theatre for the demonstration at their New York mansion. He went to France to settle some family business and on September 16th 1890 Louis Le Prince boarded a train from Dijon to Paris - he never arrived. A metal plaque was unveiled on his workshop in Woodhouse Lane in 1930 by his daughter Marie and is displayed in the vestibule of BBC Radio Leeds: the plaque states that Le Prince was assisted by his son and by Joseph Whitley, James William Longley and Frederick Mason of Leeds. His son Adolphe was born in 1872 and was found shot on Long Island in 1901.

LEE, DENNIS was a stone and marble mason with his workshop at the end of Cobourg Street Woodhouse Lane. His mid-19th century work included monuments, tombs, tablets and gravestones with ornamental stone work and chimney pieces. Dennis Lee was responsible for the statue of Robert Hall (1857) in Leeds Town Hall.

LEEDS BABIES' WELCOME ASSOCIATION The first Welcome was opened on October 6th 1909 using four houses on Ellerby Road (Central) set up by the Yorkshire Ladies' Council. St Peter's Welcome opened in 1910 in The Good Shepherd Mission Rooms on St Peter's Square. In May 1913 the LBWA was formed and there were five centres by the end of 1912 with Armley Babies Welcome opening on August 9th 1928 by the Princess Royal. By the 1920's there were 18 centres with offices in Market Buildings Vicar Lane. In 1946 the National Health Service Act was passed - it started in July 1948: the Leeds Babies' Welcome Association ended in 1974 and in May 1988 a memorial was unveiled in the Clarendon Wing at the LGI.

LEEDS CLUB on Albion Place was established at a meeting held on March 23rd 1849 as the Union Club in the Leeds Stock Exchange - built on the site of an early reservoir. The Club leased two houses on the north side of Albion Place from Mr Martin and these were purchased in 1861 for £5300. Plans for extensive alterations were submitted by both Cuthbert Brodrick and Perkin & Backhouse although it was the scheme by Thomas Ambler which was accepted and completed in 1864. There were initially 150 members who paid a 15 guinea entrance fee and an annual subscription of 4 guineas. This private club still occupies the building at which ladies were accepted as members in 1984.

LEEDS CROSS There was a church in Leeds from the 7th century probably built in wood by Paulinus, burnt by King Penda of Mercia in 633 and was then rebuilt in stone. Proof of the Saxon churches is shown by the fragments of six crosses and the reconstructed free standing cross in St Peter's Church today. The Leeds Crosses are early 10th century of local stone: they survived to the 15th century and were cut up for use in the central tower. In 1838 Robert Chantrell produced plans for repairs to the old church and during the dismantling of the tower many pieces of carved stone were discovered. In reconstruction new stones were carved and he added a cross from another structure - the completed pillar featuring Wayland the Smith was erected in his garden at Oatlands House Little London. In 1863 he moved it to his retirement house Ivy Cottage at Rottingdean, east of Brighton East Sussex. Chantrell died in 1875 and after negotiations son Francis Chantrell agreed that the reconstructed cross be returned to Leeds Parish Church. Dr John Gott (Vicar 1873-1886) had asked for the cross to be returned to Leeds, where it was placed in the church in 1880. Six pieces of crosses discovered during the dismantling of the old church were donated by Chantrell to the Museum in 1856. A further section was found at Bramham in 1987, probably originating from the Parish Church and showing a priest flanked by acolytes, holding a chalice and a paten.

LEEDS DEVELOPMENT CORPORATION was formed in 1982 by the Leeds City Council and private enterprise: it was disbanded in March 1995.

LEEDS FLOWER SHOW had its conception in 1924 as the Ayrsome Terrace Show due to the site location. This became The Roundhay Show and later Roundhay Leeds Show and in 1976 The Leeds Show was held on Soldier's Field Roundhay under the auspices of the Leeds Horticultural Society. Financial difficulties caused the 1999 Show to be member's only and in 2000 the LHS held The Leeds Flower Show at Leeds Grammar School Alwoodley Gates, where the 25th Show was held in 2001.

LEEDS IN BLOOM The annual competition is part of the Leeds Flower Initiative which was established in 1991. The Initiative creates a partnership between the people of Leeds, the business community and the City Council. Leeds in Bloom includes the Gardens Competition and the children's Design Competition.

LEEDS PALS were formed by the Lord Mayor and the City in September 1914: the Pals were members of the 15th (Service) Battalion (1st Leeds) of The Prince of Wales Own (West Yorkshire Regiment): 93rd Brigade/31st Division. On December 7th 1917 they amalgamated with the 17th Battalion to form the 15th/17th Battalion. Initially the main recruiting offices were in Hanover Square and in the Tramway Depot in Swinegate but the main Pals recruitment was held at the Victoria Hall in the Town Hall from September 3rd 1914. The Battalion trained at a special camp site in Colsterdale where a memorial was unveiled and dedicated on September 28th 1935. A memorial at Leeds Parish Church was unveiled on July 1st 1931.

LEEDS POTTERY was founded c1770 by Richard Humble, John Green and Joshua Green on Jack Lane Hunslet: the factory produced Leeds creamware. The factory closed in 1881 and all the buildings were demolished.

LEEDS RIFLES was first raised in 1859 when the Volunteer Force was formed to meet the threat of invasion by France as the 7th Yorkshire, West Riding (Leeds) Rifle Volunteer Corps. Their first barracks were in Park Street and in the 1880's The Leeds Rifles became a Volunteer Battalion of The Prince of Wales's Own (West

Yorkshire Regiment). The Leeds Rifles bought the old militia barracks at Carlton Hill and in 1888 completed a new drill hall - the old entrance on the present Carlton Hill still bears the name Leeds Rifles. The Leeds Rifles saw active service in the Boer War where they were awarded their first battle honour - a memorial to those who died was unveiled in Leeds Parish Church. The Volunteer Force became the Territorial Force in 1908 and the unit became two battalions-the first line serving in the Great War in Flanders. The second line battalion saw active service in 1917 and fought to recapture Marne - they were awarded the Croix de Guerre in 1918 for gallantry in capturing Bligny Ridge; about 2050 members of The Leeds Rifles died on active service. Both Leeds Rifles Battalions reformed in 1920 and in the late 1930's the 8th Battalion was converted to the anti-aircraft role as the 66th (Leeds Rifles) Heavy Anti-aircraft RA (TA) seeing active service in Britain and the Far East. The 7th Battalion became a tank unit, which was expanded to form two regiments: they fought in both North Africa and Italy. In 1961 the Battalions became infantry and were amalgamated to become The Leeds Rifles The Prince of Wales's Own Regiment of Yorkshire (TA) and in 1967 a new Volunteer Regiment (Yorkshire Volunteers) was formed. In 1969 The Leeds Rifles became E (Leeds Rifles) Company at Leeds and the C Company was formed in Castleford in 1971. In 1993 The Leeds Rifles were serving as a Company of 3rd Battalion The Prince of Wales's Own Regiment of Yorkshire. As a consequence of The Strategic Defence Review of 1998 The Leeds Rifles were reduced to a platoon of Imphal Company the East & West Riding Regiment based at Harewood Barracks on Regent Street/Skinner Lane. The Leeds Rifles comrades hold an annual service and march past at Leeds Parish Church.

LEEDS UNITED FOOTBALL CLUB The first football club in Leeds was in 1885 founded by Leonard Cooper. In 1887 Leeds played at Kirkstall and Leeds Albion at Brudenell Road and thence to Armley. In 1894 the West Yorkshire League was formed with the Leeds club formed on February 22nd 1894. Leeds transferred to Headingley in June 1894 and ceased to exist as a club. Hunslet Club played adjacent to the Rugby Club at Parkside but the club ended in 1902: the first match at Elland Road was Hunslet v Harrogate on April 23rd 1898. The new club which came out of the

Hunslet Club was Leeds City: they took over the Hunslet Club's Elland Road site in 1904: in November 1904 a lease was signed and the match Leeds City v Hull City took place. In April 1905 Leeds City Co Ltd was formed and the new company built the west stand. The first match in the Football League was held on September 2nd 1905. In 1913 the Leeds City Club ceased to exist following a scandal and the new club as Leeds United was elected to the Midland League on October 31st 1913 and in 1920 was elected to the Football League with eventual promotion to the first division. The club was elected to Division Two and entered the First Division in 1924 and in 1964 stayed in the top division for 18 years: Leeds United won the FA Cup in 1972. The parent company of Leeds United FC is Leeds Sporting. It was proposed in 2001 that a new £40 million stadium be built on a different site.

LEEDS & YORKSHIRE ASSURANCE COMPANY was founded in 1824 for the transaction of fire, life and annuity business and they established fire brigades in Leeds, Bradford, Halifax, Huddersfield and Wakefield. Their headquarters were on the corner of Albion Street and Commercial Street designed by Bristol based architect William Bruce Gingell using millstone grit from Bramley Fall, Pool Bank and Rawdon Hill quarries. In 1864 the Leeds & Yorkshire was sold to The Liverpool & London Fire and Life Insurance Co (established 1836). The company also acquired the Globe Insurance Co of London and altered its name to The Liverpool & London & Globe Insurance Ltd. In 1864 the Head Office of the Leeds & Yorkshire became a branch office of Leeds & London & Globe and remained until 1964. The shares had been acquired in 1918 by Royal Insurance and in 1964 the two staffs were merged with a new building on Park Row.

LEEMING & LEEMING John Leeming (1849-1931) and brother Joseph (1841-1929) were the sons of Alfred Leeming of Halifax. They started their architectural practice in Halifax in 1872: their work in Leeds was the new Leeds Market building (1904) with the Potts clock removed to Oakwood (marked by a Civic Trust blue plaque) in July 1912.

LEGAL & GENERAL ASSURANCE SOCIETY LTD is based in Zicon House on Wade Lane: it was founded in 1836 by six London lawyers and incorporated in 1920. The firm was once on South Parade: the building opened as Son Carlo Restaurant in Autumn

2001.

LEIGHTON STREET runs south from Great George Street and was named after Isabel Leighton who founded a charity for the schooling of poor children in the 17th century: she was married to Dr Alexander Leighton. Centaur House and the new Nuffield Hospital are features of the street.

LEISURE SERVICES department of Leeds City Council is made up of six divisions. *Support Services* provides finance, human resource, administration and property management; *Library & Information* has a network of 57 local libraries and 7 mobile libraries; specialist services include Local and Family History, Braille and large print services and a prison library service; *Museums & Galleries* manages Abbey House & Kirkstall Abbey, Armley Mills Industrial Museum, Art Gallery, Lotherton Hall, Temple Newsam House and Thwaite Mills; *Arts, Promotions & Tourism* is responsible for a programme of annual events including the International Concert Season and Breeze, Party/Ballet and Opera in the Parks and the Leeds Lights: the department operates Leeds Town Hall, Civic Theatre, Pudsey Civic Hall; *Parks & Countryside* involves managing the city parks, 440 sports pitches, 156 nature reserves, 3500 allotments, 12 national plant collections, 185 playgrounds, 4 million trees, 25 cemeteries & crematoria together with many miles of public rights of way: the division also manages the Home Farm at Temple Newsam, Lotherton Bird Garden and Roundhay's Tropical World; the *Sport Division* includes a network of 24 sports centres and pools including the International Pool and South Leeds Stadium. Leisure Services make a financial contribution (£2.25 million annually) to organisations including the Grand Theatre, Opera North, Northern Ballet, Phoenix Dance, West Yorkshire Playhouse and Yorkshire Dance.

LEWIS'S was opened on September 17th 1932 as one of the largest department stores in the North of England: only the lower floor was opened at first with completion of the remainder in 1938. The site cost £160,000 and the building cost £750,000 with design by architects Atkinson & Shaw. The department store locked its doors and turned away staff and shoppers on February 1st 1991 after the company went into receivership; Lewis's Department Store was sold to Allders in 1996.

LEYLANDS was an area bounded by Skinner Lane, North Street, Regent Street and Lady Lane. The name derived from a farm in the area in the early 18th century. It was in a slumlike area with back-to-back housing that the dedicated and hard working Jewish community lived and prayed. Jewish immigrants from Russia and Poland settled in The Leylands most being attracted to the developing clothing industry. The Russian pogroms of 1881 brought more Jews to Leeds and the community numbered c20,000 by 1914. One of these immigrants was Michael Marks who lived in Trafalgar Street and started his market stall in Leeds in 1884. Education in The Leylands was served by Gower Street School (1875) - now a Chinese restaurant; Lovell Road School (1901)- closed in the early 1990's; Darley Street School (1895) where Jacob Kramer was educated and Newtown School (1875). The Jewish population moved north from the Leylands area which was gradually demolished from 1907-08 starting south of Trafalgar Street: in 1937 the remainder of the area was demolished. There were two Anglican churches in The Leylands area: St Thomas's Church on Melbourne Street (1852/1893) and St Luke's Church (1841) on the corner of Skinner Lane - both have been demolished.

LIBRARIES The *Leeds Library* in Commercial Street started in 1768 when it occupied the ground floor of the Rotation Office Kirkgate. It was Rev Dr Joseph Priestley of Mill Hill Chapel who was the inspiration for a private library, which moved to the new building by Thomas Johnson on Commercial Street in July 1808- the site had been bought in 1806. The library was on the top floor while the ground floor had a newsroom and shops; Robert Chantrell made alterations to the library building in 1821-35 with extensions in 1881 by Thomas Ambler. A new subscription library was opened in Albion Street (Park Row 1826) in 1793 mainly for those who came out of the Leeds Library membership. The Public Libraries Act was adopted in Leeds in March 1869: the Lending Department opened on April 8th 1872 at the *Central Library* Infirmary Street and moved to the Municipal Buildings in 1884. The Municipal Buildings was given a £2.3 million refurbishment between July 1999 and July 2000. The project revealed the original Victorian features as designed by George Corson: included a barrel vaulted ceiling with columns, intricate mosaics, decorative fireplace and terracotta carved arches and window frames.

LIGHT A £100 million development by Halifax & St James Securities (Clerical Medical Investment Group) in The Headrow including the former Leeds Permanent Building - Bovis Lend Lease. The complex of Life Café, restaurant, late night venue, fashion store Proibito and offices. The 1960's annex attached to the Grade II listed building was demolished and replaced by a 13 screen 2900 seat multiplex cinema (Ster Century Cinemas) with underground car parking. The original LPBS building was built in 1932 by architect Sir Reginald Blomfield and this is linked to the new section by a glass roofed street which will house a restaurant, bar and fitness club. The Light opened on Monday November 12th 2001 and features the 150 bedroom four star Radisson SAS International Hotel.

LIGHTDOWN, ASPINALL & CO were manufacturers of paper hangings on Gascoigne Street Boar Lane: opened in 1891.

LINDLEY, SIMON (born 1948) was appointed organist and Master of the Music at Leeds Parish Church in 1975 succeeding Dr Donald Hunt having been the first full time assistant organist at St Alban's Abbey. He was born in London the son of an Anglican priest and a writer. He was educated in Oxford and the Royal College of Music. Simon Lindley became deputy organist at the Roman Catholic Westminster Cathedral (1969-73) and was appointed Leeds City Organist in January 1976. Simon Lindley presented a 25th anniversary concert on the Town Hall organ on Monday January 8th 2001. He was senior lecturer in music at Leeds Polytechnic until 1987 and is a senior assistant music officer for the City Council, concerned with the International Concert Season. He is also Music Director of St Peter's Singers and Chamber Orchestra and is closely involved with many aspects of music making in the county. Simon Lindley was president of the Royal College of Organists for a two year period and is a respected soloist, author, composer, accompanist and recording artist. He was awarded a Doctorate by the Leeds Metropolitan University in 2001.

LIPTON'S was established at 18 Kirkgate c1882 by Thomas Johnstone Lipton in the former premises of Reuben Wormald. The shop was initially a tea merchant but developed into a general provisioner: it closed on February 4th 1984 having been taken over by Argyle Foods of London in 1983.

LITTLE KING STREET features a single stone pillar from the original Leeds Infirmary on Infirmary Street and there is a gas lamp on the corner of a building. The junction of Little King Street with Wellington Street features Wharf Street public house and Wellington House - opened by Ron Todd (General Secretary of the TG&WU) on January 31st 1990; it is the headquarters of the WYPTA.

LITTLE LONDON is a residential area centred on Lovell Park Road/ Claypit Lane and the Oatlands: the estate was first occupied in January 1972. Little London was named because it was a fashionable area with interesting architecture and expensive mahogany used in many houses: comparable with parts of London. St Matthew's Church was on Camp Road and was consecrated on August 13th 1851: there was a vicarage, schoolroom and parish room - demolished in June 1967. Carlton Hill is a redeveloped road now starting on the north side of the Inner Ring Road but once started from Woodhouse Lane: Carlton Barracks are still occupied but the Carlton Cinema was closed and demolished in 1965 for redevelopment. The Victory Cinema on Camp Road was opened in August 1920 and closed in January 1959 prior to demolition. Little London Primary School was opened in 1974 and re-opened on September 8th 1999 following an arson attack on the original building in November 1995. The first Little London Gala was held in July 1973 and the Community Centre opened in 1979. The demolished Windsor Castle public house was rebuilt on Carlton Parade and renamed The Leeds Rifleman in July 1984 - on the 125th anniversary of the founding of The Leeds Rifles regiment.

LITTLE WOODHOUSE is the area centred round Woodhouse Square, where the statue of Sir Peter Fairbairn faces the Town Hall. The area was developed with fine merchant's houses at the end of the 18th century and the 19th century: Woodhouse Square was being developed in the 1820's. Little Woodhouse Hall on Clarendon Road was first built in 1740 as a manor house for Christopher Thompson and in 1793 was with Thomas Coupland. In 1822 John Atkinson had the Hall - his son lived at Waverley House on Woodhouse Square. In 1855 the Hall was sold to the Council as a Judge's Lodging and later it became an art college and in 1973 was divided into six apartments with further development in 2001. The Hostel of the Resurrection or Priory of St Wilfrid on Springfield Mount was designed by Temple Moore in 1908 and finished by his son in law Leslie Moore in 1928. The Community of the Resurrection was founded at Oxford by Charles Gore in 1892 being a community of priests and one of the few Anglican monastic orders. Charles Gore (1853-1932) was Bishop of Worcester (1902-05), Bishop of Birmingham (1905-11) and Bishop of Oxford (1911-19): under his influence the Oxford Tractarian Movement based on authority and tradition reached a reconciliation with a modern critical scientific and liberal outlook. In 1898 the Community was established at Mirfield where a College for training candidates for holy orders was set up in 1903. The Community of the Resurrection opened their Leeds establishment to provide training for a degree in Theology for students prevented through lack of money from going to Oxford. In 1976 the building was bought by Leeds University for the Department of Continuing Education. The University Department of Adult Education was established in 1946 set up by Sidney Raybould (1904-77) and Fred Sedgwick (1910-76). Sidney Raybould was Director of Extramural Studies at the University from 1946 and the Professor from 1953 to 1969. Fred Sedgwick was the District Secretary of the Yorkshire North District of the WEA. Springfield Place was developed by Quaker stuff merchant Newman Cash who bought Springfield Lodge in 1839; Hillel House dates from the mid 19th century and was the home of oil merchant RJ Ellershaw; Belle Vue House was built in 1792 and the home of Thomas George: Mayor of Leeds in 1855 and 1868; Highfield House was built in 1862 for dyer George Hirst. Hyde Terrace once had the Maternity Hospital opened on May 23rd 1910 by actress Mrs Kendall and Lord Mayor William Penrose-Green in the former home of J Ellershaw Pepper, who gave the property to the Hospital committee. The Leeds Maternity Home was first opened in December 1905 by the Marchioness of Zetland in Spring House Caledonian Road, which was endowed by the March sisters. The maternity hospital closed on November 19th 1983 and former Mount Hotel (closed November 1975 and bought by the Leeds Area Health Authority, demolished 2001) are to be replaced with the building of a four storey community mental health residence and day centre (Leeds Community & Mental Heath Services). George Corson built 9/13 Hyde Terrace for WD Heaton. The Little Woodhouse and Clarendon Road CAP Scheme is a Conservation Area Partnership initiated in 1996 by Leeds City Council, English

Heritage and Heritage Lottery Fund. Projects costing £300,000 have restored Swarthmore Education Centre, 37/38 Hanover Square, Claremont and Fairbairn House. (ref: Clarendon Road/ Hanover Square/Swarthmore/Woodhouse Square)

LITTLEWOODS STORE was opened in 1952 in the closed Hitchen's store building; the former corner shoe shop of Stead & Simpson was later included. The store was rebuilt and was reopened on May 21st 1970 by the Lord Mayor Ald Arthur Brown. This Littlewoods Store was closed in 1997 with transfer to the White Rose Centre. The building in Kirkgate was taken by Marks & Spencers in 1998 - they closed this branch in 2001. The Littlewoods Organisation was started in 1923 as Littlewoods Pools by John Moores, who was knighted in 1972: he was born in 1896 at Eccles and retired in 1982. In 1932 they started a retail mail order business and in 1937 opened their first store at Blackpool.

LIVETT, RICHARD ALFRED HARDWICK (1897-1959) was born at Balham London and became Deputy Director of Housing in Manchester; in Leeds he lived on Gledhow Valley Road. He was appointed Leeds Director of Housing in 1934 and in 1946 was appointed Leeds City Architect: he was responsible for the design of the Quarry Hill Flats and estates including those at Gipton, Seacroft, Belle Isle, Halton Moor and Ireland Wood. He became a member of the RIAB in 1922 and was later awarded the OBE.

LOFTHOUSE PLACE to the east of Blackman Lane is the site of Blenheim Primary School and Nursery. On the north side was the home and business of ice cream maker Michael Ambrose whose carts were a frequent sight in Leeds; the Eldorado Ice Cream Co had their premises at 89 Woodhouse Lane.

LOIDIS IN ELMET was the name given to the "regio" or district by the Venerable Bede (c673-735) in his Historia Ecclesiastica Gentis Anglorum (731) - the Venerable Bede is buried in the Galilee Chapel in Durham Cathedral. The name he gave (Regio Quoe Vocatur Loidis) was later restricted to the main place in the district and refers to the river: later spellings were Ledes (1086), Leddes (1108) and Leedes (1185).

LOINERS probably refers to the yards and closes of Briggate whose back entrances were called "low-ins" or loins (lanes).

LONGLEY, WALTER (1846-1930) commenced working in the family business in 1865 which had been founded by Joseph

Longley in 1835 in a first floor room on Lands Lane; in 1886 the business moved to another building on Lands Lane. In 1871 he married Emma Dearden (died 1908) living at Park View Newton Road - he bought Larchfield Mills Hunslet which he remodelled and was involved in other property transactions including two sites on Vicar Lane (Coronation and Crown Buildings). He bought an old skating rink on Reginald Terrace and used this as his own factory. In 1896 he paid £35,000 for the Marshall & Snelgrove building in Bond Street and in the same year sold it to Eagle Life Insurance for £48,750. In February 1896 he bought the National Provincial Bank on Albion Street/Bond Street corner and a month later sold it to Pearce Jewellers: it later became the Yorkshire Post office. In 1888 Walter bought premises on New York Street which were gutted in a fire in 1894 - he rebuilt and reopened a year later. Walter Longley opened his Lands Lane premises in 1903 and then opened the Borough Mills factory in 1919 on Great Wilson Street - Longley's Bedding Specialists closed in 1964 having involved five generations of the family.

LOOKER'S OF LEEDS were a car dealership based at Central Garage in Woodhouse Lane - now the site of St John's Shopping Centre. The business opened on Burley Road in 1966 and closed their central Leeds branch on February 11th 1983.

LORD MAYORS were appointed from June 1897 being a title bestowed on the chief magistrate. The first Lord Mayor was Sir James Kitson MP who had been appointed Mayor of Leeds in 1896. The second Lord Mayor was Thomas Walter Harding followed by John Gordon - his wife Mary was remembered in the name of a steam boat on Waterloo Lake Roundhay Park.

LOVELL PARK on North Street was the site of Smithfield Market (1855-1886) and was landscaped to be opened in 1888: it once had a bandstand and bowling green.

LOWRY, MORGAN was born in Leeds with premises on Briggate and Boar Lane. He was responsible for the repair of the clock of St John's Church for the sum of 13 shillings and made a longcase clock c1730 on display in Abbey House Museum.

LUCCOCK, JOHN DARNTON (1808-84) was for 42 years an alderman of Leeds: he is buried at Lawnswood Cemetery. He was Lord Mayor in 1845-46 & 1864-65 and laid the foundation stone for the Dispensary on North Street on October 19th 1865. His father was John Luccock (1770-1826) who was a merchant and wool stapler of Leeds. His portrait by Sydney Hodges is in Leeds Civic Hall.

LUPTON It was Francis Lupton who bought the Goodman's House estate at Roundhay in 1860: renamed it Beechwood and engaged George Corson to design the lodgehouse. Francis was born in 1813 and married Frances Greenhow in 1847 and their family lived at the Hall, which became a centre for both cultural and civic activities. During the 18th century the family were involved in marketing cloth in Europe with a Lupton surviving the great earthquake in Lisbon in 1755 - he was in Lisbon on business. Arthur Lupton (1748-1807) was a schoolfellow of the German poet Goethe. Frank Lupton (1848-1901) was involved with slum clearance and held office on Leeds City Council, promoting the modernisation of houses for a moderate rent. Charles Lupton (1855-1935) gave the impetus for The Headrow redevelopment - he gave 50 years of service to the LGI and was made a Freeman of Leeds in 1926. Arthur Greenhow Lupton (1850-1930) was the first Pro-Vice Chancellor of Leeds University (1904-20) and a pioneer in the supply of electricity for the city. He was a senior partner in William Lupton & Co - he died on February 8th 1930. His brother Hugh Lupton (1861-1947) served many years on the City Council; members of this great Leeds family are buried on the south side of St John's Church Roundhay. Darnton Lupton was the Mayor of Leeds in 1844; Charles Lupton was Lord Mayor in 1915 and Hugh Lupton in 1926.

LYDGATE was the area north of The Headrow to Woodhouse Lane: it once featured Woodhouse Bar stone-the northern boundary. Lydgate was an area of houses, crofts and tenter with gardens and orchards. One of these houses was Fairfax House on the corner of Wormald Row and other well known Leeds families with properties in Lydgate were Blayds (Calverley), Brown and Sheepshanks. The Lydgate area also once featured the original reservoir for Leeds fed by pumps from Leeds Bridge.

MABGATE links Skinner Lane with Eastgate/Regent Street: Mab was the name of a female fairy and bringer of dreams. The name could have been given to a "loose woman" with Mabgate being an early days "red light area". Mabgate Beck runs to the west of

Mabgate and is part of Sheepscar Beck. The Hope Foundry which occupied both sides of Mabgate was founded in 1812 by Samuel Lawson - closed 1930: the firm were iron and brass founders. The impressive gateway with an inscribed stone announcing "Hope Foundry" is now the entrance to small businesses and Hope House. Hope House on the corner of Hope Street and Mabgate is dated 1910. The two public houses on Mabgate have historical connections: The City of Mabgate with its green tile façade dates c1857; the Black Horse was originally Mabgate Hall (1673) later the Black Bull Inn and was rebuilt in 1868. There is a cholera burial ground opposite the City of Mabgate inn - many of the worn graves date from the cholera outbreak in 1832; Joseph Wainwright died in June 1832 aged 33, Naomi Oates of Pudsey who was raised as a Moravian at Fulneck died in September 1832 aged 32 and Charles Wain of Derwent Hall Derby died of cholera in August 1832 aged 77. Mabgate Mills is now a commercial centre on the corner of Skinner Lane: it was the premises of Walter Albrecht (c1901-c1922) and later saw a mixed use including H Taylor & Sons (1938-1978) as well as rag merchants, glaziers and printers. Mabgate was also the site for the clothing manufacturer JA Corner Ltd from c1935 to c1984 - the business was taken over by Firstneat and Topflight Leisure wear.

MACE The Great Mace of Leeds was made in 1694 by goldsmith Arthur Mangey of Briggate at a cost of £60/11 shillings and is insured for £20,000. It is inscribed and made of silver-gilt weighing nearly 6 kilograms. Arthur Mangey was executed in York on October 2nd 1696 being convicted of clipping coins: although he said he was innocent a pair of clipping shears was discovered in his Briggate workshop after his death. The Mace is an emblem of Royal Authority and is carried before the Lord Mayor at official ceremonies by the Sergeant-at-Mace.

McLAREN, SIR JOHN (1850-1921) was born near Sunderland and later lived at Highfield House Headingley. He was the Chairman of the Board of Control and pioneer in the establishment of the National Ordnance Munitions Factories at Armley and Barnbow. He ran the Midland Engine Works making agricultural machinery and steam ploughs on Jack Lane Hunslet which he founded with brother Henry McLaren: Sir John was the President of the Leeds Chamber of Commerce. He was knighted in 1919 and was the

Chairman of the Leeds Chamber of Commerce (1918).

MACLEA, CHARLES GASCOIGNE JP (1793-1864) was Mayor of Leeds in 1846 and succeeded by Sir George Goodman. He lived on Blenheim Terrace and was a member of the family firm of Maclea & March Dewsbury Road - makers of flax spinning machinery. He married a daughter of Matthew Murray and with no children he left much property to the children of JO March- he was buried at St Mark's Church Woodhouse in which there is a Caen stone font which he presented to the church.

MAGUIRE, TOM (1866-95) is remembered in a plaque in the bus station: *"pioneer socialist and trade unionist was born, lived and died in this area of Leeds"*. The plaque was erected by the Ford Maguire Society.

MALCOLM, JOHN COOPER (1831-1924) was born in Leeds of Scottish parents and for 44 years (1876-1920) was the Leeds Coroner who had been concerned with 30,000 inquests.

MALMAISON HOTELS were launched by Ken McCulloch with the backing of Robert Breare's Arcadian International Group: Arcadia and Malmaison were taken over in 1998 by Patriot American Hospitality with plans to expand the chain under the Wyndham International banner. The property owner Marylebone Warwick Balfour in 2000 paid £65 million for Malmaison Hotels and set up Malmaison Holdings with Scandinavian Airlines System (SAS). The Holdings purchased the Malmaison brand for £11 million with rights to worldwide expansion: in 2002 the former Birmingham Mailbox sorting office will open as a 180 room Malmaison Hotel.

MANDELA, NELSON ROLIHLAHLA (born 1918) was the organiser of the African National Congress and was imprisoned from 1964 until February 1990 becoming a symbol of unity for the anti-apartheid movement. He was president of the ANC from 1991 and in April 1994 he was elected President of South Africa: he was awarded the Nobel Peace Prize in 1993. The City of Leeds opened the Mandela Gardens in front of the Civic Hall on December 10th 1983 and Nelson Mandela came to the City to re-open the new gardens in Millennium Square on Monday April 30th 2001 when he also became an Honorary Freeman of Leeds.

MANNING WARDLE was an engineering business established in 1858 and was bought out by the Hunslet Engineering Works in

1926.

MANOR OF LEEDS was the name given in 1086 in the Domesday survey to the system operated by farmers who lived in their dwellings along Kirkgate. The manor was run from the moated manor house - on the site of the Scarbrough Hotel in the area of Mill Hill. The Leeds Park was a medieval enclosure from Park Row to the end of Wellington Street; the wooded Woodhouse Ridge was in the north and an area of "common land" was Woodhouse Moor. The manorial mill was sited on the River Aire and complete with goits - the Kings Mills. The Manor of Leeds was given to Ilbert de Lacy by William the Conqueror; most of this manor was given by Ilbert de Lacy to the Norman baron Ralph Paynel. The 162 manors of Ilbert de Lacy formed the basis of the Honour of Pontefract - the castle is known to have existed from 1088. Ilbert de Lacy acquired the estate c1076 and commenced the building of what was to be one of the largest castles in the north of England. In the first de Lacy period lands were lost in 1106 when after a rebellion Robert de Lacy was dispossessed by Henry I - they were returned after Henry's death in 1135. Henry de Lacy held the Honour of Pontefract from 1177 to 1194 and was the patron of Kirkstall Abbey which he had founded in 1152. Henry died without a male heir in 1311 and the lands passed to Thomas of Lancaster (nephew of Edward I). The Manor was a feudal estate which for 500 years from 1066 was the basic unit of local government. The Manor was held by the Lord of the Manor from the King and was worked by villeins with administration by a Manor Court (Court Baron and Court Leet).

MANOR HOUSE was on the site of the Scarbrough Hotel Bishopgate Street: in 1836 while excavating the foundations for a warehouse south of West Bar workmen discovered the moat which had a semicircular form terminating at mill goit.

MARATHON, LEEDS is run on a Sunday in May and was started in 1980: it is one of the top ten events in the country welcoming runners from all parts of Britain and abroad.

MARKETS A market in Leeds started in 1258 with an annual fair in Briggate from 1322. The Central Market on Duncan Street designed by Francis Goodwin had the foundation stone laid by Lepton Dobson on November 26th 1824 and it opened in 1827 costing £30,000 and had 67 shops and a covered hall with 56 stalls.

The South Market was designed by Robert Chantrell; the foundation stone was laid by George Banks in October 1824. The Market opened in 1825 at a cost of £22,000 on Meadow Lane -there were nearly 50 shops and 88 stalls: the cost was £22,000. The first quarterly leather fair was held there on October 17th 1827. The Bazaar and Shambles on Briggate were completed in 1826 and included butchers shops and a fish market. *Fish Market* started by selling produce in Briggate and then moved to the "free market" on Vicar's Croft: there were fish stallholders in the Central Market on Duncan Street. There were fish traders inside and outside the covered market (1857); the fish market was a row of buildings east of the complex of 1875. The *wholesale* fish market was opened at the junction of George Street and East Lane in 1894 due to a shortage of accommodation. *Kirkgate Market* had its origins in the purchase of the old Vicarage on Vicar's Croft on the corner of Kirkgate and Vicar Lane; the market stalls transferred to the site in 1826. The Leeds Improvement Act allowed for the expansion of the Kirkgate Market in 1846. In 1854 it was decided to erect the first Kirkgate Covered Market which opened in May 1857 with advice by Joseph Paxton; it was expanded in 1875 to the east and south (Leeds New Market: Butcher's Row, Game Row and adjacent rows). The market hall extended further east in 1888 and after a fire damaged the building in 1893 the market was extended again in 1898-1900; a new wholesale fish market was added in 1894. The roofing of the open square of the market was completed in 1901. John and Joseph Leeming of Halifax won a competition to rebuild the market, which was started in 1901 at a cost of c£80,000: the market was opened on July 1st 1904. The central clock made in iron of the new market hall was by Potts & Sons, which was removed to Oakwood in July 1912 by the Parks department when a central entrance was created on Vicar Lane with the re-arrangement of the stalls. There was damage to the market by an air raid in March 1941 and a new butcher's row was completed in 1954. On Saturday evening December 13th 1975 the market hall was nearly all destroyed by a fierce blaze. The 3.5 acre site was cleared by February 1976 and the new replacement hall was completed by July 19th with a further building ready on November 27th 1981 - all at a cost of £1.6 million. The fire affected the eastern end of the main market although the 1904 façade on Vicar Lane remained intact. The market had a £10 million refurbishment in 1993/95 as a joint venture with Norwich Union and the City Council and in 1996 there was a £2 million restoration of the 1875 building. The market today houses 450 indoor businesses with 220 outside stalls attracting 250,000 shoppers weekly. A Leeds Civic Trust blue plaque was unveiled by Richard Wainwright MP in January 2001. The *Kirkgate Outdoor Market* was opened on October 25th 1997 by Lord Mayor Coun Linda Middleton. The *Victoria Cattle Market* on Gelderd Road was opened on June 1st 1886 having transferred from North Street (opened 1853). The *Wholesale Market* on Pontefract Lane opened in 1965 with many tons of earth taken to Temple Newsam for landscaping - the market was closed in April 1988 and sold in 1990 followed by demolition the following year. The £4 million *Yorkshire Produce Centre* which replaced the former Leeds Wholesale Market was formally opened in August 2000 by Lord Mayor Bernard Atha. It is a privately run market which supplies caterers, retailers and wholesalers throughout the region; the market was bought by Leeds firms Gilbert Thompson and Ernest White Ltd.

MARKET CROSS was provided by merchant John Harrison in the top part of Briggate in 1619 for the sale of produce in sheltered conditions. This was replaced by a larger cross in 1776 on Briggate.

MARKET DISTRICT BOY'S CLUB was started by Rev Mackie c1920 above an archway at the end of Harper Street, moved to an alley near the Parish Church and then moved into their premises on Marsh Lane. The Club was to finally close in 1994; in 1993 the building became The Market Place and this was closed in 1998.

MARKS AND SPENCERS originated in Michael Marks Penny Bazaar in the Leeds covered market (1857) in 1884. It was Isaac Dewhirst who had met Michael Marks in Kirkgate and lent him £5 with which Marks bought some goods from Dewhirsts for sale on his rounds. By 1884 the 25 year old Michael Marks had a stall in the Leeds Market with the popular slogan *"Don't ask the price - it's a penny"*. The second location in the market was in two brick built shops in 1896; while Marks visited other northern towns with his wares, the Leeds stall was looked after by Charlie Backhouse with some of the girls from the Dewhirst warehouse. Michael Marks was born in Russian Poland in 1863 and arrived in Leeds from

London looking for a job with Barran's clothiers. His stall at Leeds market sold cotton reels bought from Dewhirst's at 11 shillings a gross for just one penny. In 1886 Michael Marks married Hannah Cohen: Simon was born in 1888 and Rebecca in 1890. In 1894 Michael Marks asked Isaac Dewhirst to be his partner but he was too much involved with his own business: he suggested a partnership with Skipton born 43 year old Tom Spencer-Dewhirst's cashier and good book keeper. On September 28th 1894 Marks & Spencer was born: Michael Marks married Hannah Cohen in 1886 at the Belgrave Synagogue. Simon Marks (1888-1964) married Miriam Sieff in 1915 and became Lord Marks and Chairman of Marks & Spencer Ltd. In 1897 a Manchester warehouse became the new headquarters and the Marks family moved across the Pennines. The firm became a limited company in 1903 and Tom Spencer retired - he died in 1905; Michael Marks died in 1907 leaving over £25,000. In 1914 there were 140 shops and in 1926 became a public company with St Michael becoming the trademark in 1928; there were 234 stores by the outbreak of the last War and by 2000 there were nearly 290 stores in Britain. The Original Penny Bazaar opened in Cross Arcade in 1904 with five years later a new shop in Briggate: this was extended to Queen's Arcade in 1926. A new Briggate store was completed in 1940 on the site of the old Rialto Cinema but was requisitioned by the Ministry of Works: it was opened in 1951; the extension of Marks & Spencer on Briggate opened on January 23rd 1973. The former Littlewoods Store on Kirkgate/Briggate was bought by Marks & Spencers in 1998 and refurbished at a cost of £7.5 million: it was closed on May 5th 2001 following a £2 million refurbishment of the main Briggate store, which was officially re-launched on May 10th 2001. The Kirkgate store opened as Zara in October 2001 and Benetton is expected to open in 2002.

MAROCHETTI, BARON CHARLES (CARLO) (1805-67) was born in Turin and died in Paris having become a French citizen. He studied at the Ecole des Beaux Arts and worked mainly in bronze, marble and plaster. He sculpted the equestrian statue of Queen Victoria for George Square Glasgow and the equestrian statue of the Duke of Orleans for the courtyard of the Louvres Museum Paris. Marochetti sculpted the statue of the Duke of Wellington, which was bought by Leeds in 1855 at a sale of works of art from the Great Exhibition of 1851. It was erected outside the Town Hall on November 31st 1855 and was covered up prior to the opening by Queen Victoria in September 1858: it was moved to Woodhouse Moor in 1937.

MARSDEN, HENRY (HARRY) ROWLAND (1823-76) was born at Holbeck and educated at a Methodist Sunday School. He was apprenticed to a tool maker and machinist but emigrated to the USA in 1848 to make a fortune patenting Black's Stone Breaker. He returned to Leeds (Soho Factory) and became a Liberal councillor and was Mayor of Leeds (1873-75); he was the initiator of the Leeds Music Festival in 1874 and was buried in Holbeck Cemetery - his family are also remembered on the large memorial. The Carrara marble statue on Woodhouse Moor, transferred from the bottom of Woodhouse Lane, shows him in mayoral robes (John Throp 1878) and the stone included some remaining from the Albert Memorial in Hyde Park London. The statue was unveiled in March 1878 and cost c£900: transfer to Woodhouse Moor took place on June 17th 1952. Two silver candelabra were presented to Harry Marsden in November 1875 by the people of Leeds in recognition of his service; his portrait by Richard Walker is in the Civic Hall.

MARSH, JONES & CRIBB was established as John Kendell & Co in 1760 on Boar Lane/Basinghall Street. In 1850 the firm was bought by Edward Jones and Henry Cribb being cabinet makers, artists, decorators and upholsterers: the firm was the painting contractor for many palaces in St Petersburg (Russia). In 1890 new warehouses were built on Basinghall Street designed by Edward Birchall; they made high quality furniture and closed down in 1991.

MARSH LANE. The area was built up with housing and public houses; Marsh Lane railway station was the end of the Selby to Leeds line on opening on September 22nd 1834. The station was rebuilt when the line was extended to Leeds New Station in 1869; the station was closed on September 15th 1958.

MARSHALL, JOHN (1765-1845) had started in his father's Mill Hill premises and took over in 1787: changing from drapery to flax spinning. He leased Scotland Mill at Adel and with the help of Matthew Murray he changed the machinery from cotton to flax spinning. He moved to a water powered mill on Water Lane by

1792 with the addition of a wide range of new buildings. The mills were changed to steam power and John Marshall took on Thomas & Benjamin Benyon - increasing the product range and eventually had the largest and most successful flax spinning firm in England. Further expansion brought architect Ignatius Bonomi to design a new mill in 1838-40 with the office block having an Egyptian design based on the Temple of Horus at Edfu, completed in 1843. John Marshall was an active member of the Leeds Philosophical & Literary Society and the Leeds Mechanics Institute; he was elected Liberal MP for Yorkshire in 1826 and served until 1830. In 1832 his son John Marshall was elected as one of two Leeds MP's; his eldest son William was MP for Carlisle; third son James Garth was MP for Leeds (1847-52) and his fourth son Henry Cowper was Mayor of Leeds in 1842-43. John Marshall had married Jane Pollard and they had five sons and six daughters: he lived at New Grange - rented from the Wade family and later bought by William Beckett and renamed Beckett Park. He bought the Hallsteads estate on Ullswater in the Lake District as well as owning estates on Buttermere, Crummock Water and Loweswater: his sons were owners of estates on both Derwentwater and Coniston Water. Marshall Mills have been restored to office use while the Egyptian style factory is now Kay's Mail Order and the temple style office block remains in use as offices.

MARSHALL & SNELGROVE were founded in 1837 and incorporated in 1898; they opened their Leeds shop in 1870 being "silk mercers, drapers with carpets and furnishings": directors included EJ Marshall and ER Debenham. This high class Leeds store was on the corner of Bond Street and Park Row having a restaurant; an additional storey was later added. The store became part of the Debenham chain of stores: the building was demolished after closure on February 13th 1971 and in 1973 the building of the new Lloyds Bank was started which was opened three years later.

MASONIC HALLS on Great George Street: the first opposite the Town Hall was built in 1865-66 at a cost of £2500 and designed by Perkin & Sons: there were shops on street level and lodge and supper rooms on the first floor. The building became Leeds Juvenile Courts and in December 1995 opened as the Felon & Firkin. The second Masonic Hall was built in 1900 designed by JM Bottomley and is now Cathedral Chambers; sold in 1988 and opened as offices in June 1994. The third Leeds Masonic Hall was on Carlton Hill: opened in 1872 designed by William Bakewell.

MATCHAM, FRANK (1855-1920) was the London based architect who designed the re-development of east Briggate for the Leeds Estates Company - including the Leeds Empire Palace Theatre, opened on August 29th 1898; Matcham also was responsible for the London Palladium. He is buried in Highgate Cemetery London.

MATERNITY HOSPITAL was opened on May 23rd 1910 in the former home of JE Pepper on Hyde Terrace, who gave the property to the Hospital committee. The Leeds Maternity Home was first opened in 1905 by the Marchioness of Zetland in Spring House Caledonian Road. In 1918 St George's Vicarage was bought as a nurses home and the need for extra accommodation was sought. The foundation stone for the extension was laid by Princess Mary Viscountess Lascelles on January 26th 1928 (as Princess Royal she died in 1965): the extension was opened in 1930 by Mrs Stanley Baldwin. The hospital was closed and remains empty.

MATTISON, ALFRED (1868-1944) was educated at Jack Lane School and in 1888 joined the Leeds branch of the Socialist League and remained in the Labour Movement for 50 years. He was a prolific local historian who published an account of the first visit of Charles Dickens to Leeds in December 1847 when he spoke at the Leeds Mechanics Institute & Literary Society. Alf Mattison also compiled the Chronicles of Leeds and cuttings about Leeds Theatres; he published *The Romance of Old Leeds* in 1908 with Walter Meakin based on articles which had appeared in the Yorkshire Daily Observer. He died on September 4th 1944 after he was knocked down by a tramcar in Leeds.

MAY, PHIL (1864-1903) was a cartoonist who was born in New Wortley on April 22nd 1864 and died in London on August 5th 1903. He became well known for his work for Punch; he was educated at St George's National School and after a period living in Australia came back to Britain in 1888.

MAY, JOSEPH were clothing manufacturers of Whitehall Road. The firm was founded by Joseph May in 1859 on Wellington Street and became the producer of Maenson (May & Son) men's wear. The firm moved to Bean Ing Mills and then to New Park Street Mills until 1907; the firm ceased trading in 1970.

MAYORS OF LEEDS were first appointed in November 1661:

Thomas Danby was the first Mayor of Leeds to be followed in September 1662 by John Dawson. The appointment of the Mayors of Leeds followed the granting of the second charter in 1661 by King Charles II.

MAYORAL CHAIN was presented to Leeds in 1836 by James Kitson (1807-85) and is made of 24 carat gold: it is normally worn by the Lord Mayor on duty during the daytime.

MECCA LOCARNO BALLROOM in Cross Arcade/County Arcade opened on November 3rd 1938 and once featured Sir Jimmy Savile as the DJ. The Store opened in the old ballroom in 1983 and in 1994 this became a cafe.

MECHANICS INSTITUTE The Mechanics Institution and Literary Society was established on January 1st 1825, meeting first off Park Row. It amalgamated with the Leeds Literary Institute in 1842 and moved to new premises on South Parade. The Leeds Institute on Cookridge Street was designed by Cuthbert Brodrick with the foundation stone laid on August 31st 1865 by John Darnton Luccock; it was opened on June 1st 1868 at a cost was £20,000. The principal auditorium was the Albert Hall which was converted to the Leeds Civic Theatre after the last war.

MEDICAL SCHOOL was founded by a group of surgeons and doctors on October 25th 1831, hiring rooms in the Dispensary on the corner of Templar Street and Vicar Lane (North Street). The school was one of the first provincial medical schools in England - in 1834 they transferred the School to East Parade. A new school was built in Park Street (later Thackrays): designed by George Corson and opened by James Paget FRS on October 3rd 1865. This was followed by WH Thorp's larger School of Medicine opened in 1894 by the Duke and Duchess of York on Thoresby Place taking three years to complete. The large house of Mount Pleasant had been sold to the Yorkshire College by the Board of the Infirmary. In 1884 the Leeds School of Medicine and the Yorkshire College amalgamated and in 1910 the clinical teaching was transferred from the Infirmary to the University's control. In 1930-33 the west wing of the Medical School opened and the Algernon Firth Laboratories were added.

MELBOURNE STREET leads east from North Street to Bridge Street being parallel with Nile Street and Byron Street. St Thomas's Church was consecrated on February 2nd 1852 designed by William Butterfield costing £7000 paid for by the Rhodes family who owned the area. The chancel had the foundation stone laid on November 14th 1891 by the Countess of Harewood and consecrated on April 25th 1893. The church was closed and demolished for redevelopment. The street was named after Viscount Melbourne (1779-1848). William Lamb was Home Secretary (1830-34), Prime Minister (1834 and 1835-41) and married Lady Caroline Ponsonby - Lady Caroline Lamb; he was adviser to Queen Victoria.

MEMBERS OF PARLIAMENT were appointed by Leeds following the Reform Act of 1832. During the 19th century until the Redistribution Act of 1885 there were two members for Leeds and these included Edward Baines (Liberal), Sir John Beckett (Conservative), Sir George Goodman (Liberal), John Barran (Liberal), William Jackson (Conservative) and William Gladstone (Liberal). In 1885 the Act divided the borough into five divisions with one MP for each division; 1918-1950 there were six divisions and seven until 1955 with a reversion to six divisions until 1983. In this era were Sir Keith Joseph (NE Conservative), Denis Healey (East Labour), Hugh Gaitskell (South Labour), Alice Bacon (SE Labour) and Sir Donald Kaberry (NW Conservative). A reorganisation in 1983 had eight divisions with George Mudie representing Leeds East from 1992.

MERRION was the name chosen by William Lupton who built Merrion Street: it was the name of a castle 3 miles south east of Dublin City centre and remembered his company's links with Ireland. The castle was the home of the Fitzwilliam family (Earls of Pembroke & Montgomery) who acquired the Manors of Merrion and Baggotrath in the 15th century: Merrion Square was built in 1762 on the former manor lands. Merrion Castle dated from 1334 and was a ruin by 1729 when the family moved to Mount Merrion. The origin of the name Merrion is probably from Meirion meaning a dairyman.

MERRION CENTRE was formally opened by Mrs Marjorie Ziff on May 26th 1964: the cost was £6 million and the architects were Gillinson Barnett & Allen. The Chairman of Town Centre Securities was Marjorie's husband Arnold Ziff. The Centre's escalator was first used in February 1963; the first shop was opened in the Centre on December 4th 1963; the Bowling Alley was opened by Brian Close on March 25th 1964, Locarno Ballroom on May 29th 1964 (Tiffanys 1974) and the Odeon Merrion Centre opened on August 17th 1964: closed October 1st 1977 and seats removed in November 1984. The Merrion Centre is a property of Town Centre Securities plc.

MERRION STREET links New Briggate with Woodhouse Lane/ Great George Street. The street was created by the Luptons in 1830: a cloth factory and plots were taken up from 1832 with land sold for Belgrave Chapel in 1836. The small St John's Garden of Rest is a public space on glebe land with an impressive entrance and adjacent is St John's House opened in February 1930 in the mock Tudor style. This style is also seen at Nash's Fish Restaurant which occupies Kemplay's Academy for Young Gentlemen. On the corner of New Briggate was Lawson Hardy (mens outfitters) and Arthur Clues sports shop with adjacent S Woolfson furniture store are both now Harvey's cafe-bar.

MERRION STREET GARDEN OF REST is north of St John's Church and was created and is maintained by the Trustees of Wade's Charity as a memorial to Thomas Wade. The garden was created as a result of his will of February 1530 where money was left to be spent for the benefit of the citizens of Leeds. In 1890 a scheme for the application of the charity was confirmed under which the funds were to be applied in providing open spaces in Leeds - the Garden of Rest was one of the spaces created. The three quarter acre garden was opened in March 1933 and once featured a sundial.

MERRION WAY is the new name for Cobourg Street: the name was changed in 1967. The Brunswick Building of the Leeds Metropolitan University, Yorkshire Bank, Merrion Centre and the Grosvenor Casino all feature on this street. Tower House was opened in 1968 and JD Wetherspoon's Stick or Twist bar opened on November 28th 1997.

METRO is the other name for the West Yorkshire Passenger Transport Authority & Executive (WYPTA) based on Wellington Street. The Authority is made up from 22 councillors: it oversees and co-ordinates public transport (trains and buses) in West Yorkshire. They deal with 30 operators including FirstBus Leeds and Arriva.

METROPOLITAN DISTRICT of Leeds covers 562 square kilometres and is the second largest MD in Britain.

MIDDLEBROOK, SIR WILLIAM (1851-1936) was born at Birstall: his father John was a woollen manufacturer. He was a solicitor, married Alma Jackson in 1880 and lived in Morley until 1921. He was the Mayor of Morley, knighted in 1916 and raised to a baronetcy in 1930. He was the Lord Mayor of Leeds in 1910/1911 and was Chairman of the Leeds Workpeoples Hospital Fund and President of the Leeds Permanent Building Society; with Charles Lupton William Middlebrook MP raised a fund of £130,000 to enlarge the LGI as a memorial to King Edward VII.

MIDDLETON RAILWAY was started in September 1758 with a waggonway linking Charles Brandling's coal pits to the coal staith at Casson Close near Leeds Bridge. Brandling had started coal mining at Middleton c1701 with staiths at Thwaite Gate linked by a waggonway to the collieries - Ralph Brandling died in 1749 and Charles died in 1802. John Blenkinsop came to Middleton c1808 and ran a steam engine for the first time on a test track at the Round Foundry on August 12th 1811; this was on a rack and pinion railway, which he had patented in April 1811. The engine was tried on the waggonway on June 24th 1812. In January 1920 land was sold to the City of Leeds for an electric tramway: the Middleton Light Railway opened in November 1925 and closed in March 1959. The Trustees of Wade's Charity bought the land and buildings transferring the site to the City of Leeds: Middleton Park was opened and some land was sold for housing. The Middleton Railway Preservation Society was founded in 1959 and in June 1960 the Middleton Railway was operated by unpaid volunteers. Middleton finished as a pit village with the closure of the Broom Colliery in May 1968 and the preservation of the railway was run by the Middleton Railway Trust. The Coal Board left Broom Pit in February 1970 and the Trust took over the buildings: the first train on a regular weekend basis ran in June 1969, which later operated on a seasonal basis.

MILES, JAMES (1847-1924) was the son of a joiner born near Stratford on Avon; he started a bookshop at Leamington in 1870 and came to Leeds to open his bookshop on Lower Head Row. The shop moved to 80 Woodhouse Lane c1930 in the premises formerly occupied by Leeds Technical School; the name was taken by Austick's Bookshop on Great George Street prior to closure, demolition and the site for the offices of the LMU.

MILLENNIUM SQUARE in front of the Civic Hall cost £12 million with £5.4 million granted from the Millennium Commission: there is an arts cinema, luxury flats, offices, exclusive shops and concert space. The new square was three years in planning and construction and features a second fountain for the civic area. The Ice Cube was an ice rink experience from January 26th to February 25th 2001 which is to be an annual event. There is a smaller version of the Victoria Quarter in the former 19th century Stansfeld Chamber/Portland Chambers/Electric Press Building which features a glass covered atrium; part of the concept occupies the site of Brodrick's Oriental Baths on Cookridge Street - the street was closed to through traffic. Historic buildings in the area were restored and floodlit and the square was decorated with new trees including those in containers which can be moved to accommodate various events in the square. A pair of art-deco owls which were unveiled on April 11th are placed on 12 feet high obelisks flanking the ceremonial area in front of the Civic Hall and a £23,000 16' high bronze sculpture entitled Both Arms by Leeds born sculptor Kenneth Armitage is a main feature of the new square. The first public event in Millennium Square was held in the afternoon of Sunday December 17th 2000 with Carols by Candlelight - with brass bands and the choirs of St Anne's Cathedral and Leeds Parish Church. Millennium Square was officially opened by Nelson Mandela on his first visit to Leeds on Monday April 30th 2001 - he became an Honorary Freeman of the City of Leeds and re-dedicated Mandela Gardens in Millennium Square - they were first named in 1983 when Nelson Mandela was in prison for his championship of the anti-apartheid movement. The Brotherton Wing of the LGI is part of a redevelopment plan with demolition and completion of a hotel on the site by 2006: the complex (planning permission applied in February 2001) will include a hospital extension, multi-storey car park, 160 bed residential units, with leisure and retail outlets. A multi-purpose art complex will include a 350 seat theatre.

MILLGARTH was the area west of Sheepscar Beck in the Quarry Hill area (bus station and police station): the mill was based on a goit produced by a dam on Sheepscar Beck, which once took traffic to the Sheepscar works from the river. The mill garth was mainly used as tenter fields: where cloth merchants would stretch their material on tenterframes being held by hooks: the possibility of the cloth not stretching properly gave rise to the expression "being on tenterhooks". The Mill Garth was the property of Thomas Falkingham of the manor of North Hall and it was he who built a new mill on his land to relieve pressure on the manorial corn mills at Swinegate. This caused a long law suit resulting in the production of the first map of Leeds in 1560. Millgarth Street has the modern police station replacing the old building and to the west was Union Street public baths.

MONK BRIDGE IRON WORKS were started by Stephen Witham in 1851: it was bought by James Kitson of the Airedale Foundry in 1854 for the manufacture of Yorkshire iron - hammered and rolled into bars and plates for many products including boilers. In 1882 the manufacture of steel was commenced using the Siemens-Martin process for many items for the locomotive industry: the factory was closed in 1969.

MONTEITH, JOHN (1868-1930) came to Leeds with his father Alexander from Largs (Ayrshire) in 1888 to found the well known department store The Grand Pygmalion of Boar Lane/Bank Street/Trinity Street. The firm was founded with his uncle Andrew Hamilton: John Monteith retired in 1927 and the shop was sold. The manager at Monteith, Hamilton & Monteith Grand Pygmalion was Thomas Duncan who retired in 1922 and died in 1930.

MOORE, HENRY SPENCER (1898-1986) was born at Roundhill Road, Castleford on July 30th 1898 the son of Raymond and Mary. He studied at Castleford Grammar School and served in the Civil Service Rifles (15th London Regiment) for two years-he was at the Battle of Cambrai. He became the first student of sculpture at the Leeds College of Art (1919-1921) and moved to London for the Royal College of Art. Henry Moore married Irina Radetsky in 1929 and in 1940 moved to Perry Green Hertfordshire, where his only child Mary was born in March 1946. His output included 919 sculptures, 5500 drawings and 717 graphics. In 1972 he formed the Henry Moore Trust which received charitable status in 1976: on his death everything went to the Trustees of the Henry Moore Foundation. He was made a Companion of Honour in 1955, received the Order of Merit in 1963 and was made an Honorary Freeman of the City of Leeds on July 3rd 1981. The figure outside the Art Gallery is Reclining Woman (Elbow) dating from 1980. The

£1 million Henry Moore Gallery was opened by HM The Queen in November 1982. Henry Moore died on August 31st 1986.

MOOT HALL was in the centre of Briggate and was built in 1618 being used as the town hall and courthouse. The Moot Hall was rebuilt on the same site in 1710/11 to the design of William Etty of York at a cost of £210: the Carpenter statue of Queen Anne was added in 1713. The meeting room was on the top floor with butchers shops at street level, known as Middle Row. The Moot Hall was demolished by May 30th 1825 and the statue of the Queen transferred to the Corn Exchange (start of New Briggate) when it opened in 1829.

MORRISH & CO is a firm of solicitors now based in Oxford Row: started by Harold James in North British Buildings on East Parade: in 1919 Eric Morrish became a partner and after the death of Harold James in 1932 Eric Morrish took Clarence Nelson as partner. In 1940 Morrish Nelson & Co merged with the Pullan Davies practice (Sir Charles Davies); Priestley Kirby and Leonard Skirrow were taken into partnership after the War with John Morrish (1951) and in 1961 Richard Morrish joining the firm - they were the two sons of Eric Morrish who died in 1952. In 1963 the Albion Street firm of Wade, Kitson and Rigg merged with Morrish & Co - the firm moved to the CU premises on Park Row. In 1976 John Morrish retired from the practice and was appointed chairman of the Industrial Tribunals (Employment Tribunals); Leonard Skirrow retired in 1982 with his son Ian Skirrow being the present senior partner; Richard Morrish retired in 1995 and his son Tom became a full partner in 1998.

MORRISON, SIR KENNETH DUNCAN (born 1932) founded a chain of supermarkets based in Bradford. Morrison's in the Merrion Centre was opened on November 21st 1972 and expanded after purchase of the Tesco store in 1976. Morrison's Merrion Centre is one of 106 stores across England: the company is the country's fifth largest supermarket operator. William Morrison (1875-1956) was born in Wakefield and ran his own shop in Bradford in 1899; his second wife was Hilda Ryder of Hull and Wm Morrison (Provisions) Ltd became a successful company which Ken Morrison took over in 1952. In the 1960s he opened his supermarket in the old Victoria Palace Cinema Girlington bought in July 1969 and converted the Woodroyd Laundry and a bowling alley into his supermarkets - in 1967 the company became listed on the stock exchange and then known as Wm Morrison Supermarkets Ltd. Hilmore House became the head office at Girlington and in 1975 they opened a fuel station at Morley. Ken Morrison was awarded the CBE in 1990 and knighted in the New Year Honours List 2000.

MOTORWAYS The MI opened to Leeds in December 1972 with the completion of the section from Stourton - the motorway was opened to Staples Corner North London in August 1976; the M62 had the first contract awarded in 1966 and the first section in Lancashire opened in September 1970: the summit section was opened in December 1970 - officially opened by HM The Queen in 1971 and the whole motorway was completed in May 1976. The A58(M) is the Inner Ring Road which opened in the 1960's. The £8 million South East Urban Motorway was opened on December 15th 1972. The second stage of the Stanningley Bypass was opened by Ald. Frank Marshall in May 1971. The M621 was opened in November 1973 linking the M62 with Leeds City centre via the inner ring road. The £21 million East Leeds Link Road started construction from Cross Green in late 2001: the junction with the A1/M1 Link Road was already completed. The A1/M1 Link Road was opened in February 1999 at a cost of £190 million (PFI).

MOYNIHAN, LORD (1865-1936) George Andrew Berkeley was knighted in 1912 and became the first Baron Moynihan of Leeds (1929) and a respected surgeon at the LGI. He came to Leeds as a boy and studied at Leeds Medical School: he qualified in 1887. Lord Moynihan was elected a Fellow of the Royal College of Surgeons in 1890 and was Professor of Clinical Surgery at Leeds University. He was the president of the RCS from 1926 to 1932 and Emeritus Professor of Surgery at Leeds. He married Isabella Wellesley, daughter of TR Jessop JP (died 1936) in 1895 and his heir was Hon Patrick Moynihan. He became an Honorary Freeman of the City of Leeds on October 6th 1926: the family home was Carr Manor. Lord Moynihan's statue in the LGI was sculpted by Sir William Reid Dick in 1931 and was due to be unveiled in October 1939 but was delayed due to the Second World War.

MUNICIPAL BUILDINGS were designed by George Corson with the foundation stone laid by the Mayor of Leeds Francis Carbutt on October 14th 1878. The buildings were opened by the Lord Mayor

Edwin Woodhouse on April 17th 1884 with the library transferring from the old Infirmary building on Infirmary Street. The new building had the civic offices and on November 6th 1969 the Leeds City Museum opened in the old police department: the Museum was transferred from Park Row in 1966. The building was closed in 1999 and re-opened after a complete refurbishment on Saturday June 10th 2000.

MURRAY, MATTHEW (1765-1826) was born in Stockton-on-Tees and came to Leeds in 1789 to work at Marshall's Scotland Mill. In 1795 he founded an engineering factory at Holbeck with James Fenton and David Wood. This was the Round Factory of Fenton, Murray & Wood producing textile machinery, steam engines and locomotives. The factory produced the world's first commercially successful steam locomotive for John Blenkinsop's Middleton Colliery in 1812. In 1804 Matthew Murray built Steam Hall west of Leeds railway station and installed a steam operated central heating system.

MUSEUMS Ralph Thoresby had an extensive museum in his house on Kirkgate and John Calvert's Natural History Museum opened on Briggate in 1826 and transferred to 11 Commercial Street corner a year later. Calvert was a gunsmith, bird and animal preserver who had a collection of 15,000 specimens: collection sold c1875. The *Leeds Philosophical & Literary Society* was founded in 1818 and the foundation stone for their new Philosophical Hall was laid by Benjamin Gott on July 9th 1819: the building on Park Row by Robert Chantrell opened on April 6th 1821. The building cost £6150 and had a lecture room, museum, library and a laboratory. The museum was enlarged in 1861-62 with a new main entrance on Park Row - transferring from Bond Street. There was a new lecture theatre designed by architects Dobson & Chorley used by many groups until it closed in December 1965. An air raid on March 14th 1941 severely damaged the Hall losing the whole frontage on Park Row as well as many exhibits. The museum reopened with a concrete rendering and included a miniature coal mine and popular Saturday film shows in the hall. The Museum closed in late 1965 and demolition followed in summer 1966: the site became the HSBC Bank (Midland) and a Civic Trust blue plaque was unveiled by Dr Peter Evenett on June 28th 2001. The transfer to the Municipal Buildings took place from Park Row and occupied the level formerly with the Police: the museum was opened by Princess Margaret on November 6th 1969. The City Museum was closed in the Municipal Buildings in 1999 with the collection housed on a temporary basis in the Resource Centre Moorfield Road Industrial estate, Yeadon. There are plans to develop the Leeds Institute (Civic Theatre) as the new Museum by 2006. The other museums of Leeds are Armley Mills Industrial Museum on Canal Road - a woollen mill built in 1805 for Benjamin Gott - the Council bought it in 1969, Abbey House which was reopened on 20th January 2001, Lotherton Hall, Temple Newsam House and Thwaite Mills.

MUSGRAVE, JOHN MUSGRAVE SAGAR (1835-1906) was a brewer who lived at Red Hall Shadwell. In 1860 he married Clara Brooksbank and in 1863 added his maternal Musgrave name to his own. He ran the Musgrave & Sagar Kirkstall brewery.

MUSIC & OPERA *City of Leeds Youth Orchestra* was founded in 1964 by the Education Department for the best school players aged from 13 to 19 years and performs concerts in Leeds - one as part of the Leeds International Concert Season - and throughout the UK and Europe. The orchestra is part of City of Leeds Youth Music supported by the City Council's Department of Education through the Leeds Music Support Service. The principal conductor from 1997 was Paul Mountain who also founded the *Academy of Leeds* in 1984 and is the Leader of the *City of Leeds String Quartet.* *College of Music Symphony Orchestra* is one of several ensembles presenting public concerts; chamber music, jazz and the choral society all offer events as a part of the annual programme. The orchestra developed from the Leeds Music Centre which changed name to the College of Music in 1972. *Headingley Amateur Operatic Society* was founded in 1950. *Leeds Amateur Operatic Society* was inaugurated on October 4th 1890 at The Grand Restaurant Boar Lane from an idea suggested at a gathering at The Fenton Hotel Woodhouse Lane. The first production was HMS Pinafore presented at Carlton Barracks in December 1890 and future presentations were at the Coliseum (1891) and The Grand Theatre from 1892; the 2001 production was My Fair Lady. The society won the Waterford glass trophy in the International Festival of Light Opera in 1966 and 1967. *Leeds Festival Chorus* was founded from the Leeds Madrigal & Motet Society (1850) and Leeds

Choral Society (1857) - the new chorus gave the first concert at the opening of the Town Hall in 1858. This was the first performance for the Leeds Triennial Musical Festival featuring a performance of Mendelssohn's oratorio Elijah. It is one of the leading amateur choirs in the country with about 160 singers trained by Simon Wright: the choir sings twice a year in the Leeds International Concert Season and visits Bridgewater Hall in Manchester and the BBC studios in Manchester. The Leeds Festival Chorus Youth Choir is a branch of the main chorus. *Leeds Gilbert & Sullivan Society* was founded in the pre war years as the St Silas (Hunslet) Choral & Operatic Society: in 1952 it became the Leeds G & S presenting annual shows at the Civic Theatre. *The Leeds Girls Choir* was founded by Walter Bradley in 1949 - he retired in 1997 when he was 80 years old. *Leeds International Concert Season* was created in the present form in 1980 - part of that first programme included Sir Simon Rattle conducting Mahler 2nd symphony. The season incorporates the concert series at Leeds Town Hall, International Chamber Music at Leeds Civic Hall, Best of Brass and Jazz at the Playhouse. *The Leeds Conductors Competition* was started in 1984 with the first competition won by Sian Edwards. *The Leeds Light Opera Group* was founded in 1975. *Leeds Peoples Choir* was founded in October 1990 by a group of Leeds people with an interest in music and community causes. *Leeds Philharmonic Society* was founded in 1870 and contributes to the Leeds International Concert Season. Music Directors have included Sir Charles Villiers Stanford (1852-1924), Sir Edward Bairstow appointed in 1917 (organist of Leeds Parish Church 1906-13 and then appointed organist at York Minster at the age of 39), Sir Malcolm Sargent (1895-1967) who conducted a performance of Belshazzar's Feast (William Walton) as part of the Leeds Musical Festival in October 1931 and Sir Charles Groves; Chorus Master Elisabeth Jane Wild was appointed in 1997. *Leeds Schools Choir* was formed in September 1995 as one of the central ensembles run by the Leeds Schools Music Association. *Leeds Symphony Orchestra* was founded in 1891 as an amateur orchestra for the city: the first concert was given at the Albert Hall (Civic Theatre) on November 30th 1891. The performances of the orchestra remained unbroken in the world wars with an average of three concerts a season between 1891 and 1980 - now there are 8 or

9 annually. The 11th conductor of the LSO from September 1970 is Martin Binks who has conducted 170 concerts - the programmes are presented at Notre Dame College, King James School Knaresborough and at Wetherby Festival. *Leeds Triennial International Pianoforte Competition* was founded by Fanny Waterman and Marion Countess of Harewood in 1961; Jack Lyons donated a substantial sum and chaired the committee until his retirement six years later. The first Competition was in September 1963 when the prizes were presented by the Princess Royal who died in 1965. Sir Arthur Bliss Master of the Queen's Music was the chairman of the jury in the first competition. The finals were played with the Royal Liverpool Philharmonic Orchestra with John Pritchard - a member of the jury. In 1966 the RLPO was conducted by Sir Charles Groves; the BBC Northern SO was conducted by Norman del Mar in 1978; the Philharmonic Orchestra under Sir Charles Groves (1981) and the first appearance of the City of Birmingham SO under Simon Rattle was in the finals on 1987. The 13th competition was held in September 2000; the winner Alessio Bax of Bari Italy. *Leeds Triennial Musical Festival* was founded in 1858 for the opening of Leeds Town Hall: the performance of Mendelssohn's Elijah (composed for the Birmingham Festival 1846) took place on Wednesday morning September 8th sung by Leeds Festival Chorus in aid of the General Infirmary. The next festival following the opening was in 1874 with Sir Arthur Sullivan as conductor until 1898: in 1886 Sullivan conducted his own "Golden Legend". The festivals continued with breaks for world wars until the 1960's. *Leeds Youth Opera* was set up in 1971 and encourages young people to take part in professionally staged opera productions. *Opera North* was established as an Arts Council Initiative with Leeds City Council at the Grand Theatre in 1978 as English National Opera North: the first performance was at the Grand Theatre in November 1978. The touring company changed to Opera North in 1981 and has a turnover of £9 million: there is a chorus of 36 and the ENP with 54 members. *Orchestra of Opera North* is the resident orchestra of Opera North and was formed in 1978; the orchestra present concerts in the Town Hall and in other English locations and also travel abroad; the first concert appearance was in February 1979. The founder conductor was David Lloyd-Jones and Paul Daniel

CBE was Opera North's Music Director and Principal Conductor from 1990 to 1997. There is a Student Training Scheme initiated in 1983 and a New Composers Forum launched in 1993. The name changed from the English Northern Philharmonia in 2001. *St Peter's Singers* were founded in 1977 by Harry Fearnley: a chamber choir with a close link to Leeds Parish Church; the music director is Simon Lindley. The *Sinfonia Leeds* was originally formed as an amateur city orchestra in 1972 by Graham Bennett: the Musical Director from 1990 is ENP leader David Greed. *University of Leeds Symphony Orchestra* and *Leeds University Philharmonia* present regular concerts in the University halls. *West Riding Opera* (Patrons: Earl & Countess of Harewood) was founded by a group of enthusiasts in 1939 with the first opera performed at the Civic Theatre in 1954 (The Bartered Bride); Martin Binks was appointed Artistic Director and Conductor in 1968 and has conducted nearly 200 performances of over 32 operas at Leeds Civic Theatre: several operas were given their first performance in the North of England. The *Yorkshire Philharmonia* made its debut on May 26th 1990 presenting concerts locally. The *Yorkshire Symphony Orchestra* with conductor Maurice Miles was founded in 1947 and played at the Festival Hall (Festival of Britain 1951) and frequently at the Leeds Town Hall before disbanding in 1955.

MUSIC HALLS The *Albion Street Music Hall* dated from 1792/93 and included an Irregulars Cloth Hall (apprentices with less than 7 years experience) with the lower hall known as Tom Paine's Hall. The Leeds Madrigal & Motet Society (President:William Beckett) held a concert in the Music Hall conducted by Mr Spark - a poster to this effect is on display in the Abbey House Museum. The Music Hall was closed and sold on February 9th 1870 having already been occupied in part by the Albion Carpet Warehouse from 1850. In 1876 it became Denby & Spinks furniture store and was demolished on April 10th 1973 - the site became part of the Leeds Shopping Plaza. *New Music Hall* was opened by the publican Charles Thornton in June 1865 who had to compete with other music hall locations in public houses. This music hall in a converted inn became the City Varieties Music Hall in 1894. *Royal Casino* was a music hall opened by Joseph Hobson in King Charles Croft in 1849 and in 1856 this became legitimate theatre. *Tivoli*

Music Hall in King Charles Croft was operating in 1898 and became the Hippodrome theatre in 1906. In 1901 they screened short news films on an "Improved Flickerless Barrascope" invented by Tom Barrasford of Jarrow.

NASH'S FISH RESTAURANT on Merrion Street is based in a house built in 1720 for Matthew Wilson and once was a minister's house in St John's Place; in 1817 the house was taken by Richard Kemplay for his academy and later was a synagogue and the Victoria Club (1877-1960). The restaurant was originally at 42 Park Lane and moved to Merrion Street after closure on November 18th 1963.

NATIONAL EXHIBITION OF WORKS OF ART was held in the new General Infirmary buildings to mark their opening. The Prince of Wales opened this grand exhibition on May 19th 1868 and it had attracted over half a million visitors by the time of closure in October 1868. Many exhibits were borrowed from the royal collections and from the South Kensington Museum in London. Edward Prince of Wales was born in 1841 as the eldest son of Queen Victoria and Prince Albert: he became King Edward VII on the death of his mother and was crowned in 1902. He married Princess Alexandra of Denmark in 1863 and they had six children. King Edward VII with Queen Alexandra and Princess Victoria came to Leeds on July 7th 1908 to open the new Leeds University buildings.

NEILSON, LILIAN ADELAIDE (1849-1880) was born in St Peter's Square and moved to Guiseley. When she was 17 years old she played Juliet on the London stage and her portrait is now displayed at Abbey House Museum. She married Philip Lee who was a clergyman's son and she died in Paris.

NEVILE, SIR JOHN was the patron of St Katherine's Chantry (Clarell Chantry) in Leeds Parish Church and in 1501 appointed William Sheafield to be priest of this chantry. He allowed William Sheafield to use the income from his estates as a schoolmaster's salary thus re-endowing Leeds Grammar School in 1552.

NEVILLE STREET features the Leeds Hilton Hotel with access to Granary Wharf by the dark arches. Green Flag opened their headquarters at Victoria Gate on July 16th 1998 - the building was Privilege Insurance (part of Direct Line who bought Green Flag based in Croydon) with Green Flag being part of Direct Line and

Royal Bank of Scotland. The building is on the site of the former Leeds Co-op coal depot, which was sold for £3 million. The architects were the TP Bennett Partnership and the building was Commended in the Leeds Awards for Architecture. KPMG offices were opened by The Princess Royal on January 28th 1990 at No 1 Embankment for Peat Marwick McLintock (from 1999 KPMG).

NEW BOND STREET was originally Wood Street and then was renamed Queen Victoria Street.

NEW BRIGGATE was agreed to be started on May 8th 1867 and was completed in 1869 at a cost of c£30,000: prior to this it was known as New Street and St John's Street - it was originally a footpath to the church. The new street involved the demolition of the Moot Hall and St John's vicarage. The half timbered houses/shops which were a feature of New Briggate were built in 1901 and demolished for the completion of the Inner Ring Road in the early 1960's.

NEW MARKET STREET links Vicar Lane with Call Lane/Duncan Street/Crown Street. This was the continuation of Vicar Lane proposed in 1865; the street was improved in 1910.

New Market Street and Vicar Lane

NEW STATION STREET was a new route opened in 1873 and once featured a covered arcade. The New Station Street Social Club

(National Association of Railway Clubs) opened in 1946 on Aire Street and transferred in 1968 to New Station Street. The Club closed on March 31st 2001.

NEW YORK ROAD was proposed in 1907 and construction started in October 1908 with completion on July 1st 1910 from York Road to North Street/Vicar Lane, replacing slum dwellings of Hope Street - the new road also included a roundabout at Mabgate which was constructed in June 1910. Heaton's clothing factory was once a main feature of the west end of the new road: converted to luxury apartments. Tate of Leeds was founded by Thomas Tate in 1922

New York Road roundabout c1932

and moved to their new premises on New York Road in 1932 - expanded to Trafalgar Street: this was opened on June 18th 1937. The company left the site in 1975 and the Trafalgar Street block was acquired by British Gas in the 1980's for car parking: until recently it housed the BGNE Sports & Social Club, standby mainframe computer, office space and storage areas. The Club was closed in late 1996 and the computer was removed - British Gas Trading use some of the block for car parking. The premises demolished for the construction of the Inner Ring Road included Hepton's, Crompton Parkinson electrical engineers, Oldham Signs and the Central Yorkshire Salvation Army.

NEW YORK STREET is the continuation of York Street from Church Lane to Kirkgate. The corner building was opened as a showroom and warehouse for Pilkington's glass in 1936: it was opened as the Mayfair Bingo Hall on May 9th 1990. St James Hall was designed by Thomas Ambler and opened on November 3rd 1877 by WJ Armitage of the Farnley Iron Co at a cost of £7000 as a workmen's club and recreation centre. The building included the Westminster Temperance Hotel, dining rooms and public hall and was enlarged in 1884 - the building became known as Westminster Buildings & Chambers. St James Church who originally administered the Hall was built in 1794 on York Street and used by the Huntingdonians as Zion Chapel; it was consecrated in 1801 for use by the Anglican Church - the church was demolished in 1952; after demolition the site became a bus station. New York Street once featured the abattoir on the north side - now the Harper Street multi-storey car park, York Buildings is the large block by the entrances to the Markets and the south side which includes the Post Office once featured Scarr's ironmongery store and the corner Yorkshire Bank.

NEWSPAPERS The *Leeds Express* is a free weekly published by Johnston Press at the offices of the Yorkshire Weekly Newspaper Group in Southgate Wakefield-the editorial office is on Austhorpe Road Cross Gates. On April 10th 1886 the Roundhay Gazette was first published and incorporated the Shadwell, Seacroft, Thorner and Cross Gates Courier: the title soon became the Roundhay Gazette and Skyrack Courier. The Skyrack Courier was published on June 4th 1887 published in Albion Street Leeds and closed in 1923 to be followed by the Skyrack Express in mid-October 1923: printed in Wakefield. In January 1978 the title changed to Skyrack and East Leeds Express and became a free newspaper; 1982 saw the title changed to the Leeds Skyrack Express and in 1984 became a tabloid. The present title is the Leeds Express (incorporating the Leeds Skyrack Express): changed in November 1996. The *Leeds Weekly News* is a free weekly paper founded by YPN in 1980. *The Yorkshire Evening Post* was first published in 1890. The *Yorkshire Post* was founded in 1754 as The Leeds Intelligencer: a weekly newspaper. In 1866 the title changed to the Yorkshire Post and it began daily publishing at Commercial Street: this was a year after the formation of the Yorkshire Conservative Newspaper Ltd. The corner shop on Bond Street/Albion Street was a branch of the National Provincial Bank and later Pearce's Jewellers: on September 23rd 1931 it became the YP Central Advertising

Department and later Austin Reed's mens outfitters. In 1969 the paper became a part of United Provincial Newspapers who acquired the Daily Express and Sunday Express and Star in 1985; Yorkshire Post Newspapers are part of the Regional Independent Media. The newspaper was published in Change Court, Albion Street until September 26th 1970; the Albion Street building was by Chorley & Connon (1886-87). The move from Albion Street took place on Saturday September 26th 1970 and the new building opened on September 28th. The official opening by HRH Prince Charles was held on December 10th 1970. The building was designed by the John Madin Design Group: the site had formally been Bean Ing Mill on Wellington Street.

Newspapers which have ceased publication include: The *Leeds Mercury* was published as a weekly in 1718 and became a daily in 1861 - the paper was acquired by the Yorkshire Post in 1923; the last edition was published on November 26th 1939. Sir William Linton Andrews was the editor of the Leeds Mercury (1923-39) and Yorkshire Post (1939-60). The *Leeds Other Paper* was first published as a monthly in January 1974, became a weekly in October 1980 and became The Northern Star in February 1991 - the paper closed in January 1994. The *Leeds Times* was published from 1833 and other papers included The Magnet, Sporting Chronicle, Sunday Guardian and Leeds Saturday Journal. *North Leeds News* was founded in 1912 and published at Victoria Chambers South Parade. *Sporting Pink* was first published in 1895 with the last issue on November 30th 1963. The *Yorkshire Evening News* was published and printed in Trinity Street (Trinity Court): it was first published in November 1872 as the Leeds Daily News and changed title in 1905. In 1929 the News became part of Provincial Newspapers and the last issue was published on December 3rd 1963 with the printing works sold and demolished.

NEXT SHOPS were founded by George Davies (born 1929): he grew up in Liverpool and attended Bootle Grammar School - played soccer for England Schoolboys and had a trial for Liverpool FC. He studied dentistry for a short period at Birmingham University and soon worked for Littlewoods as a stock controller. It was Sir Terence Conran who employed George Davies to transform the Hepworth's chain of menswear shops into Next. He designed the George range of clothing for ASDA and in 2001 was appointed to design a new Marks & Spencer range. Next opened on Commercial Street in 1980 and acquired the adjacent shop for expansion in 1986. The store in Lands Lane opened in 1988 and a branch opened later in the White Rose Shopping Centre. On March 29th 2001 Next opened a new store on the corner of Bond Street and Albion Street - the old Yorkshire Post office and later Austin Reed site: the two other city centre shops were closed on March 24th 2001.

NICHOLSON, THOMAS (1764-1821) was born at Chapel Allerton and worked in London in insurance, where he married Elizabeth Jackson in 1786. He bought the Chapel Allerton Hall estate in 1799 and with fellow Quaker Samuel Elam bought Roundhay Park from Philip, Lord Stourton on August 4th 1803. The estate was inherited by his half-brother Stephen Nicholson (1778-1858) and then by William Nicholson Phillips (Nicholson) (1803-68). After his death and inheritance by Emily Armitage (Farnley Hall) the estate was auctioned at the Great Northern Hotel on October 4th 1871. It was purchased by John Barran for £139,000 and offered to the Town Council who accepted the estate for the people of Leeds: HRH Prince Arthur opened the park on September 19th 1872.

NICHOLSON, WILLIAM GUSTAVUS (1845-1918) was educated at Leeds Grammar School and had a distinguished military career becoming Chief of the Imperial General Staff, Field Marshal and Baron Nicholson of Roundhay in 1912.

NILE STREET was laid out in 1809 by the Bischoff family off North Street and like the adjacent Copenhagen and Trafalgar Streets was named after one of Admiral Lord Nelson's victories. Viscount Horatio Nelson (1758-1805) won victories over the French at the Battle of the Nile (Aboukir Bay) in 1798, over the Danish fleet at the Battle of Copenhagen in 1801 and over the Franco - Spanish fleet at the Battle of Trafalgar near Gibraltar in 1805: he died from his wounds and is buried in St Paul's Cathedral London. The Nile Street Synagogue was opened in March 1908: the congregation having used converted houses. The Beth Hamedrash Hagadol moved to Newton Road Chapeltown in 1937 and the original premises were sold to the Salvation Army. The present Beth Hamedrash Hagadol on Street Lane was opened in 1969 by Chief Rabbi Jacobovits. The Nile Street Synagogue was demolished in 1988 and the Leeds Central Salvation Army Worship and

Community Halls were opened by Commissioner Harry Read on September 8th 1990: the foundation stone was laid on September 8th 1989.

NOBLE, MATTHEW (1818-76) was the sculptor of Sir Peter Fairbairn in Woodhouse Square, Queen Victoria (1858) and Prince Albert (1865) in the newly tiled vestibule of Leeds Town Hall together with the busts of Edward Prince of Wales and Alexandra Princess of Wales (1872) commissioned by Alderman Kitson for the Town Hall. Matthew Noble was born at Hackness near Scarborough and died in London: he exhibited at the Royal Academy from 1845 until his death.

NORMAN, ANN BATHURST (1907-2001) was the fourth daughter of Sir Gervase Beckett who was the Leeds North MP from 1923-29: succeeded by Sir Osbert Peake. Her elder sister Beatrice married Anthony Eden (Prime Minister 1955-57). Ann married Lt Col Harry Bathurst Norman in 1936 - he died in 1966.

NORTH, COL JOHN THOMAS (1841-96) was born in Hunslet: his father was a coal merchant. He was apprenticed to Shaw, North & Watson and worked at John Fowler Steam Plough Works. In 1869 Fowlers sent him to the west coast of South America to erect and commission equipment. He started distilling water for domestic purposes at Valparaiso Chile and patched up a wrecked tramp steamer as a water tank. He bought some land at Tarapaca in the northern part of Chile and started the extraction of nitrate of soda for fertilisers and also worked the guana deposits. Col North developed the silver mines and gas works accumulating a fortune: he returned to England in 1882/83. He worked in London and was the Honorary Colonel of the Tower Hamlets Voluntary Engineers. In December 1888 the Trustees of the Earls of Cardigan offered the Kirkstall Abbey ruins for sale by auction. The Borough Council bid £6100 although the reserve of £10,000 was not attained and the lot was withdrawn. Col North was visited by two friends who persuaded him to buy the ruins for the City of Leeds and he added extra lands valued at £900. John North presented Kirkstall Abbey to the Borough of Leeds at a special ceremony in the Victoria Hall on January 25th 1889 and he became the first Honorary Freeman of Leeds in the same year. He made donations to the Yorkshire College (University), General Infirmary and acquired Hunslet Moor as a public park. Col North died in his Gracechurch Street London offices on March 5th 1896.

NORTH HALL The manor of North Hall was created at the end of the 12th century and the house was at Vicar Lane/Lady Lane with lands to the Sheepscar Beck to the east. The land was taken from that of the Manor of Whitkirk which held property in the east part of the town: marked with a Templar cross to denote exemption from grinding corn at the manorial mills at Swinegate.

NORTH STREET was once known as Sheepscar Lane and was the continuation of Vicar Lane from Lady Lane bar stone to Sheepscar. The workhouse was on the east side - site of the bus station and the Grammar School on the west side on land once belonging to John Harrison. Sheepshanks Yard was on the east - demolished for the inner ring road; the yard was once a tram depot and in 1874 was the property of the late William Sheepshanks - the land was auctioned and bought by William Turton who built stables and yard in 1878 for his bus business. In 1882 Turton was bought out by the Tramways and a tram track was laid on Sheepshanks Yard to North Street. In 1902 this arrangement ceased when the lease expired and the property including the Hope Inn was all demolished in 1967. The Chest Clinic (Dispensary) site was near the first toll bar for the Leeds-Harrogate Turnpike Road opened in 1752. Crispin House is being developed into luxury apartments in

Old Hope Inn and Sheepshanks House (*Vicar Lane (North Street)*)

the shell of the Heatons clothing factory - sold to HW Poole in 1979. The Leeds Public Dispensary opened in 1904 and is now restored being the home of the Leeds Blind and Hard of Hearing on Hartley Hill (Centenary House). On the west side of North Street by the 1960's slip road for the Inner Ring is Lovell Park: in 1855 this was Smithfield Cattle Market which was closed in 1886 and moved to Gelderd Road. The area was landscaped and opened as a public park in 1888 with bandstand and bowling green. On the opposite side was Thomas Green's Smithfield Works - the iron works were established on the site in 1835; the firm manufactured steam trams, steam rollers and lawn mowers. The business closed in 1975 and most of the site was redeveloped: the façade of the Smithfield Inn, closed in the early 1900's is retained on the North street frontage. A large area on the east side of North Street was known as The Leylands - Skinner Lane, Regent Street and Lady Lane - where the Jewish population of Leeds settled prior to their movement to Chapeltown by the start of 1939. There were three Anglican churches in the area: St Thomas was consecrated in February 1852, St Luke was consecrated in October 1841 and St Clement designed by George Corson was consecrated in September 1868 and demolished for the Sheepscar Interchange in 1976.

NORWICH UNION operated in Leeds from their main office in City Square - previously the Standard Life Assurance Building (Standard House) north of the square. Norwich Union occupied the building with Standard Life and the Norwich Union rebuilt this in 1969 and this was demolished in 1995 to be replaced by No 1 City Square. The Norwich Union was founded in 1797 by Thomas Bignold who as a wine merchant and banker moved to Norwich from Kent. He formed the Norwich Union Society for the insurance of houses and stock from fire - this was followed by the Norwich Union Fire Insurance office and in 1808 he established the NU Life Insurance Society - in 1821 the NU had 25 fire brigades. In 1866 the NU acquired the Amicable (1706) and in 1908 the Norwich & London Accident Insurance Association. In 1959 the NU bought the Scottish Union & National Insurance Company and in 1990 they formed NU Healthcare with NU Direct following in 1996. In 1998 the NU bought the London & Edinburgh Insurance Co. The CGU and the Norwich Union merged on May 30th 2000; the CGU was formed in June 1998 through the merger of the Commercial Union and General Accident. The Commercial Union was founded in 1861 after a disastrous London dockland fire: in 1905 the Hand in Hand (founded in a London coffee house in the reign of King William III) became a part of CU.

OASTLER, RICHARD (1789-1861) became known as the Factory King with his fight against cruelty to children in the factories and mills. He was born in St Peter's Square becoming a cloth dealer and when his father died in 1820 he managed an estate near Huddersfield. About ten years later Richard Oastler started his campaign against children working in the mills: his main object was a ten hour day, which he achieved in 1847 before retiring from public life. He died in the corner house on Raglan Street/West Park at Harrogate on August 22nd 1861 and buried at Kirkstall Parish Church.

OBSERVATORY The Cecil Duncombe Observatory was opened on May 4th 1906: the telescope was the property of Cecil Duncombe and was housed in the adapted stone built reservoir keeper's lodge on Reservoir Street. The observatory was run by the University and remained for about 30 years.

ODDFELLOWS is an Independent Order of the Manchester Unity Friendly Society formed in 1810. It was a group set up as a society that would protect themselves and their families in times of need - at a period when there were no trade unions or welfare state. There were many trade societies but the new society had no such affiliation and were known as the Odd Fellows - members from different trades and all walks of life. The branches of the Oddfellows are known as Lodges and it is a mutual non-profit making Friendly Society owned by the members; the profits are returned to the members as benefits. The Oddfellows make annual donations to medical research and support charities in local areas. The Oddfellows started in Leeds in 1825; the Kingston Unity of Oddfellows (Leeds District) had 7000 members in 48 branches and The Kingston Unity Club & Friendly Societies Hall opened on Union Street/Bernard Street in 1892. They had centres in Queen's Square and Park Square in the 1920's and moved to Stonegate Road and then to their present headquarters at Unity House Meanwood Road in the 1990's. The local Lodges were amalgamated in 1989: there are some Oddfellows staffs on display in the Abbey House Museum.

OLD MONK COMPANY was founded in May 1994 by Gerald Martin who is the Chairman and Managing Director. The company opened their first Leeds pub in the old Lloyds Bank building on Park Row in June 1999.

OWEN & ROBINSON were jewellers in Lower Briggate/Blayds Yard - one of four branches of which the largest was at 23 Boar Lane and another on Duncan Street. The firm was established in 1839 and was taken by William Owen in 1898 when it became a public company. The name Owen first appeared over the shop in the 1870's - William Owen was born in the living quarters at the shop. The Briggate shop closed in July 1972 and the headquarters moved to York (1975). The firm was taken over by Richard Ratner in 1986 and in 1995 was acquired by Philip Owen.

OXFORD PLACE features the old Bridewell entrance in the Town Hall (east) and Oxford Place Methodist Church (west) featuring Oxford Chambers (in the 1920's this was the home of the Caxton Publishing Co), together with the Britannia Buildings dating from 1868 designed by Charles & John Fowler who had their offices in the building.

OXFORD ROW is a pedestrianised street between the Methodist Church and the new Court Buildings. The street mainly featured offices such as Oxford Buildings and Oxford Offices-the site to the north of the Church has been redeveloped as offices-Oxford House includes the firm of Morrish & Co Solicitors.

PACKER, RT REV JOHN RICHARD (born 1946) was appointed the Bishop of Ripon and Leeds in 2000. He was born in Blackburn, educated at Talbot Road PS Leeds until the age of seven, grew up in Bolton and attended Manchester GS. He studied for the ministry at Ripon Hall Oxford and was ordained in 1970 - he was Vicar of Wath-Upon-Dearne (1977-86) and Sheffield Manor (1986-1991). He was Archdeacon of West Cumberland (1991-96) and the Bishop of Warrington from 1996. The Bishop has pastoral oversight of 160 parishes and 266 churches served by 193 stipendiary clergy; the Diocese covers 1359 square miles and has a population of 780,000.

PARISH COUNCILS There are 30 parish councils in the Leeds MD: Leeds City includes St Peter (Parish Church), Holy Trinity Boar Lane, St Mary's in St Peter's School Hall and the Deaf Centre at

Centenary House.

PARK CROSS STREET was paved and re-opened on February 17th 1987 by Lord Mayor Rose Lund. Following the demolition of the west side of the street, a £700,000 office block was opened in March 1987.

PARK ESTATE It was in 1768 that the first house was built in the west end of Leeds: the grant of land for building was in 1767 on the Wilson estate. In 1797 the estate included East Parade, Park Place, Park Row, Park Square and South Parade - there were 122 houses. Richard Wilson inherited the Park estate from his father in 1761 - he rebuilt his manor house on Mill Hill: the old house had been inherited by Richard Wilson in 1694. Thomas Wilson inherited in 1776 and moved into the Manor House. Rev Christopher Wilson inherited the estate in 1789 (died 1792) from his brother and it was in 1780 that East Parade first saw houses.

PARK LANE was first known as Upper Head Row and was once the main bridlepath route to Bradford via Boar Lane, Park Row,and Burley: Park Lane linked Park Row/Cookridge Street with Burley Road. The turnpike road was opened in 1827 along Burley Road, Spen Lane and along a new road which cut through the Kirkstall Abbey precinct thus isolating the gatehouse - the turnpike proceeded towards Guiseley and Ilkley. It was in the 20th century that the eastern section became part of the Headrow and Westgate. Park Lane now links Westgate with Burley Road with Park Lane College as a prominent feature. Marlborough Towers were built in 1973: Park Dale Hall was opened on Park Lane for the Marlborough Residents Association of Marlborough Towers/Grange by the Lord Mayor on March 3rd 1997. St Andrew's Church was consecrated on March 26th 1845 to designs by Sir George Gilbert Scott. Work by constructors Balfour Beatty started in November 2000 on the £25 million scheme for No 1 Park Lane being a development by Haslemere Estates with architect Carey Jones: the 7 storey building has an underground car park (77 spaces) with steel and glass used for the main building which opened as offices in November 2001. The block replaced the 7 storey Telecom House which was blown up on February 18th 1990.

PARK PLACE was started in 1785 as a part of the Park Estate by Thomas Wilson (died 1789) and was completed by 1800. Many of the houses were built by master carpenter William Hargrave between 1788 and 1794. No 18 Park Place was erected in 1788 as a Georgian merchant's house and restored in 1988 by MEPC Ltd. No 30 Park Place was by Thomas Ambler (1863) for NP Nathan - a German export house. No 6 was the home of Rev Dr Walter Hook Vicar of Leeds and other Vicars of Leeds Parish Church: in later years it became WT Robinson & Co and is now Insignia Richard Ellis. In the mid-19th century the area between Park Place and York Place was gardens: later becoming warehouses.

PARK ROW was started in 1767 and completed in 1776 on the site known as Park Butts on the route from the Manor House to Park Lane (The Headrow). The Square was originally an open area bounded by South Parade, Park Row, Infirmary Street (West Street) and East Parade: the area was offered for building purposes in 1805. The street is known as the financial district with banks and insurance companies, although many original buildings have been demolished or changed.

The Standard Life Assurance building north of the square was opened in 1901 - it became the Norwich Union Building and it was rebuilt in 1969. This was demolished in 1995 to be replaced by No 1 City Square (HQ Global Workplaces): this opened in April 1998 and was designed by Abbey Hanson Rowe. On the east side is the office block of No 1 Park Row which was opened on November 26th 1999 with the official opening in April 2000. It was designed by Fletcher Joseph with original owners NatWest selling to Bastinien and in 2000 they sold the property to the Scottish Mutual. The offices are those of Pinsent Curtis Biddle: Simpson Curtis was an old established law firm in the 19th century - in May 1995 they merged with Biddle & Co and in February 2001 they merged with Pinsent & Co of Birmingham. The new block had replaced the NatWest building of Priestley House - on the site of the original Priestley Hall of the Mill Hill Chapel. The Post Office ran their administrative centre on Park Row (opposite Lloyds Bank) from 1939; the foundation stone was laid by the Postmaster General on April 28th 1938 with Portland Stone used in the main construction; the building became the offices of Sun Alliance in 1986 and was recently converted into new offices. Lloyds/TSB bank on the corner of Bond Street and Park Row replaced Marshall & Snelgrove's store in 1976: the bank was designed by Abbey Hanson Rowe with Peter Tysoe's steel Black Horse sculpture at the entrance. The Woolwich Building was originally built for the York City & County Bank in 1892: the branch transferred from Bond Street in 1988. The Woolwich was founded in 1847 as The Woolwich Equitable Benefit Building & Investment Association: it became a bank in 1997. HSBC (Hong Kong & Shanghai Banking Corporation) bought the Midland Bank in 1987 and changed the name to HSBC in 1998. The office (Midland Bank House) on Park Row/Bond Court was opened in June 1969 on the site of the Leeds Museum & Philosophical Hall. An air raid on March 14th 1941 severely damaged the Hall losing the whole frontage on Park Row as well as many exhibits. The museum reopened with a concrete rendering and included a replica coal mine and Saturday morning film shows in the hall. The Museum closed in late 1965 and demolition followed in summer 1966. National Westminster started as Beckett's Bank on the same site opening on June 3rd 1867 designed by George Gilbert Scott (foundation stone laid August 19th 1863): it had transferred from Beckett & Blayds Old Bank Briggate. The building was demolished, rebuilt and opened in January 1967. Cala Homes altered No 8 Park Row into 78 apartments. In between Russell Street and Greek Street is Greek Street Chambers being the old William Williams Brown bank building, complete with initials. The bank transferred to Park Row in 1898 and was designed by architect Alfred Waterhouse: it was taken over by Lloyds Bank in 1900. The building was partially converted into the Old Monk Bar which was opened in June 1999 and offices. The Old Monk Company's Managing Director and Chairman is Gerald PH Martin (his brother Tim is the owner of JD Wetherspoon's chain of bars) and the Leeds branch uses the old Lloyd's vaults in the basement as toilets and offices. Abbey National was opened in December 1959 as Abbey House: the Building Society became a bank in 1995; the Park Row building was demolished and the new building was opened in January 1967 and refurbished in 2001. The offices of the Hand in Hand Fire & Life Assurance Society (Commercial Union) were opened c1902 on the site of a cabinet maker's shop: the building was demolished in 1958 and rebuilt. This was sold in June 1989 to Town Centre Securities and was converted: the Parisa bar-restaurant occupies the building converted into 14 apartments by KW Linfoot of York. Barclay's Bank opened on Park Row in 1967 in a building built in 1923 - the branch closed on September

3rd 1999. Beckett's Bank is a JD Wetherspoon Free House which opened in the building on January 17th 2001. The plate glass office building on the east side was designed by Carey Jones and commended in the Leeds Awards for Architecture in 1997: it replaced the premises of Barclay's Bank and later Scottish Mutual House of the 1960's. Abtech House was built in 1900 as the West Riding Union Bank and designed by architect Edward J Dodgshun. Park Row House was the original Prudential Assurance offices designed by Alfred Waterhouse in 1894 and was altered and restored including alterations to the roofline; it was sympathetically restored in 1990-1992 by architects Abbey Hanson Rowe into a modern office block. St Andrew's Chambers was built in 1869 by George Corson for the Scottish Widows Fund and has been restored by Kevin W Linfoot of York into 19 apartments at a cost of £5 million - completion was in November 2001. St Andrew's House is at the north end of Park Row and was designed by Edward Dodgshun and was once Peacocks Furnishing Store. The Royal Bank of Scotland building on the corner of South Parade was built in 1909 by Perkin & Bulmer for the Scottish Union & National Insurance Company: it used white Marmo blocks. The old Bank of England (Sovereign House) on the west corner of Park Row and The Headrow was opened in 1864 designed by Philip Hardwick and is now offices for Hays accountancy and recruitment agency with The Bankers Draft occupying the old vaults. Park Row was closed to through traffic in May 2000.

PARK SQUARE was being developed on the east side from 1788 - the first service in the estate church of St Paul's was held in 1793. The church was on the south east corner of Park Square and was built on land donated by Bishop Wilson by architect William Johnson: the first burial in the crypt was in 1796 and the church was demolished after closure in May 1905. In 1938 Rivers House was built: Yorkshire Water Authority and now the home of the Environment Agency; the underground car park uses the old church vaults. Houses were built on the west side in 1795 and architects included John Cordingley and Thomas Johnson. Houses in the north west of the Square were built by Benjamin Wilson in 1791-97. Park Square was completed in 1810. Thomas Ambler built the Moorish-Venetian clothing warehouse for John Barran on the south side of the Square in 1878: restored by Booth, Shaw &

Partners. A branch of the Midland Bank opened in Park Square (west) in 1964 and remained for ten years - the property became the home of Kingston Unity Friendly Society. The statue of Circe is in the small park-sculpted by Alfred Drury in 1894. The statue was exhibited at the Brussels International Exhibition (1898) and the Paris Universal Exhibition (1900). In Greek mythology Circe was an enchantress who turned the followers of Odysseus into pigs when she held their leader captive (Homer's Odyssey-8th century BC).

PARK STREET links Great George Street with Westgate (continuation of The Headrow) and is now the location for the court buildings. On the east side were once Oxford Mills (boot & shoe) and the West Riding Police Station - in later days this side became the Fire Station (1883). On the west side were the Working Men's Hall (1867) and the Medical School (1865-94) - later to be taken by Charles Thackray. On the west corner at the south end was once Stewart & McDonald's clothing factory replaced by the City Treasury (Rates Office) - including the Leeds Corporation Collection Office, Electricity Meter Inspectors Department, Leeds Rating Authority and Gas Meter's Inspectors Department. The building was demolished to prepare the site for the new courts.

PARKING METERS first appeared in Leeds on April 5th 1964; they were approved for street parking in 1962 and phased out from 1996; yellow lines were already in Leeds by 1958.

PARKS *Armley* was opened in 1892: Charlie Cake Park is a small Armley parkland associated with a local vendor. *Bramley* opened in 1870 and *Burley Park* opened on September 8th 1900. *Chapel Allerton* opened in July 1900; *Cross Flatts Park* is 44 acres and opened in 1891; *East End Park* opened in 1886 and *Gipton Wood* on Roundhay Road was acquired in 1923. *Golden Acre* opened in March 1932 and the amusement park was closed in 1939 and in 1945 the City Council bought the site. *Harehills Recreation Ground* was opened on October 1st 1904 and *Holbeck* opened in 1877 with Holbeck Moor in 1900. *The Hollies* was opened on June 24th 1921 being presented to Leeds by George Brown in memory of his son Major Harold Brown. *Hunslet Moor* was purchased in 1879. *Lotherton Hall and Park* was opened in 1968: the gift of Sir Alvary Gascoigne. *Meanwood Park* was opened in 1922 and *Middleton Park* was opened on July 23rd 1920 being a gift of Wade's Charity and *New Wortley Park* opened in 1884. *North Street*

(Lovell Park) was opened in 1888 on the site of Smithfield Market, which was closed on May 27th 1886 and **Potternewton Park** opened in 1901. **Rodley** was opened in 1889. **Roundhay Park** was opened by Prince Arthur in September 1872: the result of £139,000 purchase by Sir John Barran in 1871. **Temple Newsam House and Park** were opened in 1923: the result of a purchase from Lord Halifax for £35,000 in 1922. **Woodhouse Moor** was bought for £3000 in 1855 and opened as a public recreation area in 1857. **Woodhouse Ridge** was purchased in 1876.

PARKINSON, FRANK (1887-1946) was a student at the Yorkshire College who became the chairman of Crompton Parkinson Ltd the manufacturers of electrical goods. He donated £200,000 for the Parkinson Building at Leeds University, which was started in 1938 and completed in 1951 using Portland stone. The architect was Thomas Arthur Lodge: during the War it was used as a Ministry of Food storeroom. Frank Parkinson was a Baines Scholar, Doctor of Law and an Honorary Graduate.

PAYNEL It was Norman baron Ralph Paynel who was granted the manor of Leeds by the de Lacy family of Pontefract Castle. It was Ralph Paynel who founded the Priory of the Holy Trinity at York and he gave to this Priory the churches of Leeds and Adel in 1089. When Ralph died c1109 he was succeeded by his son William Paynel who confirmed the gift of the churches to the Priory: he later founded the Priory at Drax near Selby for the monks of the order of St Augustine. In the late 12th century Robert de Gant (husband of Ralph Paynel's great grand daughter) held the manor. His son was Maurice Paynel who gained the manor of Leeds and in 1207 he granted a charter creating the Borough of Leeds: this included the 60 burgage plots created on Briggate.

PEACOCK'S STORE at the junction of Park Row and The Headrow was founded as a soft furnishings business in 1849: the store was refurbished and reopened in 1964: the store was closed in 1977 but continued to operate from Kirkstall Bridge Mills until taken over by Durastic Ltd in 1981. The Headrow store is St Andrew's House and retains the original Park Row façade with a new development on The Headrow; it is now offices.

PEARL LIFE ASSURANCE was founded by Patrick James Foley who was the President and MP for West Galway. Pearl Building (Pearl Chambers) on The Headrow had the foundation stone laid on July 14th 1910 and was opened a year later using Portland stone (one of the earliest uses) and granite. The architect was William Bakewell who had his business in East Parade. It was William Bakewell who was concerned with the layout of City Square, Oriental Baths and Coliseum Cookridge Street, Lloyds/TSB Kirkgate as well as Ilkley Town Hall. Pearl Assurance sold the building to EMCO Estates Holdings Ltd on September 29th 1995 -they also own the building on the opposite corner of East Parade/Headrow. The building has entrances on three streets and the four floors include the offices of the Coroner together with two bar-cafes.

PEARSON & DENHAM were photographic dealers who were established in 1898 on New Station Street and transferred to Bond Street c1924 in the former premises of photographer Josef Rosemont: the business was closed in 1971.

PEEL, SIR ROBERT (1788-1850) was Home Secretary 1822-27 and again in 1828-30 founding the modern police force; he was Prime Minister 1834-35 and 1841-46 - in his last year he repealed the Corn Laws. The bronze statue of Sir Robert Peel by William Behnes was donated by Walter Wainwright and is at Hyde Park corner on Woodhouse Moor; it was first unveiled on August 20th 1852 outside the Court House Park Row and then taken to Victoria Square outside the Town Hall prior to removal to Woodhouse Moor in 1937.

PENROSE-GREEN, WILLIAM (1860-1941) was the son of plumber William and Sarah Anne Penrose (1826-1908), educated at Harrogate College and married Pattie Green, daughter of Willoughby Green in 1886. He was the stepson of Thomas Green and Chairman of Thomas Green of North Street and Kirby Banks Screw Ltd. William Penrose-Green was Lord Mayor of Leeds in 1909 and an Alderman from 1910 until 1924; he lived at Rosenheim (Springwood Road) and Towerhurst where he died and was buried at the nearby St John's Church. The large family monument is inscribed *"Life's work well done; Life's race well run; Life's crown well won-now cometh rest"*. He was the Chairman of the Leeds Public Dispensary (retired 1922), A West Riding magistrate, Chairman of the Central War Conservative Association, one of the earliest members of the Yorkshire Automobile Club and President of Leeds Golf Club; he presented a silver ball cigar lighter in an African Ivory tusk to the City of Leeds in 1910.

PERKIN, WILLIAM JOSHUA BELTON (fl 1860-74) was in partnership with Elisha Backhouse moving his architect's practice from White Horse Yard to Commercial Buildings. He was the architect for St Luke's Church North Street, Armley Gaol, Moral & Industrial Training School, Manston New Hall (Seacroft Hospital site). His son **HENRY PERKIN** (1847-1925) entered his father's practice and took George Bertram Bulmer as a partner - his works include Atlas Chambers in 1910.

PETTY PRINTERS were founded in 1865 with their factory on Whitehall Road: from an initial workforce of 5, by 1900 there were 400 workers at the factory. In 1982 they took over printers Tapp & Toothill. William Petty died in 1956 and son Frank Petty died in 1984 aged 69.

PHILLIP, E W & S was a firm of jewellers in The Headrow, founded in 1880 in a yard off the same street. The founder was Lewis Edward Phillips born in Leeds and died in 1945. His sons Edward, Walter and Sidney carried on the business which became an incorporated company in 1947.

PHILLIPS is a firm of valuers and auctioneers based on East Parade in Hepper House. The Leeds business was originally founded in 1825 by John Hepper (died 1851) who moved to Trinity Street. In 1862 the business moved to East Parade where an auction room was built. The firm became Hepper & Watson in 1974 and the salerooms were operated by Phillips of London from 1976.

PHILOSOPHICAL HALL was on the corner of Park Row and Bond Street: the foundation stone was laid by Benjamin Gott on July 9th 1819; it was opened on April 6th 1821 to the designs of Robert Chantrell. This was the meeting place of the Leeds Philosophical & Literary Society founded on February 5th 1819 and included a museum which became the nucleus of the Leeds City Museum. The Hall was enlarged and reopened in 1862 but suffered a direct hit in an air raid in March 1941.

PHOTOPRESS (LEEDS) LTD was opened by Jimmie Waite (1912-82) c1949 on East Parade moving to New Station Street in 1960: the firm was one of the first tenants of the Merrion Centre in 1964 - the business was closed in 1976. He was born in Meanwood and went to Leeds Modern School: married Edith Woodward in 1938 and served in the Royal Navy and Fleet Air Arm Photographic School. Jimmie Waite trained with Robert Ledbetter and in c1939 was a partner in Ledbetters/Leeds Press Agency.

PINSENT CURTIS is one of the Big Four corporate law firms in Leeds based at offices at No 1 Park Row: they merged with City of London firm Biddle (founded c1850) in early 2001. Pinsent Curtis was formed in May 1995 from the merger of Simpson Curtis which was formed in Leeds in 1850 and Pinsent & Co founded in Birmingham in 1876. It is the 18th largest law firm in Britain based on turnover.

PITFALL STREET is a narrow access to the riverside from Call Lane near Leeds Bridge. There were two fulling mills which became a Rape Mill and a water engine worked by George Sorocold pumping water through lead pipes to a reservoir north of The Headrow (Lydgate).

PITMAN, ISAAC (1813-97) published his own shorthand system in 1837: he invented the idea while teaching in Queen Street in Barton-on-Humber. His ideas led to the foundation of many Pitman secretarial schools and colleges of commerce including one in Leeds.

POLICE The Leeds Police Force started on April 2nd 1836 and ceased to exist on March 31st 1974 on merging with the West Yorkshire Metropolitan Police. The Police first occupied the Court House in 1813 (13 cells) on Park Row/Infirmary Street and in 1836 it became the first headquarters of the Municipal Police and remained so until 1858. The headquarters were transferred to the Town Hall in 1858 and remained there until 1934 when they were moved to the adjacent Municipal Buildings. These new headquarters were officially opened on July 25th 1934 by the Chairman of the Watch Committee Councillor Hamill. They occupied the area later the home of Leeds City Museums: Brotherton House on Westgate became the new headquarters in 1965, bought by the Corporation in 1963 from a chemical manufacturing company for £325,000. The Police transferred to their new Millgarth Headquarters which were officially opened on March 17th 1976 by County Councillor KH Steeples JP Chairman of the WYMPA. The original Millgarth Street Police Headquarters opened in 1878 and included a barracks and mortuary. The old Millgarth station was closed on January 14th 1976. The Leeds Police occupied the Central Fire Station Park Street in 1883 until 1941: stables at the rear were used by the Police mounted section until 1972 on transfer to Temple Newsam: the building was demolished. The Police left Temple Newsam in 1987 for Carr Gate Wakefield. Other city centre stations included Kirkgate Market (1872-73) and Marsh Lane (1872-1907) rebuilt 1907 (closed 1961).

PORTLAND CRESCENT links Woodhouse Lane with Portland Gate to the east of Leeds Civic Hall. A new apartment block on the corner of Portland Crescent and Portland Gate was designed by architects West & Machell as part of Millennium Square.

PORTLAND PLACE is a block of 20 two bedroom apartments including five penthouses built by the Crosby Group and a restaurant developed by Rushbond: the project was completed in 2001, facing Millennium Square. Portland Gate is north of the Civic Hall, Portland Way links Calverley Street with Woodhouse Lane the name changed from St James Street in June 1960. Portland Street is a one way system linking Calverley Street and Great George Street.

PORTLAND STONE comes from the Isle of Portland on the Dorset coast and is a fine hard oolitic limestone. This area is linked by the A354 from Fortuneswell (Isle of Portland) with Weymouth: Portland Harbour is to the east and Chesil Beach to the west. The stone was used by Inigo Jones in 1619 for the Banqueting Hall Whitehall and by Christopher Wren for the rebuilding of St Paul's Cathedral. Portland stone was used to build the Civic Hall in 1933 and the Brotherton Wing of the LGI together with other Leeds buildings including the Parkinson Building at Leeds University, the Post Office building on Park Row and the Parish Church War Memorial on Kirkgate.

POST CODES for Leeds were first used on November 11th 1968 (LS).

POST OFFICE in Leeds was on Boar Lane in converted premises before 1800 and moved to Call Lane/Duncan Street in 1800-06 in Ald Atkinson's House (built c1720) and opened in Mill Hill in 1824. The Post Office opened on Albion Street on January 21st 1846. The office occupied the Court House on Park Row (1813) in 1861: the building was bought by the government for £6000 and had an added storey in 1872 for the use of the postal telegraph. The General Post Office (Head Office and Sorting Centre) in City Square was designed by Sir Henry Tanner and opened at a cost of £75,000 in April 1896. The Post Office ran their administrative centre on Park Row (opposite Lloyds Bank) from 1939 - the foundation stone was laid by the Postmaster General on April 28th 1938 with Portland Stone used in the main construction; in 1986 the building became Sun Alliance. Royal Mail House on Wellington Street was opened on the site of Leeds Central Railway Station in 1974: it closed in 1998 when the Post Office transferred to Stourton leaving a post counter service at City Square. The Stourton complex was designed by William Saunders Partnership at a cost of £30 million and was officially opened in 1999. The corporate name for the Post Office became Consignia in March 2001.

POTTER, THOMAS (1643-98) was a Leeds merchant whose wife Mary founded the almshouses near St John's Church in 1729. They were buried at this church and they have a memorial plate on the east wall of the chancel.

POTTS, WILLIAM (1809-87) It was Robert Potts who was apprenticed to a Darlington clock maker in 1790 and his son William founded his clock making business in Pudsey in 1833. In 1862 the business transferred to Guildford Street: the Guildford Clock Works; a turret clock factory opened on Cookridge Street and the mass production of clocks for schools, offices and railways was carried out behind the Guildford Street factory in Butts Court. Three of William's sons joined the firm (William Potts & Sons Ltd): Robert Potts (1843-1917) was the second son of the founder who became the Leeds head of the firm. Brother Tom left in 1928 to set up on his own while Charles left in 1930 to set up a turret clock making business at Marshall Mills, where it remained until the 1950's latterly under Anthony Potts; William ran the Newcastle branch. James Potts (1838-1910) lived at Holmleigh Headingley. The original firm was sold in 1935 to John Smith of Derby and is today trading at Bankfield Terrace as a subsidiary company: the Group also own JB Joyce of Whitchurch. The Potts family have no connection with the present company, although Michael Potts is a family member with a great interest in the history of clocks. There are many Potts clocks in Leeds still maintained by the firm - in 1864 Potts made the clock for Roundhay Park stables.

POWOLNY, ERNEST ADOLF (1839-1915) ran the catering firm on Bond Street: the firm presented the banquet which featured at the opening of Leeds Town Hall in 1858.

PRESTON, WADE (died 1789) was the owner of fields between

Woodhouse Lane and Little Woodhouse in the late 18th century. He was a wealthy merchant of Leeds whose father and grandfather were Mayors of Leeds: John Preston (1691) and Croft Preston (1715). It was his sister's daughter Julia Silly (died 1828) of Boston Spa and Bath who inherited the estate. She married Captain William Lyddon (died 1844) in 1807 and lived in Park Square - she was responsible for the development of the Preston estate whose streets were named after both Preston and Lyddon.

PRICE, SIR HENRY (1877-1963) was born in Leeds and started work at 12 years old and after training as a tailor became general manager of the Grand Clothing Hall at Keighley. He married seamstress Ann Elizabeth Craggs in 1899 and they set up a market stall and later used their front room at their Silsden house; their factory was on Templar Street and Vicar Lane and Lennox Road (1923). In 1932 the business was known as Fifty Shilling Tailors and in the 1930's they extended their factory onto Cardigan Crescent and in the following decade a factory on Burton Road Beeston opened. In 1947 the Harper Street factory was opened and in the 1954 Henry Price sold out to Joseph Collier and prepared for retirement. The Leeds shop on Boar Lane/Briggate corner occupied the Trevelyan building built by Thomas Ambler for Sir John Barran. This was one of more than 500 shops employing 12,000 staff which Henry Price owned at the height of the trade: the shops were restyled John Collier and Leeds manufacturing stopped in 1983 as the business was bought by the Hanson Trust: the shops were relaunched briefly as Collier. He furnished his mansion of Wakehurst Place Sussex and his London home of Wilbraham House Sloane Square with many antiques. The collection of antiques was auctioned at Sotheby's in November 2000 on behalf of the executors of the will of his second wife Eva.

PRICEWATERHOUSE COOPERS started in London in 1849 when Samuel Lowell Price set up his business: in 1854 William Cooper became established which in 1861 became Cooper Brothers. In 1865 Price, Holyland and Waterhouse were in partnership and in 1874 the business became Price, Waterhouse & Co. In 1898 Robert Montgomery, William Lybrand, Adam & Edward Ross became Lybrand, Ross Bros and Montgomery. In 1957 Coopers & Lybrand were formed and in 1982 Price Waterhouse World Firm was in business: in 1990 Cooper & Lybrand merged with Deloitte, Haskins

& Sells in a number of countries and in 1999 Price Waterhouse and Coopers & Lybrand merged to form Pricewaterhouse Coopers. The chartered accountancy business operates in 150 countries with the Leeds branches at 9 Bond Court (Sun Alliance House) and Benson House Wellington Street from October 1997. Coopers Lybrand were originally based in the Church Institute (Albion Court) with branches on Park Row and Albion Street; Price Waterhouse were based on South Parade and in Minerva House East Parade.

PRIESTLEY, REV JOSEPH (1733-1804) was the Minister of the Unitarian Mill Hill Chapel from 1767 to 1773. He was a founder of the private Leeds Library and a respected scientist - he discovered Oxygen in 1774. Joseph Priestley was born on March 13th 1733 at Fieldhead Birstall: his father was a cloth dresser. He was educated at the local grammar school and the dissenting academy at Daventry. He was appointed minister at Needham Market and three years later Nantwich: in 1761 he taught at Warrington until his move to Leeds. In 1773 he was appointed librarian and literary companion to the Earl of Shelburne: he stayed in Calne and worked at Bowood House in Wiltshire until 1780. Priestley went to Birmingham and after much trouble due to his support for the French Revolution, went to Hackney but on April 7th 1794 embarked with his family to Northumberland Pennsylvania USA: his wife died in 1796. In 2000 an International Historic Chemical Landmark plaque was unveiled at Bowood Hall by the Royal Society of Chemistry and American Chemical Society to mark the discovery of Oxygen on August 1st 1774.

PRIESTLEY HALL was built in 1858/59 by George Corson as the school for Mill Hill Chapel; it was adopted for wartime use in 1915-19. In 1956 the Hall was sold to Ocean Accident Assurance with the top floor leased for chapel use. It was sold and demolished in 1968 by new owners National Provincial Bank: the hall was reopened at the south end of Mill Hill Chapel.

PRINCES SQUARE features the new entrance to the Leeds railway station and car parks. Princes Exchange was opened on December 22nd 1999 and is owned by the German company Credit Suisse: a £32 million development designed by Carey Jones for Teesland Development Ltd and built by Kier Construction. Prince's Exchange won a top prize in the 14th City of Leeds Awards for Architecture.

PRISONS The first prison was on Briggate by the market cross prior to 1655 and prisoners were transferred then to a borough jail at the top of Kirkgate. This was replaced with another prison on Kirkgate with 5 or 6 cells in 1726 - long stay prisoners went to Wakefield. Leeds facilities improved with the Court House on Park Row (1811-13) with 13 cells in the basement. The opening of the Town Hall in 1858 saw the first use of the Bridewell. The Leeds Borough Gaol at Armley was completed in July 1847 at a cost of £43,000 for both land and buildings: the architects were Perkin & Backhouse.

PRUDENTIAL ASSURANCE had their offices on Park Row designed by Alfred Waterhouse in 1894 at a cost of £600,000. This was the first building in the city with lifts: later years saw the top floor altered and this was restored as part of Park Row House by architects Abbey Hanson Rowe. The project was commended in the Leeds Awards for Architecture in 1992. The Prudential Assurance bought a large area of the city centre which included the County and Cross Arcades on July 28th 1955, sold to Paul Sykes in 2001.

PUBLIC HOUSES The most interesting of the many public houses in the city centre include *The Adelphi* by Leeds Bridge and dating from 1839 although the present inn dates from the turn of the 20th century by architect Thomas Winn (died 1908) - Alfred Bellhouse bought the inn in 1889 and stayed there to 1920. *Angel Inn* was open c1870 to 1903 and was then used as business premises: these included jewellers TS & H Davis who moved from Bank Street in 1966 and closed in 1992. There was a conversion of the building to the present Angel Inn by Sam Smith of Tadcaster - opened June 2000. *Courtyard* is a Bass outlet on Great George Street/Cookridge Street, which was opened in November 1994. *Duncan (Admiral Duncan)* is a 19th century inn on the south side of Duncan Street completed following the demolition of the original properties and widening of the street. It is named after Adam Duncan (1731-1804) who defeated the Dutch at Camperdown in 1797. *Dry Dock* (Bass) is the old gravel barge Lambda which was taken to the Woodhouse Lane site in December 1993 and refurbished in 2000. *Duck and Drake* was originally The Brougham Arms standing by the railway bridge across Kirkgate. A brougham was a one horse closed carriage and named after Baron Brougham & Vaux (1778-1868) in 1851. *Felon & Firkin* on Great George Street was opened in the original Masonic Hall (1865) in 1995. The Firkin chain of pubs was founded by David Bruce. *General Elliott* on Vicar Lane dates from the early 19th century and was built on the site of a c1700 house - the public house was restored c1982. Gen George Elliott (1717-90) who became Baron Heathfield defended Gibraltar from the onslaught of Spain in 1779-83. *Harvey's Bar* was opened on May 18th 1985 in the former premises of a furniture shop and a sports shop. *Horse & Trumpet* was built c1875, "Hotel" is in stone over the entrance. *Hogshead* on Lower Briggate opened in 1997 in the former premises of Watson Cairns Cycles: previously Lockhart's Cocoa Rooms. *The Junction 7* on Wade Lane was re-launched on January 17th 2001: it was previously The General Wade, Nautical Wheel from November 1978 and The Box Office. *Palace* by the Parish Church was rebuilt on the site of an 18th century house and inn; *Pack Horse Inn* started business in 1615 as the Nag's Head and was a part of the Manor of Whitkirk displaying a Templar cross. In the 18th century the name changed to the Slip Inn and a new façade was placed in the 1940's but the inn closed in 1987 with rebuilding by 1989 on the site of the old cellars and the repositioning of the old cross; *Rat & Parrot* (Scottish & Newcastle) opened in May 1998 in the Sunday School (1888) of the Woodhouse Lane Methodist New Connexion Chapel opened in April 1858 and designed by William Hill (Leeds) - the schoolroom was originally under the chapel which closed in 1928: in later years it was used by the School of Architecture of Leeds Polytechnic. *Scarbrough* on Bishopgate Street is named after Henry Scarbrough who opened the hotel on July 17th 1823 in the 1765 manor house and stayed until 1847: the hotel was demolished c1935. The inn was first known as the King's Arms (1815); the interior was restored in 1996. *Ship Inn* off Briggate is a Georgian building. *Square on the Lane* (Boar Lane) was opened by Greenall's Brewery in December 1996. *Templar Hotel* in Vicar Lane was built in the Leylands area c1710 and became a public house c1828 with its own brewhouse: it was bought by the City of Leeds and sold to Tetley's Brewery in 1964. *Three Legs* on The Headrow is on a site once owned by John Harrison and in trust until 1897: built c1743. The inn was sold to the Leeds Estates Company who sold the next year to SW Wood of the Scarbrough Inn: he sold to Tetley's in 1902. The building was restored in the

20th century; in between this and the neighbouring Horse and Trumpet was once The Haunch of Venison which was demolished in 1873 for the completion of Thornton's Buildings. *TGI Fridays* on Wellington Street was opened on February 12th 1996. *Victoria* was opened in 1864 with 28 bedrooms to serve the courts in the Town Hall and was a popular meeting place for lawyers, journalists and politicians - in 1897 it was owned by the Victoria Hotel Co Ltd and Brown Carson Hotels (1897) - it was bought by Tetley's in 1901 and had a complete restoration in 1981 and another £300,000 restoration in 1997. *Wharf Street* on Wellington Street was the West Riding Hotel - closed and reopened as a Vittle Inn in 1977 and became Wharf Street in April 1999. *Whip* dates from c1830 and was built on one of the old burgage plots - it is visited from both Lower Briggate and Duncan Street; The Whip became a Tetley's public house in 1896 and was originally men only but this changed in the late 1970's. *Whitelocks* started life in 1715 becoming the Turk's Head c1784 and changed in 1880 to the present name when Percy Whitelock bought the establishment with the First City Luncheon Bar - the inn was rebuilt in 1886. *White Swan* (Blue Bar Café) started in the early 18th century as a coaching inn and c1765 included a singing room - Thornton's New Music Hall was built above the inn (City Varieties). *The Wrens* opened in 1880 by Alfred Wren. *Yates Wine Lodge* on Woodhouse Lane occupies the Woodhouse Lane Chapel which was opened on April 29th 1858. It was designed by William Hill for the Leeds First Circuit of the Methodist New Connexion. *Hoagy's Bar* on Eastgate was opened as The Yorkshire Hussar in 1939, changed to be the Tam O'Shanter in June 1971 and in 1983 acquired the present name.

The many public houses which no longer exist include the *Bay Horse* off Briggate which retains the stone plaque above the yard entrance inscribed *"Bay Horse Hotel-Molineaux"*. *Central Market* (building dated 1904) on Duncan Street had various names from 1969 including *The Admiral, Barbarellas and Hollywood Days & Nights* - in 1986 Sam Smith's sold it to Websters Brewery. *Cock & Bottle* was on The Headrow opposite the end of Woodhouse Lane (Dortmund Square) dated from the 18th century - in 1938 it was bought by Snowden Schofield, demolished in 1961 and the site became part of the growing department store. *Crown & Fleece* is a corner building on Crown Court/Crown Street opened in 1830 and when closed gave its name to Crown Wallpapers - it once had its own brewhouse. **Golden Cockerel** on the north side of Kirkgate (Vicar Lane/Briggate) opened c1740 and in the 1980's was renamed *The Precinct*: it closed and the premises taken by Superdrug. **Hope Inn** on Vicar Lane was an early 19th century public house, rebuilt in the early 20th century and demolished for the construction of the Inner Ring Road. **King Charles** on Lands Lane opened in 1845 and was closed on May 5th 1965: demolished for Schofields development in January 1975. **Lloyds Arms** (John Smiths) on the corner of York Street/Duke Street by the railway arch was demolished in June 1994 to make way for the Inner City Loop development. **Malt Shovel Inn** was on Lower Headrow near the corner with Vicar Lane opened c1798 and closed c1927 to be replaced with Barclays Bank in 1936. **Market Tavern** on George Street/Harewood Street was built c1806 as a private house and became a public house c1850: it closed in 1995 and was demolished - now a car parking area. **Marquis of Granby** opened on Lady Lane, rebuilt in 1897 and was closed for road widening on February 9th 1933, this public house had its own brewhouse which was closed in late 1931. This was replaced with a new building on Eastgate opened on February 10th 1933. The new inn was closed and was converted into offices in August 1984 - the Marquess of Granby was John Manners (1721-70) who was the Colonel of the Royal Regiment of Horse Guards by 1758 and C in C of the British Army (1766): he set up his men as inn keepers when they left the army. **The Mitre** on Commercial Street was designed by Thomas Winn in 1899 and was closed on March 25th 1961: it was built on the site of the Horse & Jockey (1744) by Henry Child (1850-1921). **Observatory** was opened as The Yorkshire Crown on January 12th 1977 in the old bank building in City Square/Boar Lane: this was followed by The Observatory which opened on March 31st 1989 and went into receivership in 1992. **Old George** (17th century) was on the east of Lower Briggate below the railway bridge: it was known as Ye Bush to about 1714 and became The George - the addition of Old followed the opening of the George & Dragon c1815; Simpson's Commercial Hotel where Charlotte Bronte stayed and closed after 1919. **Old Kings Arms** was on the north corner of Duncan Street prior to widening c1904 when the building was demolished - it was built as a private house for John Harrison and later became a house and shops. The building became the Mercury office and it was the headquarters of the military when in Leeds; it was the Kings Arms Tavern in the 17th century: the magistrates courts and turnpike commissioners had their meetings at the Old Kings Arms. *Old Railway Inn* was by the railway bridge on Marsh Lane: owners Bass closed it and it was demolished in July 1994. *The Peel* on Boar Lane was closed in November 1983. *Rose & Crown (Binks Hotel)* was an old coaching inn on the west side of the upper part of Briggate: demolished in 1889 for the Queen's Arcade. *The Scotsman* on Kirkgate closed in 1993 and is now Storey's. *Smith's Arms* on Marsh Lane was closed by Tetley's and it was demolished in July 1994. *Smithfield Hotel* was on North Street was built in 1848/50 and was closed in the early 20th century becoming part of the ironworks. *Star & Garter* on Duncan Street/Call Lane was closed in August 1984. The façade was restored and became listed in 1975. *White Horse* was an important coaching inn on Boar Lane: demolished for the road widening scheme. *White Swan* in Call Lane is now brb café bar and retains the original façade.

PYGMALION, GRAND was opened by Monteith, Hamilton and Monteith in 1888 on Boar Lane: it was one of the most successful early department stores. The store was demolished to make way for the first building used by C & A store, which was replaced in the 1960's: C & A ceased operations in the UK in May 2001.

QUARRY HILL is said to be the oldest inhabited site of Leeds: once called Quarrel Hill and the suggested site of an ancient settlement. Between 1786 and 1789 the area became the scene of intense building development using back to back housing, although in 1789 more valuable housing was being built in St Peter's Square. Quarry Hill became an unhealthy area and the houses were demolished by 1930: the cholera outbreak of 1832 spread through unpiped water from sewage infected wells. There were three wells on Quarry Hill and baths were built on the site of St Peter's Well-still flourishing in the early 20th century; the baths included a Turkish Bath with supplies from a 66 feet deep well - they were demolished in 1908 as part of a slum clearance started in 1895. At one time Quarry Hill was supplied with 53 public houses and there were chapels with St Mary's Church (1826-1979) on the north side of New York Road. The Ripon & Leeds Diocesan Office was opened in October 1981 on the site of St Mary's Church. Quarry Hill features West Yorkshire Playhouse (1990), Quarry House (1993), Leeds College of Music (1998), BBC Media Centre (2002) and a new £9 million home for the Northern Ballet Theatre and Phoenix Dance Company, designed by Carey Jones included in an 11 storey building with 100 apartments bar and restaurant. A new £40 million four star hotel will be developed by Metro Holst for Derby based Menzies Hotels: work started in autumn 2001.

QUARRY HILL FLATS started building in August 1936 and the Lord Mayor opened the first flat in March 1938: there were 938 self contained units housing 3000. The expense of continuous repairs, poor waste disposal and structural deterioration resulted in the demolition from September 25th 1975 (Jackson House) - completed in June 1978. Later development included the West Yorkshire Playhouse (1990), Quarry House (1992-93) and the College of Music (1998).

QUARRY HOUSE is the £55 million headquarters of the National Health Service Management Executive (Department of Health and Social Security) including the Benefits Agency, re-located from London. The block took eight years to build and was opened in 1993.

QUAYS is a development by KW Linfoot on Concordia Street: luxury apartments. The first £1 million apartment was sold in 2001.

QUEBEC was an area of old Leeds centred around City Square with the housing originally from c1759.

QUEBEC HOUSE was the home of the Leeds & County Liberal Club (founded 1881): it is faced with Burmantofts terra-cotta and had the foundation stone laid by Sir James Kitson on March 12th 1890 being built at a cost of £24,000 from designs by Chorley & Connon. William Gladstone made several public addresses from the corner balcony to crowds in Quebec Street below. The building was placed on sale in 1979: owned by Norwich Union and became National Employers House. The £3.8 million conversion includes the restoration of five stained glass windows as part of Quebecs: a 45 guest room/suite four star Town House by the Eton Town House Group which opened in Autumn 2001. The Eton Town House Group operates three London hotels and will open The Glasshouse in Edinburgh in Autumn 2002.

QUEBEC STREET was opened on September 13th 1872: Quebec was the name given to this area of Leeds and named after General Wolfe who captured Quebec Canada in 1759 after a battle of Plains of Abraham, in which Wolfe and the French commander Montcalm were killed. On the corner with King Street is Kings Court: offices opened on December 14th 1990 by the Secretary of State for the Environment Rt Hon Michael Heseltine. On the opposite side of the street is Cloth Hall Court: the first phase was opened by the Lord Mayor in September 1980 on the site of part of the Coloured Cloth Hall. Quebec House was the Leeds & County Liberal Club designed by Chorley and Connon in 1890 using terracotta.

QUEEN'S COURT is a restored courtyard off Lower Briggate (east) and features an early 18th century merchant's house: the Oates family bought their cloth on Briggate and the finishing process was carried out in Queen's Court. In the 19th century Queen's Court was occupied by wool staplers - they bought fleeces and after sorting sold them to weavers. In the late 19th century Queen's Court had a small temperance hotel, a printer, tea warehouse and grocery warehouse. The Court was completely restored in the 1970's by Brian Prideaux.

QUEEN'S HALL was the Swinegate tram depot on the Isle of Cinder estate - made into a permanent way yard in 1908-10. Architects Connon & Chorley of Park Place designed the new depot with construction by William Airey - it opened on June 29th 1914: the first trams were taken to Swinegate on October 12/13th 1914. This was short lived as the new depot was taken over by the military as an army clothing store from November 30th 1914 until September 26th 1919. The depot was enlarged using the property of the Gas Committee in 1927-29 with the demolition of both Kings Mills and the old bus garage in late 1929. The extensions were completed in March 1931 and the depot ceased to be of use after the last tram ran in Leeds in November 1959. The depot was renamed Queen's Hall and became an exhibition centre and indoor concert arena which included a concert by The Beatles: the first exhibition was the Yorkshire Ideal Homes on May 6th 1961 and another was Anthony Porter's *"colossal flea market"*. The Queen's Hall was demolished by October 7th 1989: Criterion Place opened in 1995 on part of the site which includes a car parking area.

QUEEN ANNE (1665-1714) reigned from 1702 until her death: she was married to Prince George of Denmark in 1683. In 1712 the statue by Andrew Carpenter was placed on the Moot Hall in Briggate at the expense of merchant and alderman of Leeds William Milner JP. William Milner JP married Mary Ibbotson daughter of Joshua Ibbotson (Mayor of Leeds 1685). On its removal to the new Corn Exchange in 1828 the statue was re-chiselled and in 1868 was transferred to the Town Hall. In commemoration of Queen Victoria's Jubilee in 1887 the statue was transferred to the Art Gallery by Sir Frederick Milner and other members of his family: the statue is displayed in a niche within the main foyer. There is an inscription on the base: "Carpenter fecit 1712".

QUEEN SQUARE was projected in 1803 by John and George Bischoff of Claypit House. In 1806 houses were being completed and in 1815 the west side and some of the north were built: the east side was completed after 1815: in 1822 the centre of the square was bought to be maintained as an ornamental garden. The properties are now part of Leeds Metropolitan University: The LMU invested £1 million in the refurbishment and redevelopment of Queen Square House and the purchase of adjoining property to improve and consolidate accommodation for the Faculty of Health and the Environment.

QUEEN STREET was first mentioned in 1817 and was named for Queen Charlotte, wife of King George III. The street features amongst much recent building Prince William House opened in April 1983, Elizabeth House and Coronet House. The west side of the street once featured the Queen Street Congregational Chapel built in 1825 with the burial ground and Chapel Square at the north corner. The Chapel was demolished by December 1st 1936 - including the school and clearance of the burial ground. The area also featured the Angus Iron Foundry and a flax mill in the 19th century. Darley House was built in 1937 and was the offices of the DHSS; it was practically rebuilt from 1988 and opened in March 1988 as Government Offices.

QUEEN VICTORIA (1819-1901) became Queen in 1837 and in 1840 she married Prince Albert of Saxe-Coburg and Gotha - he died in 1861. They had four sons and five daughters and she died at Osborne House Isle of Wight on January 22nd 1901 and was buried at Windsor. The Queen and Prince Albert came to Leeds for two days in September 1858 to open the Town Hall where there is the

Victoria Hall and the Albert Room. The statue of Queen Victoria by George J Frampton was unveiled outside the Town Hall on November 27th 1905 by Lord Mayor Edwin Woodhouse: it replaced a fountain from Vicar's Croft, which was removed in 1902. The large statue was moved to Woodhouse Moor in 1937. The statue in the Town Hall vestibule of Queen Victoria (Matthew Noble 1858) was once at the centre of the vestibule and was paid for by Sir Peter Fairbairn; the statue of Prince Albert was by Matthew Noble and commissioned in 1865 after Albert's death.

RADIO There was a BBC Radio relay station on Claypit Lane (1924) with the Leeds & Bradford Relay Station on Basinghall Street opened in July 1924. *Galaxy 105* is a commercial station serving Yorkshire which opened at midnight on September 29th 1997: the station is based at Kiss House, Joseph Well on Park Lane. *Radio Aire* started broadcasting from their Leeds studios on September 1st 1981. *BBC Radio Leeds* moved to studios in the Merrion Centre on May 8th and first broadcast on June 24th 1968 - the site became Jessop's Photographic Store and a bookmakers on Wade Lane. Radio Leeds moved to the old Friends Meeting House on Woodhouse Lane in 1980; in 1978 the BBC offered to buy the property from the Friends and the final meeting for worship was held on April 22nd 1979. BBC Radio Leeds is intending to move to purpose built new studios on Quarry Hill in 2003.

RAILWAY FOUNDRY occupied an extensive site: Charles Todd worked at Matthew Murray's works and moved to Kitson's factory. He founded the Railway Foundry (Shepherd & Todd) which in 1846 was bought by Edward Brown Wilson who created the world's largest locomotive works manufacturing 75 a year with 650 workers. The works closed in 1858 with the property divided and auctioned: the site became the home of some famous engineering factories in Leeds.

RAILWAY STATIONS *Central Station* was opened on Wellington Street on September 18th 1848 and closed on May 1st 1967. The station was completely demolished by April 1968: the site became the Royal Mail headquarters. *City Station* was formed from an amalgamation of *Leeds Wellington* and *Leeds New*. Leeds Wellington was opened on June 30th 1846 by the Midland Railway and Leeds New opened on April 1st 1869 to the south and slightly higher than Wellington. The new site was built on land once occupied by King's Mills and was built on arches across the goits and weirs. The Leeds New and Leeds Wellington stations were merged to become Leeds City on May 2nd 1938: the main concourse was built in 1937 but it was used for car parking from 1967 until the recent £3 million restoration. The New Station was jointly operated by NER and L & NW: from 1975 it was known as Leeds Station. It was rebuilt with the demolition of the old booking office at a cost of £4.5 million and opened by Lord Mayor JS Walsh on May 17th 1967. The whole station complex was expanded and restructured in 2000/2001 at a cost of £165 million by Railtrack. The 1970 track layout catered for 500 trains a day and in 2001 there are over 900 trains daily. There were two new tracks and overhead power lines on the west end with four new bridges; the new signalling system at the west end together with new lines cost £95 million. The completion of the project is expected to be in December 2001. New passenger facilities include four new platforms, new roof and lighting and new waiting rooms: this cost was £12 million. *Holbeck* was on two levels opening in July 1855 and both closed in July 1958; there was a pedestrian tunnel under an embankment linking two sides - the tunnel exists today to the east of the Armley Gyratory. *Marsh Lane* was opened on September 22nd 1834 as the terminus of the Leeds & Selby railway: the station was closed and re-sited on the through route to Leeds on April 1st 1869 - the station closed on September 15th 1958. The original site is used as private sidings while platform are visible at the later station.

RAMSDEN, ARCHIBALD (1835-1916) was a choirboy at Leeds Parish Church and started his pianoforte business in 1864 on Park Row: he also formed a choir which performed at many churches. New showrooms were opened at 12 Park Row designed by George Corson in 1871-demolished for redevelopment: the business closed in 1970.

RANSOME ARTHUR (1884-1967) was born at Ash Grove Hyde Park. His father was a professor of history at the Yorkshire College. He was schooled in Leeds and Rugby and wrote Swallows and Amazons in 1929 while living in Cumbria.

RAWCLIFFES opened in Leeds at 130 Woodhouse Lane c1912 taking over from the well established clothiers Maxwell Carter. In

1914 Rawcliffes moved to 7 Duncan Street the former premises of Hopkin & Hall Cash Drapery Stores. The Duncan Street building had been completed in 1905 having been designed by Percy Robinson. The firm was started in 1897 by RT Rawcliffe of Blackpool and in 1910 became a limited company. Rawcliffe's could be the oldest commercial concern in Leeds trading under the same name: the firm was taken by the Maxwell family with whom it remains.

RED HALL was probably the first brick building in Leeds being built in 1628 for Alderman Thomas Metcalfe (appointed 1630); the grounds and orchards spread to Albion Place and the garden became King Charles Croft. On February 9th 1646/47 King Charles 1st stayed at Red Hall as a prisoner: it is said that John Harrison brought the King a tankard of gold coins - an event shown in the stained glass of St John's Church. The room became known as the King's Chamber. During the 18th century it was the home of Richard Thornton and Sir Henry Ibbetson and in the 19th century Samuel Blakelock was living at Red Hall. In the early 20th century the house became offices; it was bought in 1912 by Snowden Schofield with internal restoration and the King's Chamber was converted to a restaurant. Red Hall was demolished in 1961.

REDMAYNE-BENTLEY is a firm of stockbrokers based at Merton House Albion Street. John Redmayne worked for the Yorkshire Banking Company in City Square and set up his own stockbroking business in 1876 with premises on Albion Place: he lived at Grove House Headingley. In the 1960's the firm merged with FW Bentley & Co who had their premises in the Yorkshire Post Building and took over the business of JW Granger & Co.

REED, AUSTIN LEONARD (1873-1954) was the London born son of William & Emily Reed: he married Emily Wilson in 1902 (she died 1953) and had one son and four daughters. Austin entered his father's retail hosiers & hatters shop on Fenchurch Street in 1888 and afterwards studied on an American tour including a visit to John Wanamakers for early inspiration. The first shop was opened as Austin Reed in London in 1900: he founded the shop with a £600 loan from his father. The firm expanded and became a private limited company in 1910 and went public in 1920 entering the provinces by 1913. The Regent Store store in London was the world's first department store for men in 1926: the store retains the barber's shop with art deco features. The store's customers have included the Duke of Windsor, Dean Martin, Peter Sellers, Gary Cooper and Cary Grant. Austin Reed in Leeds opened at 1 Bond Street in 1922 (Boots today) and in 1974 transferred to the opposite corner (former Pearce Jewellers & Yorkshire Post site and later Adams). The firm moved in 1985 to the old YMCA building on the corner of Albion Place/Albion Street; the previous site was opened in March 2001 as a Next store. Austin Reed was one of the first stores to use photography in advertising and hired Tom Purvis as an advertising illustrator-he was well known for his Shell, BP and Bovril images. The Leeds store closed on January 27th 2001 for refurbishment: it was reopened on March 5th 2001. The building's freehold interest was acquired by Town Centre Securities from Countrywide Investments in February 2001 in a £7.6 million deal. The property is leased to Austin Reed, Electronics Boutique and Bass Taverns-Town Centre Securities own all the south side of Albion Place between Lands Lane and Albion Street.

REID, SIR GEORGE (1841-1914) was a portrait painter and illustrator who studied at Edinburgh, Utrecht and Paris: he was knighted in 1891. He painted the portrait of Frederick Spark which is displayed in the Albert Room at the Town Hall.

REGENT STREET links Eastgate to Sheepscar Street South/Cross Stamford Street - Roseville Road. The Regency Period was from 1811-1820 when the future George IV was the Prince Regent during his father George III's insanity. The street was known for The Melbourne Brewery demolished in 1973 for new development as well as the premises of the Marsham Tyre Co and Joseph Hobson's Black Beer Manufacturers. The Harewood Barracks were opened in 1963 as replacement for the Harewood Barracks on Woodhouse Lane.

REGISTER OFFICE was opened on Park Square in 1933 in what was the former Town Clerk's Office. This office closed on February 2nd 1979 to become a branch of Barclay's Bank and two days later opened in Belgrave House on Belgrave Street; the new office was officially opened by the Lord Mayor Harry Booth on March 3rd 1979.

REINHARDT, JOHANN CHRISTIAN (1848-1913) had a pharmacy in Queen Victoria Street, where he was a senior partner in the business, which had been founded in 1774.

RESERVOIRS supplying Leeds are Eccup with work starting in 1879 and opened in April 1898 after a delay; Fewston opened in 1879; Leighton opened in 1929; Lindley Wood (1875), Swinsty (1876) and Thruscross (1966) which drowned the village of West End in the Washburn Valley; Weetwood was on the site of the filter beds and linked Eccup by a tunnel under Adel Moor and across Adel Beck by the Seven Arches viaduct which was redundant by 1866 when a cast iron pipe was laid; Woodhouse covered reservoir opened in 1863 linking Eccup.

REYNOLDS & BRANSON were chemists founded by William West in 1816 (died 1851) at 13 Briggate. In 1841 Thomas Harvey joined the firm and in 1854 William Harvey was joined by Richard Reynolds and the partnership lasted until Harvey's death in 1867. In 1883 FW Branson joined the firm with RF Reynolds and it became a limited company in 1898. They added other outlets on Commercial Street and Trinity Street and expanded the site to the rear of the Briggate shop and factory. The surgical and photographic shop on Briggate continued until 1973 - the works transferred to Larkfield Laboratories at Rawdon. The firm was taken over by Hildreth & Co Ltd of Horsforth.

RING ROADS *The Inner Ring Road* was started in January 1964 with the 1200' tunnel opening on January 14th 1967; Woodhouse Lane/Quarry Hill section opening in August 1968 and from Westgate to Wellington Road completed in 1974. The Westgate tunnel opened in February 1974 and the Wellington Flyover was opened to traffic on November 6th 1974; the completed road was fully opened in February 1975. The Woodpecker flyover was opened in January 1992 and the roads completed to the M1 in 1996. Stage 6 from the Woodpecker Junction to Cross Green was completed in January 2000 and Stage 7 will be completed by 2007 to the East Leeds Link Road. *The Outer Ring Road* had seven miles completed by 1924 - including Tongue Lane to Harrogate Road which used some of the graveyard of St John's Church and from Shadwell Lane to Roundhay Park Lane. The Seacroft by pass was opened in 1964 joining with the Cross Gates and Halton Ring Road - using Station Road which had used a wider railway bridge from 1955.

ROBERTS MART was founded by William Roberts in 1852 in Lady Lane transferring to Alfred Street and in 1892 moved to Bank Mills. In 1877 William Mart was taken into a partnership and in 1888 the firm became Roberts Mart & Co. The original paper business changed to concentrate on making polythene bags and carriers and at present supplies supermarkets with printed packaging. The subsidiary company is Romar Packaging of Newmarket Lane set up in 1983 and extrudes and converts polythene film used to manufacture bags for duvets and pillows.

ROBERTS, PETER (1914-2000) joined Robert Mart & Co in 1930 as a junior manager becoming chairman and managing director in 1954. He was educated at Ghyll Royd Preparatory School Ilkley and Scarborough College. He joined the Duke of Wellingtons regiment in 1939 and was posted to India in 1941: during the journey he met his future wife Grace. They had three children and John Roberts is the managing director of Roberts Mart and his two sons William and Ben both work for the company.

ROBINSON, MATTHIAS JP (1849-1929) was born at Constable Burton near Leyburn and founded his firm at West Hartlepool in 1875. He opened shops at Stockton and Leeds where he took over the adjacent milliners and furriers of H & D Hart. Hart's premises were part of the Leeds Estates Company's development which became Charles James Fox (piano dealer) and G Cooke outfitters; Hart's shop transferred from Lower Briggate in 1926. Matthias Robinson bought Hart's shop in 1938: the popular department store was sold to Debenhams in 1962 with a name change in 1972. Matthias Robinson died at his home Landieu Hartburn near Stockton on Tees.

ROBINSON, PERCY (1868-1950) started his architecture practice in Leeds in 1881 after working for GW Atkinson and Thomas Winn. His work includes Rawcliffes Store Duncan Street, Leeds Exchange Briggate (1907) and firemen's flats in Park Lane (1909).

ROCKINGHAM STREET once linked Wade Lane with Woodhouse Lane - it was opposite Belgrave Street and became the site of the 1960's Merrion Centre. The street also featured the Rockingham Arms public house and a short lived bus station: opened in 1954 and closed c1962.

ROCKLEY HALL YARD is off Lower Head Row and features a gas lamp together with an old stone sign for The Nag's Head public house. Rockley Hall was the home of the Rockley family who had links with the Parish Church (Rockley Quire). John Harrison bought the Hall from the Falkingham family with the rents obtained put to "pious uses"; a picture of the hall taken in 1923 appeared in a newspaper.

ROMANS There has always been conjecture that Quarry Hill was the Roman Cambodunum - Ralph Thoresby (1715) suggested that Quarry Hill had a Roman camp. The nearest settlement to Leeds was at Adel (Burgodunum) on the Roman road from York to Ilkley: remains of gravestones were discovered in 1702 together with many stone fragments of pillars, altars and monuments. During the 18th century a cellar on Briggate revealed the probable remains of a Roman road. In 1818 some Roman coins were discovered in an old house on Wade Lane and in May 1819 workmen found a Roman ford in Simpson's Fold (Dock Street) on a line with Call Lane. The Roman road followed The Calls to New Market Street and Vicar Lane: round pits were discovered in the area containing iron blades and wooden handles from Roman times. Other Roman remains found in the Leeds area include an altar discovered in 1880 at Chapel Allerton: it was inscribed *"To the Mother Goddess deservedly"*.

ROSSINGTON STREET links Cookridge Street and Woodhouse Lane including the Civic Theatre (Leeds Institute), site of Leeds Boys Modern School and the former Central High and Thoresby Schools - both now restored and altered as council offices. The Leonardo Building on the corner of Cookridge Street is an extension of the listed site completed in 1998 with the original printing works (Chorley & Pickersgill) dating from 1892. A dome on the corner tower was recreated by city architect John Thorp with contractors Wildgoose Construction and MJ Greeson Group.

ROTATION OFFICE was established on Call Lane in 1775 - where magistrates met in rotation to deal with routine concerns. In 1796 a new office was opened in the upper part of a house in Kirkgate - the ground floor had the Leeds Library. It was in this Rotation Office that the Leeds General Eye & Ear Infirmary opened in August 1829 transferring from St Peter's Square. In 1842 this moved to Park Lane and in 1870 patients were transferred to the Infirmary.

ROTHWELLS was a furniture store on New Briggate which was founded in Leeds c1905: the shop closed on December 31st 1958.

ROUND FACTORY was set up on Water Lane by Matthew Murray in 1795: Fenton, Murray and Wood was known for their steam engines, textile machinery and locomotives: John Blenkinsop's locomotive was made at the Round Factory. The premises were affected by fire in 1875 and were restored in 1991: Matthew Murray House was completed in 1992. The site is to be included in a £30 million regeneration scheme known as The Round Factory, creating an urban village by developers Ctp St James.

ROUNDHOUSE was opened by the Leeds & Thirsk Railway in 1847: the oldest of this type to survive in England. The building is now Leeds Commercial Van Hire.

ROYAL ARMOURIES were officially opened on Clarence Dock by HM The Queen on Friday March 15th 1996 - opening to the public on April 1st 1996. A start had been made on the site in February 1994 with the foundation stone laid by the Duke of Kent on September 23rd 1994 - the Duke of Kent was also present at the official opening which was followed by lunch at Leeds Civic Hall. This £42.5 million award winning museum in Leeds designed by Danish architect Henning Larsen had transferred a valuable and interesting collection from London.

ROYAL EXCHANGE on the corner of Boar Lane and Park Row in City Square - the area was once known as Park Stile - was opened on August 31st 1875 on the site of the Commercial Buildings: the architect was Thomas Healey. A replacement Exchange was opened on Briggate by Lord Mayor Wilfred Lawrence Hepton on November 12th 1907: the design was by Percy Robinson. The original Commercial Buildings were built in 1826-29 with an impressive entrance flanked by columns; the present Royal Exchange House was started in 1964 and opened two years later: it was topped out on February 8th 1966. It is intended that the Park Plaza Hotel is to be opened in 2001.

ROYAL MAIL HOUSE on Wellington Street opened in 1974 and was the sorting office until transfer of the facility to Stourton in 1998. Developers Teesland Group plc and Leeds based Sterling Capital is transforming the building into a mixed use complex: the Royal Mail depot will be demolished and the 14 storey tower will have a new terracotta and glass façade. The development of West Central is centred around a piazza with a 200 bed hotel, restaurants, bars and shops costing £120 million. There will be three ten storey blocks of offices and flats and there will be access from both Whitehall Road and Wellington Street. Work on the site will commence in 2002 with the new building completed in 2004.

ROYAL & SUN ALLIANCE was founded in April 1710 as the Sun Fire office and in Liverpool in 1845 as the "joint Stock Fire & Life Association" or Royal. In 1824 the Alliance was formed and this was followed with the incorporation of the Westminster Fire Office (1717), London (1920) and Phoenix (1782). In 1996 the Royal Insurance merged with the Sun Alliance.

ROYAL VISITS TO LEEDS There have been many royal visits to Leeds and these have included Queen Victoria and Prince Albert on September 7th 1858 to open the Town Hall; Prince of Wales on May 19th 1868 to open the National Exhibition of Works of Art at the new LGI; HRH Prince Arthur on September 19th 1872 who opened Roundhay Park; Duke & Duchess of York on October 6th 1894 to be entertained at Temple Newsam House by Mrs Emily Meynell Ingram; King Edward VII and Queen Alexandra in 1895 and again on July 7th 1908; King George V and Queen Mary in 1912 - the King was again in the city in May 1918 at Beckett Park; Queen Elizabeth The Queen Mother (as Duchess of York) on July 13th 1932 visiting the Great Yorkshire Show at Temple Newsam Park; King George V and Queen Mary on August 23rd 1933 to open the Civic Hall; King George VI and Queen Elizabeth with the Princess Royal on October 21st 1937; HM The Queen Mother on April 26th and April 27th 1954 to mark the Jubilee Celebrations at Leeds University; Princess Margaret on July 3rd 1954 to present prizes to student nurses at St James Hospital; HM The Queen in October 1958 for the final concert of the Leeds Centenary Musical Festival at Leeds Grand Theatre; The Princess Royal on March 22nd 1961 who was Chancellor of Leeds University: she married Viscount Lascelles in 1922 moving to Harewood House in 1930; The Duke of Edinburgh on November 3rd 1961 to open the Martin Wing and Link Block Laboratories at the LGI; The Queen opened Seacroft Centre on October 22nd 1965 and afterwards lunched at The Civic Hall; Princess Margaret and Lord Snowdon had lunch with the Lord Mayor on June 24th 1966; The Queen Mother was in Leeds for the HMS Ark Royal Freedom Ceremony on October 24th 1973; on December 17th 1975 Prince Charles visited the aftermath of the Leeds Markets fire; on July 12th 1977 The Queen and Duke of Edinburgh were in the city; Prince Charles came on November 16th 1978 and again with Princess Diana on March 30th 1982 to visit St

Gemma's Hospice; The Queen opened the new Art Gallery extension on November 26th 1984; Prince Charles and Princess Diana visited Cookridge Hospital on November 19th 1985; Diana Princess of Wales visited the city in September 1991 and in April 1993 she attended a conference at the West Yorkshire Playhouse and the Princess was again in Leeds on May 20th 1993. The Queen visited Chapeltown with the Duke of Edinburgh on February 23rd 1990 and in February 1995 The Duke unveiled a plaque at Kirkgate Market - he was again in Leeds on November 16th 1995; HM Queen on March 15th 1996 to open the Royal Armouries; Prince Charles visited the city on April 17th 1999; Prince Charles came to Leeds on February 9th 2001 to open the £1.5 million refurbished Accident and Emergency unit at St James Hospital.

RSPCA was founded in 1824 and has been in Leeds from 1836 first on Kirkstall Road and on Cavendish Street from 1967 with a new centre built at Rothwell.

RUSSELL STREET features the former premises of William Williams Brown's bank - including the stone WWB on the building, which is now offices and The Old Monk bar. Capitol House is owned by Evans of Leeds and includes the offices of King Sturge who transferred from Park Place in 1995. King Sturge & Co is an independent partnership of chartered surveyors and property consultants (senior partner:Malcolm King). Evans of Leeds also have Minerva House (refurbished 1990's), Greek Street car park and retail/office property on Vicar Lane. Pennine House was opened c1995 and was refurbished in the 1990's.

SADLER, MICHAEL THOMAS MP FRS (1780-1835) was born in Derbyshire and with his brother Benjamin (twice Mayor of Leeds in 1822 & 1833) ran a Leeds business for the importing of Irish linen. He was a social reformer who worked with Richard Oastler to regulate the working hours of children in the factories, promoting the Ten Hour Bill. He was married to the daughter of Samuel Fenton and had seven children: he died at New Lodge Belfast. He was a partner in the linen firm of Sadler, Fenton & Co Belfast.

SADLER, SIR MICHAEL ERNEST (1861-1943) was born in Barnsley and was educated at Rugby and Trinity College Oxford. He married Mary Harvey in 1885 - she died in 1931; his second marriage was to Eva Gilpin in 1934 - she died in 1940. He was Professor of History and Administration of Education at Victoria

University of Manchester (1903-11) and was the Vice Chancellor of Leeds University (1911-23); he had a knighthood conferred in 1919. He was an Hon Freeman of the Clothworkers Company. Sir Michael Sadler's schemes included the commissioning of Eric Gill's War Memorial for the University and generous gifts of pictures to the City Art Gallery and the University; his home was Buckingham House.

ST JOHN'S CENTRE Work started on the building in September 1982 and the foundation stone was laid on September 20th 1983 by Lord Mayor Martin Dodgson. The development was by French Kier Property Investments and Scottish Amicable Life Assurance Society - architects were The Gillinson Partnership. The first shops were occupied on September 5th 1985 - the car park opened in April 1985. The Post Office opened in June 1986 and a sculpture by Stephen Hines was placed in the Centre on November 24th 1986 (removed 1990). Scottish Amicable sold the Centre to Argent in 1995 and there have been other changes in ownership. The Centre occupies Kelsall Street and Wade Street with the site including Central Motors and parts of the glebe land of St John's Church - during the site preparation numerous human remains were discovered and re-interred; the church still retains a holding in the area.

ST PAUL'S HOUSE was built on the site of demolished Georgian houses on the south side of Park Square in 1878 by Thomas Ambler for John Barran. In 1904 the warehouse and cloth cutting works was sold to the Public Benefit Footwear Company. The construction used terracotta and glazed tiles and wrought iron entrance gates - the factory was crowned by colourful terracotta minarets. The building was sold in 1963 and restored in 1974-75: the new office accommodation was opened by Sir Nikolaus Pevsner (1902-83) on July 16th 1976. The main entrance on St Paul's Street was blocked off and the wrought iron gates removed to the present north entrance with its canopy - it won the 1979 Civic Trust award. In 1976 the terracotta minarets were wind damaged and replaced in fibreglass. St Paul's House was sold again in January 1986 to Norwich Union Pensions Management for £4 million. The sculpture outside the main entrance is "*Wound*" (1963) by Austin Wright (1911-97). St Paul's House is owned by Norwich Union; the Bar Med was opened in the basement on January 5th 2001. It is part of a chain of more than 30 outlets across Britain owned by the SFI Group and features a steel exterior entrance from Park Square.

ST PETER'S BUILDINGS are on York Street and partly derelict awaiting redevelopment - Munro House is on the corner of St Peter's Street; West Yorkshire Arts Marketing occupies St Peter's Buildings on St Peter's Square which is also the location for Yorkshire Dance studios and The Wardrobe. Coss & Morris opened their clothing works in 1906 and remained until 1917. Hirst

St Paul's House, Park Square 1978 *(Leeds Express)*

& Thackray were raincoat manufacturers at St Peter's Buildings c1917 to 1924 when they moved to Dewsbury Road Potterdale Mills. Frazer Bros were wholesale clothiers who moved from Concord Street to St Peter's Buildings c1915 and remained there until 1936. Berwin's clothing manufacturer opened the business by 1921 on Coburg Street and later Templar Street-by 1936 they moved to St Peter's Buildings and in 1938 moved to Roseville Road (Berbourne House) previously Heaton's factory. In 1962 a factory opened on Harehills Lane and the firm closed in 2000.

ST PETER'S SQUARE connects St Peter's Street/Duke Street with St Peter's Place on Quarry Hill. It is the entry to St Peter's Buildings, College of Music and West Yorkshire Playhouse. In the times prior to the building of Quarry Hill Flats in the 1930's the area was a slum site: the buildings included a cholera and fever hospital which became a school for orphans, Parish Church Sunday School, National Day School and a Parish Church Mission.

Vicar of Leeds Rev John Gott pulled down the buildings in St Peter's Square and opened the Good Shepherd Mission and School in June 1882.

SALVATION ARMY The Leeds Central Salvation Army Worship & Community Halls were opened on Nile Street by Commissioner Harry Read on 8th September 1990: the British Commissioner laid the foundation stone on 16th September 1989. The first building on the Nile Street site was the Nile Street Synagogue (1869) and the Salvation Army used this for many years before it was demolished in 1988. The Yorkshire Divisional Headquarters are in Cadman Court Morley and there are local Corps and Community Centres on Kirkstall Lane (Burley), Waterloo Road (Temple), and in Morley and West Hunslet (Hunslet Hall Road). There is a Counselling Centre & Charity Shop on Meanwood Road together with the Furniture Project on Penraevon Street. The Salvation Army has a Families Centre in Bramley and an Outreach Centre in Wetherby. The Salvation Army was founded in 1878 by William Booth (1829-1912) who was its first general. He was born in Nottingham and in 1865 founded the Christian Mission Whitechapel East London which became the Salvation Army. He married Catherine Mumford (1829-90) in 1855: their eldest son was William Bramwell Booth (1856-1929) who became general from 1912 until 1929. There is a membership of over 43,000 in Britain: it is a Christian Church with ordained ministers.

SAVAGE CLUB was founded in London in 1857 and in Leeds during 1898 meeting in Owen Bowen's studio on Cookridge Street. The first formal meeting took place on January 6th 1899 with Edmund Bogg elected Chief at the occasional "pow wows". The annual dinner was first held at the *"wigwam"* at 3 Woodhouse Lane and in 1908 a new Leeds Savage Club was formed when Edmund Bogg retired and the last meeting was held on October 11th 1912.

SAVILE, SIR JOHN (1556-1630) of Howley Hall became the first Alderman of Leeds following the Incorporation of Leeds by Charles 1st on July 13th 1626. The three owls were a part of the crest of Sir John Savile and are part of the Leeds coat of arms; the fleece on the original Corporation Seal was included to mark the importance of woollen manufacture in Leeds. Sir John Savile was often unable to be present at meetings and clothier John Harrison often deputised and himself became an alderman in 1634.

SAXONE was a shoe store on the corner of Briggate and Boar Lane. The whole building was demolished in March 1982 and replaced with a replica of the original 19th century building. Habitat was opened in the redevelopment in September 1983. Saxone moved into the building c1908 taking over from Sutton's mantle shop, previously Pullan's Central Shawl & Mantle Warehouse; the corner shop is now Macdonalds (Richard & Maurice McDonald)-incorporated 1955. Saxone is part of the Stylo Group together with Barratts (265 shops) and Priceless (104 shops).

SAXONS On the departure of the Romans in 410AD the area which included Leeds became known as the Kingdom of Elmet based at Barwick-in-Elmet: this Kingdom lasted until the defeat by King Edwin of Northumbria in 617AD. Edwin was baptised in a wooden church at York in 627AD by Paulinus and this was followed by the conversion of ordinary people by Paulinus and James the Deacon - Edwin was killed at Hatfield in 633AD. The subsequent heathen rule by the Mercians ended with the defeat of Penda at Whinmoor in 655AD and at the Synod of Whitby in 664AD the church adopted the Roman church: there are many Saxon crosses to be found in Yorkshire churches. The Saxon settlement of Leeds could have been on Quarry Hill and there would have been a 7th century wooden church - burnt by Penda in 633AD and rebuilt in stone on the site of the present Parish Church. The church remained until the Normans rebuilt in the 11th century. The end of the 8th century saw raiders from Denmark and Norway attacking the coast and the Norse Vikings reached Yorkshire from Ireland and built on their toft - a piece of land for a house. The stone crosses in the Parish Church and in the museum date from the 9th/10th century and were probably memorials to important local folk.

SCARR, ARCHIBALD WITHAM (1827-1904) was born in Burnley and moved to Addingham and then to Leeds where he had a greengrocer's stall in 1845 in the old market. He developed the business with shops in Kirkgate dealing as General Merchants and known for their hardware, dried fruit and biscuits. Archibald Scarr was Mayor of Leeds in 1887/88 and was responsible for inaugurating the new Art Gallery - he lived at Clarendon House - his wife Isabella died aged 57 in 1895. Scarr's business on New York Street closed in 1963 and the shop on Kirkgate closed in 1974.

SCATTERGOOD & JOHNSON was founded in 1900 by Bernard Scattergood being joined by Claude Johnson as a partner in the electrical equipment firm. They moved to Cookridge Street in 1912 when JN Hargreaves merged his business with the firm. Christopher Hargreaves had his apprenticeship at Peckfield Colliery and in 1956 moved the firm to St Paul's Street: in 1966 the firm moved to Lowfields Road.

SCHOFIELD, PETER (1917-96) was the son of Snowden Schofield and became the head of the firm after his father's death in 1949.

SCHOFIELD, SNOWDEN (1870-1949) opened a drapery shop at No 1 Victoria Arcade on May 4th 1901: adjacent property was acquired in 1903 and 1908 with Red Hall bought in 1911 - the King's Chamber became a restaurant. The Leeds Hippodrome Theatre which had closed in 1933 became a warehouse and was demolished for store extensions in 1967. The Theatre Royal closed in March 1957 and was bought by Schofields and demolished in May. A new building was completed in October 1962 as the Furnishing Centre. In 1938 the old Cock & Bottle public house was bought and demolished in 1961; in 1947 Snowden Schofield had bought the Victoria Arcade. In 1984 Schofields was sold to Clayform Properties (London) for £15.8 million and the Schofields Shopping Centre was opened in 1987. The store moved temporarily to the Woolworths store on Briggate in May 1987 and the old Schofields store closed in August 1987. The business was bought by Mohammed al Fayed's House of Fraser in 1988 for £6.95 million. The £16 million Headrow Centre was built on The Headrow/Lands Lane site to designs by Crampin & Pring and was opened on September 6th 1990 by the Lord Mayor Bill Kilgallon. Snowden Schofield's wife Mabel died aged 34 in 1909: Snowden died on March 24th 1949.

SCHOOL STATISTICS There are 298 schools in Leeds (2001) with 117,000 pupils; the schools include 18 Infants, 14 Junior, 212 Primary, 43 High, 11 Special and 37 Early Years Centres.

SCHOOLS *Central Higher Grade School* was founded by the Leeds School Board in 1885 as the co-educational Leeds Central Higher Grade School. It occupied the schoolroom of the Oxford Place Chapel from June 1st 1885 prior to transfer to the £48,000 purpose built school with a controversial flat roof on Woodhouse Lane: it was formally opened in October 28th 1889 by George J

Cockburn. The headmaster David Forsyth was at the school from the opening in the new building until December 1918 - he died in August 1934 and was buried at Lawnswood. In 1928 Central High became City of Leeds School until the war: the school was evacuated to Lincoln and the building became the government headquarters for the Ministry of Food. The school opened again on Woodhouse Lane in 1944 as Central High School and in 1972 it amalgamated with Thoresby School. The school remained in these premises until December 1993 and moved to Bedford Field on Woodhouse Cliff opening in January 1994. The old school on Woodhouse Lane was converted and opened as council offices in February 1995: the building retains some glazed tiles by the Wortley Fireclay Co. *Leeds Girls High School* first opened in September 1876 in St James Lodge on Woodhouse Lane -it became Harewood Barracks and was demolished in 1966. In 1902 the Morley House estate (Obadiah Nussey) was obtained in Headingley and a new school was designed by Harry S Chorley: the building was started in 1904. The foundation stone was laid on July 10th 1905 and the school was opened by the Duchess of Argyll on September 29th 1906. In 1899 a kindergarten was opened in Chapel Allerton and in 1900 it was enlarged to admit girls to 13 years old - in later years it was Allerton High School. The extensions were opened in 1959 with a Sixth Form Centre (1976), Sports Hall (1983) and Arts Centre (1986). *Leeds Grammar School* The school was traditionally founded in 1552 although there is evidence that the first Grammar School in Leeds dated from about 1341. It was at the start of the 14th century that the Parish Church was burnt down and a replacement was soon completed. It is likely that when the new church had been finished lessons were conducted by the parish priest in the chantries and it is here that the origins of the famous school lie. The school became linked with the Chantry of St Katherine founded by the will of Sir Thomas Clarell in 1469. In 1547 there was a danger of school closure as the chantries were dissolved. The Master of the School Rev William Sheafield entered into an agreement with the local sheriff Sir John Nevile that the allowance generated by the chantry lands should revert to Sheafield for the remainder of his life. After his death the lands should be vested with 16 trustees to provide a salary for a schoolmaster to succeed Sheafield. Sheafield thus kept the school intact and gave it the principle benefaction under the terms of his will dated July 6th 1552. Sheafield died a year afterwards and the trustees quickly re-established the school and new premises were found in The Calls. In 1555 Sir William Ermystead gave some more land to the school and in 1580 a building in Lady Lane was bought by the Leeds people and turned into a Grammar School. It was not until 1624 that the school received its proper home when John Harrison re-located the school to one of his own fields north of the Head Row. John Harrison built the school from his own personal fortune - he was a great benefactor to Leeds and rich merchant. The school was built between Vicar Lane and New Briggate near St John's Church, which Harrison also financed and in which is his tomb. In 1691 Alderman and Mayor Godfrey Lawson gifted the school library - the first in Leeds. By 1791 the Trustees wanted to introduce other subjects and the debate resulted in a suit in Chancery in 1795. In 1805 other modern subjects were able to be taught including languages with Latin and Greek. By 1820 Leeds Grammar School was teaching Religion, Classics, Maths and English with foreign languages available. Dr Alfred Barry became headmaster in 1854 at the age of 28 - son of the architect Charles Barry who had designed the new Houses of Parliament after the fire. In 1856 Dr Barry suggested that the school should be re-located to Woodhouse Moor from the city centre. Barry's brother was another architect Edward Middleton Barry and he was appointed to design the new buildings. The sale of the old site brought in £4200 and about £7000 was raised by public subscription: the old building was sold to Samuel Denison who used it as a foundry. The foundation stone was laid on April 6th 1858 by the Bishop of Ripon. The new school was opened on June 27th 1859. St Wilfreds chapel was designed by Barry and opened in 1863 being consecrated on January 13th 1870. The boarder house opened in 1862 with the fives courts in 1876. The school colours were adopted in 1885 with the coat of arms already in existence by 1820: the hanging ram (connection with Leeds) and three books-Homer, Virgil and the New Testament. The motto Nullius Non Mater Discipline means *"Mother of all Knowledge"*. A clock was placed by William Potts & Co on the tower in 1889 and in 1897 the school song was first sung. The school was extended in 1904/05 designed by Austin & Paley of Lancaster. The foundation stone was laid in April 1904 by Lord Mayor Arthur Currer Briggs: the new wing included classrooms and science block. The Lawnswood playing fields were bought for £5000 in 1923 with the Tetley Pavilion from 1925. Between 1924 and 1926 more classrooms were added to the 1904 wing. The War Memorial Fund swimming bath and shrine were built in 1926-28: foundation stone laid November 1926 by Charles Tetley. More reconstruction and addition to buildings followed in 1936 including a new gymnasium; in 1937 an independent Junior School was opened. The Junior School moved into Sheafield House on Clarendon Road and in 1939 a lease was taken on Hartlington Hall near Burnsall. In the 1950' s a further expansion scheme was initiated with the foundation stone laid by the Lord Mayor in December 1956 for buildings on the north side. A new building on the east side of the school precinct entailed the demolition of the old island block (1881 laboratory) and was formally opened in May 1965. In 1971 the 6th Form Centre was opened as the first part in an extension plan which included another storey on the 1904 wing. In 1976 the new sports hall was in use and in 1987 the theatre was opened with the science wing in 1991. The University was looking to expand and it proved possible to negotiate a deal, which enabled the school to re-locate and rebuild on a site at Alwoodley Gates owned by the University. The new Leeds Grammar School was opened on September 11th 1997 in the £18.5 million complex - the old school closed on July 4th. The school was officially opened on June 4th 1998 by the Rt Hon Earl of Harewood: in November 1998 the chapel was dedicated in the new building - retaining some stained glass from the original chapel on display in the corridor. *Notre Dame Sixth Form College* In 1898 Canon Croskell of St Anne's Cathedral invited the Sisters of Notre Dame to take charge of St Anne's School and Holy Rosary School: the Notre Dame Pupil-Teacher Classes started on March 24th 1903. A convent was acquired in St Mark's Avenue and building of a day/boarding school started on October 23rd 1904 - the school was opened in October 1905. The school became a College on Roman Catholic schools reorganisation in 1991. The chapel was opened in 1929 to the designs of Henry Smart following the use of a temporary chapel. *St Michael's College* was opened as the Leeds Catholic College on September 18th 1905 in the Diocesan Seminary. St

John's Lodge was bought in January 1906 and the school was occupied in June. The foundation stone for a new building was laid on June 29th 1908 and the school opened at Easter 1909 - the old house became the home of the Jesuit Community. In 1933 the school became known as St Michael's College - the Jesuits left in 1970 and the college was handed over to the Leeds Diocese. A new chapel was consecrated on November 3rd 1991 on the top floor of a divided chapel area. It is proposed that the school be closed under Roman Catholic schools reorganisation.

Schools that have closed include **Blenheim School** opened on August 11th 1879 and closed as Blenheim Middle School in July 1990 with eventual demolition - the site is now University buildings including the Student Medical Practice. *City School of Commerce* established in 1923 at Portland Chambers Woodhouse Lane moving in 1924 to Portland Crescent. In 1931 partners Leonard Kaye (1878-1941), Joe Lee and Frank Wood who started the Leeds school from Huddersfield bought Clark's College on Blenheim Terrace; Clark's College started on Hillary Place in 1912 and transferred to Blenheim Terrace in 1922. De Grey College was also acquired in 1931 also located on Blenheim Terrace: from the mid-1930's the courses offered were Commercial or High School. In 1939 the school had classes for 11 to 16 year olds with a separate junior department. The uniform was dark green blazers with gold and white stripes and ties and caps for the boys: the uniform sported the school badge with motto *Ne Plus Supra* (Nothing Better). Extensions were completed in 1940 and post war emphasis changed to being mainly high school courses: the school was known as City High School & School of Commerce. The school closed in July 1964 and a year later the site was sold to Austick's bookshops for their University branch: the bookshop opened after alterations in October 1965. *Leeds Church Middle Class School* had the foundation stone laid by Sir Francis Sharp Powell of Bradford on April 5th 1875. The £7000 building on Vernon Road followed the earlier site on Basinghall Street and was designed by Charles Chorley on land bought from the Lyddon estate. The new school was opened by the Earl of Wharncliffe on August 5th 1876: the girl's entrance was on Willow Terrace Road and the boys entered from Vernon Road with the school rooms on the upper floor. In 1879 a new wing was opened in the school

Leeds Church Middle Class School - Vernon Road

which concentrated on commerce and science. The school closed in 1907 and from 1908 to 1932 was used by the Leeds Girls Modern School when the school transferred to West Park (Lawnswood School). *Leeds Boys Modern School* was founded in 1845 and opened in the basement of the Leeds Institute; it transferred to a new purpose built school built to the rear of the Leeds Institute and opened in 1888 on Rossington Street. The school transferred to West Park where it was officially opened by Prince George on September 27th 1932. The old school became part of the Technical College and later was part of the Leeds College of Art & Design. *Leeds Girls Modern School* was established in 1854 as an education department at Leeds Institute and moved to Vernon Road in 1908. The school was opened by Rowland Barran MP in May 1908 - transferring to new buildings at West Park in 1932. *Leeds National School* had the foundation stone laid on May 8th 1812: it was opened in 1813 for poor children on the site of a tithe barn near the Parish Church. *Royal Lancasterian Free School* was in the old assembly rooms on Kirkgate in 1811 with the foundation stone laid for a new building designed by Thomas Taylor on Alfred Street (parallel street to New Station Street) on January 24th 1812. The school opened a year later: the trustees included Thomas Bischoff, Richard Kemplay and Samuel Clapham. The school was run on the principles of Joseph Lancaster. **Thoresby High School** started on June 1st 1885 as a school for girls in the School Board Offices on Calverley Street as Leeds Central Higher Grade School. The boys who were accommodated at Oxford Place Chapel transferred to their new building on October 28th 1889. In 1901 the pupil-teacher college was created, designed by Walter Samuel Braithwaite and in September 1904 they moved to the new building on Great George Street adjacent to Central; the schools became separate boys and girls schools in 1910. Thoresby became a Secondary Technical School in 1946 (Grammar Technical) for Girls. The school became a girl's secondary school and in September 1972 the girls of Thoresby and boys of Central amalgamated to create City of Leeds School; Thoresby became the home for the Lower School and Sixth Form.

SCHOOL BOARD in Leeds was first elected on November 28th 1870 with Chairman Sir Andrew Fairbairn: the first Board School was Bewerley Street built in 1872-73 by George Corson. The school board building on Calverley Street was built in 1878-81 designed by George Corson; the Education Offices were transferred to Merrion House in 1986. The building was restored in 1994-95 for £2.25 million as Civic Court and Carpe Diem (sieze the day) ale & wine bar was opened in 1995 (Punch Retail) in the basement.

SCHWANFELDER, CHARLES HENRY (1773-1837) was a Leeds artist (Albion Street) who worked between 1809 and 1826: a painting of Benjamin Goodman hangs in the Civic Hall. He exhibited 11 paintings at the Royal Academy, including a portrait of a dog (1809) and Grasmere (1816); he was appointed animal painter to both the Prince Regent and King George V. The St Peter Window in the Parish Church contains glass designed by the artist, which originally featured in the old church.

SCOTT, SIR GEORGE GILBERT (1811-78) was the architect of the Leeds General Infirmary (1868-69). He was the architect of All Soul's Blackman Lane: the foundation stone was laid on September 2nd 1876. This was the last church he designed and due to ill health passed over the project to his son John Oldrid Scott.

SECOND WORLD WAR EXPERIENCE CENTRE was opened in York Place in 2000 with director Dr Peter Liddle. The Centre was visited by HRH Prince Charles on Friday February 9th 2001. Volunteers help the Centre with the cataloguing of the experiences of men and women during the last War. The Centre is part of York Place Buildings (1902).

SELLERS, WILLIAM (1887-1950) was a severely handicapped man who used two wooden blocks to move about: his patch was outside Holy Trinity Church Boar Lane. He had nine children including Catherine and Allan Sellers of Belle Isle: most of the children married. He lived near the Pineapple public house near the Pottery Field at Hunslet.

SEWERAGE IN LEEDS The development of good water drainage and sewers in Leeds originated from the cholera outbreak of 1832. The Chadwick Report of 1842 prompted action and a new scheme by John Wignall Leather was accepted in 1846.; houses were to be connected to the street sewers with new earthenware pipes. The Leather scheme suffered delays but was completed in 1855. The 26 acres of land at Knostrop had been acquired on July 6th 1848 and in 1870 the Council bought a further 26 acres from Mrs Meynell Ingram of Temple Newsam to extend the low level works. In 1873/74 the product was purified prior to entry into the River Aire and as a consequence the works for the chemical purification of sewage were constructed at Knostrop's outfall. Following Mrs Meynell Ingram's death in 1904 the Council bought 600 acres and included eight miles of new city sewers. After the Great War the high level works were restarted in 1921 and a sewer constructed to Pontefract Lane parallel to Waterloo Colliery to Cross Green Lane and then to York Road. A new pumping station opened in October 1923 and the whole Knostrop project was completed in March 1936. In 1972 work was completed on a new heat treatment, pressing and incinerator unit with new low level primary tanks) 1971) and high level inlet works (1975). In 1985 a scheme costing £19 million closed eight smaller sewage works: the official opening was in December 1988. There has been further modernisation and the Knostrop works today spread over 500 acres.

SHAMBLES were to the east of Briggate: the name derives from "sceamol" meaning a bench for sale or display of meat. The new Shambles & Bazaar was financed by Joseph and Frederick Rinder and had the foundation stone laid by Frederick Rinder on June 15th 1823 and it was opened in 1824. The development was sited between Fleet Street and Cheapside with the bazaar being above a block of shops. The whole unhealthy area of The Shambles was bought by the City Council in 1898 and passed on to the Leeds Estates Company Ltd for redevelopment.

SHAW, JOHN HOPE (1792-1864) was a solicitor of Leeds and an alderman: he was the Mayor of Leeds in 1848-49 and 1852-53; he laid the foundation stone for the Town Hall on August 17th 1853. He was President of the Leeds Philosophical & Literary Society and President of the Leeds Mechanics Institute. He acquired sites in Headingley after the 1829 Act of Parliament for enclosure of lands: his name is remembered in Shaw Lane.

SHEAFIELD, WILLIAM (died 1553) was the first benefactor of Leeds Grammar School under the terms of his will dated July 6th 1552. The Grammar School originated in Leeds Parish Church in the mid-14th century and became associated with the Chantry of St Katherine, which was dissolved in 1547. The schoolmaster Rev William Sheafield agreed with the local Sheriff Sir John Nevile that the allowance from the chantry lands would be reverted to Sheafield for his life and after his death it would be invested in trustees for a schoolmaster's salary. It was after Sheafield's death that the trustees started re-establishing the school with new premises in The Calls.

SHEEPSCAR once had a toll bar on the site of the branch library which closed in 1976 and is now the West Yorkshire Archives. The Sheepscar Interchange was approved in 1980 and opened in June 1983. Sheepscar is derived from Old Norse meaning a marsh: Sheepscar Beck flows through the area and under Timble Bridge. St Clement's Church designed by George Corson was consecrated in September 1868 and closed in 1974: it was demolished in 1976 with the site becoming a part of the Interchange. Other buildings that were demolished for the redevelopment included the Roscoe Place Methodist Chapel and The Roscoe public house which was a private house in 1831 - closed in 1982 with a plaque unveiled on the site a year later.

SHEEPSCAR BECK has its origins as Meanwood and Adel Becks and becomes Sheepscar Beck following its confluence with Gipton Beck. The beck which features in Breary Marsh, Adel Dam and Seven Arches once had several mills. It was once described as one of the dirtiest waterways in Leeds, due to the presence of the dye works at Sheepscar bridge; the tunnels through which the stream passes in the Sheepscar area were given various names including Laundry, Cannonball, Egg & Bacon and Giants Coffin. The water once flowed under Timble Bridge east of the Parish Church and joins the River Aire: the diversion and covering of Lady Beck was completed in September 1913. There had been improvements made to the beck in 1869 with further work in 1937/38; the beck through Leeds is now channelled under the roads.

SHEEPSHANKS was the name of a family of merchants of Leeds who lived at various dwellings including Sheepshanks House (built for Robert Denison c1720 probably by William Thornton) at Town End. The site eventually became The Ritz Cinema: Sheepshanks Yard was sited north of the cinema by the Inner Ring Road slip road. Rev William Sheepshanks (1740-1810) was the Vicar of St John's Church Leeds: he was born at Linton near Grassington. William was the son of Richard Sheepshanks (died 1779) and his brothers were Whittell Sheepshanks who became an eminent Leeds merchant (1743-1817) and was twice Mayor of Leeds (1795 & 1815), Richard (1747-1797), Joseph (born 1755), James a merchant of Leeds (died 1789) and John (born 1765) who was a curate at Holy Trinity Church Leeds. Rev Richard Sheepshanks (1794-1855) was descended from this Leeds woollen family and a distinguished astronomer. He was the brother of John Sheepshanks (1787-1863); his uncle was Ven John Sheepshanks Vicar of Holy Trinity Church Leeds (died 1844). The son of Whittell Sheepshanks was Richard York (change of name by licence) who lived at Wighill Park and married Lady Mary Lascelles daughter of the Edward 1st Earl of Harewood.

SHERRATT & HUGHES opened their Albion Street bookshop in July 1987 and were bought by Waterstone's Bookshops in 1989.

SHORT STREET links Butts Court with Albion Street.

SILVER, LESLIE OBE (born 1926) founded Kalon Paints and retired as Chairman of the company in 1991. He was the Chairman of Leeds United Football Club from 1983 to 1996. He was the Yorkshire Businessman of the Year in 1983 having been awarded the OBE in 1982. Leslie Silver donated funds to refurbish the City Art Gallery and was a member of the Fund Raising Committee for the West Yorkshire Playhouse. He was the driving force behind the Leeds Metropolitan University of which he became the first

Chancellor: he was also the Chairman of the Board of Governors until appointed Chancellor.

SKINNER LANE links Regent Street and North Street: on the north side are Churchill and Harewood Barracks for the Territorial Army. The barracks are the headquarters of the Leeds Detachment (Leeds Rifles) Imphal Company, the East & West Riding Regiments - this status of the Leeds Rifles was created in early 1999 as a result of the Strategic Defence Review (1998).

SKYRACK was the wapentake in which Leeds was included: this old administrative division of Yorkshire was created by the Danish-Norse kings and centred at the Old Oak at Headingley. The word is derived from *"bright oak"* with meetings being by the tree - the original fell down in May 1941. An engraving by Ellis c1850 and a knarl from the old Shire Oak tree are displayed in Abbey House Museum. A new oak sapling was planted in 1985 on the site by the Original Oak inn. The Skyrack wapentake stretched from the A1 to Otley, Ilkley and Addingham - north to Collingham, Harewood and Arthington; south to the River Aire: Rawdon, Baildon and Bingley. The Skyrack Express was a name taken by a weekly newspaper-now The Leeds Express with the editorial office in Cross Gates and published in Wakefield.

SMEATON, JOHN FRS (1724-1792) was born at Austhorpe Lodge, educated at Leeds Grammar School and went to London in 1742 to train as an attorney to follow in his father's footsteps. He was to resign from these studies and in 1750 he started a London business as a mathematical instrument maker. He was elected an FRS in 1753 and was asked to design the third Eddystone Lighthouse (the previous one was burned down in December 1752) with the building completed in October 1759. He planned the navigation of the Calder, the Firth-Clyde canal, Spurn Lighthouse together with many bridges and mills. John Smeaton died after paralysis on October 28th 1792 and was buried at Whitkirk Church in which there is a lighthouse memorial on the north chancel wall.

SMILES, SAMUEL (1812-1904) was born at Haddington and came to Leeds to practice as a surgeon in 1836 but his heart was in literature: he edited the Leeds Times (1838-1844) and wrote "Self Help" in 1859; he gave many lectures at the Mechanics Institute and was the Secretary of the Leeds & Thirsk Railway Co.

SMITH, STEPHEN ERNEST (1845-1925) set up his architect's practice in Leeds in 1868: his partner from 1878 to 1903 was John Tweedale. He was responsible for warehouses in York Place (1874), City & County Bank Park Row (1892) and the Grand Arcade (1897).

SMITH, WILLIAM HENRY (WH) (1825-91) followed his father's interest in book selling: he sold books on the Birmingham railway and opened a bookshop in Strand London in 1827 - he retired in 1857 and died aged 73 in 1865. WH Smith entered his father's shop in 1841 and became a partner in 1846 obtaining a monopoly of all the bookstalls on the London & North Western stations and by 1862 on all the other stations (109). He founded a circulating library and became MP for Westminster (1868-85), Secretary to the Treasury (1874-77), First Lord of the Admiralty (1877-80), Secretary of State for War (1885-87) - he was also Leader of the House of Commons (1887-91) and Warden of the Cinque Ports: he died at Walmer Castle. In Leeds WH Smiths opened their first station bookstall by 1901 in both stations; by 1901 they opened a shop at 5 Commercial Street and in 1926 moved to the Leeds Library Building - taking over the shop run by Richard Jackson bookseller. In 1983 WH Smiths bought the old County Court building on Albion Place and demolished the Lands Lane property to rebuild a modern store with internal communication with the court building. The new shop was opened in November 1987 and stands on the site of the first Leeds Permanent Building Society branch in Leeds.

SMITHFIELD was the cattle market, which opened on North Street on May 15th 1855: the market was closed on May 27th 1886 and moved to Gelderd Road (established 1883). The area on North Street was landscaped as Lovell Park. The Smithfield Market was remembered in Thomas Green's Smithfield Works and in the Smithfield pub - this ceased to be an inn in the early 1900's and became a part of the ironworks. Thomas Green established the iron works in 1835: they manufactured steam trams and steam rollers as well as lawnmowers. The firm closed in Leeds in 1975 with most of the land being redeveloped.

SOROCOLD, GEORGE Leeds was one of the first towns in Britain to have a piped water supply to housing: it started in 1694 designed by George Sorocold of Derby and surveyor Henry Gilbert of Leicester. He also built the first multi-storey mill in Leeds for the Thomas Lombe silk mill.

SOUTH LEEDS STADIUM   The £3.6 million stadium had the foundation stone laid in June 1995 and was opened on September 30th 1995.

SOUTH PARADE links Park Row with East Parade and once featured the South Parade Baptist Chapel. The Baptists founded their church in Leeds in 1779 holding meetings at the Kirkgate Assembly Rooms. They built a stone chapel in St Peter's Square opened in 1781 and the foundation stone for the new South Parade Chapel was laid in February 1825. The Chapel was opened on October 25th 1826 and the building was enlarged in 1836. It was decided in 1905 to move to the suburbs and the last service at South Parade was held on June 17th 1909 and the property was auctioned in 1914. The premises became the New Gallery Kinema opening on March 22nd 1920 and closing on June 10th 1922 - the premises were used as a billiard hall and ballroom prior to demolition and redevelopment. South Parade Baptist Church was opened in Headingley in June 1909 and extended in 1927 - the new street was named in 1909. In the late 19th century South Parade also featured the Mechanics Institution. South Parade was also once the site for the Leeds & County Conservative Club - in the building adjacent to the old Bank of England - now Phoenix House. Phoenix House was built c1965 by Phoenix Assurance (now part of Royal Sun Alliance) and Eagle Star (Zurich) Insurance. Crusader House was built c1972 with AW Bain moving in during the following year - the building is owned by Britannia.   Fountain House was completed c1948 as the new offices of the Yorkshire Insurance Co Ltd following use by the War Office.   Yorkshire Insurance was taken over by General Accident and they vacated the building c1968.   On the south side were the offices of the Friends Provident & Century Life - the inscription remains today. The Son Carlo restaurant opened in late 2001 in the former premises of the Legal & General Insurance.

SOVEREIGN STREET was named after Queen Victoria and included Goodall, Backhouse & Co (now new office development) and Victoria Mills (1836) - the Mills have had a variety of uses from being a drysalters, dyeware manufactury and a flour business. The Mills were restored and reopened in August 1992 as Victoria Wharf and partly provides the premises for the Leodis Restaurant. The Embankment constitutes four main office blocks by Quarmby

Construction for St James Securities (architect: David Lyons) including KPMG, No 2 Embankment opened in 1992 and Sovereign House; this had the foundation stone laid by Mrs S Marshall of Marshall Holdings on June 6th 1996. The firm of Addleshaw Booth & Co opened in the building in June 1998, transferring from the old Bank of England on Park Row. There is entry to the Queen's Hall car park opened on the site of the old complex after demolition. The Criterion Place multi-storey car park opened on November 8th 1999 and No 1 Sovereign Street was built for Royal London Mutual Insurance Society.

SPARK, FREDERICK R (1831-1919) of Hyde Terrace ran a printing business on Cookridge Street with son Henry Spark (1866-1920). He was the assistant secretary to the first Leeds Triennial Musical Festival in 1858 and was the honorary secretary until 1907. He was the founder of the Leeds Workpeople's Hospital Fund in 1887, a magistrate and governor of Wade's Charity and Leeds Grammar School. His portrait by George Reid (1841-1913) is in the Albert Room at the Town Hall.

SPARK, WILLIAM (1823-97) was the younger brother of Frederick Spark and after being organist at Tiverton Parish Church became the Leeds City Organist for 40 years.

SPEED, POLICE SERGEANT JOHN (1945-84) was killed on October 31st 1984 during the course of his duty near the Parish Church, where there is a memorial in Kirkgate. There is also a memorial plaque in the Millgarth Police Station.

SPRUCE, EDWARD CALDWELL (1849-1923) was born in Knutsford Cheshire and became a modeller for the Burmantofts Pottery Company and was to study in Paris, where he exhibited at the Paris Salon. He set up his studio on Cowper Street where he modelled many personalities including Sir James Kitson the head of the Airedale Foundry and Monkbridge Iron Works - the bust is displayed in the foyer of the Leeds Civic Hall. There is a bronze bust of Sam Wilson by Caldwell Spruce in the Leeds Art Gallery and he also was responsible for the bronze memorial to Sam Wilson at Lawnswood Cemetery. He sculpted The Alarm for Sir Edward Brotherton's home in Gledhow and was a member of the Leeds Savage Club.

SRI CHINMOY PEACE CITY the City of Leeds was dedicated to world peace on October 24th 1995 the 50th anniversary of the UN: the peace plaque is in Park Square.

STANDARD LIFE ASSURANCE COMPANY was incorporated in 1825 as the Life Insurance Company of Scotland (Fire Office: Edinburgh). The Leeds offices were designed by Archibald Neill and opened in 1901 on the site of the former court house/post office - on the north side of City Square. The building was replaced by the Norwich Union in 1969: demolished in 1995 to be replaced by No 1 City Square - opened in 1996 and designed by Abbey Hanson Rowe.

STANSFELD, JOHN was an iron merchant with premises at 6 Great George Street which were closed in November 1955 and sold to Chorley & Pickersgill printers. The business was established in 1857 and Stansfeld Chambers were converted in 2000/2001 to include an enclosed square with a glass atrium.

STAPLERS were merchants who graded and sold wool; staple towns were appointed by the king.

STARBUCKS The coffee bar chain was initially opened in Seattle's Pike Place Public Market in 1971. The two coffee bars in Leeds are on the station concourse (1999) and in the Yorkshire Assurance/ Britannia BS building on Commercial Street/Albion Street, opened in September 2000.

STEANDER is derived from "a stony place" and is the area created by the junction of Sheepscar Beck and the River Aire, the area includes Fearne's Island. The Sheepscar or Timble Beck was at the eastern edge of the medieval village of Leeds and flowed under Timble Bridge driving a water mill and supplying water for the beckside dye houses. Nether Mills was powered by the river dammed by a weir at Crown Point: the tail races of these two mills effectively isolated Steander and Fearne's Island - named after the owner of Nether Mills. In the 19th century there was a coal staith, timber yard, a coal and sand wharf and Crown Point Dye Works - closed 1942. Leeds Dam probably originated in medieval times with Nether Mills from 1636 having five water wheels by the late 18th century. The Mills had a varied use from grinding dyestuffs, cotton spinning and fulling cloth to carpet manufacture and James Richardson's chemical works; the Mills were demolished in 1957. Steander was also the site of Fred Dyson' s Steander Foundry.

STEVENS, SIR ROGER BENTHAM (1906-80) was educated at Wellington School and Queen's College Oxford. He married Constance Hipwell in 1931 (died 1976) and Jane Chandler in 1977.

He was in the Consular Service from 1928 and in the Foreign Office from 1946-1948; he was Assistant Under Secretary of State at the Foreign Office 1948-51 and was the British Ambassador to Sweden (1951-54) and to Persia (1954-58). He was knighted in 1954 (KCMG) and was the Vice Chancellor at Leeds University from 1963 until 1970. There is a stained glass window to remember his contribution to the University in the foyer of the Rupert Beckett Lecture Theatre; he had houses at Thursley Surrey and at Giggleswick.

STOCK EXCHANGE in Leeds was founded on December 5th 1844 and the first daily share list in Leeds was published on October 4th 1845. The headquarters building was built in 1846-47 at the junction of Albion Street and Albion Place: part of the building was used by Denby & Crowe in later years. The site became the new building for the YMCA designed by WH Thorp with the memorial stone laid by Lord Kinnaird in December 1906: the YMCA was opened on October 5th 1907 and officially on February 8th 1908 - the building is now partly Austin Reed. A new Stock Exchange building was opened on Albion Street in 1875 as Exchange Rooms due to a declining membership for the large building; this was demolished to make way for West Riding House.

STRONG, FREDERICK set up a business making clay pipes in 1882 on Cottage Street (York Road) with his wife Angelina; their son Samson Strong ran the business from 1895 until 1950. The shop and contents were acquired by the Leeds Museums who re-erected the shop in the Abbey House Museum.

STUDENTS IN LEEDS Leeds University has about 25,000 students, LMU has 34,000 full time and part time students (1999) with 8 Further Education Colleges having 45,000 students. The colleges include Park Lane College with 21,600, Thomas Danby has 10,749 -there are 3672 courses offered.

SUPERTRAM was approved by the government on March 28th 2001 at a cost of £500 million with the first routes opened by 2005/2006 and being fully operational in 2007: plans were first drawn up in 1988 costing £38 million. There will be three lines to Tingley (South Leeds), Whinmoor (East Leeds) and Lawnswood (North West Leeds): the length will be 28 km with 49 stations. There will be four park and ride facilities served by a fleet of 40 electric trains powered from overhead wires suspended from masts or buildings.

Each train will carry 270 running on roads or reserved track.

SWAN STREET is the main entrance to the City Varieties and was restored by September 1993. Mallorie & Co were wine and spirit merchants established in 1812 who had a shop at the Lands Lane end of the street.

SWARTHMORE EDUCATIONAL CENTRE was established on Clarendon Road (now Burley House) in 1909 by a Quaker family who named the Centre after Swarthmore Hall in Cumbria in which lived a family of Quaker sympathisers: George Fox (1624-91) was to marry the gentleman's wife after her husband's death. The Centre moved to No 4 Woodhouse Square in 1919: a house designed by Richard William Moore (1840-49). There was a homeopathic dispensary in the house from 1907 to 1953. The Centre own Nos 2, 3, 4, and 5 Woodhouse Square and have a lease at a peppercorn rent from 1969 on Nos 6 and 7 from Leeds City Council who bought them in 1961; No 1 was demolished for road improvements and was once the home of private detective Charlie Crystal; No 2 was bought as a derelict house in 1972 being once used as apartments; No 3 was the home of Bernard Lyons; No 5 was once the home of Sir Berkeley Moynihan (1896-1906) after his marriage to Isabel Jessop - now the coffee bar; No 6 was the home of Ellen Heaton and was where the poet Christina Rossetti (1830-94) stayed when she visited the National Fine Arts Exhibition at the LGI in May 1868; No 7 was the home of Sir John Rothenstein who became the Director of the Tate Gallery in London. The first warden of Swarthmore was Gerald Hibbert (1909-20). It is a non profit making charity with over 2000 people enrolling annually: two members of the Society of Friends remain on the elected council of trustees.

SWINEGATE is part of the City Loop Road and links Bridge End and Bishopgate Street. The name derives from the pigs once herded along the route. The most notable feature from the past on Swinegate were the Kings Mills - the only reminder today is a stone slab set into the river wall. Brassfounders S Dixon Ltd had their premises on Swinegate - they were established in 1825. The Malmaison Hotel was opened in the former Leeds City Transport Offices in June 1999. The Queen's Hall was built in 1914 as the Swinegate Tram Depot, closed in 1959 and became a concert and exhibition centre prior to demolition in 1989.

TATE OF LEEDS was founded by Thomas Tate when he left Ireland and joined the transport departments in Glasgow, Newcastle and Bradford: moving to the public transport department at Wakefield dealing with horse drawn vehicles. In 1922 he obtained the Ford franchise and moved to Armley Road and later to a sales and showroom on Albion Street. In 1932 the firm moved to New York Road and five years later built additional space on Trafalgar Street - used for War Department and Air Ministry contracts during the last War. The business was then run by sons Tom and Frank Tate and in 1962 the business became a company and in 1966 moved to Balm Road Hunslet. In 1975 the Yorkshire Ford Centre was created with Thomas's grandson Thomas and the business expanded to West Park Garage. In 1983 Thomas Tate formed a private company - Tate Family Holdings Ltd. The New York Road showroom saw a change in use and is still owned by Tate of Leeds.

TAYLOR, ERIC (1909-99) was head of design at Leeds College of Art (1949-56) and Principal (1956-69): he designed a mosaic for the Merrion Centre.

TAYLOR, THOMAS (1778-1826) was the architect of the Court House on Park Row in 1813, Lancasterian School on Alfred Street (1813), Union Bank Commercial Street (1813), National School Kirkgate (1813), Mansion Roundhay for Thomas Nicholson (1819), St Mary's Church Quarry Hill (1826), St John's Church Roundhay for Stephen Nicholson (1826) and the Roundhay Almshouses and School (1833) on Wetherby Road. He died after catching a cold while at St Mary's Church and was buried in his own church at Liversedge (1816).

TAYLOR'S DRUG STORES were founded by William Barber Reason (1850-1921) who worked for Goodall & Backhouse and then opened his shop in Thornton's Arcade in 1881 using his wife's maiden name. He opened a warehouse on Albion Street and the shop moved to Guildford Street and then to Burley Hill - he retired in 1912 when there were 130 shops. In 1935 the business merged with druggists Timothy White (started in Portsmouth in 1848) and Boots bought out Timothy, White & Taylors shops in 1968 for £35 million: the Briggate store closed on July 5th 1969. In 1983 the shops were sold by Boots in a £40 million deal. Taylor's Drug Company Ltd was opened in Stephen Harding Gate in the new Abbey House Museum in 2001 - replacing the original WT

Castelow chemist of Woodhouse Lane. The contents include fittings from a Goole chemist's shop with enamel and glass containers from Frederick Hayes of 13 Woodhouse Lane and John Benn of 65 Meadow Road.

TELEPHONE AREA CODE FOR LEEDS was changed from 1532 to 0113 with numbers to commence with 2 on April 16th 1995.

TELEPHONE BOXES They first appeared in 1921 with type K1 made of concrete with red wooden doors; Type K2 were introduced in 1927 made from cast iron; K3 came in 1929 and K4 followed in 1930 in cast iron. Type K5 in concrete came in 1935 but was immediately superceded by K6 designed Sir Giles Gilbert Scott in 1935. There are six of the c 20 boxes in Leeds preserved red cast iron K6 boxes outside the Post Office in City Square and they are classed as listed buildings.

TELEVISION STUDIOS The *BBC* opened their first temporary interview studio in All Souls Church parish hall in 1968, prior to the move to a small studio to the rear of the Friends Meeting House. The new studios to the west of the Friends Meeting House on Woodhouse Lane were opened in 1974: this involved the demolition of a garage, workshop where Louis Le Prince worked, Fielding's shop, Dr Denton and Dr Moorhouse's surgery and Mason's Yard with Roberts signs, a small clothing works and Featherstone's panel beaters. *Yorkshire Television* studios on Kirkstall Road were officially opened by the Duchess of Kent on July 29th 1968. The work on the new £4 million studios had started in July 1967; the fourth studio was opened in spring 1969 and colour transmission started in November 1969. A modern studio was opened on January 1st 1997 and is the largest in Britain: Yorkshire Television became part of the Granada Media Group in 1996 and holds its own broadcasting licence.

TEMPLAR CROSSES were displayed on the houses of the Manor of Whitkirk to indicate their exemption from grinding their corn at the King's Mills on Swinegate. A re-sited cross is on the restored Pack Horse Inn and the cross once on the Old George public house Lower Briggate is now re-positioned high up on the adjoining property south of the railway bridge (once Rycrofts which was affected by fire in April 1967). There were originally six on Lower Head Row and Lady Lane with ten on Templar Street: there were at one period 19 Templar Crosses in the city. Crosses exist today on houses at Whitkirk and Halton and a stone cross probably from a house on Templar Lane has been restored on the Hark to Rover Inn Stephen Harding Gate Abbey House Museum.

TENTER FIELDS were areas where the tenter frames were placed-on these frames pieces of cloth were hooked on and stretched and dried to certain sizes. The saying "on tenterhooks" derives from the possibility that cloth could be ruined during the process.

TERRACOTTA is unglazed earthenware containing "grog" which is previously fired earthenware ground to a powder. The material was introduced from Italy during the 16th century and the "baked earth" is used on many Leeds buildings manufactured at the Burmantofts Works. The Rock Colliery became the Burmantofts Pottery opened in 1842 producing materials from the local clay. The business developed under James Holroyd (1839-90) who founded the Burmantofts Faience Works: pottery manufacture ceased in 1904 and the company closed in 1957.

TESCO STORES opened in the Merrion Centre in the 1960's and closed in 1976 - the store was sold to and it became an extension to Morrison's Supermarket, which had opened in 1972. Tesco derives from tea supplier Thomas Edward Stockwell and the founder John Edward Cohen in London in 1919. It was Jack Cohen who opened a grocery stall in 1919 and in 1931 founded Tesco Stores Ltd with 1947 bringing the first self service store and the first supermarket in 1956. The first superstore was opened in 1968 and by 1976 there were 900 supermarkets: in 1983 Tesco plc was created.

TETLEY, CS had a tobacconist's shop at the junction of Lowerhead Row and Vicar Lane: it was established in 1795 and was demolished in the early 20th century redevelopment.

TETLEY, JOSHUA (1778-1859) was the son of William Tetley (1749-1834) and was responsible for the purchase of the Hunslet brewery from Wllliam Sykes in 1822. Joshua married Hannah Carbutt in March 1808 at Sheffield Parish Church and they had seven children; they lived in Albion Street, Park Square and in Salem Place. Joshua's brother was William (1776-1831) who married Sarah Anne Tetley and lived at Armley Lodge - she died in 1871 aged 89.

THACKRAY, CHARLES FREDERICK (1877-1934) bought a retail pharmacy in Leeds with Henry Scurrah Wainwright in 1902: this was the business of Samuel Taylor who took over a fruit and game shop in 1862 in Great George Street. Charles Thackray's father had a butcher's shop on the corner of Great George Street and Oxford Row and Charles was born here and lived there until he was 11: he was sent to Giggleswick School. He was an apprentice at Rimmington's pharmacy in Bradford and then went to Squire & Son in London: Charles Thackray qualified in 1899. In 1903 he married Helen Pearce - a Leeds jeweller's daughter and their son Charles Noel was born in 1905 and William Pearce in 1907 with Douglas (1909) and Freda (1911). The first surgical instruments were supplied by Selby's of London and sold in 1908 to the LGI. In the 1920's the firm was changing from pharmaceuticals and dressings to surgical supplies and extra space was needed. Thackray bought the premises on Park Street that belonged to the Yorkshire Archaeological Society and Thoresby Society in the old Medical School: built originally in 1865. Thackrays took over the new premises in 1926 retaining the Great George Street shop as the retail outlet. Thackray died on a walk in Roundhay Park near his house and his body was recovered from Waterloo Lake. This successful Leeds company was sold to Corange in 1990 and their premises on Park Street were demolished to become the site of the new courts.

THACKRAY MEDICAL MUSEUM was opened on March 25th 1997 in the old workhouse which became part of St James Hospital. The collection is based around that of Paul Thackray of the firm of surgical instrument makers.

THEATRES *City Varieties* started as a rebuilding of the White Swan Inn singing room in 1865. The White Swan was a coaching inn built in 1762 with a singing room opened in 1766: it was demolished and rebuilt in 1799. Charles Thornton rebuilt the old singing room over The White Swan and opened Thornton's New Music Hall in June 1865 but in 1876 it was closed and offered for sale. Thornton leased the theatre to John Stansfield and used the money to build Thornton's Arcade. Charlie Chaplin appeared on stage in 1897 and a year after the theatre was bought by Fred Wood (he owned the Scarbrough Hotel and Queen's Theatre Holbeck) who held the Varieties for 15 years. The new owners were Hewitt's Brewers of Grimsby and in 1923 was sold to the City Palace of Varieties Co of Leeds. In 1933 the theatre and inn were sold to Tom Lawton and in 1936 sold again to the White Swan Estate Co of Leeds-the lease was taken by Harry Joseph in 1941. In 1947 it was sold to Harry Joseph with a holding company British Union Varieties and a programme of restoration was started. From 1953 to 1983 it was used for recordings of the popular TV programme The Good Old Days featuring Leonard Sachs, Bernard Herrman and his Orchestra and members of The Player's Theatre. Harry Joseph died in 1962 and sons Stanley and Michael took over the ownership. In January 1988 the Joseph brothers vacated the theatre: it had been bought by Leeds Grand Theatre & Opera House Ltd (Leeds City Council). The Good Old Days is revived on stage twice a year to sell out audiences and there is a continuous programme of restoration. *Civic Theatre* is used for local drama groups and meets in the old lecture hall of the Leeds Institute of Arts & Sciences (Mechanics Institute). The Institute ceased in 1939 and the building was bought by the City of Leeds. Post war alterations included the change of use of a lecture hall to a theatre and in 1983 the theatre was refurbished and redecorated by Clare Ferraby. This was followed by the formation of the Leeds Civic Arts Guild to co-ordinate the activities of the many societies using the theatre and rehearsal rooms, including the Leeds Childrens Theatre formed in 1935. *Leeds Grand Theatre* was designed by George Corson (with James Watson) and opened on November 18th 1878: the site had cost £21,102 in 1876. The City Council bought the theatre in 1973 despite being sold in 1971 to Howard & Wyndhams for £380,000. The theatre was redecorated by Clare Ferraby in 1982. *West Yorkshire Playhouse* was founded in 1970 as the Leeds Playhouse: using part of the University Sports Hall which was designed by W Houghton Evans and James Ashcroft and completed in September 1970. The theatre was also used by the Leeds Film Society which had transferred from Cookridge Street. In 1984 a site on Quarry Hill was chosen for a new theatre designed by the Ian Appleton Partnership. The foundation stone was laid by Dame Judi Dench in March 1989 and the £13.5 million West Yorkshire Playhouse was officially opened by Dame Diana Rigg on March 8th 1990. The first play performed in the 750 seat Quarry Theatre was John O'Keefe's "Wild Oats"; the adjacent Courtyard Theatre seats 350.

Theatres which have been closed and demolished are the *Albion Street Music Hall* erected in 1792 and ceased operating in 1870; *Empire Palace Theatre* on Briggate opened on August 29th 1898 designed by the London architect Frank Matcham. The theatre was a Stoll Moss theatre, which was a popular music hall; it closed on February 25th 1961 and demolished in January 1962. The site became the Empire Arcade and is now Harvey Nichols store. *Hippodrome* in King Charles Croft (1848-1933) started as the New Theatre opened by Billy Thorne. This was demolished and rebuilt and opened on December 24th 1864 as The Princess Concert Hall. The theatre became The Tivoli c1898 on the opening of The Empire Theatre and it was refurbished and reopened in August 1906 as the Hippodrome closing in summer 1933 - it was bought by Schofields Store as a warehouse and demolished 1967; *Old Leeds Theatre* on Hunslet Lane was designed by John Battley and first opened on July 24th 1771 for Tate Wilkinson: it was destroyed by fire in 1875; *Prince of Wales Music and Concert Hall* was in Kirkgate and this small establishment was destroyed by fire in 1868; *Queen's Picture Theatre* was opened as a theatre in Meadow Road Holbeck in 1898 and became a cinema in December 1924: it closed in 1957. *Theatre Royal* in King Charles Croft/Lands Lane was originally built in 1849 by Joseph Hobson as the Royal Casino on a bowling green. In 1856 it became the Royal Alhambra and on August 6th 1864 became The Royal Amphitheatre; in 1864 it was remodelled but was burnt down in March 1876. Hobson rebuilt the theatre as the New Theatre Royal and Opera House which was opened in October 1876 to designs by Thomas More & Sons. Francis Laidler came to the theatre in 1909 and was responsible for the successful pantomimes. The theatre was closed on March 30th 1957, bought by Schofields Store and demolished in May 1957.

THEOSOPHICAL SOCIETY was founded in Leeds in 1892 and bought their present Queen's Square (north) building by donations in 1900: their centenary was held on September 19th 2000. The first president was J Rust and a founder member was Leeds bookseller WH Bean. The Theosophical Society studies comparative religion and was the first to develop a universal brotherhood.

THISTLE HOTELS as Mount Charlotte Hotels moved their head office from London to 2 The Calls in Leeds in 1976 with a re-location to another Leeds site planned for 2002. The company has its origins in 1932 as Lonah (Rhodesia) Gold Mines Ltd and interests shifted from Africa to Australia - the Mount Charlotte Mine at Kalgoorlie produced more than half the gold in Australia - the company name changed to Mount Charlotte (Kalgoorlie) Ltd. By 1954 all the gold mine leases had been sold and the company changed to Mount Charlotte Investments. Between 1957 and 1960 they acquired a group of London outlets and in the 1960's and 1970's hotels were being acquired, which became the sole interest of the Group. In 1974 Gale Lister of Leeds became part of the Group - they were a Leeds based wine & spirit shipping company. In 1979 the Golden Lion and Wellesley hotels were purchased and in 1986 Kingsmead Hotels were taken over-their properties included the Merrion Hotel. In 1989 thirty four Thistle Hotels were bought from the Scottish & Newcastle Breweries and the Group acquired its present name; in 1990 the company was acquired by Brierley Investments Ltd., with Robert Peel appointed to the Board - in 1978 he had become the joint managing director and was appointed Director of the London Tourist Board in 1994. In 1991 Brierley sold 20% of the shares to the Government of Singapore and 10% to Tamasek Holdings. In 1995 Mount Charlotte Investments was renamed Thistle Hotels plc and the Central Reservations Office was moved from London to Leeds in 1995; in 1998 Robert Peel stepped down as Chief Executive. In the same year a sale of 30 provincial hotels included the Golden Lion.

THOMPSON, FRANK TEMPLE (1897-1950) was born in the family home on Harehills Lane and became a house builder: he lived for a while in a house he built on land bought from Charles Ryder of Gledhow Hill. The Thompsons bought the Golden Acre estate: the amusement park was opened by Lord Mayor Fred Brown Simpson on March 24th 1932 and closed 1939 - it featured The Blue Lagoon, dance hall and a miniature railway. Frank Thompson's Parkway Hotel was opened on November 25th 1938: Jarvis Hotels bought The Parkway in 1990 and invested in improvement and expansion.

THORESBY, RALPH (1658-1725) was born in Kirkgate in the house built by grandfather in 1610. He was educated at Leeds Grammar School and married Ann Sykes of Ledsham. He had a great interest in local history and wrote Ducatus Leodiensis in 1714 (dated July 30th 1714 and dedicated to the Lord Marquis of Carmarthen son and heir of the Duke of Leeds) - it was the first history of Leeds. Thoresby had a museum in his home: he died on

October 16th 1725 and was buried in the medieval Parish Church. His memorial in the present church had been transferred and included the canopy from an old piscina. His father who died in 1661 was John Thoresby: remembered in the Parish Church by a plaque/bust by Andrew Carpenter.

THORESBY SOCIETY was formed in July 1889 on the initiative of Col Edmund Wilson of Denison Hall: for 29 years the Society - named after Ralph Thoresby - occupied rooms in the old medical school on Park Street. In 1925 they bought 16 Queen Square which was the old home of William Boyne. In July 1968 the Thoresby Society moved to the YAS premises of Claremont Clarendon Road - the old home of Dr JD Heaton. The publications of the Thoresby Society are an essential part of Leeds history and offer a unique local history resource - the first published work was in 1891.

THORNE, HENRY had their cocoa & toffee works on Lady Lane: established in 1837 and incorporated 1889. The factory was closed in 1972 and the building was demolished to create a car park where the foundations are exposed. A chocolate tin c1880 from the firm is on display in the Abbey House Museum.

THORNTON & CO were manufacturers and retailers of India Rubber and started in Leeds in the Exchange Buildings at the corner of Basinghall Street and Boar Lane in 1848: they were incorporated in 1897. They moved to their grand new premises on the west side of Briggate adjacent to the entrance to Turks Head Yard on the site of the last bow-fronted shop in Leeds which had been demolished - the building is two shops on street level. The pillared building used Burmantofts Marmo imitation marble and was designed by S D Kitson in 1922; John and George Thornton ran the retail Leeds outlet during the 1930's and the business closed on Briggate in October 1964, transferring for a few years to Seacroft prior to closure. Thornton's had one factory in Edinburgh and the Leeds shop was for retail selling wellington boots and fashions.

THORNTON, CHARLES (1820-1881) was the proprietor of Thornton's Buildings (1873), Varieties Music Hall and Thornton's Arcade (1877). He died on August 4th 1881 at his Blenheim Terrace home after confinement to bed for 3 weeks.

THORNTON, THOMAS (1874-1970) was the solicitor for 41 years with Leeds Corporation: he was Town Clerk from 1924 until 1938 having joined the Corporation in 1897. He was educated at the Leeds Parish Church Middle Class School and was elected as an Honorary Freeman of Leeds in 1937.

THORP, WILLIAM HENRY (1852-1944) set up a Leeds practice in 1876 and was later in partnership with GF Danby and then with his son Ralph Thorp and George Foggitt. He designed the Leeds Art Gallery, School of Medicine, remodelling of Oxford Place Chapel, YMCA Albion Place and Nurses Home LGI.

THRIFT STORES was started in 1881 when Wright Popplewell opened a grocer's shop eight years after JW Jessop had opened his grocer's shop in Holbeck. The two men joined to create Thrift Stores with Ideal Stores of Wellington Road (1873) and by c1962 there were 150 stores in Yorkshire. The Thrift opened their Halton shop on Cross Green Lane c1900 and their supermarket opened by the Irwin Arms in 1964. The headquarters and warehouse was on Bridge Road Kirkstall which became Clover and is now Allders; the furnishing and ladies outfitting departments on Albion Street were closed in February 1958.

THROP, JOHN (1820-1889) sculpted the statues for the Royal Exchange Building (demolished 1964) and that of Henry Rowland Marsden now on Woodhouse Moor. He lived at Beeston Hill with works on Victoria Road: John Throp exhibited at the Royal Academy from 1857 to 1880. He was buried in Holbeck Cemetery on January 15th 1889 in the family vault - the same cemetery in which Henry Rowland Marsden is buried.

THWAITE MILLS started as a fulling mill in 1641 with eight fulling stocks using four waterwheels; the Aire & Calder canal company had bought the mills and rebuilt the site 1823-25 with two large waterwheels designed by Thomas Cheek Hewes at a cost of £15, 876. In 1825 the mills were operated on lease by W & E Joy seed crushers and oil refiners specialising in rape oil for lubricating and lighting. Exotic woods were also crushed at Thwaite Mills and the extract was used to make colour dyes for the textile industry. In 1872 the Horn family came to operate Thwaite Mills grinding flint and china stone for glazing pottery and whiting-ground chalk used for whitewash. Thwaite Mills ended their working life with the manufacture of putty from whiting and linseed oil having use in the re-construction of London property after the Blitz. On January 29th 1975 the weir collapsed in a flood and the waterwheels could no longer work.

Thwaite Mills Society was formed in 1978 to restore the site by September 1989 and the Mills are now owned by Leeds City Council as a museum. Thwaite House was built in 1823 for the mill manager and after restoration became an exhibition centre.

TOD, ALLEN (NK Allen & IJ Tod) is an architect's practice based in The Calls - formed in September 1977. The business has been concerned with the Leeds Design Innovation Centre on The Calls, the restoration of the Northern School of Contemporary Dance in 1997 (officially reopened by Mark Fisher in January 1998), the Yorkshire Dance Centre in St Peter's Buildings - the practice has been working with the Yorkshire Dance Centre Trust from 1980 and the waterfront's Fletland Mills conversion to 42 The Calls for A Way of Life Ltd.

TOLLS on the turnpike roads were completely abolished on December 31st 1870 and toll bars were banned in 1873.

TOWER WORKS were built for Col Thomas Walter Harding in 1864 on Globe Road: Tower Works produced pins for the textile mills: used in the carding and combing of the wool. The well known landmark is the tower designed by Thomas Shaw in 1864 after the 12th century campanile of the Palazzo del Commune in Verona and the other dust extraction chimney was by William Bakewell in 1899 designed on the 1334 Giotto Tower at the Cathedral in Florence. The firm was amalgamated with two other firms in 1895 and became Harding, Rhodes & Co. The works were closed in 1981 and many buildings were demolished: the site is now home to many small businesses.

TOWN CENTRE SECURITIES was established on March 17th 1959 by Arnold Ziff and floated on the stock market in 1960. The first major development was the Merrion Centre, which was officially opened by Marjorie Ziff. The business is involved in property redevelopment in Leeds and remains in the Ziff family control: the offices are at the Merrion Centre.

TOWN HALL was first proposed in 1850 and two years later a competition judged by Sir Charles Barry was held for a design: won by 29 year old Hull architect Cuthbert Brodrick who won £200 for the design. The land had been bought from John Blayds for £9000 and a tender from Samual Atak was accepted for £41,835 without a tower - construction commenced in July 1853. The tower was to be added at an additional cost of £5500 and the two lions by William

Day Keyworth Jnr (contract awarded December 1865) were added at a cost of £603: the two lions at the east end were unveiled on February 15th 1867 and the two at the west end of the Town Hall steps were unveiled on June 7th 1867. The foundation stone was laid on August 17th 1853 by Mayor John Hope Shaw. The stone for the Town Hall included gritstone from Rawdon Hill, Pool Bank and from Calverley Wood with some from Derbyshire. Queen Victoria opened the new Town Hall on September 7th 1858 - a ticket for the opening is on display in the Abbey House Museum. The Town Hall was completed when the bell was hung in the tower on January 3rd 1860. The clock was designed by Edmund Beckett Denison later Lord Grimthorpe and was made by EJ Dent of London: there are 320 steps to the clock tower. The organ was designed as a five manual by Henry Smart of London and William Spark of Leeds. It was built by Gray & Davison of London between August 1857 and April 1859 with the case designed by Cuthbert Brodrick and made by Thorp & Atkinson of Leeds - ornaments were carved by Matthews of Leeds; the original estimate was £4000. The organ was first played by Henry Smart with performances of the National Anthem and the Hallelujah Chorus - it was inaugurated on April 7th 1859 by Smart and Spark. The echo organ was added in 1865 with rebuilding in 1898 and 1908 with a complete reconstruction in 1972 - the manuals were reduced to three and the console moved to the stage area to be raised and lowered by a hydraulic lift. There was a new gallery added in 1877 designed by Alfred William Morant (1828-81) - replaced in 1890 designed by WH Thorp; in 1878 new light fittings replaced the original chandeliers - the present lights in the Victoria Hall date from the 1930's. The fountain in front of the Town Hall in Victoria Square was removed in June 1902: George Frampton's statue of Queen Victoria was unveiled by Lord Mayor Edwin Woodhouse on November 27th 1905 - removed to Woodhouse Moor in 1937. There was an alteration/restoration of Victoria Square in 1937 by J Proctor, when the main steps were changed from a bow shape (1864) to being straight. A memento of this event is on display in Leeds Civic Hall - dated May 12th 1937. The Victoria Hall was restored from September 1978 until re-opening in late 1979. The Town Hall was washed and netted to prevent problems with roosting starlings in 1992 and was closed again for a few months in

2000 for a £2 million renovation with new seating and four audience boxes creating 48 additional seats - the boxes were part of Brodrick's original plan; the orchestra rises which had been re-modelled in 1904 by James Fraser were re-seated and restored. The first event after re-opening was the Final of the 13th Leeds International Pianoforte Competition. In February/May 2001 6300 Minton-Hollins encaustic tiles were laid on the front vestibule floor matching the originals from 1858.

TRAMWAYS The first tramway in Leeds started on September 16th 1871 from Boar Lane to Headingley (Original Oak Inn) hauled by horses which operated tram services opening to 1901. Steam powered cars operated from May 1891 (Sheepscar-Oakwood). The first electric tramcar was opened in Leeds on October 29th 1891 from Sheepscar to Oakwood with the public service operating from November 10th. The Crown Point Tramways Generation Station was opened in 1897. New routes were opened from 1897 and 1949 including City Square-Headingley (1900) & Woodpecker Inn-Victoria Road (York Road in 1900, Whitehall Road (1901), Canal Gardens (1902), Lower Wortley (1903), Churwell and Killingbeck (1904), Rothwell (1905), Pudsey (1908), Yeadon (1909), Lawnswood (1913), Halton (1915), Temple Newsam and Cross Gates routes in 1924, Gipton Estate (1936). The last tram ran on November 7th 1959 with the services from Cross Gates and Temple Newsam/Halton.

TRANSPORT OFFICES The first office was in the Standard Assurance Building on City Square with administration in an office on Boar Lane - transferred to City Square in 1902/05. A larger office was suggested at either the Market Buildings on Vicar Lane or the old Dispensary on North Street/Vicar Lane. In 1912 a new central office on Swinegate was suggested and plans by George Bowman were completed and approved in June 1914. The new offices were occupied from December 31st 1915. The use of the Swinegate/ Concordia Street offices came to an end and the building was restored and altered to become the Malmaison Hotel. The WYPTA offices are in Wellington House on Wellington Street-opened by Ron Todd General Secretary of the TGWU on January 31st 1990.

TREVELYAN SQUARE features the entrance to the Marriott Hotel and new offices - sold in 2000 by MEPC for £15 million. The Talbot Hounds Fountain was commissioned by Cpt Joseph Edwards for his home Castle Carr in Halifax; the house was demolished in 1961 and the fountain was rediscovered and restored by Crowther of Syon Lodge: it was bought by MEPC in 1991 for Trevelyan Square, where the Trevelyan Chambers/ Temperance Hotel were on the site. The name of the temperance hotel and later square is derived from either Sir Walter Trevelyan (1797-1879) who was the President of the United Kingdom Temperance Alliance or Sir Charles Trevelyan (1807-86) who was the Governor of Madras and Secretary of State to the Treasury.

TRINITY STREET was cleared by March 1967 for a development by Laing: it was made into a pedestrian precinct in February 1973; the street once linked Commercial Street and Boar Lane having the headquarters of the Yorkshire Evening News. This paper was founded in November 1872 as the Leeds Daily News becoming the YEN in 1905; the paper was closed on December 3rd 1963. In earlier times the street had the premises of Ross & Co paint manufacturers, Johnson's Engravers, Pygmalion Arcade Chambers and the Ostler's Arms.

TUNNICLIFFE, REV JABEZ (1809-65) was the founder of the Leeds Band of Hope in 1847: he is buried at Burmantofts Cemetery.

TURK'S HEAD YARD to the east of Briggate represents one of the burgage plots and is the location of Whitelock's Public House (First City Luncheon Bar).

TURNPIKE ROADS were opened from Leeds to Birstall (1824), Leeds and Bradford & Halifax (1741), Leeds and Elland (1741), Leeds to Selby (1741), Harrogate(1752), Otley & Skipton (1755), Tadcaster and Halton Dial (1751), Wakefield (1758), Wetherby by Roundhay (1808) & Collingham (1824) and Leeds and Whitehall (1826). The tolls were removed to Roundhay and Harrogate in 1867; to Elland in 1868; to Whitehall in 1870; to Otley in 1873. The turnpikes were the gated entries to walled towns where travellers were checked by a sentry with a pike: he would lower his pike to prevent entry. In 1633 an act provided finance for the Great North Road and the first toll gate or turnpike was erected. In later years turnpike trusts were formed with tolls paid at numerous toll bars and the keeper was responsible for the receipt of tolls and turning of the gate to allow entry. Prior to the 1773 Turnpike Act about 2000 turnpike bills were presented at Parliament. It was the advent of both canal and rail transport that caused the abolition of all turnpike roads by 1895.

TWINNINGS The City of Leeds has twinning agreements with Dortmund, Siegen and Lille and it has special links with Jullundur (India), Ulan Bator (Mongolia) and Hangzho (China).

UNION STREET to the north of Millgarth Street police station once featured the Baths, Yorkshire Hussars public house and the Kingston Unity Club & Friendly Society Hall. The car park area is to be developed as a £50 million mixed use facility as the Harewood Quarter by Town Centre Securities, including apartments and a 100 bed hotel.

UNIVERSITY *Leeds University* The Yorkshire College was opened with 24 students on Cookridge Street on October 26th 1874 - formally inaugurated by the Duke of Devonshire on October 6th 1875. In 1877 the Beech Grove estate was bought for £13,000 from John Lawson: Beech Grove House now houses the Education Department. Alfred Waterhouse was appointed to build on the new site; on October 23rd 1877 the foundation stone for the first part of the Clothworker's Building was laid by the Archbishop of York and it was completed in 1879 at a cost of £70,000 by the Worshipful Company of Clothworkers for the City of London - including lecture room, museum and weaving sheds. In 1878 it became known as The Yorkshire College and in 1884 was combined with the Medical School which was opened on October 5th 1894. The College became part of the Victoria University in 1887 as a partner of the colleges in Manchester and Liverpool. The principle frontage on University Road (College Road) at the south east corner was the Edward Baines Memorial Wing - a testimonial to the Chairman of the Council of the Yorkshire College Sir Edward Baines and opened in his presence by HRH Albert Edward Prince of Wales on July 15th 1885. The engineering department was opened by Jeremiah Head on October 18th 1886. The Great Hall was opened in October 1894 by the Duke & Duchess of York: reopened by Richard Horne MP on May 7th 1992 after refurbishment. On April 25th 1904 the Royal Charter was signed creating Leeds University. Extensions were opened on July 7th 1908 by King Edward VII who was accompanied by Queen Alexandra and Princess Victoria. The University Road buildings covering 8 acres cost £250,000 of which £250,000 was contributed by the Worshipful Company of Clothworkers. The Textile

Department building designed by Paul Waterhouse was opened in April 1912; the Department of Agriculture dates from 1925 and Paul Waterhouse also conceived the Mining, Fuel and Metallurgy building. In 1926 plans were presented to build on Woodhouse Lane and the foundation stone for the Brotherton Library was laid by Lord Brotherton on June 24th 1930 and it was opened on October 6th 1936 by Archbishop of Canterbury Cosmo Gordon Lang and the Duke of Devonshire - builders William Airey used Swedish marble for the interior of the £100,000 building. The University Union was opened by W Riley-Smith on July 3rd 1939. The Lanchester & Lodge (Thomas Arthur Lodge) Parkinson Building in Portland stone was completed in 1951 and opened by the Princess Royal on November 9th 1951 on the occasion of her installation as Chancellor: the height of the tower is 189 feet. The University Refectory was opened in 1954 and the Man Made Fibres Building opened on June 29th 1956 and the Engineering Building on Woodhouse Lane dates from 1960-61. The University Hall of Residence at Bodington Hall was opened in November 1961 with Morris Hall opening in January 1966. The Arts Building dates from 1957-64, Houldsworth School of Applied Science (1960-64) and Engineering Building (1957-63). The University architects in 1958 were Chamberlin, Powell & Bon who succeeded Lanchester & Lodge: the new firm designed Chancellor's Court as a centrepiece of the complex - an RIBA award was granted in 1973. The Henry Price Building for student accommodation on Clarendon Road (Reservoir Street) was opened in June 1965 and the first Sports Hall dated from 1967. The University Central Television Service was officially opened in August 1970 and the new £115,000 Textile block opened in May 1971 by the Duchess of Kent. The Clinical Sciences Building opened in 1979 and the new Sports Hall was opened in September 1986. The University of Leeds Institute of Education was founded in 1948; the Leeds University Business School and Leeds Innovation Centre are both on the site of Leeds Grammar School. There are c25,000 students at Leeds University (2001) with 6185 staff (1999) including 2154 academic and research staff. *Leeds Metropolitan University* can be traced back to 1824 with the foundation of the Leeds Mechanics Institute. In 1868 this became the Leeds Institute of Science, Art and Literature; later Leeds College of Technology. Leeds College of Art had origins in a government school of design founded in 1846; Leeds College of Commerce started in 1845 as the Mathematics & Commercial School; the Yorkshire Training School of Cookery was founded in 1874 and by the 1960's had been renamed the Yorkshire College of Education and Home Economics. In the early 1950's the Leeds LEA decided to house the four colleges on a central site - City Campus. The Central Colleges with the departments of Building and Mechanical Engineering of the College of Technology were housed in buildings north of the Civic Hall. The Leeds Polytechnic came into being in 1970 and was enlarged in 1976 with the addition of the James Graham College and the City of Leeds & Carnegie College - now the 94 acre campus at Beckett Park. City Campus Brunswick Building (Faculty of Health and Environment) was opened by Sir Hugh Casson (President of the Royal Academy) on April 24th 1979. The Polytechnic was a constituent part of the Leeds LEA until it became an independent Higher Education Corporation on April 1st 1989. University status was granted to Leeds Polytechnic in September 1992 with a change of name to Leeds Metropolitan University; inauguration followed on February 12th 1993. In 1998 the LMU became one of only two English Higher Education Institutions to merge with a general purpose Further Education College - Harrogate College at Hornbeam Park. A £20 million LMU New Learning Centre (City Campus) was opened by the Earl of Harewood on September 22nd 2000 - this is named after the first Chancellor Leslie Silver. *Open University* has a regional centre in Leeds: there are 13 Regional Centres with 300 study centres and 5000 students in the region. The Open University was established in the UK in 1969.

UNIVERSITY ROAD was once a bus route through the University precinct and was closed to traffic on April 1st 1963. The road was originally College Road in 1874 and changed with the status in 1904.

VALENTINE, SAINT according to tradition was a Bishop of Terni who was martyred at Rome. Although probably non-existent his festival on February 14th coincided with the Roman mid-February festival of Lupercalia (February 15th). The name derives from the Lupercal, which was the cave in which Romulus and Remus were suckled by the wolf. The Leeds Valentines Fair has taken place on the streets and squares from February 1992.

VAUGHAN, FRANKIE (1930-2000) was Frank Ephraim Ableson and raised in Leeds starting his professional career at the Leeds City Varieties: married to Stella Kesselman for nearly 50 years - they had a son David and daughter Susan. Frankie Vaughan achieved fame as Mr Moonlight and was remembered in February 2001 at a memorial service held at the West End Synagogue at Bayswater; he was a King Water Rat of the Royal Variety Club. He was the son of Leah and Isaac Ableson, a student at the Leeds College of Art and sang at The Leeds Empire and with Nat Temple's Band. Frankie Vaughan was a great supporter of the Boy's Clubs and was awarded the CBE in 1997.

VENTURA is based at Hepworth House on Claypit Lane and is a customer services outsourcing company set up in October 1995. In 1968 Hepworths set up its own department to provide credit for folk wishing to buy a Hepworth suit and by 1977 it became Club 24 with customers receiving up to 24 times their monthly repayments. The business grew and in 1982 Hepworths re-launched 78 of their stores as Next and in 1984 the company provided credit for 3000 high street shops. By 1988 the customer base grew and Club 24 formed a joint company with the Kingfisher Group called Time Retail Finance: clients included Woolworths, B&Q and Comet being based at the back of Hepworth House. In 1991 the Co-operative Business Unit was launched which was eventually to be a Customer Service Management group with a move away from credit. In 1994 the company bought Clydesdale Financial Services. In November 1995 Providence House was opened being named after the original name of the factory - Providence Works, and the whole site is to have a multi-million pound refurbishment. Ventura manages over 8 million accounts including BT Cellnet, Northern Rock, Co-operative Bank and The Woolwich. Ventura with its staff of 3000 was awarded the Customer Service Call Centre of the Year accolade in 2000.

VERNON ROAD In 1875 land from the Lyddon estate was purchased by the managers of the Leeds Church Middle Class School in Basinghall Street. The foundation stone was laid for a new school in April 1875 and the school was opened by the Earl of Wharncliffe on August 5th 1876. A new west wing was opened in 1879 and the main building was later extended with the newer wing demolished: the school closed in 1907. The following year the school was used by the Leeds Girls Modern School who remained until they transferred to Lawnswood in 1932. In 1913 the School of Housewifery was opened by the Leeds Education Committee at Vernon Road: the Leeds School of Cookery and Domestic Economy was founded in 1874 by the Yorkshire Ladies Council of Education in Albion Street and in 1907 transferred to the Leeds Education Committee. This became the Yorkshire Training College of Housecraft in 1936 and in 1966 was the Yorkshire College of Education and Home Economics. The building was vacated in 1967 and in 1980 became the Department of Law until 1993. On February 7th 1997 the single building (1875) became the North Yorkshire Regional Office of the NHS Executive; Vernon Road became known as Willow Terrace Road. The Department for NHS Postgraduate Medical and Dental Education (transferred from Harrogate) provides training and recruitment for Yorkshire doctors. It was officially opened on July 11th 1997 by Sir Kenneth Calman (Chief Medical Officer for Health). The New Jerusalem Church had the foundation stone laid by Alfred Backhouse on May 7th 1884 for the Swedenborgians and was opened on January 28th 1885 - the church building is now the University Outdoor Centre. The first church of the Swedenborgians was constituted in London in 1787 and the Albion Chapel in Leeds was opened on Albion Walk in 1794/1796.

VICAR LANE is one of the original streets of Leeds and was originally King Street and renamed on the building of the vicarage in 1717. One of the buildings was the Vagrant Office established in 1818; the buildings on the west side were demolished in 1899 for road widening and the street was enhanced with the rebuilding of the Leeds Covered Market in 1904 and the Coronation Buildings in 1902. Vicar Lane once continued to Lady Lane and the North Bar stone before becoming North Street. Vicar Lane was remodelled in 1993.

VICARAGES The vicarage for the Leeds Parish Church was at the corner of Vicar Lane and Kirkgate on Vicar's Croft being built in 1717. Richard Fawcett who was Vicar of Leeds from 1815 to 1837 agreed to the sale on August 28th 1823. The site became the Leeds Free Market in 1824 - extended in 1843 onto the yards including the Boot & Shoe. The vicarage was sold for £8000 and with part of these proceeds the parishioners bought the large house at 6 Park

Place from the widow of Mr Knubley: restored and altered with a new frontage as offices. It was here that a few Vicars resided including Rev Walter Farquahar Hook (Vicar 1837-59): the vicarage moved to No 5 Hillary Place until the University bought the property in 1926.

VICTORIA CROSS HOLDERS are remembered by a bronze plaque in the Garden of Remembrance on The Headrow, which was unveiled in November 1992. The men who were born in Leeds included the first VC in Leeds awarded to Private John Pearson 8th Hussars who won the VC in the Indian Mutiny on June 17th 1858 - he was born in Leeds on January 19th 1825 and died in Ontario Canada on April 18th 1892. The second VC was awarded to Colour-Sergeant Edward McKenna of the 1st battalion 65th Reg (later Yorkshire & Lancashire Regiment) who won the VC in the New Zealand Maori War on September 7th 1863. The subsequent holders of the VC were Sgt Alfred Atkinson of the 1st Bn The Yorkshire Regiment in South Africa on February 18th 1900 - he died at Paardeberg on February 21st 1900; Private Charles Ward 2nd Bn KOYLI who won the VC in South Africa on June 26th 1900 - he was born in Hunslet on July 10th 1877 and died in Glamorganshire on December 30th 1921; Cpl (later Captain) George Sanders West Yorks Reg (Prince of Wales Own) won the VC in France on July 1st 1916 - he was born in New Wortley on July 8th 1894 and died in Leeds on April 4th 1950 and was buried at Cottingley; Lance Sgt Frederick McNess 1st Bn Scots Guards won the VC in France on September 15th 1916 - he was born in Bramley on January 22nd 1892 and died in Bournemouth on May 4th 1956; Acting Cpt David Philip Hirsch 4th Bn West Yorks Reg won the VC in France on April 23rd 1917 - he was born in Leeds on December 28th 1896 and died in France on the day of the award; Private William Boynton Butler 17th Bn West Yorks Reg won the VC on August 6th 1917 in France - he was born in Leeds on November 20th 1894 and died on March 25th 1972: buried at Hunslet Cemetery; Sgt Albert Mountain 15/17th West Yorks Reg won the VC in France on March 26th 1918 - he was born in Leeds on April 19th 1895 and died on January 7th 1967: cremated at Lawnswood; Sgt Laurence Calvert 5th Bn KOYLI won the VC in France on September 12th 1918 - he was born in Hunslet on February 16th 1892 and died in Dagenham Essex on June 7th 1964; Private Jacob Weiss (Jack White) of the 6th Reg King's Own

Royal Lancashire was born in The Leylands (Templar Street) in 1896: his parents were Russian Jews who moved to Edinburgh and Manchester - he won the VC in 1917 on the battle for Baghdad under General Maude when he showed bravery in crossing the River Diala; Acting Flt Sgt Arthur Louis Aaron RAF won the VC during a bombing flight from Turin to Algeria on August 13th 1943 - he was born in Leeds on March 5th 1922 and died as a result of injuries on the day of the flight - he was buried at Bone War Cemetery on the Algerian coast near the Tunisian border. The holders of the VC who were not born in Leeds but are buried in the City are Pt Smith Charles Hull 21st Lancers who won the VC in India on September 5th 1915 - he was born in Harrogate on July 24th 1890 and died in Leeds on February 13th 1953 - buried in Woodhouse Cemetery; CSM (later Cpt) Harry Daniels Rifle Brigade won the VC on March 12th 1915 in France - he was born in Wymondham Norfolk on December 13th 1893 and died in Leeds on December 13th 1953: buried at Lawnswood; Sgt Major John Crawshaw Raynes 71st Brigade RA won the VC on October 11th 1915 in France - he was born in Eccleshall Sheffield on April 28th 1887 and died in Leeds on November 13th 1929: buried at Harehills Cemetery; Pte (later Cpt) Wilfred Edwards 7th Bn KOYLI won the VC in Belgium on August 16th 1917 - he was born in Norwich on February 16th 1893 and died in Leeds on January 4th 1972 - buried in Wortley Cemetery; Pte Arthur Poulter 1/4th Duke of Wellington's (WR) Reg won the VC in France on April 10th 1918 - he was born at East Witton Wensleydale on December 16th 1893 and died in Leeds on August 29th 1956: buried at New Wortley Cemetery.

VICTORIA PLACE is a new development on Manor Road south of the river which includes Energis House. The Yorkshire Bank Leeds Regional Business Centre was opened on October 26th 2000. There is the NatWest Leeds Account Management centre together with the offices of Yorkshire Forward opened on January 28th 2000 and chartered quantity surveyors Richard Boothroyd & Associates.

VICTORIA QUARTER was developed by enclosing Queen Victoria Street and including County and Cross Arcades; the new name was first used in March 1989. The refurbishment project included the covering of the street with a stained glass roof by Brian Clarke (May 1990) and cost £6 million. The original arcades and flanking buildings on Queen Victoria Street were by Frank Matcham in

1902 (Leeds Estates Company). The late 1970's saw a one way traffic system introduced along the street from Briggate to Vicar Lane and in later years the traffic was banned to make a pedestrian precinct. The Victoria Quarter project received an award in the Leeds Awards for Architecture in 1991 - the architect was Derek Latham for Prudential Portfolio Managers, it was sold in 2001.

VICTORIA QUAYS is south of the river on Dock Street: the development was launched by William Waldegrave MP on September 21st 1987. The £3.8 million complex by Barratt's Urban Renewals (Northern) transformed the 1880 warehouse once used by the Waterways for storing flax, hemp, grain and flour. The development included 120 apartments completed in 1987/1988 with conversion of a listed building and three new blocks.

VICTORIAN SOCIETY (West Riding Group) was founded at Claremont in April 1974 affiliated to the Yorkshire Archaeological Society - the inaugural meeting took place on November 20th 1974 with Sir Nikolaus Pevsner (1902-83) as the speaker.

WADE, GENERAL MARSHAL (1671-1751) led forces who came north in an attempt to protect the country from possible invasion following Bonnie Prince Charlie's landing in Scotland in July 1745. Henry Ingram at Temple Newsam organised the defence of the Leeds district with Henry Ibbetson of Red Hall and other local folk. Wade came north with 10,000 men in October and marched to Newcastle being forced to retreat. The Scots reached Derby and avoided Leeds on their own retreat - General Wade set up a camp for his troops on Woodhouse Moor.

WADE HALL was built in 1630-40 for Thomas Jackson and named after benefactor Thomas Wade (1530): much was demolished in 1863 for the formation of Kelsall Street from Woodhouse Lane to Wade Lane, later the site of the Merrion Centre. The remaining part of the Hall was the Old Hall Hotel prior to demolition.

WADE LANE links Merrion Street with Lovell Park Road having the Merrion Centre and Hotel together with Fairfax House and the site of Brunswick Chapel (Yorkshire Bank). In 1818 a number of copper Roman coins were discovered in an old house on Wade Lane. Fairfax House was opened in 1972 with this office building owned by Great Bear Properties of London.

WADDINGTON, JOHN was the founder of a printing firm who

started with theatrical advertising c1896 on Wade Lane. In 1902 the business had also started on Great Wilson Street: the two branches merged in 1920. In 1905 John Waddington Ltd was established and soon Victor Hugo Watson (1878-1943) was appointed as lithographic foreman. In 1913 a plant was established on Elland Road which burnt down in 1915 and Union Mills on Dewsbury Road were bought: it became a plc in 1921. The four sites of the firm were brought together in 1922 when the business moved into the premises of the Conqueror Typewriter Co on Wakefield Road Hunslet. The firm manufactured playing cards from 1921 with Lexicon produced in 1932 and Monopoly in December 1935. The firm moved into carton, light bulb packaging (1949), greeting cards, Green Shield Stamps and postage stamps in 1970/80.

WALDEN'S was founded in Leeds in 1896 by Sam Walden and the handmade bed specialists have their shop in Grand Arcade/New Briggate. The shop were first based on New York Road and transferred to the Stock Exchange Building on Albion Street (with neighbours Martins the Cleaners and Pobjee's fruit and flower shop) later to become West Riding House; they took over the former Chinese Restaurant in the Grand Arcade, which was enlarged in 1984. The firm was bought by Benson's of Warrington in 1990 and in February 1997 became a part of the Roseby Group.

WALSH, JUDGE BRIAN QC (1935-2000) was educated at Leeds Grammar School and became President of Cambridge Union. Between 1990 and 1994 he was the leader of the North Eastern Circuit of the judiciary; from 1996 Brian Walsh was the Recorder of Leeds and since 1998 was Deputy Lieutenant of West Yorkshire; he was Chairman of Yorkshire Cricket from 1986.

WAPENTAKE is derived from Old Norse "vapnatak" meaning a flourish of weapons: a sword was raised to signify assent in a judicial assembly. Leeds was in the Skyrack Wapentake centred on the Old Oak at Headingley where early meetings were convened. A wapentake was an administrative district in the former Danelaw shires and was the equivalent of the Hundred: a 10th century division of a shire where administration was by the shire reeve (sheriff). The Danelaw was the north eastern area of England occupied by the Danes in the 9th and 10th centuries which included the kingdoms of Bernicia, York and East Anglia together with the five boroughs (Derby, Lincoln, Nottingham, Leicester and Stamford). In 1894 the Local Government Act established District Councils which were the successors to the wapentakes.

WAR MEMORIALS The first site for the *City war memorial* was in City Square unveiled by the Earl of Harewood on October 10th 1922; this was moved to the Garden of Rest designed by JE Procter on The Headrow opened on October 28th 1937. The Winged Victory on the top of the Portland stone war memorial by Henry Charles Fehr was removed twice for repair in 1940 and 1965 when the Angel became unstable during a gale. In 1967 a marble capping was introduced and the bronze taken to Lawnswood Cemetery: removed in November 1988 and the Head of Victory was displayed in the Art Gallery. In 1992 the Angel of Peace sculpted by Ian Judd was placed on the top. The protective surrounding railings were positioned in 1997. *The University War Memorial* was sculpted by Eric Gill in Portland stone entitled *"Our Lord driving the money changers out of the Temple"* and dedicated on June 23rd 1923 by the Bishop of Ripon in the presence of the Prince of Wales: it had been commissioned by University Vice-Chancellor Sir Michael Sadler and donated by Frances Cross. In 1961 it was moved from near the Baines Wing entrance to the New Arts Centre and is in the entrance foyer of the Rupert Beckett Lecture Theatre. The *War Memorial at Leeds Parish Church* was designed in Portland stone by Sir Edwin Lutyens as a memorial to the men of the 7th and 8th battalions of the West Yorkshire Regiment (Leeds Rifles). The dedication was held on November 13th 1921 and unveiled by Cpt G Sanders VC MC.

WARD, SIR JOHN (1844-1908) of Moor Allerton House joined his father's business as a provision merchant on Kirkgate. He became an alderman in 1886, a magistrate in 1890 and was knighted in 1906. He was a great supporter of the provision of a new Dispensary and was involved with the progress of slum clearance in the Marsh Lane area. He was the Lord Mayor of Leeds in 1902.

WASH HOUSES were first opened at Holbeck in 1928 with the one at Armley opening in September 1932 by Prince George. The Armley wash house was closed on July 30th 1977.

WATER SUPPLY IN LEEDS Leeds was one of the first towns in Britain to have a piped water supply to housing: it started in 1694 designed by George Sorocold of Derby and surveyor Henry Gilbert of Leicester. A water wheel near Leeds Bridge pumped water to reservoirs at Lydgate by St John's Church and in Albion Place (YMCA site) where the lead piped water served the houses of those who could afford the system. In the mid-18th century new works were built at Pitfall Mills and in 1795 a new reservoir was completed in New Briggate (Harrison Street). Most of the Leeds inhabitants were relying on water from wells, boreholes, water carriers and the river. A more powerful engine was used in 1809 with the number of houses supplied increasing; a steam engine was introduced at Pitfall in 1815 and river water was used for drinking until 1837 when new works were built: the Leeds Waterworks Company was incorporated in 1847. In 1852 the company was bought by the Leeds Corporation and they constructed Eccup Reservoir with service reservoirs at Weetwood and Woodhouse Moor (Reservoir Street - now Clarendon Road). Three new impounding reservoirs were built at Fewston, Swinsty and Lindley Wood in the Washburn Valley: the four reservoirs hold 5100 million gallons. There are also pumping stations on the River Ouse at Moor Monkton and River Wharfe at Arthington. The Headingley Treatment Works opened in 1995 at a cost of £33 million with 26 million gallons a day provided for Leeds. The supply of water is controlled by Yorkshire Water - the name was changed to the Kelda Group in August 1999 - the name is Norse for "clear water".

WATERHOUSE, ALFRED (1830-1905) was the architect of the first buildings of Leeds University.

WATERMAN, DR FANNY (born 1920) is the daughter of a Russian émigré who became a jeweller in Hatton Garden London. She was educated at Chapel Allerton High School and Leeds University: she married Dr Geoffrey de Keyser at the Beth Hamedrash Synagogue in 1944; she played the piano in concert during the war at Leeds Museum on Park Row. In 1950 she gave up her concert career when her son Robert was born and she became a teacher with pupils including Alan Schiller and Michael Roll. Fanny Waterman launched the Leeds International Piano Competition in 1961: the winner at the first concert in 1963 was Michael Roll - at the age of 17. Fanny Waterman was awarded the CBE in June 2000 and in 2001 was awarded the Distinguished Musician Award by the Incorporated Society of Musicians in recognition of her achievements as a pianist, teacher and founder of one of the world's top piano competitions. The latest award was set up in 1976 to acknowledge outstanding contributions to British musical life.

WATERSTONE, TIM founded the chain of bookshops in 1982: the first opened in London. In 1988 the first bookshop-café was opened in Bath and in 1999 Waterstones opened the largest bookshop in Europe in the old Simpson's store on Piccadilly. The 80 shops were sold to WH Smith in 1989, who sold together with Dillons Bookshops (merged with Waterstones in April 1998) to HMV Media Group's book division in April 1998. Tim Waterstone became the non-executive chairman of HMV Media: in July 1989 Waterstone's Investments was formed incorporating WH Smith's Sherratt & Hughes bookshops and they were re-branded as Waterstones - as were the Dillons stores. Waterstone's have two stores in Leeds on Albion Street - the larger top store opened on November 19th 1991, while the lower shop on Albion Street was originally opened as Sherratt & Hughes in July 1987 who had taken over the Chelsea Girl store; the shop became a branch of Waterstones in 1989. The main store was refurbished and enlarged-reopening on April 22nd 1999 with a first floor coffee shop.

WATSON, JOSEPH (1873-1922) founded the soap factory on Whitehall Road (Soapy Joe's) where the product was produced from the 1860's until 1987. In the early days the Matchless Cleanser was the main brand until the firm became a part of Unilever in 1930: Joseph Watson's shares were sold to William Lever in 1917. Soap production ceased at Whitehall Road after the last War and the firm concentrated on toiletries: shampoos, shaving creams and toothpastes. In 1962 Watson's business merged with D & W Gibbs and Pepsodent Ltd: renamed Gibbs Proprietories Ltd in 1965 - further changed on the merger with the Austrian firm of Elida. Elida Gibbs was trading in 1971. In 1969 some of the production went to the factory at Seacroft where all production was concentrated after 1987. The company became Elida Fabergé and from early 2001 was Lever Fabergé. He was born on Monkbridge Road Headingley and inherited the business from his father. He was educated at Repton School and Clare College Cambridge. Joseph Watson was the third generation of Watsons at the Whitehall Factory; in 1911 he bought the mansion of Wood Hall (hotel from 1988) and later moved to Linton Springs. He received a peerage in the New Year Honours 1922. Joe Watson bought an estate at Compton Verney in Warwickshire and estates at Manton, Offchurch, Barlby near Selby and Thorney near Peterborough together with Sudbourne Hall Suffolk. Joe Watson Lord Manton was the Chairman of the Directing Board who was in charge of the Barnbow Shell Filling Factory, a member of the Leeds Infirmary Board and director of the Lancashire & Yorkshire Railway. Lord Manton died as a result of a riding accident on his Compton Verney estate and was buried at Offchurch near Leamington: there were memorial services held at Leeds Parish Church and Wetherby Parish Church. Linton Springs was bought by Major Hon Edward Lascelles and is now a hotel.

WATSON & CAIRNS was a cycle shop on Lower Briggate: it opened in Leeds in 1920 and was closed in January 1997; re-developed as the Hogshead café bar. On the upper floor of the lower building (1894) was once Lockhart's Golden Cup Cocoa Rooms - later City Restaurant (Walter Fairburn).

WATT, JAMES (1736-1819) was a Scottish engineer who developed the steam engine; he made Thomas Newcomen's steam engine more efficient by cooling the used steam in a condenser separate from the main cylinder. The bronze statue of James Watt in City Square was by Henry Fehr and unveiled in 1903 when City Square was first opened. The work was paid for by engineer Councillor Richard Wainwright.

WEATHERALL, GREEN & SMITH are chartered surveyors and property consultants. The business started in 1833 by Thomas Hardwick who was joined by Joshua Bramham in 1843. In 1870 the firm became Bramham & Gale when Walter Gale joined the business. Hollis & Webb amalgamated with Bramham & Gale in 1969 and in 1973 with Wetherall Green & Smith. The business moved into 25 Wellington Street in February 2001 in new offices refurbished by pension fund landlords PRICOA.

WELLINGTON, DUKE ARTHUR WELLESLEY (1769-1852) was an Anglo-Irishman (born Arthur Wesley) and the 5th son of the Earl of Mornington: born at Merrion Street Upper in Dublin. He was educated at Eton and at Angers Military Academy in France serving in India and Denmark. He became the 1st Duke of Wellington in 1814 - the year in which he expelled the French from Spain during the Peninsular War. Wellington defeated Napoleon

Bonaparte at Quatre-Bras and Waterloo in 1815; he was Prime Minister 1828-30. He died at Walmer Castle in Kent - he was Lord Warden of the Cinque Ports - and was buried at St Paul's Cathedral. Wellington's bronze statue by Baron Carlo (Charles) Marochetti was first unveiled when the Town Hall was opened in 1858 and was later removed to the south east corner of Woodhouse Moor. There were many streets and sites named after Wellington together with his victory at Waterloo: in Leeds and Pudsey there are the Wellesley Hotel (City Central), Wellington Bridge, Hill, Road and Street with Waterloo featuring in Bramley, Roundhay Park and the former colliery near Temple Newsam.

WELLINGTON STREET was known first as Wellington Road as the route of the new Wellington Bridge Turnpike of 1817 - the Bradford Turnpike of 1794 was the continuation of Park Place. The extension of Wellington Street westwards in 1818 included the demolition of buildings on Drony Laith. The new roads mainly used land on the Wilson estate much to the displeasure of Park Square residents. The Central Railway Station and extensive goodsyards were once features. St Philip's Church on the north side at Bean Ing (Wellington Street/St Philip's Street) had the foundation stone laid on November 10th 1845 and it was consecrated in October 1847 on land donated by the Gott family. The architect was Robert Chantrell and the church was closed and demolished in 1931: the site is now part of the Westgate flyover.

The north side of Wellington Street: Majestic Cinema (dated 1921) opened in June 1922 and closed as a cinema in July 1969: now the Majestyk; No 36 was the former office of WT Avery of Sherburn-in-Elmet who made weighing machines; Wharf Street was the West Riding Hotel, reopened as a Vittle Inn in 1977 and became Wharf Street in April 1999; Wellington House - the offices of the WYPTA opened by Ron Todd on January 31st 1990, King's House on the corner of King Street, Waterloo House which opened in 1985, St Martin's House on the corner of Britannia Street, Springfield House designed by architects Goddard Wybor was built in 1997 on the site of the Wellington Street Bus Station - in the course of contruction an old well was revealed on the site; Apsley House was built in 1903 by Corson & Jones: it was restored in the 1990's; Central Station Hotel is now Wellingtons public house and Regent House; 100 Wellington Road incorporates shops and the BT

Business Centre (Lisbon Street), Bank of Scotland occupies a new building prior to the end of Westgate by the flyover: Ebor Court, Compton House and Bridge House. The Wellington Picture House was opened near the bridge in November 1920 and closed in November 1941 prior to demolition.

The south side of Wellington Street: City Square House is a development replacing shops and offices (demolished 1979) on the corner of Aire Street: it includes the offices of AXA Insurance. City Central is a new development of apartments based in the old Great Northern (Wellesley) Hotel. Taywood Homes completed a £4.8 million restoration programme to create 65 apartments; Royal Mail House was the sorting office in the 1960's until transfer of the facility to Stourton. Developers Teesland Group plc and Leeds based Sterling Capital is transforming the building into a mixed use complex: the Royal Mail depot will be demolished and the 14 storey tower will have a new terracotta and glass façade. The development of West Central is centred around a piazza with a 200 bed hotel - costing £120 million; Wellington Place (St James Securities for Hermes) is an office development, restaurants and an NCP multi-storey car park opened in summer 2001; Benson House is one of the offices of Price Waterhouse Cooper opened in October 1997; Crowne Plaza Hotel was opened on May 31st 1990 by the Earl of Harewood as The Crest and in 1997 it became a Holiday Inn - the name changed to Holiday Inn-Crowne Plaza and then dropped the Holiday Inn; The Yorkshire Post moved from Albion Street on Saturday September 26th 1970 and the new building opened on September 28th - the official opening by HRH Prince Charles was held on December 10th 1970. The building was designed by the John Madin Design Group: the site had formerly been Bean Ing Mill.

WESLEY, SAMUEL SEBASTIAN (1810-76) was the organist of Leeds Parish Church for 7 years from 1842: he composed the morning and evening service in E major: the memorial's music is from The Wilderness.

WESTGATE is the continuation of The Headrow (Upper Head Row) from Oxford Place to the Inner Ring Road (A58M): the extensions was completed by February 1958. The road continues as Park Lane. Westgate Point dates from 1988 and is an office block designed by David Lyons & Associates (commended 1989): the first occupants were in September 1989. One of the companies at Westgate Point is the Equitable Life Assurance Society, which was founded in 1767.

WEST RIDING HOUSE on Albion Street dates from 1976 and was refurbished by 2000 as Grade A office accommodation: it is the tallest office building in the city with 19 floors.

WEST YORKSHIRE ARCHIVES opened in the old Sheepscar Branch Library in 1965 and became a part of the WYAS in 1982. The collection includes the records of Leeds Corporation, archives of the Diocese of Ripon & Leeds, areas of Craven, Ripon, Harrogate and the old West Riding. There are family collections, maps, estate records and businesses - open to the public on booking. The library building stands on the site of the former police station (1872) which closed in 1930 and the foundation stone for the new library building was laid on October 29th 1936 - it opened on April 26th 1938.

WETHERSPOON JD is a leading public house chain in Britain founded in 1979 by 24 year old law student Tim Walker who opened his first pub in North London and named it after JD (Hogg) from Dukes of Hazzard on TV and his former teacher in New Zealand. In 1982 he opened a pub in a converted brewery in Holloway and in 1991 opened in a former ballroom at the Great Eastern Hotel at Liverpool Street Station - which had been empty for 40 years. In 1988 Scottish & Newcastle bought a 20% share of the business - they sold this in 1992 when JD Wetherspoon was floated on the Stock Exchange. The 100th pub was opened in 1994 and a year later the largest pub in the UK was opened in the former ABC Cinema in Manchester; the first budget hotel was opened in 1998 in Shrewsbury. The company announced plans in January 2001 to create 3000 jobs in an expansion programme, investing £140 million on developing new sites including one in a former bank in Park Row. Barclay's Bank opened on Park Row in 1967– the branch closed on September 3rd 1999: Wetherspoon's Beckett's Bank opened in January 2001. There were 110 new pubs opened during 2001 throughout the country and there are plans for 1000 pubs to be opened prior to 2010. The company operates 466 public houses (2000) in Britain employing 12,500 workers prior to the expansion plans. In 2001 there were four branches in Leeds: Lloyds Number 1 opened December 7th 2000 on Great George Street - before this was Browne's Bar (Mansfield Breweries) which had been opened in November 1996, City Station concourse opened April 26th 2000, Stick or Twist on Merrion Way opened November 28th 1997 and the latest branch on Park Row. The name Lloyds No 1 was taken as Wetherspoons opened a few branches in old bank buildings.

WHITAKER, REV THOMAS DUNHAM (1759-1821) was the author of the important history of Leeds *Loidis and Elmet* and the 1819 edition of Ralph Thoresby's *Ducatus Leodiensis.* He was born at the parsonage of Rainham Norfolk and in 1774 was placed with Rev William Sheepshanks at Grassington. He was educated at St John's College Cambridge and was ordained a priest in 1785. He was the Vicar of Whalley in 1809 and in 1818 was Vicar of Blackburn; he married Lucy Thoresby and they had four children. He died at Blackburn on December 18th 1821 and buried at Holme.

WHITEHALL is a riverside development in two phases: the foundation stone for Whitehall 1 (Yorkshire Electricity) was laid by the Lord Mayor on April 12th 1996 and is occupied by MWB Business Exchange. Plans for Whitehall 2 were passed in March 2001: it is a development of a head office building with a start in July 2001. The development of 149 luxury riverside apartments by Crosby Homes were opened in Autumn 2001. The architects for the whole project are Abbey Holford Rowe for Miller Gregory: there will be a 180 bedroom Novotel Hotel (Accor) to be opened in early 2002. Riverside Business Park (Town Centre Securities) are to complete an office development with residential apartments, leisure and retail outlets on an existing car park.

WHITEHALL ROAD commences at Aire Street/Thirsk Row and becomes the main route (A58) to Halifax. This was the turnpike road from Leeds to the Whitehall Hotel at Hipperholme - the road was opened in October 1833 by an Act of Parliament passed in 1825: the road ended at the White Swan Inn Halifax - a distance of just over 14 miles from Leeds. The tolls were removed in 1869. One of the main factory complexes at the Leeds end of Whitehall Road was Watson's soap works, together with J Bannister of Britannia Mills - the premises were built in 1836 and occupied by Bannisters from c1863. Whitehall Road also had the large premises of J Hudson's North of England Preserve Works founded c1863 for the processing of fruit; William Lupton's Whitehall Mills and Petty & Sons Printers. The road now features the Aireside Retail Centre and much redevelopment including Crosby Homes 13 storey block which has flats, offices and a hotel - built on the former YEB site. Town Centre Securities is proposing to build four office blocks, two apartment blocks, two café bars, shops and a multi-storey car park on the site of a former factory; the scheme is likely to include a new £1.25 million bridge across the river linking with the proposed Holbeck Urban Village.

WHITLEY, JOSEPH (1818-91) was the father in law of Augustine Le Prince and involved in the making of centrifugal castings.

WILKINSON, TATE (1739-1803) was an actor-manager who started in London (1757) and moved to York where he died. He built the first Leeds Theatre (licensed) on Hunslet Lane in 1771 - the Old Leeds Theatre was opened on July 24th 1771. The theatre was rebuilt by John Coleman with The New Theatre Royal and Opera House opening on September 30th 1867; the theatre was burnt down in May 1875.

WILLIS LUDLOW was a department store on Vicar Lane/Sidney Street which was opened on March 24th 1960, the business was founded in 1920. The premises became Clover by 1979 and were closed in the 1980s (now Flannels).

WILSON, SIR CHARLES HENRY (1859-1930) was an alderman and at the boundary extension enquiry of 1921 declared "I am Leeds" (the bill failed). He was a member of the City Council from 1890, an alderman from 1906 to 1928 (when he retired) and the Conservative leader from 1907 to 1928. He was the MP for Central Leeds for 6 years (1923-29) and in 1923 became an Honorary Freeman of Leeds, received an Honorary LlD from the University and was honoured with a knighthood. He was born near Easingwold and worked in Leeds as an accountant: he died at Osgodby Hall and was buried at Skipwith Church.

WILSON, SAM JP (1851-1914) was a Leeds industrialist who lived at Rutland Lodge Potternewton. He was the Chairman of Joshua Wilson & Sons Ltd worsted clothing manufacturer of Wellington Street. Sam Wilson bequeathed his fine art collection to Leeds Art Gallery with the exhibition opening in a special room in 1925. Rutland Lodge was also given to Leeds and the Wilson collection includes the carved Alfred Gilbert fireplace and a grand piano by Jansen of Paris/Sebastian Erard (1900). There are plans to demolish Rutland Lodge and build a restaurant. Sam Wilson has one of the largest memorials in Lawnswood Cemetery: he died on December 13th 1914 - his wife Ann (1862-1931) was buried in the tomb whose memorial includes the words Faith and Benevolence together with the motto Mons Janva Vitae.

WINN, ROWLAND JP (1872-1959) was the motoring pioneer who became Lord Mayor in 1938/39 and was made an Honorary Freeman of Leeds in 1956. He started his motoring in the 1890's with his first garage on Cookridge Street; he was the founder of the Yorkshire Automobile Club.

WINN, THOMAS (died 1908) started his practice in Carlton Chambers Albion Street c1882 and was a member of Leeds City Council. His work included the design for the Nurses Home Burmantofts in 1893-94 built at a cost of £10,000, altering Holy Trinity Church; he also was responsible for The Mitre, Jubilee, Black Swan and Adelphi inns. Thomas Winn remodelled the Hippodrome Theatre in 1906 and built the Swinegate foundry for Dixon & Sons as well as shops and a hotel on Commercial Street.

WOOD STREET was east of Briggate and named by Joseph Wood who was a hatter: he bought two yards between Vicar Lane and Briggate to create a new street. The street had the Boot & Shoe and Boy & Barrel inns and was swept away by 1900 to make Queen Victoria Street.

WOODBINE LIZZIE or Tramway Liz (died 1947) was born Alice Porter in Stanningley having lived at New Row Lowtown, Butcher's Arms and Chapeltown. She moved to Pudsey for 12 years following her marriage to Joseph Hartley in 1907 and they had their honeymoon in Hull. She reverted to her maiden name after the break up of her marriage in 1919 - they had six children: the last child only weighed 3lbs 2oz. Alice went to live with her parents in Kirkstall and entered service in Headingley but at the age of 38 decided on a more open life and walked all the way to London and back. She became a lady-tramp and was usually based outside the Whip yard on Duncan Street after an early morning coffee from a stall on Boar Lane. She slept in a tent for a while on an allotment and was often seen behind the Imperial Picture House on Kirkstall Road (opened 1913 - closed 1940): she was often on the steps of Queen Street Chapel and used to sleep in shelters on Woodhouse Ridge and Moor. Woodbine Lizzie was once in St James Hospital following a car accident and was often taken to the Town Hall Bridewell for a wash by the Police.

WOODHOUSE LANE is a major route to north west Leeds from Albion Street to Hyde Park Corner. The turnpike road to Otley cutting through Woodhouse Moor was opened in 1754 with a toll bar at the end of Blenheim Terrace (Emmanuel Church). The city end of Woodhouse Lane was changed with the development of both the St John's Centre and Merrion Centre: in 1870 Albion Street was continued through to join Woodhouse Lane at Great George Street. On Great George Street corner was the Central High School (Council Offices) on the west and the Albion Brewery on the east. Woodhouse Lane Methodist New Connexion Chapel was built on land bought in 1853 to replace the former Baptist Ebenezer Chapel between Vicar Lane and Millgarth. The large chapel had the foundation stone laid on April 18th 1857 and it opened on Woodhouse Lane in April 1858 designed by Leeds architect William Hill. In 1888 additional school premises were opened on the north side of the chapel again designed by William Hill. Two members of the Chapel were Henry Rowland Marsden whose monument once stood nearby on Woodhouse Lane and Joseph Hepworth (1834-1911) who was the founder of the clothing firm. The Chapel closed in 1928 and went on to have various other uses including the College of Commerce in the old chapel and School of Architecture in the old school; later there were rehearsal rooms for

Woodhouse Lane 1957 *(Painting by JE Castelow)*

the College of Music. The two buildings have been developed as two licensed premises - Yates Wine Lodge (1997) and The Rat & Parrot. St Columba's Presbyterian Church had the foundation stone laid in August 1985 and the chapel was opened in October 1868 by the congregation who had once met in the Music Hall on Albion Street: the architects were Hey & Sons of Liverpool. In 1902 the congregations of Woodhouse Lane merged with Cavendish Road Chapel and the Woodhouse Lane Chapel was later demolished. The College of Technology now stands on the Woodhouse Lane/Cookridge Street junction and there has been much demolition of old properties for the inner ring road including Carlton Hill and Carlton Street, which also features Woodhouse Lane Multi-Storey Car Park. On the east side was the Friends Meeting House opened in 1868 (BBC Radio Leeds), the site of Le Prince's workshops and Blenheim Baptist Church. The first chapel was on Great George Street -demolished for building the Infirmary in 1864. The new chapel on Blackman Lane/Woodhouse Lane was opened in 1864 with the Woodhouse Lane frontage opening in 1892 - this was sold in 1980 for development as offices. On the west side opposite the present BBC TV studios was Walter Thomas Castelow's pharmacy built in 1857 (Strawberry Fields), Fenton public house (1853) and on the corner was Craven Dairies shop (1845) with the Post Office (1857) on the opposite corner of Lodge Street. Hillary Place, named by JH Hebblethwaite, has Hopewell House: built for Briggate coach proprietor Henry Littlewood and later the home of flax merchant Henry Pritchard. Blenheim Terrace was built on New Close in 1824 with the first houses erected two years later and were to feature extensive front gardens: the terrace was completed by 1881. Trinity St David's United Reformed Church was opened on the site of Hope Villa in 1902 as Trinity Congregational Chapel designed by George Danby. The church became URC in 1972 and was renamed being closed in 1991 - the University bought the buildings. Emmanuel Church was built in the gardens of Hillary House and was consecrated on September 15th 1880 to designs by Adams & Kelly; the spire was designed by Harry Chorley and added in 1906. Emmanuel Church is the University Chaplaincy for Anglican, Baptist, Catholic, Lutheran, Methodist, Quakers, Salvation Army and United Reformed Church members. The Parkinson Building dominates this section of Woodhouse Lane designed in Portland stone by TA Lodge - work started in 1938 and the building opened in 1951. The Brotherton Library was opened in 1936 as part of the Lancaster, Lucas and Lodge plans. These were the second phase of University development following the Alfred & Paul Waterhouse buildings (Great Hall, Textile Building and Baines Wing) from 1904: the second phase started in the mid 1920's and was finished in the early 1960's. The Engineering Building stands on the site of Greater Woodhouse Hall and on the opposite side of Woodhouse Lane is the Carlton Hill Religious Society of Friends Meeting House opened in 1987. The Quakers first met on Water Lane in 1699 - rebuilt in 1788. The Carlton House estate was sold in 1864 and a new Meeting House was opened in 1868 designed by Edward Birchall. The main building was later to be Albrecht & Albrecht clothiers and exporters from 1921 until their move to Lower Hanover Street in 1938 - the building became the home of the BBC with Radio Leeds moving from Wade Lane (Merrion Centre) in 1980 - the last meeting for worship was held on April 22nd 1979. On the east side was the site of Eldon Wesleyan Chapel: foundation stone laid May 9th 1889 (trowel in Abbey House Museum) and opened on November 11th 1890 to the designs of GF Danby - the building remained empty after closure and in August 1981 was destroyed in a fire and the remainder was demolished. Notre Dame Sixth Form College opened in October 1905 and the chapel was designed by Henry Smart and opened in 1929. The school became a College on Roman Catholic Schools re-organisation in 1991: there is a modern school hall in which are held the concerts of the Leeds Symphony Orchestra. St Mark's Street United Methodist Free Church was opened in 1831: it became university property and is now boarded up. The Eldon public house was opened as the Cemetery Tavern in 1839 while The Pack Horse dates from the 18th century and was rebuilt c1868. Reservoir Street (Clarendon Road) is at the eastern end of the Moor; the Library and Fire & Police Station have been converted into a public house which opened as the Feast & Firkin (Allied Domecq) in December 1994 after a £750,000 refurbishment - it re-opened after a short closure in October 2000 as The Library (Bass). The original police station was opened as a two storey house in 1857 and used as a section station until demolition in 1898. This was replaced by a

Police Station Woodhouse Lane/Reservoir Street corner

large combined police/fire station and library on the upper floor in 1902 at a cost of over £6000. It was used until 1932 and replaced by the box system and then taken over by the Public Assistance Committee as a payments centre: the last occupants were Voluntary Action Leeds who left in 1992. St Mark's Church was consecrated on January 13th 1826 and the final service was held on 15th July 2001: the architects were Peter Atkinson Jnr and RH Sharp: the church was one of the Waterloo churches. The Swan with Two Necks public house is on Raglan Road: the name derives from the nicks that are made on the beaks of Swans to denote ownership.

WOODHOUSE MOOR was an extensive open space bought by the Leeds Corporation for £3000 on November 5th 1855 and public subscriptions provided a fountain and band stand with a later cricket ground, aviary, gymnasium and bowling green (1906). The statue of Arthur Wellesley First Duke of Wellington was sculpted by Baron Carlo Marochetti in 1854 and unveiled outside the Town Hall in 1858 prior to removal to the Moor. The statue of Sir Robert Peel was made by William Behnes in 1852 and in August of that year was placed outside the Court House on Park Row, prior to being taken to Victoria Square and thence to the Moor. The statue of Henry Rowland Marsden was by John Throp (1878) and shows his mayoral robes (Mayor 1873-76): it was at the south end of Woodhouse Lane (Dortmund Square) before being removed to Woodhouse Moor. The large statue of Queen Victoria was sculpted by Sir George Frampton in 1905 for Victoria Square in front of the Town Hall and replaced an earlier fountain feature. The memorial was taken to the present position on Woodhouse Moor in 1937 together with Sir Robert Peel and the Duke of Wellington. St Augustine's Church Wrangthorne was consecrated on November 8th 1871: the architect was James Barlow Fraser.

WOODHOUSE SQUARE was developed from 1825 on the land that once formed a part of the Claremont estate. In 1817 the northern part of the estate was bought by John Hill who entered into a partnership in 1824 with Joseph Green and builder Samuel Green. John Hill's entitlement to the estate was sold in 1828 to John Atkinson (died 1833) of Little Woodhouse Hall - the new square would allow a good prospect from the Hall: it was about the same time that Green built the first houses on the square - no 1 on the south side. This was demolished for road alterations but the completed row was to become the home of Swarthmore. The north side was dominated by Claremont which became the home of surgeon Francis Chorley. It was initially proposed that St George's Church was to be sited in the Square but it was built on Christopher Beckett's Mount Pleasant estate. The gardens of Woodhouse Square were reduced with the 1897 completion of Claremont Avenue and Villas. By 1839 Clarendon Road had cut through the estate as well as the new road of Hyde Terrace. The northern end featured Woodsley Hall in 1840 for Sir Peter Fairbairn, whose statue is a feature of Woodhouse Square. In 1840 Waverley House was completed by architect RW Moore (died 1891) on the west side of the Square and in 1845 built Nos 3, 4, and 5 (Swarthmore). Waverley House became a dancing school and a temperance hotel. It was in 1855 that Little Woodhouse Hall was sold to Leeds Corporation with the gardens of the Square, maintained by the Parks department from 1906. St Ann's RC Primary School was first opened on Lady Lane in 1833 and transferred to Cookridge Street in 1841: the building cost £2000 and was opened by Daniel O'Connell (1775-1847). The school moved into their new building on Woodhouse Square in 1904 and in 1989 amalgamated with Holy Rosary RC Primary in the old St Dominic's RC School on Leopold Street.

WOODSLEY HOUSE on Clarendon Road was built for Sir Peter Fairbairn in 1840 by John Clark: Queen Victoria and Prince Albert stayed here during the opening ceremony for Leeds Town Hall in 1858; it is now the Nuffield Institute.

WOOL The sequence of the woollen process started with shearing, grading and packing in woolsacks to be sold by weight; the raw wool was sorted and washed and after oiling the fibres were loosened (carding) or combed and spun into skeins of yarn to sell to the weaver; the yarn was woven into cloth on looms - after scouring in stale urine to remove oil, the woven cloth was soaped, folded and cleaned (fulled) using drop hammers in fulling mills; the lengths of wet cloth were brushed with teasel heads and set up onto tenter frames with tenter hooks for drying and stretching to the required size. The Yorkshire Dales clothiers produced unfinished or white cloth which was sold in cloth markets and cloth halls to merchants who dyed and then finished the cloth.

WOOLWORTH, FRANK WINFIELD (1852-1919) opened his first store in Pennsylvania in 1879 and with his brother CS Woolworth (1856-1947) built up a chain of stores through America, Canada, Britain and Europe. The first store in the UK was opened in 1909 - five years after the incorporation as FW Woolworth & Co.

WOOLWORTH'S STORE was first opened in Liverpool and opened in Leeds in 1913 on Briggate in the Post Office Exchange Building (1907) designed by Percy Robinson: a new storey was added in 1920 onto the Exchange Buildings. On December 1st 1928 a new store on Briggate was opened replacing the Albion Hotel; extended to the adjacent site of The Victory Hotel (Bull & Mouth/Grand Central) in 1939. The store was placed on sale in March 1982 and was bought by Schofields for their temporary location during the rebuilding of the new Headrow Centre. The store was closed on May 23rd 1987 and Woolworths relocated to the Merrion Centre: the store in the Centre was opened on July 3rd 1987. The Woolworths/Schofields site on Briggate was opened as Rackhams and then House of Fraser.

WORKHOUSE was built on Lady Lane in 1638 and became a Charity School in 1704; it became a workhouse again in June 1726. It was closed again in 1729 and re-opened in 1738: in 1740 a workroom, infirmary, granary, brewhouse, wash house and coalhouse were added and another larger building came in c1806. The workhouse transferred to Beckett Street in 1861 (architect: William Perkin) where the trowel used to lay the foundation stone on April 5th 1858 by William Middleton is displayed in the Civic Hall. The old building was used for various businesses including the Leeds Lead Works and it was demolished in August 1936 for a new bus station. There were nearly 2000 workhouses built in England between 1723 and 1776, provided by parishes and financed out of the poor rates. Parishes were able to levy a poor rate from 1597 and the Poor Law Act of 1601 established a pattern of administration; the General Workhouse Act (1723) gave parishes the power to build workhouses with groups of smaller parishes building Union Workhouses. The Poor Law Board was responsible from 1847 with duties transferring in 1871 to the Local Government Board: workhouses became Poor Law Institutions in 1913 which were taken over by the Ministry of Health in 1919 and from 1929 authorities were encouraged to convert workhouses to infirmaries.

WORKING MEN'S HALL was on Park Street built in 1867 and demolished in 1967. The Hall offered a library, news room and wash room - all facilities costing a penny a week. The Leeds Working Men's Institute was originally opened in 1861 in the Assembly Rooms on Crown Street and this Institute was closed down on September 1st 1870.

WRIGHT, GRIFFITH (1784-1846) was a magistrate of Leeds and Mayor in 1834-35. He was a patron of the Leeds vicarage, Trustee of Leeds Grammar School and continued The Leeds Intelligencer which had been established by his grandfather in 1754. He lived on his estate at Harehills and died unmarried: buried at Chapeltown Church.

YATES WINE LODGES were founded in Oldham by Peter Yates in 1884 and there are now over 160 branches. The first Leeds site was in Bond Street (1961) opening in the former Powolny's Bar - this closed in August 1974 and was demolished for the new shopping centre. In 1977 a Yates Wine Lodge opened at 3 Boar Lane: the Boar Lane Wine Lodge was opened in a former furniture store on December 7th 1994 and in December 1997 the second branch opened on Woodhouse Lane in the original New Connexion Methodist Chapel (1858) - later the College of Commerce.

YORK PLACE is the street that is parallel to Wellington Street and Park Place: there are a few interesting 19th century houses including York Place Buildings (THR/JRR), Lion House, York House 30 York Place (JL) being the property of LCC. The street also had Hepper's Horse & Carriage Repository - their auction rooms are on East Parade. The north site at the junction with Queen Street was at one time a timber yard - the saw and moulding mills were opposite on Queen Street. The Food Emporium opened on July 4th 2001 and 30 York Place is being developed as apartments by Cala Homes.

YORKSHIRE as a name of the county in which Leeds is included was first recorded in 1055 although would have been used before this date. The shires were created by the Saxon kings where the territory of the Mercians had been taken back: shire is derived from Old English "scir" or shearing. Yorkshire was divided into three ridings by the Danes: it is derived from Old Norse "thrithi" meaning a third part. Yorkshire had the East, North and West Ridings with Leeds in the West Riding until the 1974 changes in local government which dispensed with the ridings and introduced West Yorkshire as the new division.

YORKSHIRE COPPERWORKS In 1888 Elmore's Depositing Co manufactured copper tubes at Stourton - on a site which was once a racecourse. In 1909 the company became Yorkshire Copper Works and in the Great War made munitions. In 1958 the business merged with ICI Metals Division and became Yorkshire Imperial Metals; in 1968 this was incorporated into IMI and in 1986 became IMI Yorkshire Fittings Ltd which closed in 1994.

YORKSHIRE DANCE CENTRE is a registered charity based in St Peter's Buildings on St Peter's Square: it is a National Dance Agency and includes the Cactus Café. The Centre was opened in 1985 with a new dance studio opening in January 1990; a new £1.4 million Centre was officially opened in April 1997.

YORKSHIRE FORWARD is the Yorkshire and The Humber Regional Development Agency - started on April 1st 1999 with the Headquarters in Leeds with 170 staff and a £160 million budget. The Regional Economy Strategy for 2000-2010 was approved in 1999. A partnership agreement was signed in April 2001 with the Yorkshire & Humberside Universities Association.

YORKSHIRE LADIES' COUNCIL OF EDUCATION was founded in 1876 to promote the education of girls and women. They occupied 18 Blenheim Terrace from 1928 to 1988 as the Administration Centre for the Council; the building also housed the Yorkshire Ladies Secretarial College.

YOUNGMAN'S FISH RESTAURANT was first opened by Henry Robert Youngman (1865-1930) in 1885 in Hunslet: he moved to Lower Headrow in 1914 and moved to New Briggate in 1928 and to Harrison Street in the 1970's: the firm closed in February 1989. The building became an Indian restaurant and a health club having been built in the 1960's for a tax office. Premier House was opened on April 6th 1998: officially opened as offices on May 1st 1998 by John Battle MP.

YOUNG MEN'S CHRISTIAN ASSOCIATION (YMCA) was inaugurated at a public meeting held on March 5th 1855 with the first meeting of the new Association on June 27th 1855. The first Leeds building was opened in April 1859 on Eastwood Lane and then on South Parade. The building on Albion Street/Albion Place had the foundation stone laid in December 1906 and the £50,000 new headquarters were opened in 1907 on the site of the Stock Exchange. The old Stock Exchange was occupied by Alfred Denby and GF Crowe from 1866 (later Crowe & Co) and the building was demolished from March 1905. The YMCA closed on the site in June 1984 with the Lawnswood headquarters having opened in September 1980.

ZIFF, ISRAEL ARNOLD JP OBE was the Chairman of Stylo; he registered Town Centre Securities in 1959 which went public in September 1960. The company built the Merrion Centre where the offices remain. Arnold Ziff joined the family firm in 1948 and became Chairman in 1966; he was awarded the OBE in 1981 and in March 1991 was appointed High Sheriff of West Yorkshire; he retired as a JP in 1997 after 30 years service. The Tropical House at Canal Gardens Roundhay was opened on May 6th 1988 and was financed by Arnold Ziff. The Botanical Gardens were opened on December 22nd 1993 by Arnold Ziff and the complex is known as the Marjorie Ziff Rainforest, Cacti and Orchid House. The Chairman and chief executive of Stylo is Michael Ziff; the business includes Saxone, Barratts and Priceless.

ZIMMERMAN, EPHRAIM (1873-1969) was a Lithuanian Jew who emigrated in 1889. The clothing firm started in Cross Stamford Street during the early 1900's and then opened two factories on Claypit Lane and St Anne's Street (1936-c1952). Compulsory purchase caused the move to a new factory on Meanwood Road: sold in 1970 to a Manchester company. The firm produced suits for many shops including Montague Burton until 1911.

ZOOLOGICAL & BOTANICAL GARDENS opened in Headingley (Cardigan Road) on July 8th 1840 designed by William Billington (born 1807) and Edward Davies on 20 acres having taken three years but never completed to the original design. The gardens were closed in 1846 and sold two years later to banker James Smith for £6100. He sold them to Henry Marshall whose gardens were managed by Tommy Clapham who held the Royal Gardens on lease until 1858. The gardens were closed in June 1858 and were dismantled. In September 1873 the site was sold for £16,500 as building plots and the bear pits are the only remaining (listed) building from the original gardens: Leeds Civic Trust became the new owner in 1966, new gates date from 1968 and the site was restored in 1992. Thomas Clapham opened a new site a few hundred yards to the east as the Royal Park Horticultural Gardens, which included pleasure grounds and greenhouses. These were closed in 1885 with the Royal Park public house on Queens Road being the only reminder of the venture.

ZOOS BIRD GARDENS AND FARMS There were aviaries in Cross Flatts Park and on Woodhouse Moor and a short lived zoological garden at Temple Newsam Park in 1923. It was proposed that a zoo be opened in front of the castle folly in Roundhay Park in 1924 which would have cost £4000. *Canal Gardens Tropical World* at Roundhay: the John Dunstan Tropical House was opened on April 17th 1984 with a grant from Wade's Charity. The Tropical House opened on May 6th 1988 and the Botanical Gardens were opened on December 22nd 1993 by Arnold Ziff with help from Wade's Charity. *Home Farm at Temple Newsam* is a rare breeds centre originally opened to the public in 1979: the complex dates from the late 17th century with the great barn from 1694. *Lotherton Hall Bird Garden* was opened in 1980 on the site of the kitchen gardens and extended over the years – there is also a deer herd at Lotherton Hall Park. *Meanwood Valley Urban Farm* is a registered charity with support from the City Council, trusts, businesses and the public. Preparation started in 1977 with opening in April 1980 with the education centre and café opening in 1983 and the EpiCentre was opened by Michael Meacher in September 1999.

ZURICH INSURANCE (Zurich Financial Services Group) was incorporated in Switzerland in 1872: the Leeds offices are on East Parade (St Martins Property Group). Zurich took over Eagle Star Insurance in 1999 and opened their new offices at Victoria Point in 2000. Zurich joined with Bank of Scotland in 2001 for the provision of banking services: distribution of the services will be by Zurich's existing channels which include Allied Dunbar and Eagle Star Direct.

ACKNOWLEDGEMENTS

John Gilleghan would like to thank all the kind staff at the Leeds Local History Library for their helpful involvement in the research over many hours; editor Judy Higgins and the readers of the Leeds Express who kindly have provided many of the illustrations over the years which have appeared in the paper in Scenes from the Past; the many Leeds businesses who so kindly provided me with relevant information and those I have pestered for information at so many Leeds city centre locations. Many of the illustrations date back many years mainly from private and personal collections and I am grateful that they are still possible to reproduce - my thanks to those who saw fit to photographically record our city.
Many thanks to John Boyd at BBC Radio Leeds for his excellent foreword and to the production team behind the popular Sunday Brunch.

Other titles by John Gilleghan MBE

Local History Books

Scenes from East Leeds (1991)
Highways and Byways from Leeds (1994)
Worship North and East of Leeds (1998)

Church Guides

All Saints Church Saxton (2000)
St Ricarius Church Aberford (2000)
St Mary's Church Garforth (2001)